International and Development Education

Series Editors
John N. Hawkins
University of California

Asian Pacific Higher Education Research
Partnership (APHERP) East-West Center
USA

W. James Jacob
Higher Education Leadership
University of Memphis

Department of Leadership and Center
for the Study of Higher Education
USA

More information about this series at
http://www.palgrave.com/gp/series/14849

Gustavo Gregorutti • Nanette Svenson
Editors

North-South University Research Partnerships in Latin America and the Caribbean

palgrave
macmillan

Editors
Gustavo Gregorutti
Andrews University
Berrien Springs, MI, USA

Nanette Svenson
Tulane University
New Orleans, LA, USA

International and Development Education
ISBN 978-3-319-75363-8   ISBN 978-3-319-75364-5   (eBook)
https://doi.org/10.1007/978-3-319-75364-5

Library of Congress Control Number: 2018935184

© The Editor(s) (if applicable) and The Author(s) 2018
This work is subject to copyright. All rights are solely and exclusively licensed by the Publisher, whether the whole or part of the material is concerned, specifically the rights of translation, reprinting, reuse of illustrations, recitation, broadcasting, reproduction on microfilms or in any other physical way, and transmission or information storage and retrieval, electronic adaptation, computer software, or by similar or dissimilar methodology now known or hereafter developed.
The use of general descriptive names, registered names, trademarks, service marks, etc. in this publication does not imply, even in the absence of a specific statement, that such names are exempt from the relevant protective laws and regulations and therefore free for general use.
The publisher, the authors, and the editors are safe to assume that the advice and information in this book are believed to be true and accurate at the date of publication. Neither the publisher nor the authors or the editors give a warranty, express or implied, with respect to the material contained herein or for any errors or omissions that may have been made. The publisher remains neutral with regard to jurisdictional claims in published maps and institutional affiliations.

Cover illustration: © Stef Bennett / Alamy Stock Photo

Printed on acid-free paper

This Palgrave Macmillan imprint is published by the registered company Springer International Publishing AG part of Springer Nature.
The registered company address is: Gewerbestrasse 11, 6330 Cham, Switzerland

CONTENTS

1 Introduction   1
Gustavo Gregorutti and Nanette Svenson

**2 Introducing a Bilateral Research and Innovation Agenda:
A Case Study on Mexico and the United States**   15
Gustavo Gregorutti, Beverly Barrett, and Angeles Dominguez

**3 Science Beyond Politics: Cuba-US Marine Research
and Conservation**   37
Daria Siciliano, Fernando Bretos, Julia Azanza,
and Nanette Svenson

**4 INCAE, Harvard, and International Development:
Research for Progress in Central America**   61
Nanette Svenson

**5 International Research Collaboration and Knowledge
Production in Colombia: A Qualitative Network Analysis
Approach**   87
Clara I. Tascón

vi CONTENTS

6 The Political Economy of Legal Knowledge in Action:
Collaborative Projects in the Americas   115
Daniel Bonilla Maldonado and Colin Crawford

7 Small Fish in a Big Pond: Internationalization
and Research Collaboration in Bolivia and Paraguay   141
Jorge Enrique Delgado

8 Comparing Urban Mobility and the Energy Transition
in France, USA, and Brazil: From Research Collaboration
to Institutional Partnerships   175
J. Kent Fitzsimons, Guy Tapie, Patrice Godier,
and Cristina de Araújo Lima

9 International Partnerships for Collaborative Research
in Argentinian Universities   203
Ángela Corengia, Ana García de Fanelli, Marcelo Rabossi,
and Dante J. Salto

10 Collaborative Research by Chilean and North American
Scholars: Precedents and Projections   233
Oscar Espinoza, Luis Eduardo González,
and Noel F. McGinn

11 Research Partnership Over Neocolonialism: Max Planck
Society Policy in Latin America   259
Pedro Pineda and Bernhard Streitwieser

Index   279

The *International and Development Education Series* focuses on the complementary areas of comparative, international, and development education. Books emphasize a number of topics ranging from key international education issues, trends, and reforms to examinations of national education systems, social theories, and development education initiatives. Local, national, regional, and global volumes (single authored and edited collections) constitute the breadth of the series and offer potential contributors a great deal of latitude based on interests and cutting-edge research. The series is supported by a strong network of international scholars and development professionals who serve on the International and Development Education Advisory Board and participate in the selection and review process for manuscript development.

SERIES EDITORS

John N. Hawkins

Professor Emeritus, University of California, Los Angeles
Co-Director, Asian Pacific Higher Education Research Partnership (APHERP), East West Center

W. James Jacob

Professor of Higher Education Leadership, University of Memphis
Chairperson, Department of Leadership and Co-Director of the Center for the Study of Higher Education

PRODUCTION EDITOR

Donna Menke

Assistant Professor, University of Memphis
Program Coordinator, Higher and Adult Education Program

INTERNATIONAL EDITORIAL ADVISORY BOARD

Clementina Acedo, *Webster University, Switzerland*
Philip G. Altbach, *Boston University, USA*
Carlos E. Blanco, *Universidad Central de Venezuela*
Oswell C. Chakulimba, *University of Zambia*
Sheng Yao Cheng, *National Chung Cheng University, Taiwan*

Edith Gnanadass, *University of Memphis, USA*
Wendy Griswold, *University of Memphis, USA*
Ruth Hayhoe, *University of Toronto, Canada*
Yuto Kitamura, *University of Tokyo, Japan*
Wanhua Ma, *Peking University, China*
Ka Ho Mok, *Lingnan University, China*
Christine Musselin, *Sciences Po, France*
Yusuf K. Nsubuga, *Ministry of Education and Sports, Uganda*
Namgi Park, *Gwangju National University of Education, Republic of Korea*
Val D. Rust, *University of California, Los Angeles, USA*
Suparno, *State University of Malang, Indonesia*
John C. Weidman, *University of Pittsburgh, USA*
Husam Zaman, *UNESCO/Regional Center of Quality and Excellence in Education, Saudi Arabia*

Center for the Study of Higher Education

Department of Leadership, University of Memphis
123 Ball Hall, Memphis, TN 38152 USA

Center for International and Development Education

Graduate School of Education & Information Studies, University of California, Los Angeles
Box 951521, Moore Hall, Los Angeles, CA 90095 USA

SERIES EDITORS INTRODUCTION

We are pleased to introduce another volume in the Palgrave Macmillan International and Development Education book series. In conceptualizing this series we took into account the extraordinary increase in the scope and depth of research on education in a global and international context. The range of topics and issues being addressed by scholars worldwide is enormous and clearly reflects the growing expansion and quality of research being conducted on comparative, international, and development education (CIDE) topics. Our goal is to cast a wide net for the most innovative and novel manuscripts, both single-authored and edited volumes, without constraints as to the level of education, geographical region, or methodology (whether disciplinary or interdisciplinary). In the process, we have also developed two subseries as part of the main series: one is cosponsored by the East West Center in Honolulu, Hawaii, drawing from their distinguished programs, the International Forum on Education 2020 (IFE 2020) and the Asian Pacific Higher Education Research Partnership (APHERP); and the other is a publication partnership with the Higher Education Special Interest Group of the Comparative and International Education Society that highlights trends and themes on international higher education.

The issues that will be highlighted in this series are those focused on capacity, access, and equity, three interrelated topics that are central to educational transformation as it appears around the world today. There are many paradoxes and asymmetries surrounding these issues, which include problems of both excess capacity and deficits, wide access to facilities as well as severe restrictions, and all the complexities that are included in the equity debate. Closely related to this critical triumvirate is the overarching concern with quality assurance, accountability, and assessment. As educational systems have expanded, so have the needs and demands for quality assessment, with implications for accreditation and accountability. Intergroup relations, multiculturalism, and gender issues comprise another cluster of concerns facing most educational systems in differential ways when one looks at the change in educational systems in an international context. Diversified notions of the structure of knowledge and curriculum development occupy another important niche in educational change at both the precollegiate and collegiate levels. Finally, how systems are managed and governed are key policy issues for educational policymakers worldwide. These and other key elements of the education and social change environment have guided this series and have been reflected in the books that have already appeared and those that will appear in the future. We welcome proposals on these and other topics from as wide a range of scholars and practitioners as possible. We believe that the world of educational change is dynamic, and our goal is to reflect the very best work being done in these and other areas. This volume meets the standards and goals of this series and we are proud to add it to our list of publications.

University of California
Los Angeles, CA, USA

John N. Hawkins

University of Memphis
Memphis, TN, USA

W. James Jacob

NOTES ON CONTRIBUTORS

Beverly Barrett is a Lecturer in Global Studies at the Bauer College of Business and at the Hobby School of Public Affairs at the University of Houston. Following her doctoral fellowship with the European Union Center of Excellence at the University of Miami, her research has concentrated on regional integration, international trade, higher education policy, and governance. In 2017, Palgrave Macmillan published her monograph *Globalization and Change in Higher Education: The Political Economy of Policy Reform in Europe*. Barrett teaches courses on globalization and public policy.

Fernando Bretos holds a master's degree in Marine Affairs and Policy from the University of Miami's Rosenstiel School of Marine and Atmospheric Science and a bachelor's degree in Biology from Oberlin College. He is Director of the Cuba Marine Research and Conservation (CubaMar) Program of the Ocean Foundation and has worked in Cuba since 1998 on a wide variety of marine conservation projects. He oversees a number of projects that involve multinational efforts to study coastal and marine resources shared by Cuba, the United States, and others in the region. He also oversees research with the Center for Marine Research of the University of Havana on sea turtles, coral reef health, and community preservation engagement.

Ángela Corengia is National Director of Accreditation and Academic Evaluation of the National Institute of Public Administration (INAP) in the Ministry of Modernization in Argentina. Prior to this appointment, she was an associate professor and researcher at the School of Education of the Austral University in Argentina. From 2005 to 2013, she was Director of the Office of Institutional Assessment at Austral and also led the Second Institutional Self-Assessment Process for the university (2010–2013). She received a research grant from the National Agency for the Promotion of Science and Technology (2008–2010) and was a post-doctoral fellow at the National Council of Research in Science and Technology (2010–2012). Her research focuses on issues related to quality and funding of higher education.

Colin Crawford is Dean and Professor of Law at the Louis D. Brandeis School of Law at the University of Louisville in the United States. Previously he was a member of the faculty of the Georgia State University Law School in Atlanta, Georgia, United States, where he founded and co-directed the Center for the Comparative Study of Metropolitan Growth. He then served on the faculty of Tulane University's Law School in New Orleans as the Robert C. Cudd Professor of Environmental Law and chair of Tulane's Global Development program. He is a legal and global development scholar and has published extensively and taught on subjects related to environmental management, international law, and urban development, among other topics.

Cristina de Araújo Lima is an architect and urban planner and Doctor of Environment and Urban Development. She is Associate Professor of Urban Design and Urban Environment at the Federal University of Parana (UFPR) in Curitiba, Brazil, and conducts postdoctoral studies at ENSAP in Bordeaux, France. She is also a research partner of ENSAPBx at the PAVE Laboratory (2012–2014), Vice-Director of the UFPR graduate program in Environment and Development, and founding director of the research group "City, Environment and Public Policy" at UFPR. She studies urban and metropolitan sprawl related to land consumption, mass transit systems, densities, and urban design.

Ana García de Fanelli is a senior research scholar of the National Council of Research in Science and Technology at the Center for the Study of State and Society in Buenos Aires, Argentina. She has published widely on comparative policies in higher education in Latin America, the management of public universities, and university financing. She was a senior consultant to the UNESCO International Institute of Educational Planning in Buenos Aires and Paris, the National Commission for University Evaluation and

Accreditation, the Inter-University Development Center from Chile, and the Argentine Ministry of Education.

Jorge Enrique Delgado holds a PhD in Administrative and Policy Studies in Education (with a concentration in Education Social and Comparative Analysis). He is an instructor at the University of Pittsburgh where he teaches courses in social justice, foundations of education, international education, public policy, and Latin American studies. His scholarly work consists primarily in case and sector analysis and focuses on the development of research in higher education institutions and systems.

Angeles Dominguez is a Professor of Mathematics at the School of Education and Director of the graduate Education Program at the Tecnologico de Monterrey, Mexico. She is also collaborating with the School of Engineering at the University Andres Bello at Santiago, Chile. Angeles holds a bachelor's degree in Physics Engineering from the Tecnologico de Monterrey and a doctoral degree in Mathematics Education from Syracuse University in New York. She is a member of the Researchers' National System in Mexico and has been a visiting researcher at Syracuse University, UT-Austin, and the Universidad Andres Bello. She teaches undergraduate courses in mathematics and graduate courses in education. Her main research areas include mathematical modeling, use of technology to improve learning, and gender issues in STEM.

Oscar Espinoza is a researcher at the School of Education in the University of San Sebastian. He is also an associate researcher at the Center of Comparative Educational Policies at the Diego Portales University and in the Interdisciplinary Program of Educational Research (PIIE), as well as a consultant for various Chilean universities. Previously, he worked on research funded by organizations such as USAID, UNESCO, the World Bank, UNDP, the Ford Foundation, and the Organization of Iberoamerican States. His research concentrates on issues associated with access, equity, social mobility, quality assurance, academic performance, management, and higher education policy. He holds an EdD in Education Policy, Planning, and Evaluation from the University of Pittsburgh, United States.

Patrice Godier holds a Doctorate in Sociology and is an Associate Professor at the National School of Architecture and Landscape of Bordeaux (ENSAP) and PAVE researcher associated with the Centre Emile Durkheim at the University of Bordeaux. He studies metropolitan dynamics, particularly those related to issues of housing, mobility, and territorial identifications in international comparisons.

Luis Eduardo González has been Director of University Policy at the International Center of University Development (CINDA) since 1982. He is also an international consultant and project coordinator in areas related to quality assurance, institutional evaluation and accreditation, university teaching methods, curriculum planning, professional skills analysis, and national higher education policy. He has coordinated more than 50 international projects, worked with over 80 universities and governments in 20 different countries, and edited more than 50 books. He has been an external consultant at the University of San Sebastian and in various international organizations such as UNESCO, ECLAC, OAS, the Inter-American Development Bank, and the World Bank.

Gustavo Gregorutti is a Professor at the School of Education at Andrews University in Michigan. Prior to this appointment, he has been a visiting professor in several Latin American universities teaching and carrying out various research projects. Gregorutti also conducted research at the Humboldt University Center for Higher Education in Berlin, Germany, where he is finishing his second PhD. He has published on faculty research productivity and organizational commitment to create knowledge, mainly among private universities, at national and international levels. He is presently involved with several international teams to advance comparative research.

J. Kent Fitzsimons is a doctor of architecture, practicing architect, and associate professor at the *Ecole Nationale Supérieure d'Architecture et de Paysage de Bordeaux*, where he teaches architectural design, architecture theory, and research. He is the Director of the PAVE research laboratory (*Profession Architecture Ville Environnement*), which studies architectural and urban phenomena from the perspective of the social sciences. His own research considers social and political aspects of architectural knowledge as manifested in the constructed environment. He has published on how notions of architectural design relate to social phenomena and focuses on issues such as life phases, gender, and physical impairment.

Daniel Bonilla Maldonado is an Associate Professor of Law at the Universidad de los Andes in Bogotá, Colombia. He holds a Doctorate and a Masters in Law from Yale Law School and a law degree from the Universidad de los Andes. Previously, during a three-year interval, he was also a visiting professor at Fordham Law School in New York City and at Yale Law School in New Haven. He was a Fulbright scholar and has published on topics including constitutional law, the Colombian legal system, and treatment of diversity in law, among others.

Noel F. McGinn is a Professor Emeritus of the Harvard University Graduate School of Education and Fellow Emeritus of the Harvard Institute for International Development. Most of his professional work centers on the relationship between research, policy, and practice in education systems. He has published on school effectiveness, educational planning, decentralization, and the impacts of globalization on education and is co-author of *Framing Questions, Constructing Answers: Linking Research with Education Policy for Developing Countries*; *Informed Dialogue: Using Research to Shape Education Policy Around the World*; and the *Handbook of Modern Education and Its Alternatives*. McGinn is also the editor of *Crossing Lines: Research and Policy Networks for Developing Country Education*; and *Learning Through Collaborative Research*. He is Past President of the Comparative and International Education Society and in 1998 received the Andres Bello Award of the Organization of American States for Outstanding Contribution to Education in Latin America.

Pedro Pineda is an assistant professor at the Faculty of Education at the Pontificia Universidad Javeriana and an affiliated professor at the Faculty of Psychology. He studied psychology and holds an MA in Education and a Doctorate from the Faculty of Education and Social Sciences at the Humboldt University of Berlin. He has worked for the last 14 years as a researcher and educational consultant for private companies, governmental agencies, and educational institutions. His studies contribute to education sociology, comparative education, and educational and developmental psychology.

Marcelo Rabossi holds a PhD in Education from the State University of New York, Albany, and is a full-time Professor at the School of Government of Torcuato di Tella University (UTDT) in Argentina, where he teaches courses on education finance and economics and higher education policy. Previously (1996–2003), he led the organization and development of Executive Training Courses in Educational Administration for headmasters, and was also (2000–2004) Director of Education at UTDT. His research interests include higher education governance and financing, private higher education, and academic labor markets.

Julia Azanza holds a PhD in Biological Sciences from the University of Havana and is a Professor at the Cuba Higher Institute of Technology and Applied Science, in the Department of Environmental Studies. Prior to this, from 2000 to 2014, she was a researcher and then an Assistant Professor at the University of Havana's Center for Marine Science, where she led marine turtle conservation efforts in Cuba for over a decade. Her work in marine biology continues to focus on sea turtle ecology, primarily in Cuba. Ricardo has published widely on her research, in Cuban and international scientific journals, and has collaborated with scientists and institutions in the wider Caribbean basin and around the world.

Dante J. Salto is a postdoctoral Fellow at the National Scientific and Technical Research Council (CONICET) at the Universidad Nacional de Cordoba (Argentina) and a research affiliate at the Program for Research on Private Higher Education (PROPHE). He earned his PhD and MS in Educational Administration and Policy Studies from the State University of New York at Albany (SUNY), with a Fulbright scholarship and an Organization of American States (OAS) fellowship. His research interests and publishing focus on higher education in Argentina, internationalization of higher education in Latin America, accreditation, and regulation of graduate education. His most recent work on "Education in Latin America and the Caribbean: Systems and Research" appears in the *International Encyclopedia of the Social and Behavioural Sciences* (2nd edition).

Daria Siciliano is a Research Associate at the Marine Science Institute of the University of California, Santa Cruz (UCSC). With expertise in coral reef ecology, geochemistry, and marine science synthesis and communication, she was formerly the Director of Science at SeaWeb. She holds a PhD in Biological Oceanography from UCSC and a BS from the University of California Santa Barbara. She is the Lead Scientist for the Cuba Marine Research and Conservation Program of the Ocean Foundation, where she oversees all scientific initiatives and collaborations, working closely with partners in the United States and Cuba at the University of Havana, the Cuban Ministry of Science Technology and Environment (CITMA), the National Aquarium of Cuba, and the Cuban Oceanology Institute.

Bernhard Streitwieser is Assistant Professor of International Education at the George Washington University in Washington, DC. His research looks at the impact of globalization on the internationalization of higher education and three main focus areas: research on study abroad and international student exchange; access and integration of migrants and refugees into higher education, with a geographic focus on Germany; and research on international branch campuses and education hubs. From 2010 to 2013, he was a visiting Fulbright and DAAD-funded professor at Berlin's Humboldt University; from 2002 to 2010, a Senior Researcher at Northwestern University, Lecturer in the School of Education and Social Policy, and Associate Director of the Study Abroad Office; and from 1998 to 2002, a guest researcher at the Max-Planck-Institut für-Bildungsforschung in Berlin and a Research Analyst at American Institutes for Research in Washington, DC. He has published *Internationalisation of Higher Education and Global Mobility* for the Oxford Studies in Comparative Education series (2014), the report on Germany for the European Parliament (2015), and *International Higher Education's Scholar-Practitioners: Bridging Research and Practice* (2016).

Nanette Svenson is an Adjunct Professor of Global Development at Tulane University. She is based in the Republic of Panama and also works as a consultant for the United Nations and other development organizations. Previously, she helped establish the UNDP Regional Centre for Latin America and the Caribbean, heading its research and knowledge management efforts, and taught at local universities in Panama. Recent projects include a book on *The United Nations as a Knowledge System*, a national higher education capacity diagnostic for the Panamanian government, and research for the UNDP on public administration higher education in Latin America and the Caribbean. She teaches courses on Education and International Development and on the United Nations System.

Guy Tapie is Professor of Sociology at the *Ecole Nationale Supérieure d'Architecture et de Paysage de Bordeaux* (School of Architecture and Landscape, Bordeaux, France). His research focuses on housing and habitat production, processes of city building, and architectural issues in contemporary society. He has published several books and numerous articles. He is a founding member and former director of the PAVE research laboratory (*Profession Architecture Ville Environnement*) and a member of the Emile Durkheim Research Center (CED CNRS 5116). He also supervises doctoral studies at the University of Bordeaux.

Clara I. Tascón holds a PhD from Western University, Canada, and teaches in the Bachelors of Education program. Previously, she held positions as an academic coordinator, a research coordinator, and a professor in several universities in Colombia. Her research interests include the internationalization of higher education, international research collaboration between universities in Canada and Latin America, knowledge production and interdisciplinary networks dynamics, and globalization, internationalization policy, and leadership in higher education. She is a member of the Comparative and International Education Society (CIES), the Higher Education Special Interest Group (CIES-HESIG), and the Comparative and International Education Society of Canada (CIESC).

ABBREVIATIONS AND ACRONYMS

AACSB	Association to Advance Collegiate Schools of Business
ABCE	Bolivian Academy of Economic Sciences
ABEST	Argentinian Bureau for Enhancing Cooperation with the European Community
AHCI	Arts & Humanities Citation Index
AIEA	Association of International Education Administrators
ALMA	Atacama Large Millimeter Array
ALTAGRO	Agriculture Alternative
ANII	National Agency of Research and Innovation
ANPCYT	National Agency for Science and Technology Promotion
APEX	Atacama Pathfinder Experiment
APLU	Association of Public and Land-Grant Universities
ASEAN	Association of Southeast Asian Nations
ATTO	Amazon Tall Tower Observatory
BALAS	Business Association of Latin American Studies
BCIE	Central American Bank for Economic Integration
BIO-ICE	Biodiversity in Bolivian Glaciers
BIO-THAW	Tropical High Andean Wetlands
BIOMOLECTRONICS	Biomolecular Electronics and Electrocatalysis
BMBF	German Federal Ministry of Education and Research
BRT	Bus Rapid Transit

CA	California
CAF	Development Bank of Latin America
CAFTA	Central American Free Trade Agreement
CAPSI	Central American Private Sector Initiative
CEBEM	Bolivian Center for Multidisciplinary Research
CELADE	Latin American and Caribbean Center of Demography
CEPAL	Economic Commission for Latin America and the Caribbean
CERES	Center for Studies on Economic and Social Reality
CFP	Call for Proposals
CIM	Center for Marine Research of the University of Havana
CIMA	Center for Applied Medicine Research
CITES	Convention on International Trade in Endangered Species of Flora and Fauna
CLACDS	Latin American Center for Competitiveness and Sustainable Development
CLACSO	Latin American Council on the Social Sciences
CLADEA	Latin American Council of Business Schools
CNPq	National Council for Scientific and Technological Development
COCHRANE	Database of Systematic Reviews
COLCIENCIAS	Colombian National Science and Technology System
CONACYT	National Council on Science and Technology Mexico
CONAHEC	Consortium for North American Higher Education
CONICET	National Scientific and Technical Research Council, Argentina
CONICYT	National Commission for Scientific and Technological Research, Chile
COPriResNet	Colombian Private Research Network
COPubResNet	Colombian Public Research Network
CRUCH	Council of Rectors of Chilean Universities
CV	Curriculum Vitae
DAAD-Germany	German Academic Exchange Service

DCIT	Department of Communication and Information Technologies
DETEIC	Technological Development, Innovation and Conformity Assessment Project, Paraguay
DST	Department of Science and Technology
EBSCO	EBSCO Information Services
ECLAC	United Nations Economic Confederation for Latin America and the Caribbean
EFMD	European Foundation for Management Development
EHEA	European Higher Education Area
ERA	European Research Area
EURALSUR	Europe-Mercosur Network in Advanced Materials and Nanomaterials
FCB	School of Biomedical Sciences
FLACSO	Latin American Faculty of Social Sciences
FOBESII	Bilateral Forum on Higher Education, Innovation, and Research
FONDECYT	National Fund for Science and Technology
GDP	Gross Domestic Product
GPS	Global Positioning Systems
GT	Group Turtle
GTZ	German Federal Enterprise for International Cooperation
HBS	Harvard Business School
HE	Higher Education
HIID	Harvard Institute for International Development
HU	Harvard University
IAA	International Association of Academies
IBIOBA	Institute for Biomedical Research of Buenos Aires
ICSU	International Council for Science
ICT	Information and Communication Technologies
IDB	Inter-American Development Bank
ILPES	Latin American Institute for Economic and Social Planning
IMR	Ignis Mutat Res
INCAE	Central American Institute of Business Administration

INPA	National Institute of Amazonian Research
INQUIMAE	Institute of Chemical Physics of Materials, Environment and Energy
IRC	International Research Collaboration
IUCN	International Union for Conservation of Nature
KFW	German Bank for Development
KI	Karolinska Institute
LAC	Latin America and the Caribbean
LAPOP	Latin American Public Opinion Project
LATINDEX	Regional Cooperative Online Information System for Scholarly Journals from Latin America, the Caribbean, Spain and Portugal
MBA	Master of Business Administration
MEC	Ministry of Education
MINCYT	Ministry of Science, Technology and Productive Innovation
MIT	Massachusetts Institute of Technology
MOU	Memorandum of Understanding
MP	Max Planck
MPAs	Marine Protected Areas
MPI	Max Planck Institutes
MPS	Max Planck Society
NAFSA	National Association of Foreign Student Advisors
NAFTA	North American Free Trade Agreement
NASPAA	Association of Schools of Public Affairs and Administration
NGO	Non-Governmental Organization
NMNHP	National Museum of Natural History of Paraguay
NOAA	National Oceanic and Atmospheric Administration
OECD	Organisation for Economic Co-operation and Development
PAVE	Profession Architecture, Ville et Environment Research Laboratory
PhD	Doctor of Philosophy

PIIE	Interdisciplinary Program for Educational Research
PIRE	Partnerships for International Research and Education
PREAL	Partnership for Educational Revitalization in the Americas
PROCIT	Support Program for the Development of Science, Technology and Innovation, Paraguay
PROINPA	Andean Products Promotion and Research Foundation
PRONII	National Incentive Program for Researchers, Paraguay
QS	Quacquarelli Symonds World University Ranking
R/V	Research Vessel
R&D	Research and Development
RAICES	Network of Argentinian Researchers and Scientists Abroad
RedALyC	Latin America and Caribbean Scientific Information System
RICYT	Iberic-American and Inter-American Network of Science and Technology Indicators
SACS	Southern Association of Colleges and Schools
SBS	School of Biomedical Sciences
SCI	Science Citation Index
SciELO	Scientific Electronic Library Online
SEKN	Social Enterprise Knowledge Network
SNA	Social Network Analysis
SNP	South-North Partnerships
SPI	Social Progress Imperative
SSCI	Social Sciences Citation Index
STEM	Science, Technology, Engineering, and Mathematics
STI	Science, Technology, and Innovation
TECH	Monterrey Institute of Technology and Higher Education
TOF	The Ocean Foundation
TWAIL	Third World Approaches to Law
TWAS	Third World Academy of Science

UA	Austral University
UABJB	Autonomous University of Beni José Ballivián
UAJMS	Autonomous University Juan Misael Saracho
UBA	University of Buenos Aires
UC	University of Cincinnati
UCBSP	Bolivian Catholic University San Pablo
UCNSA	Catholic University Our Lady of Asuncion
UCSC	University of California, Santa Cruz
UFPR	The Federal University of Paraná in Curitiba, Brazil
UIS	UNESCO Institute for Statistics
UK HE	United Kingdom Higher Education
UMSA	Major University of San Andres
UMSS	Major University of San Simon
UNA	National University of Asuncion
UNCED	United Nations Conference on Environment and Development
UNDP	United Nations Development Program
UNEP	United Nations Environmental Program
UNESCO	United Nations Educational, Scientific and Cultural Organization
UPB	Bolivian Private University
USAID	United States Agency for International Development
USD	United States Dollar
WEF	World Economic Forum
WHOI	Woods Hole Oceanographic Institution
WoK	Web of Knowledge
WTO	World Trade Organization

LIST OF FIGURES

Fig. 5.1   Colombia Public Research Network—COPubResNet. (Direct members (nodes) of the COPubResNet: COPubProf1 (Coordinator of the network), COPubProf2, COPubProf3, COPubProf4, COPubPostdoc, COPubDr, COPubMon. Indirect members (nodes) of the COPubResNet: COPubResFac1, COPubIntOff, COPubVicResOff, and other research networks such as EuroAsianNet, COPubUNet, CONatNet, LatinNet1, and so on)   96

Fig. 5.2   Colombian Private Research Network—COPriResNet. (Direct members (nodes) of the COPriResNet: COPriProf1, COPriProf2, COPriProf3, COPriProf4, COPriPhD1, COPriPhD2, COPriMon. Indirect members (nodes) of the COPriResNet: COPriResFac, COPriVicResOff, COPriIntOff, and other research networks such as COPriUNet, CONatNet, EuroNet1, LatinNet1, and so on)   97

Fig. 9.1   Argentinian papers produced through international collaboration, by country, 2008–2012. (Source: MINCYT 2014)   210

LIST OF TABLES

Table 2.1	Collaboration agreements with US research partners, 1981–2016	18
Table 3.1	The Ocean Foundation as a conduit for US-Cuba marine research	52
Table 4.1	Selected Central American development statistics, 2014	64
Table 4.2	List of INCAE rectors	72
Table 4.3	Types of research collaboration and associated characteristics	74
Table 5.1	Colombian Public Research Network (COPubResNet), node codes and descriptors	99
Table 5.2	Colombian Private Research Network (COPriResNet), node codes and descriptors	100
Table 7.1	Journals in SciELO Bolivia, December 2015	152
Table 7.2	Journals in SciELO Paraguay, December 2015	154
Table 9.1	Criteria and dimensions	215
Table 9.2	Number of publications and citations in relation to international collaboration at INQUIMAE and FCB, 2010–2014	224
Table 10.1	Number of collaborative research projects by university and topic (2010–2015)	244
Table 10.2	Research reports by targeted population	247
Table 10.3	Participating researchers, disciplines, and degree levels	247
Table 11.1	Development of Max Planck's partnerships with Latin America (2013–2015)	267
Table 11.2	Max Planck Research Groups currently operating in Latin America	269

xxvii

CHAPTER 1

Introduction

Gustavo Gregorutti and Nanette Svenson

Research productivity is a critical component of university output worldwide and a major determinant in global university rankings. Universities in Latin America and the Caribbean (LAC) have been consistently weak in this regard. The entire region accounts for just over three percent of global research and development (R&D), around four percent of Science Citation Index publications, and about two percent of the top 500 universities globally (Marginson 2012; PREAL 2007; Velez-Cuartas et al. 2015). Despite the lackluster figures, certain LAC university research programs are producing results. Many of these engage North-South university partnerships, with one or more institutions from industrialized countries and one or more LAC institutions.

This book explores the dynamics involved in some of these LAC North-South research partnerships and presents various examples from countries in the region as illustrative case studies. The general research questions in the studies of the cases presented revolve around: What

G. Gregorutti (✉)
Leadership and Higher Education, Andrews University,
Berrien Springs, MI, USA

N. Svenson
Global Development Program, Tulane University, New Orleans, LA, USA

© The Author(s) 2018
G. Gregorutti, N. Svenson (eds.), *North-South University Research Partnerships in Latin America and the Caribbean*,
https://doi.org/10.1007/978-3-319-75364-5_1

motivates collaboration between universities in different countries with distinct sociocultural and economic development contexts? What barriers and limitations are faced in carrying out joint research? What key factors advance research productivity for these partnerships? Much of the scholarly work done on international research collaborations (IRCs), and North-South partnerships in particular, focuses on co-authorship as a measure for increased productivity; it concentrates less on the intangible, multifaceted issues of relationships, operational mechanics, and knowledge generation. The focus of this book is the latter. It builds on the literature studying the many forms these collaborations may take, with varying responsibilities for involved parties; the different motivations— individually and organizationally driven—for entering into such partnerships; and the external and internal factors that influence collaboration parameters (Bozeman et al. 2013; Bradley 2007; Sonnenwald 2007). Through application of case study analysis, the book contributes qualitative empirical evidence to further substantiate and broaden documented theoretical claims on international, and particularly North-South, research partnerships.

This introduction to the text begins with a brief overview of the literature on IRC and partnerships. It then links this review with certain relevant characteristics and tendencies of the LAC region and its higher education and research sectors. Finally, it presents synopses of the case studies that form the basis for each of the subsequent chapters.

INTERNATIONAL RESEARCH COLLABORATION AND NORTH-SOUTH UNIVERSITY PARTNERSHIPS

The practice of research collaboration between universities and scholars in different countries is almost as old as academia itself. While formal definitions, agreement parameters, and publication on the topic of IRC, itself, are all newer phenomena, the cross-border combining of forces for expanded, improved scientific perspective and results has a long academic tradition. Even more organized associations for propelling this endeavor have been in existence for more than a century. The International Council for Science (ICSU), one of the oldest non-governmental organizations for promoting scientific partnerships between countries for the benefit of humanity, was founded in 1931—and represented a merger of earlier bodies dedicated to similar missions, the International Association of Academies (1899–1914) and the International Research Council (1919–1931).

Today, the ICSU boasts 122 members representing 142 countries around the world and lists its key priorities as IRC, development of international science policy, and the creation of a global scientific community on the basis of equity (ICSU 2016). Agreements of collaborations between the European Union and LAC have been on the rise; the Declaration of Santiago is one of the most comprehensive partnerships between the regions (Council of the European Union 2013). Projects oriented to map biodiversity and ecosystems in LAC supported by the European Research Area are new possibilities for researchers and universities to join in complex teams across continents (Olivier et al. 2016).

The focus on North-South university partnerships for research collaboration also has a fairly long tradition, though publication on the subject as such was accelerated as a result of post-World War II decolonization efforts and the more recent advent of the knowledge economy near the end of the twentieth century (Baud 2002; Binka 2005; Gaillard 1994). In this discourse, the issues revolve more around inequality, in all its facets, knowledge transfer, and pursuit of mutually beneficial agendas and outputs. Yet, in spite of the increased attention directed toward the topic, a number of important gaps persist in the literature.

First, there is a disproportionate tendency to rely on bibliometric quantification of international co-authorship as the predominant methodology for assessing international research cooperation (Bozeman et al. 2013; Katz and Martin 1997). While this means is undeniably simpler and easiest to measure, it ignores numerous aspects of the collaborative relationships and their results, as well as the associations that do not produce joint publications. Second, even studies that go beyond co-authorship metrics tend to focus on efficiency and productivity gains without exploring the more complex issues of ownership, capacity development, and sustainability (Bozeman et al. 2013). Third, to the extent that individual research partners' situations are examined, emphases are inclined toward respective financial resources (Ynalvez and Shrum 2011), organizational management characteristics (Cummings and Kiesler 2005; Fox and Mohapatra 2007; Siegel et al. 2003), and specific forms of partnership (Bukvova 2010; Morrison et al.. 2003; Sonnenwald 2007).

Among the more comprehensive activities undertaken in recent years to review the overall state of IRC and the individual elements that comprise it are the 2008 study, *International Research Collaboration: Opportunities for the UK Higher Education Sector,* conducted by the UK

Higher Education International Unit established to promote and undertake activities designed to support UK universities, and the 2011 study, *Examining Core Elements of International Research Collaboration - Summary of a Workshop,* from the US National Academies' Government-University-Industry Research Roundtable. Both studies aim to synthesize some of the major trends, benefits, support, and obstacles associated with cross-border research partnerships. Both publications highlight the considerable growth over the past decades of this type of endeavor and also the need for universities and governments to do more for facilitating and supporting these initiatives (UK HE 2008; US National Academies 2011). While these studies are welcome contributions to the international North-South research partnership discourse, both are conducted from a Northern perspective with a view to enhancing the competitiveness of the Northern institutions and countries involved. More from the South is needed for balancing the discourse and providing the view from the other side.

LAC Higher Education and Research Context

Higher education in the LAC region has made important progress over the past few decades. Enrollment has doubled and demand continues to grow; providers have multiplied and diversified; degree categories and levels have expanded considerably; university administration has become more decentralized and cognizant of the need to link with industry; and the higher education sector in almost every country has become more internationalized. Nevertheless, much remains to be done for realizing the region's vast potential in this regard. Graduation rates are still low; quality issues persist and quality assurance systems are weak; inequity is pervasive throughout the region and within each country; the academic offer is inconsistent with labor market demand; and R&D is highly underdeveloped (Holm-Nielsen et al. 2005; UNESCO 2017).

Universities in LAC were established initially in the image of those already existing in the countries of their European colonizers, run by the public sector and the Catholic Church, designed primarily to educate professionals rather than function as sources of new knowledge. Whereas the European and US universities began to orient more toward research with the Industrial Revolution of the nineteenth century, LAC higher education did not. The region's economic growth has continued to depend heavily on export of primary products requiring little intellectual innovation and its universities have been slow to adopt vigorous research agendas (Arocena and Sutz 2005). This teaching-centered model has endured even as higher education enrollment and institutional establishment (especially private) have exploded over the past 30 years. Though LAC student enrollment grew from under 23 percent in 2000 to over 44 percent of the respective age cohort in 2013, LAC expenditure on R&D continued to hover around 0.5 percent of gross domestic product over the same period (with Europe and the US steadily investing roughly five times that percentage) (UIS 2017). Additionally, unlike the situation in most developed regions where private industry finances up to 60 or 70 percent of national research, LAC funding of R&D is predominantly public with little (10–15 percent) private participation. In many places, there is still an active distrust between academia and the private sector that tends to propel separation of the two realms (Didriksson 2008).

A further hindrance to developing LAC university research capacity is the relative dearth of doctorate holders among most higher education faculties. While most developed country university professors hold a PhD, the majority of LAC university professors do not (roughly one in ten professors, on average)—and many do not even hold a Master's degree (Holm-Nielsen et al. 2005). This makes it more difficult for universities to conduct research and offer PhD coursework and degrees. This situation is reflected in the statistics on the number of researchers in R&D per million inhabitants: the LAC regional average is just over 500, compared with the Organisation for Economic Co-operation and Development (OECD) average of nearly 2500 and the US average of over 3000 (World Bank 2017). Even in countries where public policy has pursued a national strategy over time to fortify research (e.g., Mexico, Brazil, Venezuela, Colombia, Costa Rica, Uruguay, and Argentina), returns are still quite small at the global level (Didriksson 2008). Financing is part of the problem, but another part lies in the preparation and experience of the professor as well as institutional allocation of professor time to research endeavors.

In spite of the multiple challenges to fortifying R&D in the LAC university context, progress is being made. Particular success stories merit further exploration—because of the heroics of their efforts and outputs, in many cases, and also for the clues they may provide for extrapolation and replication, within the LAC region and beyond. The stories presented in the following chapters reflect LAC attempts to boost R&D efforts through North–South collaborations. Better understanding of these experiences is critical as evidence from both the region and the OECD highlights the strategic importance of expanding exchange of ideas and individuals, instead of only looking inward, for the production of new knowledge (Holm-Nielsen et al. 2005).

CHAPTER CONTENT

The following paragraphs provide a chapter-by-chapter synopsis of the book's content. After this introduction that sets the stage, the volume presents a total of 11 chapters, each of which offers a relevant case study from a particular country or collection of countries within the LAC region. The order of these is arranged geographically from North to South.

Chapter 2 begins with Mexico and is titled, "Introducing a Bilateral Research and Innovation Agenda: A Case Study on Mexico and the United States." In the chapter, Gustavo Gregorutti, Beverly Barrett, and Angeles Dominguez examine the results of several research partnerships between the Tecnológico de Monterrey (or the Tech, as it is referred to in English), a private university in northern Mexico, and various US universities and companies. The Tech has been pursuing a research agenda throughout the last decade and one of the strategies involved targets collaboration with prestigious US institutions. The study presented here is based on data from interviews with principal Tech liaisons placed in different areas of the US, and seeks to develop a deeper understanding of the motives, benefits, and limitations surrounding these collaborations. Conclusions indicate the collaborative efforts have enhanced Mexican faculty research productivity, advanced human resource capacity development, and generated useful and marketable applied research. US institutions have also expanded their research trajectories through these partnerships and improved their related knowledge bases. The chapter ends by offering alternative policies for promoting research collaboration and knowledge exchange with potential for impacting regional economies.

Chapter 3 moves to Cuba. In "Science Beyond Politics: Cuba-US Marine Research and Conservation," Daria Siciliano, Fernando Bretos, Julia Azanza, and Nanette Svenson explore the Ocean Foundation Cuba Marine Research and Conservation Program, an ongoing multiyear endeavor that brings together Cuban and US researchers—from the University of Havana, the University of California, Santa Cruz, and various other institutes—in unprecedented marine research. The initiative began in 1999, builds on prior work in the area, and combines study on species diversity, genetic connectivity, and historical ecology with conservation targets for protected areas in Cuban marine ecosystems. Two projects in particular are highlighted: the Guanahacabibes Peninsula Marine Turtle Conservation Project, and the Three Gulfs Project. The chapter focuses on how the Ocean Foundation, a US-based non-governmental organization, serves as the necessary bridge in this multinational venture to facilitate cross-border scientific collaboration in a climate of political and socioeconomic tension. It looks at the processes involved in this complex partnership, the roles and contributions of all participants, the obstacles overcome, and the resulting successes, exchanges, and scientific output achieved to date.

Chapter 4, "INCAE, Harvard and International Development: Research for Progress in Central America," looks at the subregion of Central America and the development of research activity in the Central American Institute of Business Administration (Instituto Centroamericano de Administración de Empresas, INCAE). It specifically explores INCAE's Latin American Center for Competitiveness and Sustainable Development (Centro Latinoamericano para la Competitividad y el Desarrollo Sostenible, CLACDS) and the role that Harvard University has played in the center's evolution. The chapter examines multiple aspects of this productive, half-century INCAE-Harvard partnership and the results generated. It also studies CLACDS' affiliation with key international development actors and how the combination of these inputs has propelled INCAE and CLACDS to the forefront of knowledge generation for Central American development. Key outputs in recent years include national and regional monitoring for the World Economic Forum and Social Progress Index; the Central American Private Sector Initiative for improved public policy; numerous joint projects with the United Nations for microfinance and sustainable development; and hundreds of publications in regional and international journals in both English and Spanish.

Chapter 5 moves to Colombia in South America. Clara I. Tascon presents "International Research Collaboration and Knowledge Production in Colombia: A Qualitative Network Analysis Approach," which addresses the motivations, challenges, and knowledge production associated with the IRC of Colombian universities. It provides examples of two Colombian research networks tied respectively to one public and one private university. Based on a qualitative Social Network Analysis approach, Tascon examines the configurations of these research networks and their embedded diaspora associations to reveal the relational dynamics of their interconnections and activities. This qualitative network approach allows for more in-depth exploration of the complex scenario of knowledge flows, sharing, and production involved in IRC in Colombia.

Chapter 6 focuses on a personal US-Colombia academic partnership that has worked to develop legal knowledge in the region through a broad collective of projects involving a number of LAC countries, institutions, and situations. In "The Political Economy of Legal Knowledge in Action: Collaborative Projects in the Americas," Daniel Bonilla Maldonado and Colin Crawford discuss how legal knowledge is a commodity and a product that is generated, exchanged, and used in specific contexts following prescribed norms. The set of rules and principles that shape the production of legal knowledge constitute its political economy. This examination of the political economy of legal knowledge concentrates on some of the routine academic practices that determine the ways in which legal knowledge is created, exchanged, and used. It is an exercise in the cultural analysis of law and describes a decade's worth of dynamic programming led by Tulane University Law School in New Orleans, Louisiana, and the Universidad de los Andes School of Law in Bogota, Colombia, to promote joint academic research among US and Latin American scholars. It applies conceptual tools to better understand the collaborative practices in the creation of legal thought as they play out in the legal academies of the US and Latin America and how they are typically characterized by a dominant global North partner and a subordinate global South partner. The chapter also offers a set of general normative criteria to guide truly collaborative processes for the construction of legal knowledge, distinct from both the traditional free market and colonial models of legal ideas.

Chapter 7 is set in Bolivia and Paraguay. Jorge Enrique Delgado notes in "Small Fish in a Big Pond: Internationalization and Research Collaboration in Bolivia and Paraguay" that Latin America is not a homogeneous region and is commonly described only with analyses of the largest and most studied countries—Brazil, Mexico, Chile, and Argentina—without much consideration of smaller countries such as Paraguay and Bolivia. This is as true for IRC as it is for most other topics. In response, Delgado's chapter analyzes the ways in which universities in Bolivia and Paraguay have found to develop international partnerships that serve to propel their research pursuits. The argument is that even though in these countries tendencies are toward more limited research capacity, smaller project size, and less generalizable research outcomes, there are, nevertheless, interesting initiatives involving international collaboration that show promising accomplishments and merit documentation. The chapter discusses these countries' demographic, economic, and R&D indicators, and analyzes their science and technology capacity and outputs as well as their higher education and science, technology, and innovation systems. It goes on to review international co-authorship and assess other

INTRODUCTION 9

forms of international collaboration activity in order to provide recommendations for small countries like Bolivia and Paraguay with regard to the development of international collaborations to promote national science and technology systems.

Chapter 8 discusses Brazil in a research partnership with France and the US. In "Comparing Urban Mobility and the Energy Transition in France, USA, and Brazil: From Research Collaboration to Institutional Partnerships," Kent Fitzsimons, Guy Tapie, Patrice Godier, and Cristina de Araújo Lima study how topics that concern global challenges require a novel kind of research that transcends the conventional model of case study comparison to develop a transnational understanding of their scope. This is the situation for the energy sector and sustainability, linked as they are through the problem of climate change. At the same time, urban development, in which energy use is an important parameter, is eminently tied to highly local conditions, whether they are geographical, historical, political, or cultural. The partnership discussed here began as a collective response to a French government call for proposals for the research program *Ignis Mutat Res* in 2011. A multinational, multidisciplinary research team was composed specifically for the project, and included members from three institutions in France (the coordinator), the US, and Brazil. The international collaboration aimed to study the effects of energy transition on mobility policy and practices, as well as on urban form, in three metropolitan areas experiencing demographic growth: Bordeaux, Cincinnati, and Curitiba. Alongside conventional research protocol, the team developed a methodological device in the form of a series of seminar and pedagogical events held in each of the three cities. This chapter discusses the project's results as well as its key success factors and some of the major obstacles encountered. Beyond lasting scientific results, the partnership experience produced a promising basis for future cooperation.

Chapter 9 takes us to Argentina where Angela Corengia, Ana García de Fanelli, Marcelo Rabossi, and Dante J. Salto look at "International Partnerships for Collaborative Research in Argentinian Universities" and address North-South university partnership contributions to the strengthening of national R&D. The chapter looks at the motivations behind this type of cooperation and the principal facilitators of and obstacles to success in two specific cases focused on the research units at public and private Argentinian universities with established North-South research partnerships. General conclusions indicate that international scientific cooperation between the South and the North has proven fruitful for the parties involved in these agreements; however, what triggers and grounds the association differs by case. Following a series of interviews and document analysis, findings show that while personal links generally dominate in their importance, state support is critical for sustainability. Difficulties that generate disincentives for maintaining longer-term partnerships are related primarily to internal, bureaucratic problems and external factors such as overall economic instability affecting both developed and developing countries.

Chapter 10 concentrates on Chile. In "Collaborative Research by Chilean and North American Scholars: Precedents and Projections," Oscar Espinoza, Luis Eduardo González, and Noel F. McGinn provide a snapshot of recent experiences in collaborative research between scholars in universities in Chile and the US from the perspective of Chilean researchers. IRC was severely constrained during the military dictatorship (1973–1989) but in the years following, democracy and rapid economic growth contributed to a significant increase in the number of projects of cross-border research production involving universities in Chile and elsewhere. This chapter is based on results from a survey of a non-representative sample of research projects in Chile that solicited information from directors of the projects. At least 79 collaborative research projects involving Chilean and US universities were initiated between 2010 and 2014. Data were obtained from participants in about 15 percent of the projects. Overall, Chilean participants indicated a high level of satisfaction with their collaborative research experience.

Pedro Pineda and Bernhard Streitwieser close the book with Chapter 11 entitled "Research Partnership Over Neocolonialism: Max Planck Society Policy in Latin America." They argue that the academic interest in North-South research cooperation has increased concurrently with joint scientific inquiry due to multiple factors. Noting tendencies observed in earlier chapters, they discuss how the general dynamics of research partnerships are traditionally explained through highlighting their functionality to universal scientific inquiry (Merton 1973), and also how more recent critiques (Crossley and Tikly 2004; Gaillard 1994; Nguyen et al. 2009) contend these partnerships may entail cultural controls from abroad that represent a form of neocolonialism. In this chapter, they aim to contribute to the theoretical discussion through an analysis of the Max Planck Institutes' work throughout Latin America. They find that cooperation is enforced, on the Northern side, through a programmatic regional office, two big installations with international cooperation, nine associated institutes and laboratories, and 25 research groups. On the Southern side, public and private universities and institutes with different profiles undertake joint research activities based on policies serving to strengthen their academic environment and allow researchers from the South access to high-level research and training that helps expand local knowledge. They note that ultimate success depends heavily on the level of national government support. They also discuss how research activities situated within broader research agendas run by the North may shut out Southern peers from having a more prominent influence on the methods and topics pursued. These scenarios highlight some of the tensions between functionalist and decolonial approaches to understanding the dynamics inherent in North-South research partnerships.

In short, this book aims to add to the current scholarly base on North-South research and at the same time produce evidence related to case study experience that looks deeper into the principal motivations on both sides for engaging in international North-South research collaborations, major factors that foster or hinder partnerships, and the value-added outputs of such cooperation. It adds to the literature on North-South research collaborations with regionally specific and practice-based empirical data from cases in the LAC region research context. From all of this, it also provides general policy recommendations for developing countries on engaging international partners for realizing R&D objectives.

REFERENCES

Arocena, R., & Sutz, J. (2005). Latin American Universities: From an Original Revolution to an Uncertain Transition. *Higher Education, 50,* 573–592.

Baud, I. S. A. (2002). North-South Research Partnerships in Development Research: An Institutions Approach. In *North-South Research Cooperation.* Amsterdam: KNAW.

Binka, F. (2005). North–South Research Collaborations: A Move Towards a True Partnership? *Tropical Medicine and International Health, 10*(3), 207–209.

Bozeman, B., Fay, D., & Slade, C. P. (2013). Research Collaboration in Universities and Academic Entrepreneurship: The-State-of-the-Art. *The Journal of Technology Transfer, 38*(1), 1–67.

Bradley, M. (2007). *North-South Research Partnerships: Challenges, Responses and Trends. A Literature Review and Annotated Bibliography.* Ottawa: International Development Research Center.

Bukvova, H. (2010). Studying Research Collaboration: A Literature Review. *Sprouts: Working Papers in Information Systems, 10*(3), 1–17.

Council of the European Union. (2013). *EU-CELAC Action Plan 2013–2015*. Santiago Summit, Chile, 5748/13 Presse 32.

Crossley, M., & Tikly, L. (2004). Postcolonial Perspectives and Comparative and International Research in Education: A Critical Introduction. *Comparative Education, 40*(2), 147–156.

Cummings, J. N., & Kiesler, S. (2005). Collaborative Research Across Disciplinary and Organizational Boundaries. *Social Studies of Science, 35*(5), 703–722.

Didriksson, A. (2008). Global and Regional Contexts of Higher Education in Latin America and the Caribbean. In A. L. Gazzola & A. Didriksson (Eds.), *Trends in Higher Education in Latin America and the Caribbean*. Caracas: UNESCO.

Fox, M. F., & Mohapatra, S. (2007). Social-Organizational Characteristics of Work and Publication Productivity Among Academic Scientists in Doctoral-Granting Departments. *The Journal of Higher Education, 78*(5), 542–571.

Gaillard, J. (1994). North-South Research Partnership: Is Collaboration Possible Between Unequal Partners? *Knowledge and Policy, 7*(2), 31–63.

Holm-Nielsen, L., Thorn, K., Brunner, J. J., & Balán, J. (2005). Regional and International Challenges to Higher Education in Latin America. In H. de Wit, J. Gacel-Avila, & J. Knight (Eds.), *Higher Education in Latin America: The International Dimension*. Washington, DC: World Bank.

International Council for Science (ICSU). 2016. *About ICSU*. Accessed from http://www.icsu.org/about-icsu/

Katz, J. S., & Martin, B. R. (1997). What is Research Collaboration? *Research Policy, 26*(1), 1–18.

Marginson, S. (2012, June 10). Improving Latin American Universities' Global Ranking. *University World News* (225).

Merton, R. K. (1973). The Normative Structure of Science. In *The Sociology of Science: Theoretical and Empirical Investigations* (pp. 267–280). Chicago: University of Chicago Press.

Morrison, P. S., Dobbie, G., & McDonald, F. J. (2003). Research Collaboration Among University Scientists. *Higher Education Research & Development, 22*(3), 275–296.

Nguyen, P. M., Elliott, J. G., Terlouw, C., & Pilot, A. (2009). Neocolonialism in Education: Cooperative Learning in an Asian Context. *Comparative Education, 45*(1), 109–130.

Olivier Dangles (Alcue Net/IRD), Jean Loirat (Alcue Net) and Xavier Le Roux (BiodivERsA/FRB). (2016). *Mapping the Collaboration Between Europe and Latin America/Caribbean for Research on Biodiversity*. ALCUE NETBiodivERsA Report.

Partnership for Educational Revitalization in the Americas (PREAL). (2007). *A Lot to Do: A Report Card on Education in Central America and the Dominican Republic*. Washington, DC: PREAL Task Force on Education Reform in Central America.

INTRODUCTION 13

Siegel, D. S., Waldman, D., & Link, A. (2003). Assessing the Impact of Organizational Practices on the Relative Productivity of University Technology Transfer Offices: An Exploratory Study. *Research Policy, 32*(1), 27–48.

Sonnenwald, D. H. (2007). Scientific Collaboration. *Annual Review of Information Science and Technology, 41*(1), 643–681.

UK Higher Education International Unit. (2008). *International Research Collaboration: Opportunities for the UK Higher Education Sector.* London: Universities UK.

UNESCO Institute for Statistics (UIS). (2017). *Data.* Education. Accessed from http://data.uis.unesco.org/

US National Academies. (2011). *Examining Core Elements of International Research Collaboration – Summary of A Workshop.* Washington, DC: The National Academies Press.

Velez-Cuartas, G., Lucio-Arias, D., & Leydesdorff, L. (2015). Regional and Global Science: Publications from Latin America and the Caribbean in the SciELO Citation Index and the Web of Science. *El Profesional de la Información, 25*(1), 35–46.

World Bank. (2017). *Data.* Researchers in R&D. Accessed from http://data.worldbank.org/indicator/SP.POP.SCIE.RD.P6

Ynalvez, M. A., & Shrum, W. M. (2011). Professional Networks, Scientific Collaboration, and Publication Productivity in Resource-Constrained Research Institutions in a Developing Country. *Research Policy, 40*(2), 204–216.

CHAPTER 2

Introducing a Bilateral Research and Innovation Agenda: A Case Study on Mexico and the United States

Gustavo Gregorutti, Beverly Barrett, and Angeles Dominguez

THE EVOLUTION OF BILATERAL COLLABORATION

The history of the bilateral relationship between Mexico and the United States of America (US) has been interwoven throughout the centuries, even as political boundaries have shifted over time. While the two countries have established themselves independently, meeting the need for education has been essential for economic development in both. Education

G. Gregorutti (✉)
Andrews University, Michigan, USA

B. Barrett
Hobby School of Public Affairs, University of Houston, Houston, TX, USA

A. Dominguez
School of Education, Tecnologico de Monterrey, Monterrey, Mexico

© The Author(s) 2018   15
G. Gregorutti, N. Svenson (eds.), *North-South University
Research Partnerships in Latin America and the Caribbean*,
https://doi.org/10.1007/978-3-319-75364-5_2

for elites only gave way to the massification of higher education toward the mid-twentieth century in the US and other developed countries (Burrage 2010). In Mexico, the massification process intensified in the 1980s, as the country's international economic progress was accompanied by a reduction in state provision of services, including higher education. At the time, according to Rodríguez Gómez and Ordorika (2012), national policies in higher education pursued three related objectives: (1) modernization of higher education administration to improve public educational quality, which included government investment; (2) public investment in technological institutions to promote diversity in higher education; and (3) greater institutional diversity in higher education, prompting private investment in new institutions for students not served by the stagnant public sector (pp. 237–238). These three objectives advanced over the following decades to create the context for the bilateral research and development (R&D) collaboration now taking place. The North American Free Trade Agreement (NAFTA) implemented in 1994 also served to create the policy space needed for prompting partnerships and exchanges between Mexican and US universities.[1]

When Mexican President, Enrique Peña Nieto, took office in December 2012, he promised reform in energy, finance, and infrastructure. The next year, when meeting his counterpart Barack Obama in May 2013, both pledged to continue advancing bilateral R&D as part of a comprehensive integration agenda (US Department of State 2013). Within this agenda, the Mexican Consultation Group of the Bilateral Forum on Higher Education, Innovation, and Research published "Proyecta 100,000: Towards a Region of Knowledge," in September 2013. The US-Mexico Bilateral Forum for Higher Education, Innovation, and Research (*Foro Bilateral* Sobre Educación Superior, Innovación e Investigación, FOBESII), Scientific and Technological Consultative Forum, continues this work. FOBESII was launched on May 21, 2014 during the visit of US Secretary of State John Kerry to Mexico City. During the visit of his successor, Rex Tillerson, the Bilateral Forum continued to be on the agenda, led on the US side by the Department of State in cooperation with the Departments of Education, Energy, and Commerce.[2] In the bilateral relationship, the institutional cooperation remains mostly at the discussion level. However, there has been gradual progress on cooperation among certain higher education institutions (HEIs), such as this chapter presents.

In the context of these policies and trends, some Mexican and US universities have been expanding their networks interacting with counterpart institutions. Some of those relationships have evolved into complex collaboration projects. This is the case for the Instituto Tecnológico de Educación Superior de Monterrey[3] (or the Tech, as it is known colloquially in English), a private university in Nuevo Leon in northern Mexico. Through a case study, this chapter explores the incentives this university has pursued to advance collaboration in research and innovation. This chapter proceeds as follows: an overview of the Tech's engagement in bilateral collaboration; review of institutional theory as understood by the regional diffusion of knowledge; explanation of the methodology for the empirical research and analysis of the findings; and presentation of conclusions drawn. In addition, the chapter identifies possible policies to facilitate not only collaboration, but also the application of what is exchanged for better impacting regional economies.

The Tech and Research Collaboration

Worldwide over recent dates, universities have been transforming themselves into advanced research institutions, assessed by their position in international rankings. In Latin America, modernization tends to manifest as a greater emphasis on research and technology (Díaz Villa 2012, p. 65). On the Mexican side, public institutions are leading many of these collaborations. They concentrate large groups of researchers, with faculty and students, to facilitate exchanges with highly productive US research universities. Traditionally, universities in Mexico have been predominantly public institutions. Since the rise of private institutions in the 1970s, the Mexican universities have fallen into two groups: those linked to industrial and financial entities and those affiliated with religious groups, mainly, the Catholic Church (Rodríguez Gómez and Ordorika 2012, p. 238).

The Tech has emerged as a leading private university with a visionary strategy for pursuing collaborative agreements with prestigious US universities. It is a non-profit institution that aims to transform Mexico and the world through developing leaders with an entrepreneurial spirit, a humanistic outlook, and a global vision.[4] To foster the latter, it has 18 international liaison offices around the world, five of which are in the US (in Boston, California, Miami, Texas, and Yale University). The main objective of these liaison offices is to represent the institution in each region through agreements established with HEIs, as well as with government entities and local companies. That is, each liaison office functions as a point of contact for local students who want to visit Mexico and study in any of its campuses' undergraduate or graduate programs.

Over a 25-year span, (1981–2016), the Tech signed around 400 agreements that vary in scope, length, and type of collaboration. These agreements have been with private and public US universities such as Harvard University, Massachusetts Institute of Technology (MIT), University of California at Berkeley and others of the University of California system, and Yale University, among others. More than 80 agreements have lasted more than 10 years, an indication of continuing commitment that has satisfied both parties. Currently, there are 156 valid collaboration agreements with US institutions and 644 academic agreements with universities in 53 countries. Table 2.1 shows the increasing trend on the number of agreements the Tech has signed.

As shown in Table 2.1, the number of signed collaboration agreements increased notably in the second half of the 1990s, most likely due to NAFTA. Another significant rise occurred just after the turn of the century, as the institution set up in 2003 special research groups with a strong institutional seed funding system (Cantu et al. 2009). This effort lasted for 11 years and elicited an average of 22 academic agreements with US universities. In 2013, the university developed a new collaboration strategy. A sophisticated internal review took place throughout all Tech campuses to facilitate support to undergraduate and graduate programs, promote research, and align efforts within disciplines and related areas of knowledge. The former research groups were reorganized within each school and across campuses. Under this new structure, each school coordinates efforts with similar academic programs among the 26 campuses. In addition, the institution created the "research professor status" with teaching load reductions and greater financial support for scholarly

Table 2.1 Collaboration agreements with US research partners, 1981–2016

Year collaboration started	Number of agreements
1981–1989	2
1990–1994	15
1995–1999	32
2000–2004	41
2005–2009	116
2010–2014	142
2015–2016	48
Total	396

work. This strategic model started in 2013–2014 and reached full implementation at the end of 2016. Over this short period, on average, roughly 30 academic agreements were signed annually with US universities. All these initiatives and structures consolidated research collaboration nationally and internationally with significant academic, social, and economic contributions.[5]

INSTITUTIONAL THEORY: REGIONAL DIFFUSION OF KNOWLEDGE

To better understand these exchanges among and within universities, this study uses neoinstitutional theory, emphasizing its sociological view of examining organizational behavior as it relates to and is influenced by other organizations and societal forces, to explain the motivations and processes of shared learning in R&D collaboration. Within institutional theory, there is a rational logic of consequences and a social constructivist logic of appropriateness that drive action (Fearon and Wendt 2002). This paper focuses on the latter to frame research collaboration in the bilateral relationship as a regional diffusion of knowledge concept (Berry and Berry 2014).

Rational theory's logic of expected consequences and social constructivist and sociological theory's logic of appropriateness help explain motivations, in terms of competitiveness and strengthened epistemic communities, respectively, framing the motivations for participation in shared R&D. Complementarily, sociological institutionalism and logic of appropriateness frame the socioeconomic context in each country. Rational institutionalism may be used to explain the preferences of stakeholders, internal and external, in research and innovation collaboration. Sociological institutionalism may be used to explain the influence of the sociocultural values, which are strongly linked to language. A sociological institutional approach has a sociocultural framework and includes social constructivist elements of norms, beliefs, and cognitive dimensions that act upon institutional behavior. These norms act on institutions through initial norm emergence followed by norm cascade. Currently the bilateral cooperation remains at the emergence stage. These become institutionalized or internalized before resulting in policy norm diffusion (Finnemore and Sikkink 1998).

This research draws mostly from the logic of appropriateness, which uses a historical and sociological institutional framework to understand actors' preferences (Pierson 2004) and the sharing or diffusion of knowledge-related policies (Berry and Berry 2014). The socially constructed logic of appropriateness frames research collaboration in the bilateral relationship as a regional diffusion of knowledge concept. The policy diffusion explanations are "inherently intergovernmental" in that governments implement policies to correspond with initiatives by other governments (Berry and Berry 2014, p. 308). Regional diffusion models, such as in the Association of Southeast Asian Nations and the European Higher Education Area, rely on networks of communication and influence across governments in the region, though this influence is not equal among governments given asymmetries in power and funding (Berry and Berry 2014, p. 308).

Historical institutionalism provides the perspective for understanding institutional change (Hall and Taylor 1996; March and Olsen 1984; Olsen 2010; Peters 2012). The European Commission in 2010 announcement the economic growth strategy Europe 2020, which had as tertiary education attainment as an objective for economic development (OECD 2015; Rodrik 2007). The institutions of focus in this research are HEIs, private research corporations, and government entities. Rules of appropriateness are embedded within institutions through their histories and interactions in a social constructivist perspective. Policies generated by institutions change over time, given changes in national identities and values, alongside changes in the interests of internal and external stakeholders:

> A conception of human behavior as rule- and identity-based invites a conception of the mechanisms by which rules and identities evolve and become legitimized, reproduced, modified and replaced. Key behavioral mechanisms are history-dependent processes of adaptation such as learning or selection. Rules of appropriateness are seen as carriers of lessons from experience as those lessons are encoded either by individuals and collectivities drawing inferences from their own and others' experiences, or by differential survival and reproduction of institutions, roles and identities based on particular rules. (March and Olsen 2009, p. 12)

Identifying stakeholder participants, their resources, and the policy context is essential to understanding the policy process, as it moves from policy formation to policy implementation (Gornitzka and Maassen 2000, p. 91).

In Mexico, the state has been the primary stakeholder affecting HEIs, as has been true in most regions of the world including Europe (Gornitzka and Maassen 2000, pp. 83–84). In the US, the HEIs themselves, collectively, are the primary stakeholders. The FOBESII initiative has comprehensive objectives as noted in the Joint Statement:[6]

> Through FOBESII, the U.S. and Mexico bring together government, the higher education community, the private sector, and civil society to promote workforce development, educational and research cooperation and encourage broader access to quality postsecondary education especially for traditionally underserved demographic groups, including women, and in the science, technology, engineering, and mathematics (STEM) fields. They also aim to expand student, scholar, and teacher exchanges, promote language acquisition, increase joint research, promote workforce development and share best practices between the two countries.

The global trend toward internationalization of higher education and research, has been actualized across various regional contexts (Grief 1998; Kent 1993; Loomis and Rodriguez 2009). Beyond the traditional purposes of education for civic purposes and social cohesion, there has been growing emphasis on higher education as a contribution toward economic development in knowledge-based economies (Raivio 2008). The North American context, in which the bilateral US-Mexico relationship exists and which includes Canada as well, is important given the potential for cooperation in research and innovation. The opportunities for cooperation in business, economics, and knowledge policies remain viable across the whole of North America, in addition to those unique opportunities focused on the bilateral relationship in higher education and research.[7] Advancing "the North American idea," the three countries may cooperate, to work more effectively in the world and support each other across the continent and globally (Pastor 2011).

The potential for higher education cooperation in Europe, launched with the Bologna Process since 1999, serves as a model for other world regions (Adelman 2009; Vögtle 2010; Wood 2013). In creating the European Higher Education Area, a framework for recognizing academic qualifications has been established in 48 countries (Barrett 2017). The EHEA exists complementary to the European Research Area for the countries in the European Union. The regional diffusion of knowledge in the North American context has some parallels with the regional cooperation in the European Research Area, and the framework Horizon 2020 that the European Commission established in 2013 (European Commission 2000, 2007, 2012, 2014).[8] The idea of a North American region of knowledge is similar to the idea of a Europe of Knowledge proposed by the European Commission in 1997 (European Commission 1997). In line with similar objectives to advance international exchanges in knowledge policies, the US-Mexico official support pledged since 2013 strengthens the already existing bilateral higher education and research institution initiatives and the opportunity for more partnerships in the future. The following section explains the research approach for assessing cooperation in this case of institutional cooperation with the Tech.

METHODOLOGY

Through a qualitative case study approach, this chapter explores the strategies the Tech has carried out over the years to advance international collaboration with the US through its liaison offices situated in different university and company hubs. From an institutional point of view, this case collects interview data from the five principal liaison offices based in the US, which share a mission of promoting collaboration agreements—that range from student internships, to short-term professor visits, to resource exchanges—to advance research.[9] This study limited data collection to interviews with liaison offices, assuming that they are key components for understanding the institutional strategies involved in the bilateral cooperation. The liaison offices are located in Miami (Florida), Silicon Valley (California), Houston (Texas), New Haven (Connecticut), and Boston (Massachusetts).

The data were collected between the first quarter of 2014 and the end of 2016. Using phone calls to conduct recorded interviews, the researchers used the following initial questions to guide the data collection: (1) What are the incentives and motivations for collaboration between universities with distinct sociocultural and economic development contexts? (2) What are the outcomes, thus far, that have advanced research productivity for these bilateral partnerships? (3) What are the challenges and limitations universities face in carrying out these joint projects? These questions were expanded as interviews unfolded. The recorded information was transcribed and analyzed using Nvivo version 11, a specialized software to code transcribed interviews and analyze emerging themes in the data.

The next section maps the core and global topics that emerged from the five liaison interviews, namely institutional motivations to engage in collaboration, benefits sought, and, finally, limitations faced in engaging with other institutions and businesses.

EMPIRICAL FINDINGS

Motivations and Processes to Expand Collaboration

The interviews started by asking what has motivated the Tech to explore bilateral research agreements. The interviewees explained the university had been exploring international connections since several decades ago, as liaison 1 put it, "All this started with student exchange programs. The Tech set up some student exchanges with liaison offices back in the 80s, especially in Spain. Then, these exchanges transformed into more research oriented projects." According to liaison 2, the Tech was looking for "offices that would connect groups of universities with what the Tech is doing to enhance collaboration." This is a two-way process, as liaison 4 put it, "As the Tech opens up to the world, it also wants to bring in the world. One of the missions of universities is to engage in that synergy to add and contribute globally." Moreover, as the Tech evolved, the institution managed to use multiple systems to carry out different goals. Liaison 1 explained,

> There are different kinds of links with universities in the U.S. For instance, some of these offices are located in a hub of well-developed universities, like Boston. So, that office interacts with many institutions and tries to bring students and professors based on specific needs. In my case, here at Yale we work with more structured programs to bring students and professors. We have several agreements to do so.

The same interviewee underscored also that some of the exchanges were a direct product of "a growing relationship that deepened as students and professors were exchanged over time. This led both institutions to engage in more complex projects." There was mutual interest in exploring what the other could provide. For instance, Yale saw that "through the Tech they could obtain more direct access to what was happening in Mexico and Latin America." In particular, they were seeking to build knowledge networks, as the same liaison stressed:

> Instead of assembling isolated initiatives in our areas of research, they realized that the potential to access more resources, information, and issues in developing countries was a great deal for expanding their projects and research agenda. This way, they saw that their initiatives would be more efficient. In addition, this led to relationships with individual researchers with specific interests in international projects, since they knew some of the

leading academics in Latin America. At the same time, the Tech started to use these connections to publish more on international issues, expanding and diversifying their research.

This increasing collaboration steered both universities' presidents to exchange visits that facilitated specific agreements, such as that of a liaison office housed at Yale to promote knowledge and development. As liaison 1 commented,

> It is very useful and strategic for both universities to have liaison offices. We are more visible and we can help connect and link with the Tech. As a liaison, I promote certain areas. It is common to see that when Yale has specific interests in Mexico, in the areas where we work together, they can count on me as their initial link. My task is to meet with them in order to help establish bridges between what they're doing through their research centers, and look for ways to collaborate with the Tech. In fact, this way we have created some good and sustainable initiatives for both institutions.

These bilateral linkages seemed to be highly beneficial for both universities when they generated bilateral agreements. However, not all the liaison offices operate like that. Liaison 2, in the Boston area, expressed that his strategy was more one of fostering individual exchanges that would promote research later:

> For instance, in our case, with Harvard University (HU), we don't have big agreements to exchange students and professors as we do with Yale. Here the relationship is case by case. If a professor or student comes to HU or MIT, it must be by direct invitation that a specific professor extends to that person. For that reason, there are some selection criteria that need to be unlocked when an opening is available. This kind of opening happens during the summer, and very often depends upon the candidates and their qualifications.

The rationale for this type of agreement can be found in that liaisons tend to adjust their behaviors to the institutional characteristics and culture, as liaison 2 stated:

> Each university functions in different ways with its own processes and internal culture. We have to adjust and search for the best mechanisms to operate in each case. For instance, MIT has very few undergraduate students because

they allocate more resources to graduate students and professors who conduct research sponsored by companies. Thus, professors at that institution plan over five years, hunting for the best undergraduate students who might be interested in doing their Master's and research projects. For this, we connect good students from the Tech capable of carrying out research with professors from these elite universities with which we have agreements.

This commentary shows how strategy is contextualized within the institutional characteristics to promote different types of exchanges. Reiterating this perspective, liaison 3 stated that, "Generally speaking, in my experience, successful international collaboration among universities is framed in mutual interest. Goals and motivations can be different, but if both parties persist, collaboration very often bears fruit." To this end, regional liaisons have the general task of "detecting" potential, at an individual or institutional level, for mobilizing and advancing research collaborations.

In the case of Florida, according to liaison 4, "The Tech is looking for opportunities to facilitate student internships for practicing in a semester what they have learned in class. The City of Miami is a hub of 1200 multinationals that make this strategy possible." Here, the Tech is not seeking to exchange professors or research with local universities. As the same liaison remarked, "I don't see how professors from the Tech could make significant contributions here. In this part of the country, we need young talent. Last year, Miami's mayor awarded our office and students for contributing to cultural diversity through our internship model." A similar motivation facilitated the creation of the Californian office, as liaison 5 explained, "The decision to install an office here, in northern California, was to be close to Silicon Valley and create internships for students. This is my main contribution as liaison." Although the office is exploring some academic exchanges, as the same liaison pointed out, "I had some initial talks with UC Berkeley to advance research internships, but that is still slow," the connection with companies and businesses is the central strategy for now.

The motivations to produce collaborations between the Tech and different regions of the US seem to vary with the specific environment to facilitate exchanges of students and professors for purposes that range from working internships to teaching exchanges and research projects. Liaison offices are a key strategic link for bridging organizational structures in multiple scenarios that can enhance collaboration. Collaboration is often thought of as research oriented, but it goes beyond that and also allows for institutional agreements with internship hubs to explore and advance state-of-the-art training, a central strategy the university seeks to develop through its liaisons. On the other side, US employers and universities seem more motivated to attract the best possible talent, at the same time as they advance their international networks. This is a win-win scenario for both parties. These complex interactions occur mainly among top universities and employers. The Tech has established its liaisons in strategic US locations to interact with institutions that follow a similar logic of selectivity with regard to partnerships and pursuit of prestige.

Collaboration Benefits

Underlining bilateral collaboration, the institutions on both sides are looking for general and specific results, since this is how all universities promote and position themselves. Several of these stood out as they came up repeatedly. According to liaison 4, "We've noticed that many transnational companies need well-trained students who can speak and write fluent Spanish, since those businesses have branch offices in Latin America. So, this is something that the Tech has to offer." This leads to creating an alumni network that is useful for expanding new projects, as liaison 5 underscored: "When I go to a new company for a new project we want to promote, I use the students they had from the Tech for internships to introduce it. They are my best 'business cards' to open new possibilities." This is particularly relevant given the lack of knowledge in most US companies about Mexican universities and is an important benefit for Mexico in looking for ways to connect with wealth through alumni.

Another important aspect of cooperation with advanced industries and universities is that students and professors get exposed to unique professional opportunities, as liaison 3 in Texas commented:

> Professors and students are the key beneficiaries of the international relationships created through collaboration. Without their active participation, launching collaboration agreements would have little meaning. Professors enrich their experience sharing professionally and personally with students. At the same time, students expand their experience and international vision participating as promoters for this kind of program.

Along with these exchanges, students receive unique professional training. As liaison 5 underscored, "The student is drawn by the opportunity to get a taste of the culture in a company of interest. In addition, an internship in a multinational company looks really good on their resume." Liaison 4 added a similar commentary: "Students apply these experiences to their real lives and the regions in which they are now working. They return to Mexico with a more continental and less parochial vision." This is an important "soft" benefit of collaboration, the impact of which is multifaceted and difficult to assess. The same is true for professors. Liaison 5 stated clearly that one of the goals of faculty exchange was exposure to new projects, as "Professors traveling to US absorb new ideas that they can apply in Mexico. For instance, one professor, after visiting a lab here tried to develop nano satellites with Mexican grants." A variant of this is the visiting professorship for faculty selected in Mexico to go to certain US universities to share knowledge through teaching. As liaison 5 mentioned, "For these exchanges, we open a call at the Tech and professors submit a teaching proposal. We select one and send him or her to the institution we have an agreement with." These experiences offer professors considerable opportunity for expanding their networks and furthering their research agendas as they interact with colleagues during their visits.

Generating knowledge is another benefit sought. The bilateral exchanges aim for concrete products from the research collaborations, but there are also other knowledge contributions that emerge, as liaison 1 expressed: "We try to have all scholars involved finish with a product such as a publication. Sometimes they already have their projects launched and come here (to the US) to utilize new resources and expand professional networks."

This means it is difficult to measure the actual impact of these exchanges because they continue to have an effect through the *posteriori* follow-up of the researchers. Liaison 5, for instance, stressed how some faculty participating in visiting professorships returned to Mexico with new tools for their classes that will help a multitude of future students. Collaboration is in an experimental and developing stage that offers potential benefits to researchers, students, and institutions as they grow and progress. Liaison 3 emphasized how the Tech sees this collaborative effort as merely the beginning of something much bigger:

> It is important to underscore that even though there are some collaboration initiatives, they are not abundant. Even though we are in a stage in which the Tech is showing increasing interest to carry research with other institutions, I believe the best is yet to come. The previous stages have been crucial for unfolding larger collaboration projects.

An underlining assumption seemed to be that the amount and diversity of products will be broadened to the extent the Tech facilitates more exchanges for professors and students providing better conditions and agreements that advance in-depth, complex research and internship projects. In short, liaisons understood themselves to be facilitators for collaborations that benefit students, professors, and businesses, positively impacting both North and South, sometimes in unpredictable ways.

Limitations in Collaborating

Even though the Tech has signed some important exchange agreements and established several liaison offices in key academic and business centers in the US, these bilateral agreements are in their initial stages and present challenges. Some of these are related to differences in academic management styles in both countries, as one interviewee commented:

> I believe that the most difficult part is to combine academic structures that are very different. In the U.S., the decision to carry out a research project depends, essentially, on the professor, who has the decision-making power over the financial and organizational resources he or she is given for a project. In the Tech, we have a structure that demands the approval from an immediate, and sometimes, field or area director to develop a project. This situation hinders the research process making it very slow and bureaucratic. To me, the challenge has been to ensure that every time administrators come to U.S. representing the Tech, they bring a professor who can provide the research component in a conversation, and the same is true for when Yale researchers visit Mexico.

The trick is to put the involved parties with decision-making power together to develop productive agreements and projects. But this is difficult given Mexico's hierarchical administrative tendency that can really slow and distort bilateral collaborations. Negotiating more flexibility from the Mexican institutions would be of great help. Another important aspect for Mexico to consider in advancing agreements with northern institutions is that US universities are very diverse, though they may look very much alike superficially. These differences are even more pronounced between US public and private universities. According to liaison 3, there are issues that go beyond the way agreements are set:

...we cannot establish a common working pattern for all [U.S.] universities. Things are different if we take into account their characteristics and their work processes. When we want to establish exchanges, we must first see that each university works differently and, from there, certain basic rules can be created but we must be flexible. If you cannot work with different strategies these exchanges will not be successful.

This means collaboration strategies must be "customized" according to the internal characteristics of each university, since there are issues associated with processes and resources for research projects. The same liaison also remarked how another limitation to carrying out bilateral exchanges is that time and resources are not always available for Mexican professors to conduct research. This is especially true at the Tech as the main source of revenue comes from teaching, making research a time-consuming and costly activity.

The international collaboration arrangements that allow for multiple positive outcomes must be more structured within Mexican academic procedures for them to become institutionalized. Good motivations may fall short without the right academic structures and resources to support and stimulate collaborations, as liaison 3 underscored:

Research collaboration, in general, is initiated and carried at an individual level with a professor as the central figure. Universities set priorities, but professors are the ones who are motivated to accomplish research. I think that productivity happens only to the extent that universities have the institutional policies to stimulate and compensate research, through funding, separation of time for dedicating to these projects, and clear operational guidelines.

Liaison 1 stressed that the Tech should deepen its alliances with the private initiatives without depending too much on tuition revenues, which tend to absorb the available human resources. This implies a paradigm shift to generate more productive bilateral agreements among multiple players:

Private sector corporate contribution has helped create the infrastructure for important research programs. Even so, money is not so easily available to the [Mexican] professor, because, traditionally, resources come from teaching. Thus, educational activities are the foundation for generating income and serving students is very important, generally more so than dedicating professors' time to research projects. Even though sabbaticals are part of institutional and departmental planning, teaching is still encouraged over scholarly work.

In addition to strategic limitations, the liaison offices face other complications in their promotion of the Tech brand. Liaison 5 stressed that lack of knowledge about and appreciation of the Tech in the US generates barriers: "I believe one of the most important limitations I have here in the US is the culture. I mean, if something is not made in America, people are not interested." In addition to this lack of information about the university, the institution has to operate within the context of a constantly depreciating Mexican peso.[10] This also has a negative impact on the exchange of Mexican students who find it more expensive to finance academic and employment experiences in the US Current uncertainty about immigration policies further exacerbates these challenges. In short, all liaisons pointed out that even though international research collaboration is on its way, the Tech still faces academic, management, and macroeconomic discrepancies that impede integration with northern companies and universities.

Final Discussion

International research collaboration has been shown to be beneficial for participants and a catalyst for increasing technological innovation. This, in turn, can facilitate economic development, which can then support greater flexibility in the labor market (Studer 2012a, b). Mexico's HEIs have become involved in a number of international education associations such as the National Association of Foreign Student Advisors, Association of Public and Land-Grant Universities, Consortium for North American Higher Education, and Association of International Education Administrators, among others. This involvement helps to promote Mexico's positioning with the internationalization of its higher education and research, and to further the country's pursuit of global knowledge generation.[11] However, with a new US presidential administration in place from early 2017 and a presidential election in Mexico slated for late 2018, shifts in political leadership will also influence the course of bilateral research and innovation policies. For example, renegotiating NAFTA would have implications for both economies with regard to R&D for innovation and for delivery of educational and research services.

From the results of the interviews in our case study, the Tech appears to be employing a variety of strategies to advance academic and research collaboration with US institutions. For student and faculty exchanges as well as research and internships, the collaborations seem to be generating good results and laying the groundwork for expansion into broader and deeper collaborations. Reacting to global competitiveness, companies and universities are constantly looking for the best human resources possible; the Tech offers a pool of potential employees and research capacity as a "trade in" approach that allows the institution to get a foot in the door to advance the exchange of other services. Although brain drain is always a potential threat, advancing academic collaboration is crucial for increasing knowledge, networking, and human capital potential in Mexico. In addition, collaboration strategies help the Tech promote a qualitative advantage for competing in the increasingly globalized higher education market. Tech students benefit from international learning experiences that give them access to experience in leading US companies and research with top US universities, and this gives the institution a unique positioning in Mexico and Latin America.

As the Tech pursues these bilateral collaborative agreements, there are clear challenges as well, particularly regarding how time and resources are managed for professors' involvement in research and bilateral collaborations. These require exploration of added external financing, which implies a reassessment of the current university teaching-centered orientation. In 2012, the Tech launched a realignment of its vision, organization, and culture "to continue improving and strengthening academic quality" (p. 18)[12] focused on the concepts laid out in the institution's 2020 Strategic Plan. One of the seven strategic initiatives mentioned, namely research that transforms lives, concentrates on using scientific investigation as a tool to enhance the student learning process and foster collaboration with other HEIs and companies. To that end, strategic academic alliances are key and Tech liaison offices, along with the main campus international office, focus most of their efforts on generating this type of opportunity for undergraduate and graduate students, as well as professors and researchers.

In addition, the institution is seeking areas of convergence for exploring exchanges with highly recognized universities and is trying to promote more aggressive knowledge generation and human resource development to benefit Mexico. Examples of this are the MIT agreements to support research and training programs in the areas of nanoscience and nanotechnology. This collaboration will allow students and researchers to gain access to fellowships, internships, and research stays at MIT laboratories. Actions such as these help strengthen partnerships and increase the potential for further exchanges. Expanding the base of graduate students who engage in new international cooperation projects also boosts collaboration processes. Finding additional sponsors and allocating more resources will be key as well to successfully increasing collaboration efforts.[13]

This research had some limitations, the biggest of which was the lack of a comprehensive report reviewing the overall activity of the Tech liaison offices. Although the liaisons have some kind of tracking system in place, they were not allowed to share these reports. Available information on official websites posted some input on activities but little on outcomes. Liaisons did not have detailed information of how their services were impacting the institution and regions back in Mexico. It appears the Tech believes in bilateral collaboration and is engaged in expanding horizons, in this case, through its liaison offices, but without dedicating support for generating bilateral streams of data to better inform policy making.

This study shows that some institutions do develop strategies as predicted by theories of regional policy diffusion and neoinstitutionalism, where the institutional context is influenced by the sociopolitical context (March and Olsen 1984; Peters 2012). The collaboration in research and innovation in the bilateral relationship is a regional diffusion of knowledge based on shared learning to drive mutual objectives. Mutual interests and objectives in economic growth and security continue to be important for the bilateral relationship, and advanced by public sector and private sector HEIs cooperating with the Tech. These interests and objectives in the bilateral relationship are shaped by regional ambitions for excellence, as articulated in the North American Leaders' Summits that take place each summer among the three heads of state. Highlighting an example of regional diffusion bilaterally, the liaison with Yale University highlighted the usefulness of having research activities in multiple locations. The hope expressed by the liaisons interviewed to continue to engage and to expand these collaborations will be dependent on the support available in the broader political environment (Berry and Berry 2014, p. 308).

A premise of social constructivism in the social sciences is that learning takes place through mutually constituted experiences (Wendt 1995). As Mexico and the US define the bilateral relationship in new ways, this will impact not only trade and migration policies but also research and educational exchange opportunities. The shifting political, economic, and sociocultural context will propel interest in a revisiting of this study in the coming years and with additional institutions. Future research may also draw comparisons across specific academic fields.

On the rational side, the national, institutional (academic and corporate), and individual benefits that result are seen to drive interest in collaboration. The Tech liaisons reinforced the idea that the research exchanges are mutually beneficial for all institutions involved. While participants from Mexico face particular challenges, given the fall of the peso value in recent years and more aggressive political leadership in the US, the historical attitude of the researchers from this institution is still that collaboration brings about a net gain for all involved.

NOTES

1. NAFTA was negotiated and agreed among Canada, Mexico, and the US entering into force on January 1, 1994. At the time, the regional trade agreement was historic and unprecedented given that developed countries and an emerging market country, Mexico, decided to enter into a formal trade agreement.
2. US Department of State. 2017. "The US-Mexico Bilateral Forum for Higher Education, Innovation, and Research." February 23, 2017. Available from: https://mx.usembassy.gov/education-culture/education/the-u-s-mexico-bilateral-forum-on-higher-education-innovation-and-research/
3. The full name is Instituto Tecnológico de Educación Superior de Monterrey (ITESM). However, the official website uses Tech as a short version of that name. For more information, see: https://tec.mx/en/inicio
4. For more details, see: https://tec.mx/en/tec-diference/formation-transforms-lives
5. See more about internationalization data of the Tecnológico de Monterrey at https://tec.mx/en/tecs-difference/data-and-figures
6. US Department of State. 2015. Joint Statement on Joint US-Mexico Statement on the US-Mexico Bilateral Forum on Higher Education, Innovation, and Research: Connecting Tomorrow's Leaders Today. Washington, D.C.: January 6, 2015.
7. Vassar, David, and Beverly Barrett. 2014. "US-Mexico Academic Mobility: Trends, Challenge, and Opportunities." Houston: Baker Institute for Public Policy: Rice University. Available from: http://bakerinstitute.org/files/8534/
8. See more information about the European Research Area (ERA) at: http://ec.europa.eu/research/era/index_en.htm
9. See more information about International Liaison Offices of the Tech at: http://www.itesm.mx/wps/wcm/connect/sim/study+in+mexico/about+us/our+presence+abroad/

10. Within the past 10 years, the Mexican peso was devalued more than 100 percent. In 2008, its value was $10 per US dollar, and in 2017 it is about $21.
11. US Department of State. 2015. Joint Statement on Joint US-Mexico Statement on the US-Mexico Bilateral Forum on Higher Education, Innovation, and Research: Connecting Tomorrow's Leaders Today. Washington, D.C.: January 6, 2015.
12. See the complete 2020 Strategic Plan at: http://sitios.itesm.mx/webtools/planestrategico2020/publico/EN/document/2020StrategicPlan.pdf
13. Read MIT News from October 31, 2014 at: http://news.mit.edu/2014/mit-Tecnológico-de-monterrey-nanotech-nanoscience-program-1031

REFERENCES

Adelman, C. (2009, April). *The Bologna Process for U.S. Eyes: Re-learning Higher Education in the Age of Convergence*. Institute for Higher Education Policy Report. http://files.eric.ed.gov/fulltext/ED504904.pdf

Barrett, B. (2017). *Globalization and Change in Higher Education: The Political Economy of Policy Reform in Europe*. London: Palgrave Macmillan.

Berry, F. S., & Berry, W. D. (2014). Innovation and Diffusion Models in Policy Research. In P. Sabatier & C. M. Weible (Eds.), *Theories of the Policy Process* (3rd ed.). Boulder: Westview Press.

Burrage, M. (Ed.). (2010). *Martin Trow. Twentieth-Century Higher Education: Elite to Mass to Universal*. Baltimore: Johns Hopkins University Press.

Cantu, F., Bustani, A., Molina, A., & Moreira, H. (2009). Knowledge-Based Development Model: The Research Chair Strategy. *Journal of Knowledge Management, 13*(1), 154–170.

Díaz Villa, M. (2012). The Idea of the University in Latin American in the Twenty-First Century. In R. Barnett (Ed.), *The Future University: Ideas and Possibilities* (pp. 59–70). New York: Routledge International Studies in Higher Education.

European Commission. (1997, November 12). Towards a Europe of Knowledge. COM (97) 563 Final. Communication from the Commission to the Council, the European Parliament, the Economic and Social Committee and the Committee of the Regions.

European Commission. (2000, January 18). Towards a European Research Area. COM(2000) 6 Final. Communication from the Commission to the Council, the European Parliament, the Economic and Social Committee and the Committee of the Regions.

European Commission. (2007). The European Research Area: New Perspectives. {SEC(2007) 412} Brussels, April 4, 2007 COM(2007) 161 Final. Green Paper. https://ec.europa.eu/research/era/pdf/era_gp_final_en.pdf

European Commission. (2012). Investing in European Research: The 3% Objective. European Research Area (ERA). http://ec.europa.eu/research/era/areas/investing/investing_research_en.htm

European Commission. (2014). Horizon 2020. http://ec.europa.eu/research/horizon2020/index_en.cfm?pg=h2020-timeline

Fearon, J., & Wendt, A. (2002). Rationalism vs. Constructivism: A Skeptical View. In W. Carlsnaes, T. Risse, & B. A. Simmons (Eds.), *Handbook of International Relations* (pp. 52–72). London: Sage Publications Ltd.

Finnemore, M., & Sikkink, K. (1998). International Norm Dynamics and Political Change. *International Organization, 52*(4), 887–917.

Gornitzka, Å., & Maassen, P. (2000). Analyzing Organizational Change in Higher Education. *Comparative Social Research, 19*, 83–99.

Grief, A. (1998). Historical and Comparative Institutional Analysis. *The New Institutional Economics, 88*(2), 80–84.

Hall, P. A., & Taylor, R. C. R. (1996). Political Science and the Three New Institutionalisms. *Political Studies, XLIV*, 936–957.

Kent, R. (1993). Higher Education in Mexico: From Unregulated Expansion to Evaluation. *Higher Education: The International Journal of Higher Education and Educational Planning, 25*(1), 73–84.

Loomis, S., & Rodriguez, J. (2009). Institutional Change and Higher Education. *Higher Education, 58*(4), 475–489.

March, J. G., & Olsen, J. P. (1984). The New Institutionalism: Organizational Factors in Political Life. *American Political Science Review, 78*(3), 734–749.

March, J. G., & Olsen, J. P. (2009). *The Logic of Appropriateness.* ARENA Working Papers 04/09. Oslo: The University of Oslo.

Mexican Consultation Group of the Bilateral Forum on Higher Education, Innovation, and Research. (2013). *Proyecta 100,000: Towards a Region of Knowledge.* FOBESII. Mexico City: Scientific and Technological Consultative Forum, Civil Association.

Olsen, J. P. (2010). *Governing Through Institution Building: Institutional Theory and Recent European Experiments in Democratic Organization.* Oxford: Oxford University Press.

Organisation for Economic Cooperation and Development (OECD). 2015. *Population with Tertiary Education.* https://data.oecd.org/eduatt/population-with-tertiary-education.htm

Pastor, R. (2011). *The North American Idea: A Vision of a Continental Future.* Oxford: Oxford University Press.

Peters, B. G. (2012). *Institutional Theory in Political Science: The 'New Institutionalism'* (3rd ed.). New York: Continuum Books.

Pierson, P. (2004). *Politics in Time: History, Analysis, and Social Analysis.* Princeton: Princeton University Press.

Raivio, K. (2008). University Reform – A Prerequisite for Success of Knowledge-Based Economy? In C. Mazza, P. Quattrone, & A. Riccaboni (Eds.), *European Universities in Transition: Issues, Models, and Cases* (pp. viii–xviii). Northampton: Edward Elgar Publishing Limited.

Rodríguez Gómez, R., & Ordorika, I. (2012). The Chameleon's Agenda: Entrepreneurial Adaptation of Higher Education in Mexico. In B. Pusser, K. Kempner, S. Marginson, & I. Ordorika (Eds.), *Universities and the Public Sphere: Knowledge Creation and State Building in the Era of Globalization* (pp. 219–241). New York: Routledge International Studies in Higher Education.

Rodrik, D. (2007). *One Economics, Many Recipes: Globalization, Institutions, and Economic Growth*. Princeton: Princeton University Press.

Studer, I. (2012a, December 4). *2012: A New Mexican Vision for North American Integration*. Modern Mexico Task Force, Center for Hemispheric Policy, Coral Gables: University of Miami.

Studer, I. (2012b). Mercados de trabajo y capital humano en América del Norte: oportunidades perdidas. *Foro Internacional, 209*(3), 584–627.

US Department of State. (2013, May 2). Fact Sheet. United States-Mexico Bilateral Forum on Higher Education, Innovation, and Research. Retrieved from https://2009-2017.state.gov/r/pa/prs/ps/2013/05/208579.htm

US Department of State. (2015, January 6). Joint Statement on Joint U.S.-Mexico Statement on the U.S.-Mexico Bilateral Forum on Higher Education, Innovation, and Research: Connecting Tomorrow's Leaders Today, Washington, DC.

US Department of State. (2017, February 23). *The U.S.-Mexico Bilateral Forum for Higher Education, Innovation, and Research*. https://mx.usembassy.gov/education-culture/education/the-u-s-mexico-bilateral-forum-on-higher-education-innovation-and-research/

Vassar, D., & Barrett, B. (2014). *US-Mexico Academic Mobility: Trends, Challenge, and Opportunities*. Houston: Baker Institute for Public Policy, Rice University. http://bakerinstitute.org/files/8534/

Vögtle, E. M. (2010). *Beyond Bologna: The Bologna Process as a Global Template for Higher Education Reform Efforts*. Transformation of the State, Working Papers. No. 129. University of Bremen. Konstanzer Online Publikations System (KOPS).

Wendt, A. (1995). Constructing International Politics. *International Security, 20*(1), 71–81.

Wood, D. (2013, May). *Educational Cooperation and Exchanges: An Emerging Issue*. Woodrow Wilson International Center for Scholars, Mexico Institute. http://www.wilsoncenter.org/sites/default/files/Wood_Edu_US_Mex.pdf

CHAPTER 3

Science Beyond Politics: Cuba-US Marine Research and Conservation

Daria Siciliano, Fernando Bretos, Julia Azanza, and Nanette Svenson

INTRODUCTION

This is the story of an exemplary Cuba-United States (US) academic and scientific collaboration. It explores the multi-decadal partnership in marine science between US and Cuban scientists in the face of an economic

---

D. Siciliano (✉)
Institute of Marine Sciences, University of California, Santa Cruz, CA, USA

Cuba Marine Research and Conservation Program, The Ocean Foundation, Washington, DC, USA

F. Bretos
Cuba Marine Research and Conservation Program, The Ocean Foundation, Washington, DC, USA

J. Azanza
Environmental Studies, Cuba Higher Institute of Technology and Applied Science, Havana, Cuba

N. Svenson
Global Development Program, Tulane University, New Orleans, LA, USA

© The Author(s) 2018
G. Gregorutti, N. Svenson (eds.), *North-South University Research Partnerships in Latin America and the Caribbean*,
https://doi.org/10.1007/978-3-319-75364-5_3

37

embargo (referred to as "bloqueo," or blockade, in Cuba) between the two neighboring countries in place since 1962. By limiting travel and trade across the Florida Straits, as well as the transport of equipment and samples essential to successful research projects, the embargo has made collaboration between the two countries exceedingly difficult. We describe the successes and challenges encountered in this journey and focus on two case studies: the Guanahacabibes Sea Turtle Conservation Project and the Three Gulfs Project (Proyecto Tres Golfos), created and led by the University of Havana in collaboration with The Ocean Foundation's (TOF's) Cuba Marine Research and Conservation Program (CubaMar). The first of these is a long-term monitoring research project on the population biology of nesting sea turtles in the Biosphere Reserve and Guanahacabibes Peninsula National Park at the western tip of Cuba initiated by the University of Havana and now maintained by the Superior Institute for Technology and Applied Sciences and Guanahacabibes National Park. The latter is an ongoing multi-year endeavor to study the three largest gulfs in Cuba. Both bring together Cuban and US researchers—from the University of Havana, the University of California Santa Cruz (UCSC), and various other institutes— in unprecedented marine research. Both projects concentrate on areas in Cuba directly across from Florida: the Guanahacabibes Peninsula in western Cuba, which is a component of both the Three Gulfs Project (one of the three gulfs is the Gulf of Guanahacabibes) and the site of the sea turtle monitoring and conservation project. This is no coincidence since striving to achieve an understanding of ecological connectivity between the US and Cuba is one of the scientific collaboration's main goals.

The initiatives began in 1999 and 2013 respectively, and build on previous work done in the area, including the Northwest Coastal Project (Proyecto Costa Noroccidental), an effort started in 2004 between CubaMar and the Center for Marine Research (CIM, for its acronym in Spanish) of the University of Havana to survey coral and fish in northwest Cuba. The sea turtle project represents the longest collaborative marine project between the US and Cuba since the Cuban Revolution, and is also the first project from CIM to focus specifically on species conservation. It involves studying the population biology and nesting behavior of primarily two species of sea turtles, categorized as endangered and vulnerable by the International Union for Conservation of Nature: the green sea turtle and the loggerhead sea turtle. On the other end, the Three Gulfs Project combines study on benthic diversity,[1] genetic connectivity, and historical ecology with conservation targets for protected areas in the three largest enclosed marine ecosystems of southern and northwestern Cuba: the Batabanó, Ana María, and Guanahacabibes Gulfs. Such a large-scale, comprehensive assessment of this region had not been attempted before but is critical for more accurate ecological predictions, and promises to serve as a model for future initiatives.

The chapter describes how the collaboration unfolded and has persisted in the face of logistical challenges and political adversity, and how TOF, a US-based non-governmental organization (NGO), serves as the necessary bridge in this bi-national venture to facilitate cross-border scientific collaboration. The partnership involves a number of institutions, and this chapter will describe in particular the role of two public universities involved, UCSC in the US and the University of Havana in Cuba, within a climate of intense political and socioeconomic tension. It looks at the processes involved in this complex partnership, the roles and contributions of all participants, the obstacles overcome, and the resulting successes, exchanges, and scientific output achieved to date.

TOF, an NGO founded in 2002 for marine conservation, acts as a host organization for a suite of marine science and conservation programs. CubaMar joined the TOF program in 2008 after being based at other universities and NGOs. The CubaMar mission has always been to build scientific collaboration between Cuba, the US, and neighboring countries with shared marine resources; establish locally supported ocean research and conservation efforts; contribute to the scientific knowledge base on the region's natural resources; conserve Cuba's marine ecosystems; and empower Cuba's next generation of marine science professionals (CubaMar 2016).

Following this introduction, the chapter is divided into several sections. The first provides background and context, offering a brief summary of Cuba-US relations from 1960 to the present and the implications of the US embargo for academic cooperation, in general, and marine research, in particular. It also describes the strategic importance of marine ecosystems in the Gulfs of Batabanó, Ana María, and Guanahacabibes, and the necessity for research cooperation to advance marine conservation in these areas. The next section gives an overview of the two case studies selected as most representative of this collaboration. It discusses the projects' foundations and prior complementary work, the major actors, their history and respective contributions, and plans for the future.

The chapter proceeds to look at TOF as a key facilitator for needed knowledge production and explores how the foundation acts as a bridge between academic, government, and civil society actors. This section also studies the strategic role of UCSC in the project as the driver of research in the US. It then examines the changing role of NGOs in epistemic communities, sustainable development action, and policy advocacy, and links this back to TOF and the two case study projects. It applies dynamics presented by Pohl, Rist, Zimmermann, Fry, Gurung, Schneider, Speranza, Kiteme, Boillat, Serrano, Hadorn, and Wiesmann (2010) to focus on challenges of power, integration, and sustainability as well as on the basic roles through which sustainable development researchers deal with these challenges.

The final sections of the chapter present a discussion of lessons learned, specifically with regard to the motivations for different actors' participation in the project; obstacles encountered and solutions developed; and key successes and research output. This is followed by a series of policy recommendations for institutional and national levels along with a conclusion to highlight significant achievements to date and visions for the future.

BACKGROUND AND CONTEXT

Cuba is the largest island in the Caribbean and a country rich in biological diversity. Located at the intersection of the Atlantic Ocean, Caribbean Sea, and Gulf of Mexico, it is home to clean waters, healthy reefs and beaches, mangrove swamps, dry forests, and mountains. Cuba boasts high reptile, mammal, and bird diversities, some species of which are unique or very rare. Twenty-five of Cuba's bird species are found nowhere else in the world, for example, and 17 of these are endangered (Garrido and Kirkconnel 2011). While Cuba's ecological riches are undeniable, its proximity to the US also means that the two countries share certain habitats and wildlife, both terrestrial and marine. For example, many North American birds migrating along the Atlantic coast to Latin America pass over Cuba, often stopping there to rest and feed (Cohn 2010). Most importantly, perhaps, US and Cuban waters contain many of the same marine species, including fish, corals, sea turtles, lobsters, and manatees, among others. Studies have shown that the larvae of snappers, lobsters, and corals are transported from Cuba to neighboring countries, including the US, and replenish the marine populations there (e.g., Paris et al. 2005). The movements are also two-way: some fish species hatch in US waters and swim south to feed and breed in Cuban waters, particularly large predatory fish such as sharks. This exemplifies the close ecological ties between Cuba, the US, and the wider Gulf of Mexico region where marine species, especially, know no political boundaries or economic embargoes as they actively move or are transported across the Florida Straits and Gulf of Mexico.

Outside of Cuba little is known about Cuban marine science. Much remains to be learned about the country's diverse marine and coastal areas. The country produces world-class marine scientists, yet field research and academic collaboration with its largest neighbor to the north have been limited during the past five decades primarily because of resource limitations; most exchanges ended in 1961 when the John F. Kennedy administration cut ties with Cuba and subsequently imposed an economic embargo that has been in place ever since. The US embargo has stymied the import of equipment and supplies made in the US or with US components, and it has left Cuba completely out of the informatics revolution that has taken hold globally since the 1980s (Stone 2015). Movement of people has also been challenging. Until March 2015, US scientists traveling to Cuba needed to have a specific research license from the Department of Treasury. Scientists wishing to take equipment to Cuba needed to have a permit from the Department of Commerce, along with a research visa from the Cuban government. As a result, the process of obtaining the necessary documentation from both sides often takes months. And once there, US scientists face poor communications capabilities on the island with slow and unreliable internet connections. Finally, scientists need to bring all the necessary cash for their stay and research needs since the US bank-issued credit or debit cards cannot be used in Cuba. However, the embargo weighs heaviest on the shoulders of Cuban scientists, who are left to accomplish a great deal with very few resources. As Stone (2015) eloquently summarized, with extremely limited resources Cuban scientists have kept science alive in Cuba by "cunning and daring in an isolated nation trapped in a time warp" (p. 747).

During the end of the first term of the Obama administration, the prospects for US-Cuba scientific collaborations improved, and with significant effort and determined advocacy on the part of US scientists, visas were issued more freely to select Cuban scientists for participating in formal meetings in the US for joint science, conservation, and management initiatives between the two countries, something that was practically unthinkable during the George W. Bush administration (Cohn 2010). Revised travel rules eased visits to Cuba for US scientists, and the US Department of Commerce began to allow scientific equipment to be freely donated to Cuba, so long as it did not have potential military applications. The slow rapprochement between the two countries was important, not only for managing common marine resources found on both sides of the Florida Straits but also for avoiding shared risks, from those associated with offshore oil exploration to the ecological perils of intense commercial fishing and overfishing (Friedman-Rudovsky 2013). Given that US federal funds, agencies, and resources have been prohibited from exchange with Cuba for the better part of the past six decades, most of the academic exchanges between the two countries have taken place as universities and NGOs in the US braved the bureaucratic and logistic challenges and reached out to their academic counterparts in Cuba. Much of this exchange has taken place under the principle that academic exchange is not subject to international conflicts or restrictions. For the same reason, the US Office of Foreign Assets Control, which maintains the embargo, has permitted several categories of travel to Cuba such as for research, religious, and artistic activities. Up until 2014 few US universities or NGOs had engaged in meaningful collaborations with Cuban universities and environmental agencies, and as a result, CubaMar, with staff from UCSC, was a poster child for what a US NGO with the backing of an academic institution could achieve by defying the odds and managing to establish long-lasting collaborations with Cuban scientists built on mutual trust and reciprocal respect.

A breakthrough came on December 17, 2014, when US President Barack Obama, in a joint announcement with President Raul Castro of Cuba, officially moved toward the restoration of full diplomatic relations with Cuba and the opening of a US embassy in Havana for the first time in over 50 years. This accord did not actually lift the embargo, but it did break the stalemate between the two countries and represented a policy shift—one welcomed by US and Cuban scientific communities. Academic collaborations between the two countries and even support from US federal agencies were finally on a much sought-after path to normalcy. But the decades of restrictions have taken a toll and there is much basic scientific research yet to be conducted in Cuba.

THREE GULFS PROJECT OVERVIEW

In May 2013, staff from TOF's CubaMar Program, affiliated with UCSC, met with colleagues from the Centro de Investigaciones Marinas (CIM, Center for Marine Research) of the University of Havana in their offices in Miramar, Havana, to discuss the foundations of a new, comprehensive, and collaborative project first conceived by a scientist at CIM. The project's goals were to combine basic research of biodiversity patterns and processes and climate change assessments, with conservation targets on ecosystem health, threats, education, and the enforcement and enhancement of marine protected areas (MPAs) and fisheries policies. Cuban colleagues had expressed interest in gathering a comprehensive ecological picture of the southern and western semi-enclosed marine regions of Cuba. Cuban scientists had previously studied these areas to a limited extent, at different times and as resources allowed, mostly with ad hoc expeditions involving different personnel over the years. A holistic and comprehensive ecological picture of the region, which was the focus of the proposed new collaboration with CubaMar/UCSC, was of paramount importance in Cuba to make more accurate predictions for future ecological change.

How and why was the Three Gulfs region chosen as the focus for an international collaboration of marine scientists? The collaborating institutions agreed that studying Cuba's three largest and most productive gulfs simultaneously and synergistically would allow for a comparative look at these ecosystems; support scale-dependent studies on issues such as diversity and genetic connectivity; and increase relevance for the conservation of marine resources in these bodies of water.

CubaMar would act as catalyst of the project by raising the needed funds from US foundations. The pivotal role of CubaMar included bringing into the fold US academic scientists who complemented the expertise of the Cuban scientists. Shortly after the original meeting in Havana in late 2013, CubaMar met with scientists from the prestigious Woods Hole Oceanographic Institution (WHOI) and invited them to join the Three Gulfs Project, bringing their unique expertise in microbiology and geochemistry, which complemented that of the University of Havana's CIM and UCSC. In this cooperation, UCSC and WHOI would be the academic institutions to which coral samples collected in Cuba were then transported for processing and analysis with the most advanced analytical equipment. This collaboration is now yielding the first long-term dataset extracted from coral cores in order to understand changing climatic conditions and the history and effects of nutrient runoff into Cuban reefs. UCSC and WHOI both boast large research infrastructure that Cuban institutions lack, particularly state-of-the-art mass spectrometers for geochemical analyses of the coral cores, as well as unique expertise in this discipline.

To better understand the motivations of the bi-national collaboration, it is important to understand the geographic and ecological importance of this region. Cuba has the largest insular shelf in the Caribbean. The shelf contains four relatively wide regions separated by long stretches of narrow shelf areas (Claro et al. 2001). The wide shelf areas form gulfs in the northwest (the Gulf of Guanahacabibes), in the southeast (the Gulf of Ana María), and in the southwest (the Gulf of Batabanó).

The Gulf of Batabanó is a relatively shallow platform that includes the Los Canarreos archipelago with 672 keys and islands, of which the biggest is the Isle of Youth (Isla Juventud). The Gulf of Batabanó is Cuba's major lobster fishery ground (Claro et al. 2001), so it is of the highest economic importance. Two main marine ecosystems share the gulf's sea bottom: coral reef and seagrass (Cerdeira-Estrada et al. 2008). Seagrass ecosystems provide the main energy input for guaranteeing biological and fishery productivity, with part of this energy exported to coral reefs. The southern border of this platform is fully covered by coastal coral reefs that in certain sectors emerge as crests. This region hosts other important fishery grounds, including for reef fishes, bottom dwellers such as red snappers and grunts, and some open ocean species like sardines and jacks. The area also represents an important touristic zone, comprising two large tourism centers in Cayo Largo (in the Los Canarreos archipelago) and Punta Frances (on the Isle of Youth), which operate large-scale beach and dive resorts, respectively.

The Gulf of Guanahacabibes in the northwestern region of the Pinar del Río Province is bound to the north by the Los Colorados archipelago, approximately 40 kilometers from the coast. The main shallow-water habitats in this region adjoin coral reefs, seagrass beds, and mangrove habitats. Contrary to other reefs on the north coast of Cuba, the reefs of Los Colorados are far from any urban center or land-based pollution source and show no evidence of contamination (González-Diaz et al. 2010). Small commercial vessels fish in these reefs targeting large-sized species (like the larger snappers, groupers, and jacks), which are heavily exploited (González-Diaz et al. 2010), making overfishing the principal threat to this ecosystem.

The wide shelf area of the Gulf of Ana María is fringed by the remarkable Jardines de la Reina archipelago, which separates it from the open Caribbean Sea. This archipelago hosts the Caribbean's largest marine reserve and one of the oldest and best enforced of the entire region. As a result, this Cuban MPA boasts the highest fish biomass (a measure of fish abundance and size) in the Caribbean (Pina-Amargós et al. 2014; Valdivia et al. 2017). The Gulf of Ana María has the greatest depths of inshore waters in the Cuban shelf. Along its coastal margin the gulf is fringed by estuaries fed by several rivers, so it is an ideal location for studying how changing runoff has affected the reefs within the gulf. A commercial shrimp fishery is the economic basis of the region (Claro et al. 2001), along with high catches of estuarine and reef fishes, which benefit from the protection afforded by the adjacent Jardines de la Reina marine reserve (Pina-Amargós et al. 2010).

Collectively, the Three Gulfs region defined in this project affords an unprecedented opportunity for exploration and discovery, the goal of which aims at increasing our understanding of the connectivity between the three gulfs, the ecological history, and the potential for strengthening the conservation of selected habitats. Such a large-scale effort could only be tackled by the resources and expertise represented by a bi-national collaboration of US and Cuban scientists.

GUANAHACABIBES SEA TURTLE CONSERVATION PROJECT OVERVIEW

The Cuban archipelago hosts a number of habitats suitable for the foraging and reproduction of marine turtles, and in fact of the seven species known globally, five roam Cuban waters and shores (Moncada et al. 2011). Of these five species, two are found only rarely, while the other three nest and forage regularly in Cuban waters: the green (*Chelonia mydas*), loggerhead (*Caretta caretta*), and hawksbill (*Eretmochelys imbricata*) sea turtles. All three are either endangered or threatened species (IUCN Red List 2017). Before 1998, most of the green turtle research in Cuba concentrated on the Isle of Youth (the second largest island of the Cuban archipelago), where long-term observations were conducted (1982–1996) on sea turtle nesting distribution and abundance (Azanza et al. 2013). In 1998, the late Dr. María Elena Ibarra, then director of the CIM at the University of Havana, initiated a research project in the Guanahacabibes Peninsula, the westernmost region of the Cuban archipelago (Ibarra et al. 2002). The project is staffed by university students who participate as volunteers during the nesting season to protect marine turtles against natural predators and poachers, and monitor their nesting activities on the beaches of the Guanahacabibes Peninsula, which is also a National Park and a UNESCO Biosphere Reserve. Supervised by marine scientists from CIM, the volunteers focus their efforts primarily on the more abundant green turtle (*Chelonia mydas*) and to a lesser but increasing degree the loggerhead turtle (*Caretta caretta*). Hawksbill turtles (*Eretmochelys imbricata*) are also known to nest infrequently there. The monitoring activities take place from May to October, which is the nesting season at this location.

The long-range migratory patterns of sea turtles for foraging and nesting on transnational coasts make them a prime species for which cooperation and collaboration among neighboring nations is paramount for conservation. The following year in 1999, TOF staff joined CIM as a partner in the budding initiative and provided much-needed funding, expertise, and equipment essential to continuing the sea turtle monitoring. TOF's CubaMar Program has been co-leading with CIM and park staff monitoring activities at the Guanahacabibes Peninsula ever since. This makes the effort the longest marine science collaboration between Cuba and the US, with scientists of both countries working continuously for 18 years (and counting) on shared conservation goals for threatened and endangered sea turtle species which develop and forage in the two countries. Their transnational migratory patterns were later confirmed when staff from TOF in 2012 brought to Cuba for the first time satellite tags from the US and carefully mounted them on five animals to record their movement. This was the first deployment of satellite tags in the Guanahacabibes Peninsula. Meanwhile the volunteer project, which started with the monitoring of only two beaches on the Guanahacabibes Peninsula, grew steadily in terms of both staff (the number of student volunteers involved) and scope. By 2000 it had expanded its area of operation to six nesting beaches (Ibarra et al. 2002) and currently includes a total of nine beaches on the peninsula (Azanza et al. 2013).

Beginning in 2002, TOF and CIM decided to build on the sea turtle monitoring collaboration by adding a new element: The International Sea Turtle Learning Exchanges, international workshops attended by Cuban, US, and Mexican scientists to swap information, data, and management lessons on regional sea turtle conservation (Bretos et al. 2016). The workshops would be held in Cuba, but attendance of scientists from the three countries bordering the Gulf of Mexico was essential. In subsequent years, the exchanges continued to be made possible by the Trinational Initiative, a larger effort TOF spearheaded to facilitate management and conservation of a number of marine species in the region.[2] The first two sea turtle workshops took place in 2002 and 2005 at the Guanahacabibes Peninsula. The goal of the 2002 workshop was to bring together international experts to advance the sea turtle monitoring work at Guanahacabibes that had started in 1998. The goal of the 2005 workshop was to develop CIM's wildlife tagging and community education work in and around Guanahacabibes—for the first time involving not just scientists but also the communities inhabiting the area around the park. The exchanges provided them the opportunity to interact with communities of other countries that went through similar experiences of adapting to more sustainable ways of life. They also offered the chance to better understand the role played by sea turtles in the overall health of their coastal marine ecosystems. Community education here plays an important role in trying to eradicate poaching, currently one of the primary threats to the turtles. Fishing sea turtle for their meat and shell was, in fact, a legal practice in Cuba until as recently as 2008, when the country imposed a nationwide ban after growing international pressure.

Following the implementation of this workshop, three Cuban sea turtle biologists traveled to Baja California Sur, Mexico, in 2006 to learn more about a network of fishermen and community members called Grupo Tortuguero (GT) de las Californias. GT is an NGO dedicated to protecting local sea turtles, as well as improving livelihoods for former sea turtle fishermen. The relevance of this exchange relates to the fact that in 1990 the Mexican government ceased its sea turtle fishery, which left many Mexican turtle fishermen facing an uncertain future. GT, formed by scientists and those same fishermen, is active in both ecotourism and field research. CIM director María Elena Ibarra identified GT as an ideal model for Cuba given machinations at the time toward a moratorium on Cuba's national sea turtle fishery.

In 2009, a third workshop took place in the Isle of Youth. A year prior, the Cuban government, under pressure from the Convention on International Trade in Endangered Species of Flora and Fauna, acted to permanently cease its sea turtle fisheries. A fishing community called Cocodrilo, located on the southwest coast of the Isle of Youth, was one of the two towns where turtle fishing still took place. TOF and CIM convened a "floating" workshop in which a group of 20 fishers, 16 of them representing GT, and Cuban, Mexican, and US scientists interviewed fishermen on their own fishing vessels to determine the impacts of the fishing closure on their livelihoods and understand what alternatives, such as ecotourism, were available to them using the GT perspective as a model (Bretos et al. 2016). The workshop became the first international exchange of its kind in Cuba.

A fourth workshop was organized in 2013 in the Guanahacabibes Peninsula and brought together US, Mexican, and Costa Rican scientists and community experts. The focus was on exchanging the latest science and conservation strategies as well as helping the Cuban communities develop alternative livelihoods in harmony with sea turtle conservation. A workshop invitee from Costa Rica, for example, led a session on creating artisan crafts using natural, sustainable materials commonly found on beaches, resulting in elaborate art that could be sold to visitors of the park. Another attendee directed a similar activity utilizing plastic materials strewn on beaches, thereby recycling harmful marine debris into an economic opportunity for the community.

Meanwhile, the monitoring of sea turtle nesting on the beaches of the Guanahacabibes Peninsula continues, and is making a quantifiable difference in the survival of this sea turtle population. Global threats to marine turtles include pollution, habitat destruction, by-catch (unintentional capture during commercial fishing for another species), illegal catch (poaching), and lately, the effects of climate change. Regarding this last threat, the effect of increasing temperatures affects gender proportion in sea turtles, which is determined by the temperature in their nests during egg incubation. These combined factors make sea turtle species threatened and endangered worldwide. The local efforts since 1999[3] through the binational US-Cuba collaboration in the westernmost region of Cuba, despite the challenges posed by the embargo, have been protecting the nesting and survival of female sea turtles, their eggs, and offspring in this remote corner of the Caribbean, and are a bright spot in the otherwise grim outlook for sea turtles globally. They are also a great example of science and conservation overcoming politics.

THE OCEAN FOUNDATION AS KEY CONDUIT FOR KNOWLEDGE PRODUCTION

The scientific achievement associated with the two projects described above and carried out with marine scholars of the University of Havana and UCSC was made possible by TOF and its role as a key facilitator for international research and knowledge production. This section explores how TOF as an NGO acts as a necessary bridge component between academic, government, and civil society actors. It also studies the strategic role of UCSC in the project as the driver of research and how TOF propelled the

UCSC participation. The TOF dynamics is examined within the context of the changing role of NGOs in epistemic communities, sustainable development action, and policy advocacy, all of which is highly relevant for the foundation particularly with regard to the CubaMar programming.

Much has been written in the past couple of decades about the role of NGOs in the production of critical global development and environmental research that prompts policy shifts (see as examples, Buchy and Ahmed 2007; Delisle et al. 2005; Edwards et al. 1999; Gough and Shackley 2001; Johnson and Wilson 2000; Pohl et al. 2010). Common threads throughout these discussions include how strong NGO/university collaboration offers increased potential for (1) data gathering, theorizing, and knowledge production; (2) practical intervention and civic action; and (3) advocacy, campaigning, and policy advisory.

The concept of "epistemic communities" was first introduced around 25 years ago to describe the broader union of actors—scientists, universities, associations, international organizations, NGOs, public officials, politicians, the private sector, community groups, and others—increasingly partnering for the study and political influencing of environmental issues (Haas 1992). While the concept can be applied to almost any social problem, it is especially pertinent for environmental concerns due to the facility and frequency with which they transcend national borders. This discourse is important as it relates to NGOs because it alters to some degree traditional perceptions of NGOs as grassroots delivery agents and positions them as essential knowledge partners and intermediaries in global dialogs linking academic research and policymaking, alongside programming intervention. It also has implications for NGO capacities, accountability, relationship building, and stakeholder involvement. Established NGOs are now more often seen as potential bridge partners between political actors and other sectors on the one hand, and between academic and non-academic actors on the other, with their non-profit, non-partisan status seen as an asset for driving both knowledge production and policymaking (Edwards et al. 1999; Pohl et al. 2010).

All of the issues surfacing in the expanded NGO-research production-policymaking discussion apply to TOF in Cuba. TOF was founded in 2002 as a US, 501(c)(3) not-for-profit international community foundation with a mission to support and promote other organizations dedicated to reversing the destruction of ocean environments around the world.[4] It responds to issues of marine health and sustainability, striving to strengthen the knowledge and expertise of the ocean conservation community everywhere (TOF 2017). TOF service lines include fiscal sponsorship, grant making, research, capacity building, advised funds, consulting, facilitation, and public speaking engagements. After a decade, TOF is a fiscal sponsor for over 50 projects and provides oversight for numerous donor funds. To date, TOF has awarded close to $40 million to other conservation organizations engaged in complementary work. In-house and collaboratively, TOF has produced many research reports, white papers, marine surveys, and award-winning books and films. It dedicates 70 percent of its total funding to international efforts (TOF 2017).

Important characteristics of 501(c)(3) entities that enable them to act as bridges between different actors across countries and sectors include their non-public affiliation, non-profit organizational structure, tax-exempt status, and mission oriented around benefitting society. Regarding its work in Cuba, these attributes permitted access to places from which US public and private organizations are typically barred. Specifically, scientists at public US universities (like UCSC) are directly prohibited from using state or federal funds for travel to countries that appear on the US State Sponsors of Terrorism list, which until 2015 included Cuba (US Department of State 2014). A foundation like TOF has no such restrictions with regard to hiring and/or sponsoring of academic work. Additionally, obtaining a research license from the US Department of Treasury to carry out research or professional meetings in Cuba can be a very slow process for public entities and can easily become mired in a sea of bureaucratic obstacles. Relatively small NGOs like TOF tend to be nimbler administratively with fewer layers of decision-making and bureaucracy, which means they can usually get things done much more quickly and efficiently.

For the CubaMar projects, an in-house bilingual (English and Spanish) team with experience in Cuba leads the programming and also recruits the complementary academic talent required—particularly, a bilingual marine researcher from the UCSC Institute of Marine Sciences with a trajectory of learning associated with coral reef ecology and assessment to direct the research along with various scholars from the University of Havana. TOF was able to interact directly with the Cuban Ministry of Science, Technology and Environment for the requisite permissions and arrangements, something that would have been very difficult and time consuming for any US public or private enterprise. TOF programming and professionals can also transcend US government administrations, further enabling sustainability for research projects and knowledge production.

Pohl et al. (2010), in examining the collaborative production of environmental sustainability research, highlight the importance of three major challenges to getting meaningful work done: addressing power relationships between different actors; integrating different perspectives on issues of concern to promote a common understanding of data and information; and ensuring that knowledge production serves the universal purposes of sustainable development. The authors also present three different roles routinely assumed by researchers to face these challenges: (1) reflective scientist, for validating knowledge according to quantitative and qualitative norms; (2) intermediary, for taking leadership in representing common interests and integrating divergent approaches; and (3) facilitator, for promoting joint learning and reflection directed toward common understanding of situations and collective action. To the extent they can effectively employ these roles, NGOs like TOF assume new importance for international scientific knowledge production and application. The table below attempts to synthesize how TOF has taken on all three of the roles described by Pohl et al. (2010) within the context of the CubaMar programming, and it highlights the external actors the foundation has involved as well as the activities implemented and outputs achieved in the process (Table 3.1).

DISCUSSION

For the two projects described in this chapter, Three Gulfs and Guanahacabibes Sea Turtle Conservation, started in 1999 and in 2013 respectively, the main actors from institutions on both sides of the Florida Straits had essentially the same motivations as they do today. US scientists desired to learn about Cuba's natural resources and ecosystems to fill the black hole of scientific knowledge that has existed in the western Caribbean for more than half a century and manage shared resources more effectively by exchanging data and management strategies with their Cuban counterparts. Cuban scientists, for their part, were generally thirsty for exchanges with the outside world, given the decades of relative isolation, and were particularly interested in acquiring experience and training with research equipment and infrastructure that the embargo had denied them for more than half a century, but that were needed to answer fundamental ecological questions in their own country's marine ecosystems.

Nevertheless, the forward-thinking scientists from the two countries faced many obstacles on the road to establishing successful collaborations.

Table 3.1 The Ocean Foundation as a conduit for US-Cuba marine research

TOF roles	Actors engaged	Activities implemented	Outputs generated
Reflective scientist *Validation of quantitative and qualitative processes and data* Intermediary *Leadership for integration of differing objectives and approaches*	UCSC Institute of Marine Sciences University of Havana Center for Marine Research (CIM) Woods Hole Oceanographic Institute (WHOI) Mexican and Costa Rican scientists from various institutions US State Department US Department of Commerce US National Oceanic and Atmospheric Administration (NOAA) US National Park Service Cuban Ministry of Foreign Affairs Cuban Ministry of Science, Technology and Environment Cuban National Center for Protected Areas	Project formulation and implementation for: Three Gulfs assessments on biodiversity, climate change, MPA enforcement Guanahacabibes sea turtle conservation/monitoring Joint UCSC/University of Havana monitoring missions to all three gulf areas Sea Turtle International Learning Exchange workshops Community education workshops with fishing villages	Long-term coral core geochemical analyses; biodiversity inventories; documentation of ecosystem descriptions and threats; and scale-dependent studies on species diversity and genetic connectivity for three gulf areas 18 years of sea turtle monitoring data and systems for continued data collection Design and implementation of sustainable community fishing engagement and outreach models Increased protection for endangered sea turtle species Import of more advanced technical equipment for Cuban research teams US-Cuba November 2015 MOU on Cooperation in the Conservation and Management of Marine Protected Areas (MPAs)

The principal constraints that tested their resolve over time included the following: the restrictions on travel to and from Cuba; the length of time necessary and the difficulty involved in obtaining research permits and other logistic permissions, as with navigation, from both countries; the enormous communication challenges in Cuba, such as the lack of reliable internet and constraints on mail and shipping, as well as the high costs of telecommunication both in Cuba and between the US and Cuba; the limited research vessels and other equipment and instrumentation available; the restrictions on the use of global positioning systems to locate study sites; and the limited available and allowable funding. While over the 18-year span of the projects some of these initial constraints were overcome, particularly since the rapprochement of the two countries starting in December 2014, some of the points merit additional description.

The communication challenges in Cuba are hard to imagine for US scientists before they travel to Cuba, especially for the newer generation of US scientists who have grown up in the information age. Because of the lack of reliable internet, Cuban scientists have very limited, sometimes non-existent, access to international scientific literature, while scientists from the world over are used to downloading the latest scientific articles from a variety of disciplines and countries of origin in a matter of seconds. This one constraint alone greatly limits scientific advancement in Cuba. One corollary of this is that Cuban scientists have until recently been less accustomed to publishing in established, peer-reviewed, English-language scientific journals. This, of course, greatly diminishes their visibility internationally, even if their science and ideas are at the forefront of their fields. The incredibly high costs of telephone communications have also hampered collaborations significantly. Any meaningful communication between collaborating scientists from the two countries is routinely accomplished in person, since phone calls and video calls are either prohibitively expensive or impossible (as in the case of Skype or any video conference calling system). This means that either US scientists must travel to Cuba (more commonly, because of the wider availability of funds), or, less commonly, that Cuban scientists must travel to the US, facing the familiar reality of being denied the visa and having to cancel their trip at the very last minute.

The limited field equipment and infrastructure available in Cuba also plays a considerable role in the pace and success of international collaborations. Cuba currently has only one dedicated research vessel for marine research that could host an international team of scientists: the Felipe Poey

R/V of CIM at the University of Havana. This vessel was due to retire about 15 years ago, but because of a lack of replacement Cuban scientists continue to use it, though the vessel often requires maintenance that keeps it out of the water for extensive periods. TOF and other US institutions have tried on numerous occasions to bring a decommissioned ship from the US to Cuba to replace or augment the available infrastructure in Cuba but these efforts have been curtailed by bureaucracy involving permits and paperwork from both countries. Up until 2017, for instance, CIM had only an old and inefficient dive compressor aboard the R/V Felipe Poey, which represented a struggle for the scientists on many field campaigns. TOF and other US colleagues tried to replace this by importing and donating a new and efficient dive compressor. After a year of continuous efforts on both sides, in January 2017 a new compressor finally reached the CIM offices in Havana. This piece of equipment alone will greatly enhance the productivity of all future research expeditions aboard the R/V Felipe Poey.

Despite the many challenges, this collaborative work has been highly rewarding and now has numerous successes to show for itself. Since 1999, for example, the sea turtle conservation collaboration has been producing outstanding results on sea turtle biology, demography, genetics, and environmental education with the participation of hundreds of volunteers (Azanza Ricardo et al. 2003, 2013). In addition, the Sea Turtle Exchanges were the first workshops in Cuba that brought fishermen, scientists, and managers from the US, Mexico, and Cuba together to promote better understanding of the status of sea turtle research and conservation in Cuba. They also led to increased collaboration among Cuba, Mexico, and the US regarding sea turtle work in the Gulf of Mexico. Cuban sea turtle scientists have been able to present data annually at international conferences such as the International Sea Turtle Symposium. The benefits of the exchange can also be seen in the sea turtle festivals now held on the southern coast of the Isle of Youth in a community historically dependent on sea turtle fishery.

The Three Gulfs Project has significantly increased knowledge about Cuba's southern and northwest coastal regions by undertaking a biodiversity inventory, characterizing ecosystems, and describing the major threats affecting the area's coral reef ecosystems. To date, this project has completed four research expeditions: to the Gulf of Guanahacabibes in 2014, and to the Gulf of Ana María and the Gulf of Batabanó (twice) in 2015. Thanks to the mediating and facilitating work of TOF, four institutions with complementary expertise have been involved in each of these cruises: TOF, UCSC, WHOI, and the University of Havana's CIM. UCSC and WHOI have carried out analyses on Cuban samples that have yielded a first glimpse of the changing climatic conditions in Cuba during the past 200 years (thanks to the unprecedented length of the recovered coral sample). A major boost to the project came in late 2015 when the Cuban government identified it as an umbrella project of national interest for which permits would be facilitated and streamlined.

One of the most important validations of the CubaMar success was receiving a formal acknowledgement from the US government that its work was critical for providing the necessary foundation and motivation for a Memorandum of Understanding (MOU) signed on November 18, 2015, by the US National Oceanic and Atmospheric Administration and National Park Service and by the Cuban Ministry of Science, Technology and Environment and National Center for Protected Areas. This "MOU on Cooperation in the Conservation and Management of Marine Protected Areas (MPAs)," is unprecedented since the advent of the Cuban Revolution and establishes a cooperative relationship that facilitates joint MPA scientific and administrative efforts. It also directs the formation of sister MPA relationships and propels better understanding and conservation of the interconnected ecosystems. The initial sister MPA relationship is focusing on Guanahacabibes National Park in Cuba (largely because of the Sea Turtle Conservation project), the Flower Garden Banks, Florida Keys National Marine Sanctuaries, and the Dry Tortugas and Biscayne National Parks in the US.

The talks that culminated with the signing of the MOU in 2015 started in 2012 between the US State Department and the Cuban Ministry of Foreign Affairs. These talks were first made possible as a consequence of TOF's Trinational Initiative, a project that since 2007 has brought together managers, scientists, and policymakers from the three countries bordering the Gulf of Mexico to facilitate discussions and programs. The discussions that led to the sister park agreement, for example, also included outlining strategies for joint management, with the notable inclusion of procedures and protocols in the event of an oil spill.

The two national scientific communities are now in a better position to create a formidable front for bringing about sound environmental policies and capacity building across territorial boundaries—even beyond the US and Cuba. It is hoped that through these recent efforts something along the lines of what was achieved by Cuba and the US in combating Ebola will become possible for the management of marine environments. In West Africa, recent achievements with containing the Ebola epidemic depended heavily on the combined forces of Cuban doctors and nurses, well trained for dealing with catastrophes and epidemics, and US and other countries' professional and infrastructural support. The two worked collaboratively to effectively curtail the exponential spread of the disease, and outcomes might otherwise have been far worse were it not for Cuban doctors and nurses working in cooperation with US hospital facilities (Pastrana 2015). As with this medical analogy, the collaborations established by US and Cuban marine scientists over the past two decades in the projects described in this chapter have paved the way for similar miracles to be wrought for marine knowledge and conservation. With precedents set in medicine and marine science, other disciplines should also begin to pursue US-Cuba academic collaboration. Ideally, these cooperative research efforts will foster scientific advances benefitting not only the two countries directly involved but also the wider Caribbean region and the rest of the world.

Conclusions

Cuba's size, as the largest country in the insular Caribbean in terms of land area, coastline, and population, and its geographic positioning between the Gulf of Mexico and the Caribbean Sea, make it the home of the largest collection of marine biodiversity in the entire Caribbean. Much of these ecological riches are shared across the Florida Straits. Thus, Cuban and US scientists have always appreciated the necessity for developing common scientific understanding and international policies to protect these shared resources. The recent political thaw between the two countries under the Obama administration is a step in the right direction. While the Trump administration has stalled much of the rapprochement between the two countries, the tide of change is pulling strongly. What is essential now is that foresight and careful planning work to redirect potential movement away from the rapprochement, and at the same time manage the influx of US tourism to the Caribbean island, which could bring disastrous environmental consequences.

Large US cruise ships started calling at ports in Havana and other Cuban coastal towns in 2015, and they arrive weekly with US tourists eager to discover the forbidden fruit of the past five decades. Since 2016, dozens of US commercial flights arrive daily to every major city in Cuba. Recently, the Cuban government announced its willingness to negotiate contracts for oil and gas exploration in the deep waters of its exclusive Gulf of Mexico economic zone, the region adjacent to the area selected for the sister MPA relationship in the 2015 MOU with the US government. With oil exploration and extraction activities a possibility for the near future, concurrent with the new wave of tourism that Cuba is experiencing, the need to continue to promote bilateral research for the country's coastal and marine ecosystems is clear. New collaborations with creative research design ideas are necessary for creating baseline data in anticipation of potential degradation due to increased visitation, as well as a possible oil spill. Now is the time to establish protections bilaterally and ensure that academic collaborations such as those begun by TOF and UCSC with the University of Havana and other Cuban institutions continue to provide information and infrastructure to inform progressive environmental policies in this changing era.

As illustrated in the chapter, NGOs like TOF can be increasingly important conduits for uniting academic actors from different countries and propelling necessary research, collective action, and sustainable development policy. TOF CubaMar achievements to date are impressive in this regard and lay solid groundwork and replicable examples for other NGOs and universities, in the region and globally. Looking to the future, additional collaborative research efforts are needed to identify critical ecosystem services and estimate values (both economic and non-monetized) for particular key economic sectors such as fisheries, aquaculture, and, especially, tourism. It would also behoove joint US-Cuba marine research institutions to create more opportunities for university faculty and student exchange. The same is true for the fostering of increased trade liberalization for technical equipment imports to Cuba and more joint publishing in both English and Spanish on the resulting findings of the international academic collaborations. Hopefully, too, the TOF model for US-Cuba university research can be extrapolated to other disciplines. Because of Cuba's continuous concentration on investment in education at all levels throughout its post-revolution history, there is a large pool of academic talent there waiting to be unleashed. With more US-Cuba university research collaborations across a range of environmental, social, political, and economic areas, the possibilities for joint knowledge production and innovation are endless.

Notes

1. Benthic refers to the ecological region at the lowest level of a water body like an ocean or a lake.
2. For more information on this, see the Trinational Initiative website, http://www.trinationalinitiative.org
3. These efforts that began in 1999 predate even the founding of TOF as the present TOF director of CubaMar was working previously through another NGO on Cuba marine science programming with the University of Havana's CIM that led to current TOF projects, particularly with the sea turtle conversation, and served as the de facto bridge for continuing the Cuba initiatives and the related knowledge generation.
4. The designation of 501(c)(3) standing refers to the section of the US International Revenue Service tax code that grants tax-exempt status to organizations operating for specific purposes that are charitable, religious, educational, scientific, literary, and/or related to testing for public safety, fostering national or international amateur sports competition, and preventing cruelty to children or animals (IRS 2017).

References

Azanza Ricardo, J., Ibarra-Martín, M. E., Espinosa, G., Díaz, R., & González-Sansón, G. (2003). Conducta de Anidación de la Tortuga Verde (*Chelonia Mydas*) en las Playas Antonio y Caleta de Los Piojos de la Península de Guanahacabibes, Pinar Del Río, Cuba [Nesting Activity of the Green Sea Turtle on the Beaches of Antonio y Caleta de Los Piojos on the Guanahacabibes Peninsula, Pinar Del Rio, Cuba]. *Revista de Investigaciones Marinas, 24*(3), 231–240.

Azanza Ricardo, J., Ibarra Martín, M. E., González Sansón, G., Abreu Grobois, A., Eckert, K., Espinosa López, G., & Oyama, K. (2013). Nesting Ecology of *Chelonia mydas* (Testudines: Cheloniidae) on the Guanahacabibes Peninsula, Cuba. *Revista de Biología Tropical, 61*(4), 1935–1945.

Bretos, F., Azanza Ricardo, J., Moncada, F., Peckham, S. H., Angulo Valdés, J. A., Diego, A., & Thompson, K. (2016). Fisheries Learning Exchanges and Sea Turtle Conservation: An Effort Between Mexico, Cuba and the U.S. to Engage Cuban Coastal Communities in Non-consumptive Alternative Behaviors. *Marine Policy, 77*, 227–230.

Buchy, M., & Ahmed, S. (2007). Social Learning, Academics and NGOs: Can the Collaborative Formula Work? *Action Research, 5*(4), 358–377.

Cerdeira-Estrada, S., Lorenzo-Sánchez, S., Areces-Mallea, A., & Martínez-Bayón, C. (2008). Mapping of the Spatial Distribution of Benthic Habitats in the Gulf of Batabanó Using Landsat-7 Images. *Ciencias Marinas, 34*(2), 213–222.

Claro, R., Reshetnikov, Y. S., & Alcolado, P. M. (2001). Physical Attributes of Coastal Cuba. In R. Claro, K. C. Lindeman, & L. R. Parenti (Eds.), *Ecology of the Marine Fishes of Cuba* (pp. 1–20). Washington, DC: Smithsonian Institution Press.

Cohn, J. P. (2010). Opening Doors to Research in Cuba. *BioScience, 60*(2), 96–99.

Cuba Marine Research and Conservation Program (CubaMar). (2016). *About CubaMar.* Available at http://www.cubamar.org/

Delisle, H., Roberts, J. H., Munro, M., Jones, L., & Gyorkos, T. W. (2005). The Role of NGOs in Global Health Research for Development. *Health Research Policy and Systems, 3*(3), 1–21.

Edwards, M., Hulme, D., & Wallace, T. (1999). *NGOs in a Global Future: Marrying Local Delivery to Worldwide Leverage.* Presented as a Background Paper for the Third International NGO Conference, Hosted by the University of Birmingham, January 10–13, 1999.

Friedman-Rudovsky, J. (2013). Marine Studies Show Potential for U.S.-Cuban Collaboration. *Science, 341*, 446–447.

Garrido, O. H., & Kirkconnell, A. (2011). Aves de Cuba. Illustrations by Román Compañy. Foreword by John W. Fitzpatrick. Comstock Publishing Associates. Ithaca, New York, USA. 2011. 287 pages, 51 color plates, 1 figure, range maps.

González-Díaz, P., González-Sansón, G., Álvarez Fernández, S., & Pérez, O. P. (2010). High Spatial Variability of Coral, Sponges and Gorgonian Assemblages in a Well-Preserved Reef. *Revista de Biologia Tropical, 58*(2), 621–634.

Gough, C., & Shackley, S. (2001). The Respectable Politics of Climate Change: The Epistemic Communities and NGOs. *International Affairs, 77*(2), 329–345. Available at http://www.jstor.org/stable/3025544. Accessed 21 Aug 2016.

Haas, P. (1992). Introduction: Epistemic Communities and International Policy Coordination. *International Organization, 14*(1), 1–36.

Ibarra-Martín, M. E., Díaz-Fernández, R., Konnorov, A. N., Ricardo, J. A., Valdés, J. A., López, G. E., & Roberto, J. P. (2002). Project Update: University Project for the Study and Conservation of Cuban Sea Turtles-Completion of Year 3. *Marine Turtle Newsletter, 95*, 18–20.

Internal Revenue Service. (2017). *Exemption Requirements for 501(c)(3) Organizations.* Available at https://www.irs.gov/charities-non-profits/charitable-organizations/exemption-requirements-section-501-c-3-organizations

IUCN. (2017). *The IUCN Red List of Threatened Species. Version 2017-1.* Available at http://www.iucnredlist.org.

Johnson, H., & Wilson, G. (2000). Biting the Bullet: Civil Society, Social Learning and the Transformation of Local Governance. *World Development, 28*(11), 1891–1906.

Moncada, F., Nodarse, A., Azanza Ricardo, J., Medina, Y., & Forneiro Martín-Viaña, Y. (2011). Principales Áreas de Anidación de las Tortugas Marinas en el Archipiélago Cubano [Principal Areas of Marine Turtle Nesting Activity in the

Cuban Archiapelago]. *Revista Electrónica de la Agencia de Medio Ambiente,* *11*(20). Available at http://ama.redciencia.cu/articulos/20.02.pdf

Paris, C. B., Cowen, R. K., Claro, R., & Lindeman, K. C. (2005). Larval Transport Pathways from Cuban Snapper (Lutjanidae) Spawning Aggregations Based on Biophysical Modeling. *Marine Ecology Progress Series, 296,* 93–106.

Pastrana, S. J. (2015). Building a Lasting Cuba-U.S. Bridge Through Science. *Science & Diplomacy, 4*(1). Available at http://www.sciencediplomacy.org/perspective/2015/building-lasting-cuba-us-bridge-through-science

Pina-Amargós, F., Sansón, G., del Castillo, A., Fernández, A., Blanco, F., & de la Red, W. (2010). An Experiment of Fish Spillover from a Marine Reserve in Cuba. *Environmental Biology of Fishes, 87*(4), 363–372.

Pina-Amargós, F., González-Sansón, G., Martín-Blanco, F., & Valdivia, A. (2014). Evidence for Protection of Targeted Reef Fish on the Largest Marine Reserve in the Caribbean. C. Elphick (Ed.), *PeerJ, 2,* e274. https://doi.org/10.7717/peerj.274.

Pohl, C., Rist, S., Zimmermann, A., Fry, P., Gurung, G. S., Schneider, F., Speranza, C. I., Kiteme, B., Boillat, S., Serrano, E., Hadorn, G. H., & Wiesmann, U. (2010). Researchers' Roles in Knowledge Co-production: Experience from Sustainability Research in Kenya, Switzerland, Bolivia and Nepal. *Science and Public Policy, 37*(4), 267–281.

Stone, R. (2015). In from the Cold: After Keeping Science Alive During Decades of Scarcity, Cuba's "Guerrilla Scientists" Are Ready to Rejoin the World. *Science, 348*(6236), 746–751.

The Ocean Foundation (TOF). (2017). *Our Story.* Available at https://www.oceanfdn.org/our-story

US Department of State. (2014). *Country Reports on Terrorism 2014.* Available at https://www.state.gov/j/ct/rls/crt/2014/index.htm.

Valdivia, A., Cox, C. E., & Bruno, J. F. (2017). Predatory Fish Depletion and Recovery Potential on Caribbean Reefs. *Science Advances, 3*(3), 1–11.

CHAPTER 4

INCAE, Harvard, and International Development: Research for Progress in Central America

Nanette Svenson

INTRODUCTION

Central America does not usually figure into the top ten list of anything related to education, especially at the higher levels. A notable exception, however, is the Central American Institute of Business Administration (Instituto Centroamericano de Administración de Empresas), or INCAE for its acronym in Spanish, which now consistently appears in international rankings among the top business schools in Latin America and in the world. For over 50 years, INCAE has offered graduate and executive business administration courses and conducted some of the best research in the region through its Latin American Center for Competitiveness and Sustainable Development (Centro Latinoamericano para la Competitividad y el Desarrollo Sostenible, CLACDS).

An important component of INCAE success is its partnership with Harvard University in the USA. Harvard has been with INCAE since its

---

N. Svenson (✉)
Global Development Program, Tulane University, New Orleans, LA, USA

© The Author(s) 2018
G. Gregorutti, N. Svenson (eds.), *North-South University Research Partnerships in Latin America and the Caribbean*,
https://doi.org/10.1007/978-3-319-75364-5_4

inception, providing inputs that have been instrumental in guiding the development of INCAE's educational and research programs. Likewise, INCAE has provided Harvard with a unique link to Latin America that has contributed significantly to the research on business and development in the region and worldwide. As an indication of the continuing significance of this relationship, INCAE recently marked its 50th anniversary with a celebration at the Harvard Business School in Boston to honor key individuals from both Harvard and Central America who have been vital to INCAE development over the decades and its impact on Latin America (HBS 2014).

This chapter explores the INCAE-Harvard partnership with regard to the evolution of research in INCAE, particularly as it has progressed within CLACDS. CLACDS is INCAE's principal research center and concentrates on study and training designed to produce practical solutions for regional development problems in a range of areas including energy policy, water resource management, poverty reduction, and rural and urban development. Recent INCAE President Arturo Condo described CLACDS as a "think-and-do tank," which accurately reflects the center's combined attention to both academic research and applied consultancy projects (AACSB 2011). Harvard has been an integral CLACDS partner from the beginning and numerous projects, papers, books, lectures, and conferences have been jointly developed and presented over the past couple of decades. The partnership has been extremely productive and the results generated have benefited not only INCAE, the southern participant in this North-South partnership, but also Harvard, the northern participant, and the entire Central American region. Further contributing to the success of the research partnership is CLACDS's increasingly important affiliation with major actors of the regional business community, Latin American governments, and international development organizations. Alongside the Harvard relationship, these influential linkages have served to propel INCAE and CLACDS to the forefront of knowledge generation and application to Central American, Latin American, and even global development, particularly as it pertains to competitiveness and sustainability.

Methodologically, the research for this chapter is presented as a case study (Yin 2014) and relies on extensive document analysis and key informant interviews with scholars from both INCAE and Harvard. The questions examined revolve around (1) the motivations on both sides for propelling the collaborative relationship; (2) the operational mechanics employed to maintain the joint cooperation; and (3) the factors critical to the success of the initiative and its research output over time. The study incorporates an adapted version of the collaborative research framework introduced by Smith and Katz (2000) to organize certain data related to the research partnership and also structure the discussion of factors contributing to its success.

Following this introduction, the chapter begins with a brief overview of the Central American context. It then goes on to describe the history of INCAE and the launch of CLACDS and its trajectory of work. The chapter next examines the INCAE partnership with Harvard and discusses the institutional motivations for both partners; the protocols, mechanics, and logistics involved with operationalizing the alliance; and the corresponding benefits and limitations of the partnership arrangements. Analysis of these aspects of the INCAE-Harvard partnership within the Smith and Katz framework attempts to highlight some of its critical success factors as well as implications for the future. The findings tell the story of a visionary knowledge collaboration that continues to produce and serve beneficiaries worldwide. Ideally, lessons from this experience will also inspire and contribute to the development of other North-South university research associations.

CENTRAL AMERICA

Central America is generally described as the southernmost isthmus of North America that connects the continent with South America. It is included in broader Latin America and made up of seven countries: Belize, Costa Rica, El Salvador, Guatemala, Honduras, Nicaragua, and Panama. Territorially, it covers over 500,000 square kilometers and has a combined population of around 42 million. All countries in Central America are classified as middle income by the World Bank (World Bank 2015), but this categorization belies the range of income variation within and across the countries. The same is true for other development indicators as well. Costa Rica and Panama show considerably better circumstances overall, for example, than do Honduras and Nicaragua. Discrepancies within the countries are also significant, as indicated by the high Gini coefficients for each country[1] (Table 4.1).

These tendencies toward inequality are particularly marked with education. While most countries in Central America have relatively high literacy rates and near universal primary school completion, the scenario declines rapidly with secondary and tertiary education, though both of these

Table 4.1 Selected Central American development statistics, 2014

Country	GDP per capita (US$)	Poverty (% of population)	Gini index	Literacy (% of adults)	Secondary enrollment (% gross)	Tertiary enrollment (% gross)	Researchers in R&D (per million people)
Belize	4894	–	–	–	86	26	–
Costa Rica	10,035	22	49	97	109	48	1289
El Salvador	3951	30	42	85	70	26	–
Guatemala	3703	54	52	78	65	19	25
Honduras	2347	65	57	85	71	21	–
Nicaragua	1914	–	–	–	69	–	–
Panama	11,771	26	52	94	74	43	111
CA (average)	5516	39	50	88	78	31	450

Based on the most recent figures available

Source: World Bank, World Development Indicators 2014

statistics have climbed noticeably in recent years (Table 4.1). Plus, quality is an issue at every level of education. Numerous reports signal serious problems across the region with regard to inadequate and outdated teacher training, curriculum development, assessment, and accountability systems (PREAL 2007; Svenson 2012, 2015; UNESCO 2007; World Bank 2005). Thus, neither the region nor any of its individual countries are well positioned to advance research and development (R&D) from a human resource perspective. Additionally, for the few countries that have figures available, the national R&D expenditure is a fraction of 1 percent of the gross domestic product (GDP), which is minimal. Most industrialized countries dedicate around 3 percent of the GDP to funding R&D (WDI 2014).

Added to these challenging development statistics—which have improved significantly since the 1960s when the INCAE-Harvard project began—the region has suffered from internal conflict (particularly in the decades of the 1970s, 1980s, and 1990s), a high percentage of natural disasters, over-reliance on natural resources for economic production, and ongoing violence related to drug trafficking. This is the regional context within which INCAE and CLACDS are working, and it is intensely difficult. The odds have always been stacked against their success—more so even in the earlier years. Incredibly, they have been able to consistently beat these odds and become increasingly productive over the years, with a range of high-quality academic programming and developmentally sound applied research.

INCAE

INCAE was founded in 1964, the realization of an idea inspired by conversations that took place with Central American governments and business leaders during the US President John F. Kennedy's visit to Costa Rica in 1963. The focus of these discussions was the strengthening of education in the region, especially at the higher levels, as a means to propelling regional development. President Kennedy returned to the USA and asked George P. Baker, dean of Harvard Business School (HBS) at the time, to explore the possibility of establishing a management program in the region similar to its Master of Business Administration (MBA) program in the USA based on the case-study method of instruction. With backing from the US Agency for International Development (USAID), the Central American Bank for Economic Integration (Banco Centroamericano de Integración Económica, BCIE), and regional business enterprises, the first private INCAE campus was opened in 1969 in Nicaragua. In 1983, INCAE opened a second branch in Costa Rica—mainly due to the instability caused by the Sandinista conflict in Nicaragua—that now serves as the school's main campus. Though initially mandated with teaching, the INCAE mission eventually came to focus on three principal activities: graduate business education through its MBA programs; executive education through seminars and corporate programming; and applied research in areas related to furthering Latin American competitiveness and sustainable development. Throughout the years, INCAE has graduated nearly 15,000 professionals from more than 50 countries around the world, educated over ten times that number of executives through its various non-degree programs, and produced thousands of case studies, papers, technical notes, and publications (INCAE 2014a).

Today, INCAE is a leading business school in Latin America and the world, as recognized by various independent rankings. For years it has been selected as the best business school in the region by *América Economía* magazine and in the top ten of Latin America for EdUniversal, the French higher education rating agency. INCAE has appeared repeatedly as tenth in the global ranking of the *Wall Street Journal* for international business and continually figures among the top 100 business schools and top 50 executive education programs in the *Financial Times* global rankings. INCAE is also accredited by three major international higher education evaluation agencies: the US Southern Association of Colleges and Schools (SACS); the Association to Advance Collegiate Schools of

Business (AACSB); and the European Foundation for Management Development (EFMD) (INCAE 2015a).

INCAE attributes a large part of its success to its international, highly educated faculty. INCAE professors come from all over the hemisphere and beyond, and nearly all of them hold doctoral degrees—many of them from Harvard University (INCAE 2015b). As alluded to in the section above, this concentration of doctoral talent is exceptional for higher education institutions in Latin America, and the percentage of Harvard-educated faculty would be difficult to match in any university. This solid academic base is also something that has positioned INCAE well for advancing its research, consulting, and publishing activities.

Another INCAE characteristic that has contributed to these activities is the school's extraordinary networking capacity. Over the years INCAE has developed very high-level alliances that span sectors and allow the institution to leverage its contacts across borders in public and private institutions, as well as in civil society and international organizations. These alliances have been the key for INCAE marketing, financing, academic programming, research, and consulting. Critical to managing and expanding this extensive network of formal and informal alliances are the INCAE Association and its National Committees that were formed at the outset in 1964 to guide and support institutional growth and development. Each country in Central America has a committee comprising distinguished individuals from private, public, and civil society entities and each committee's president serves on the INCAE Board of Directors. Additional responsibilities associated with the committees include promotion of and advice on INCAE programming, fundraising, recruiting, national contribution, and graduate employment and networking (INCAE 2014a).

Regarding academic alliances, INCAE is an active member of the US founded National Association of Schools of Public Affairs and Administration (NASPAA), the Business Association of Latin American Studies (BALAS), the Latin American Council of Business Schools (Consejo Latinoamericano de Escuelas de Administración, CLADEA), and the Social Enterprise Knowledge Network (SEKN), a collaboration of ten prestigious business schools in Iberoamerica. INCAE is also the founder of the Latin American University Network for Quality and Sustainable Development (Red Latinoamericana de Universidades por la Calidad y el Desarrollo Sostenible), a group of over 40 universities in the region. Additionally, INCAE has official agreements with dozens of top schools in the USA, Europe, and Asia Pacific, which allow for the development of joint programming and research.

INCAE's networking with the business community covers a wide range of national, regional, and global companies operating in Latin America, and much of this affiliation has been instigated and nurtured by INCAE alumni. Well-known entities among these include Dell, General Electric, Cargill, Pepsi, Procter and Gamble, Kimberly Clark, Deloitte & Touche, Nestlé, Pfizer, Coca Cola, and INTEL, among many others. These linkages are important sources of employment for INCAE graduates, donations, and scholarships, as well as potential consulting business (INCAE 2015b). Finally, INCAE's network extends to regional and international development as well. INCAE is a World Economic Forum (WEF) partner and, along with Harvard and Oxford, host to the WEF Young Global Leaders program. Similar economic-social progress-oriented partners include the World Bank Institute, Inter-American Development Bank (IDB), the AVINA Foundation, and bilateral international development agencies such as Germany's Deutsche Gesellschaft für Internationale Zusammenarbeit (the German Society for International Cooperation, GIZ) and USAID (Artavia 2008; INCAE 2015b).

CLACDS

CLACDS, INCAE's principal research center, was officially founded in 1996, but the INCAE research tradition extends back to its very early years. Because of the HBS methodology and its reliance on teaching from real-life business cases, INCAE from the start began to produce material on Latin American examples with Harvard professors to add to the HBS collective case library. The Latin cases now number close to 20,000 with over 60 new cases produced each year. Apart from the case studies produced by its faculty, INCAE research output to date has led to 58 books and roughly 500 articles, 150 professional papers, 100 independent research studies, and 200 consultancies (INCAE 2015c).

In response to the specific needs in the region, the INCAE research function quickly expanded beyond case-study investigations. Shortly after the establishment of the Nicaragua campus, the first major Harvard-INCAE research collaboration on agribusiness and rural development began under the guidance of Harvard professor Ray Goldberg and continued for several years, producing a number of books, cases, seminars, and other documentation (HBS 2014). Following the 1972 earthquake in Nicaragua and the resulting devastation, INCAE professor Harry Strachan (who would later become rector of INCAE) led the way for INCAE to contribute as a think-tank to the research and decision-making required for the national reconstruction plans. INCAE secured a US $1,000,000 grant to this end and worked with international organizations such as the World Bank and USAID on the rebuilding of the Nicaraguan economic and social infrastructure (Strachan 2007; Solis 2014). A formal INCAE Assessment Center was established with the assigned faculty, who negotiated a contract with Harvard's Development Advisory Service (later to become the Harvard Institute of International Development) and began to work with a Harvard team of scholars on government advising. A number of publications resulted from this collaboration and the effort paved the way for much of the later CLACDS planning and implementation. INCAE took on a similar government advisory role during other regional crises such as the Sandinista conflict of the later 1970s and 1980s, the post-war modernizing of the Guatemalan economy in the 1990s, the impending implications of climate change and conclusions of the 1992 Rio de Janeiro Earth Summit, and Hurricane Mitch in 1998.

At the end of 1995, a conference at Harvard University of the Central American presidents, INCAE and HBS scholars, and key regional businessmen paved the way for the consolidation of INCAE's background and experience in research activity and the channeling of this into a more permanent research center. The focus of the conference was the promotion of competitiveness and sustainable development in the region (INCAE-CLACDS 2015). Two critical participants in this presidential conference were renowned HBS professor and author Michael Porter and Swiss entrepreneur and philanthropist Stephan Schmidheiny. Michael Porter—whose 1990 book *The Competitive Advantage of Nations* focused on the differences in culture, policy, institutions, economic structure, and history that make the world's leading trading nations so successful—was instrumental in putting forth key concepts for advancing national and regional competitiveness. Stephan Schmidheiny, through his recently established AVINA Foundation, emphasized the need to devise new models for environmentally, socially, and economically sustainable development. Shortly thereafter in 1996, INCAE proposed the foundation of CLACDS as a permanent think tank within the school devoted to the issues of competitiveness and sustainable development, and the AVINA Foundation agreed to provide the initial financing (Artavia 2015; VIVA Trust 2007).

During its first five years, supported by the AVINA Foundation and HBS, much of CLACDS's research focused on the process of producing and implementing the *Central American Agenda for the 21st Century*, a long-term strategy for the region directed toward responsible development and insertion into the global economy. Building on the Agenda work, CLACDS went on to identify five strategic themes that would guide its research for the years to follow: national and regional competitiveness, rural development, challenges and implications of free trade, small- and medium-sized company competitiveness, and the impact of digital technology on the process of development (Condo and Majano 2005). For all of these topics, CLACDS received direct and indirect support from Harvard. Michael Porter continued to be very involved with the macro- and micro-level competitiveness work and Jeffrey Sachs, then head of the Harvard Institute for International Development (HIID), was closely associated with much of the work on development issues. This led to a number of joint INCAE-Harvard publications. Authorship for the *Central American Agenda for the 21st Century* is attributed to INCAE and HIID, for example, and various subsequent articles and papers, published in English and Spanish, also included authors from both INCAE-CLACDS and Harvard and/or joint research (see, e.g., Barahona et al. 1999; Jenkins et al. 1998; Pratt 2000). Additionally, CLACDS upon formation became involved with the WEF and its *Global Competitiveness Report*, through the HBS association, and was instrumental in getting more developing countries included in the index. CLACDS now handles the preparatory data collection for this report for eight countries in the region (INCAE-CLACDS 2015).

Over the past decade, the CLACDS research focus has expanded significantly to include a broader range of topics covering high potential cluster development, renewable energy proposals, corporate social responsibility, climate change, export promotion, microfinance, and foreign direct investment, among many others. Recent research and project partners include the Massachusetts Institute of Technology (MIT), Stanford University, the United Nations Environmental Programme (UNEP), GIZ, Walmart, and Philips. Among CLACDS's higher profile projects of the past several years is its Central American Private Sector Initiative (CAPSI). CAPSI started in 2011 to focus on the regional development issues related to cross-border trade facilitation, citizen security, and energy, and incorporated a 2013 summit that included US President Obama and over 200 Central American government, business, and civil society leaders. Another notable project is CLACDS's involvement with the Social Progress Imperative (SPI) launched in 2012 at the tenth annual Skoll World Forum held at Oxford University and originally conceived of within the WEF Global Agenda Council on Philanthropy and Social Investing. CLACDS currently works on the SPI Social Progress Index, an amplified societal development index, for ten countries of Latin America (INCAE-CLACDS 2015; SPI 2015).

By deciding to focus on economic competitiveness and sustainable development, CLACDS has been in a position to address a wider array of the region's most pressing issues and advise a broader group of government, business, and civil society organizations. Building on the INCAE ability to convene top players, CLACDS also leads a number of activities and events that bring together academic researchers, corporate actors, and other international entities for the purpose of examining problems and solutions for sustainable development. The annual Latin America Forum, within which global experts, INCAE faculty, and regional leaders meet to discuss organizational challenges in Latin America, is a prime example of this (INCAE-CLACDS 2015).

HARVARD PARTNERSHIP

The link with Harvard has been essential to INCAE's establishment and success. It has made major contributions in four key areas: education and training; research methods and experience; branding and prestige; and the fostering of interpersonal relationships. With education, INCAE received not only the HBS case-study methodology for teaching business administration but also training in how to teach, how to market, and how to administrate a graduate business school program. INCAE faculty members have also had privileged access to HBS for completing their own degree studies. With research, INCAE faculty—particularly those educated at Harvard—have gained valuable training in methodology for preparing case studies and for conducting various types of rigorous research on topics of importance to the region. They have also benefited from working together directly with Harvard scholars on numerous joint projects. Additionally, Harvard has provided prestigious brand recognition that has facilitated everything from fundraising and marketing to recruiting and placing students. Finally, the interpersonal relationships established between Harvard professors and their INCAE faculty students, research partners and colleagues have laid the foundation for a longer-term cooperation and a range of collaborative projects.

During the formation of INCAE, more than 50 HBS faculty contributed to its creation and growth (HBS 2014). George Cabot Lodge was the young HBS professor assigned to head the project from the Harvard side and in 1963 he led a nine-person team to Central America to survey over 400 luminaries from academia, government, business, and civil society in an effort to devise a workable plan for the INCAE implementation. Lodge is quick to point out that INCAE has always been an independent concept—independent from Harvard and from any government or organization—and as much a product of local leadership as of Harvard influence. He notes that Salvadoran businessman Francisco de Sola promptly emerged as the local actor who orchestrated the formation of the INCAE National Committees as well as the initial private sector fundraising campaign that raised over US $2 million. De Sola remained actively engaged with the National Committees and headed the INCAE Board of Directors until his death in 1983 (Solis 2014; Lodge 1999). His leadership and influence set the tone for INCAE's close connection to and management of its high-level Central American and international network. Lodge also emphasizes the relatively informal, ad hoc nature of the INCAE-Harvard partnership. Perhaps the formidable institutional mandate—coming straight from the US President Kennedy to HBS and backed by millions of dollars in technical assistance—eliminated the necessity for detailed and formalized contracts, protocol, or documentation at the outset. The INCAE faculty coming to HBS for education in combination with a number of Harvard professors' personal research interests extending to Central and Latin America over the years likely fueled the continued development of this institutional bond. At any rate, a fairly constant flow of exchange of people and knowledge continued almost uninterrupted for at least several decades.

From the beginning, many INCAE faculty members have been educated at Harvard (in both MBA and doctoral programs) before returning and taking on leadership positions at INCAE. The list of INCAE rectors presented in Table 4.2 shows the influence of this Harvard education trajectory on the evolution of INCAE administration. Alongside the trend of predominantly Harvard-trained scholars heading INCAE throughout, it is also notable that the rectors of the past several decades have come from Latin America and not from the USA as was the case in earlier years. This suggests a solid grounding in Harvard methods at the INCAE helm from the beginning and a shift toward a Latin American leadership over the last 20 years, the time period in which CLACDS has been in operation. The combination of Harvard graduate education with regional knowledge and experience is arguably a strong foundation for pursuing institutional research. Additionally, both Roberto Artavia and Arturo Condo were very involved with CLACDS prior to their assuming the position of rector. Artavia served as the first director of CLACDS and Condo subsequently directed numerous CLACDS projects. Thus, CLACDS benefitted initially from INCAE leadership that was predisposed to valuing research in the institution. This year marks the

Table 4.2 List of INCAE rectors

Rector	Nationality	Education	Years
Clark Wilson	USA	PhD, University of Southern California	1967–1968
Ernesto Cruz	Nicaragua	PhD, Harvard University	1968–1980
Harry Strachan	USA and Costa Rica	PhD, Harvard Business School	1981–1982
Marc Lindenberg	USA	PhD, University of Southern California	1982–1987
Melvyn Copen	USA	PhD, Harvard Business School	1987–1991
Brizio Biondi-Morra	USA	PhD, Harvard Business School	1991–1999
Roberto Artavia	Costa Rica	MBA/PhD, Harvard Business School	1999–2007
Arturo Condo	Ecuador	MBA/PhD, Harvard Business School	2007–2015
Enrique Bolaños	Nicaragua	MBA, INCAE	2015–

Source: INCAE

first time INCAE is led by a rector without a doctoral degree or a Harvard education. Current rector Bolaños has not been involved with CLACDS either, which could affect future prioritization of research objectives.

In addition to the formal education and administrative assistance INCAE received from Harvard, which is of a distinctly North-South nature in terms of flow and knowledge transfer, a great deal of informal learning has occurred over the years, which has been much more bidirectional. While this informal learning has involved North-South knowledge transfer, especially with regard to research methods and implementation, it has also created many opportunities for scholars from both INCAE and Harvard to broaden their knowledge and experience in areas related to researching business and development in Latin America. Specific examples of this include the early work done by Harvard professors Ray Goldberg and George Cabot Lodge on agribusiness and rural development in Central America, respectively, and the CLACDS work mentioned previously that involved Michael Porter and Jeffrey Sachs along with many from INCAE. Thus, while the Harvard participation was crucial for launching INCAE in all aspects, the resulting INCAE-Harvard partnership at the research level has been a mutually benefitting relationship, financially and academically, at least for protracted segments of the institutional interaction.

The branding and academic prestige that Harvard brings to INCAE has been another significant enabler, though more difficult to quantify and qualify. It is particularly tricky in more recent years to distinguish the branding contribution from that made by the Harvard training of INCAE professors and administrators. For instance, the Harvard branding was likely a weightier factor in the early years for convincing regional businesses, organizations, and individuals to donate and invest as well as for securing project funding from USAID and the IDB. By the mid-1990s, however, when WEF and AVINA became interested and involved with INCAE and CLACDS, the institution and its faculty had already begun to make a name for themselves in both education and research. Still, the affiliation is likely very advantageous even today for recruiting students, faculty, and high-profile partners across the spectrum of INCAE activity.

The development of interpersonal relationships fostered by the institutional INCAE-Harvard connection is also important and will be discussed in more depth in the following section. This interaction has affected all of the above and all aspects of the INCAE-Harvard dynamics.

ANALYSIS

Returning to the original questions guiding the examination of the INCAE-Harvard relationship and how it relates to research—regarding the motivations on both sides propelling the relationship, the operational mechanics for maintaining it, and the factors critical to its success—the study *Collaborative Approaches to Research* by David Smith and J. Sylvan Katz (2000) offers a fitting framework for analysis. An adapted version of the framework is useful for its categorization of collaboration models and description of institutional characteristics that facilitate research partnership efforts. Smith and Katz present three general models of collaborative research activity, constructed from the empirical data gathered from a series of institutional case studies: (1) interpersonal collaboration, (2) team collaboration, and (3) corporate partnership. In reality, most institutions demonstrate variations of these models, often with all three coexisting in varying degrees, even within specific projects. This is certainly true for the INCAE-Harvard relationship. What the separate models provide, however, is a heuristic for distinguishing basic differences in the types of collaborations based on structures, roles, objectives, and modes of operation, as well as how these affect output and success.

Table 4.3 presents an abbreviated, adapted representation of the Smith and Katz framework. It shows the three basic collaboration models along with the general characteristics, benefits, and limitations associated with

74   N. SVENSON

Table 4.3 Types of research collaboration and associated characteristics

General characteristics	Benefits	Limitations
Interpersonal collaboration		
Personal connection and intellectual interests of the people involved drive collaboration Collaborations are bottom-up, built on trust and proven ability of scholars to work together Structures are mainly informal, with collaborators working together throughout the project or selectively on parts of the investigation and publication Institutional affiliation is not always relevant as relationships often endure despite institutional changes related to career moves	Fluid cooperation based on trajectory of shared experience and study among researchers Evidence confirms this type of collaboration is more often successful, largely due to the mutual trust involved Academic conferences play a part in strengthening and expanding these alliances over time Often enhances personal and joint capacity with research, publication output, and intellectual recognition	Often unsustainable without solid and continuing sources of funding With current technology, participating researchers may not actually work together physically, which may limit capacity development Does not ensure that the "best" scholars are involved in a given study, only ones who already have a connection Authorship on joint publications may not accurately reflect individual contributions to research output
Team collaboration		
A need for multi-disciplinary skills, experience usually drives the collaboration Funding may come from various sources and act as both stimulant and problem for longer-term group stability Research output is determined by the teams and usually practitioner focused and problem/ task-based Teams may involve researchers from academia, industry, government, or professional practice, generally in semi-formalized groups without official partnership arrangements	Formation of and/or linkage to communities or networks of scholars working in a particular area Potentially applicable model for all disciplines and combinations of interdisciplinary work Enables projects of sizable scale and breadth Better access to funding through the leveraging of multiple institutions' different areas of expertise More possibility for inclusion of graduate and even undergraduate student researchers	Competition-collaboration continuum often established between researchers within and across institutions as they vie for funding Financing sources may dictate team conditions and affect longevity of team collaboration

(continued)

Table 4.3 (continued)

General characteristics	Benefits	Limitations
Corporate partnership External funding (for the university side) and specific research data (for the corporate partner) generally drives the association Research activity is usually conducted entirely by the university side Partnership structures include contracts, formal boards, or companies responsible for implementation and delivery	Advancement of individual and group interests by harnessing diverse expertise for application to common purpose Funding may serve a range of university purposes including technology infrastructure, training, travel, and fellowships Improved data/competitiveness for corporate partners Optimization of institutional complementarity/resource pools Potential cultural transformation, synergies, and spin-off projects	Selectivity of application—primarily cutting-edge scientific and technological research—that excludes many disciplines Research focus often skewed toward corporate needs

Adapted from Smith and Katz (2000)

each. The following section analyzes and discusses the INCAE-Harvard research partnership within this context. Applying this framework, the three types of models are evident throughout their 50-year history in various ways, on a number of levels, and often overlap and intertwine. The same is true for the corresponding benefits and limitations.

Interpersonal Collaboration

The importance of the interpersonal relationship for propelling collaborations is evident all the way through the INCAE-Harvard affiliation. It starts with US President Kennedy's contacting HBS Dean George Baker, Baker's assignation of George Cabot Lodge to lead the project and Lodge's connection with Francisco de Sola. How de Sola leveraged the Harvard link with key Central American business and government actors falls into this category, too, and de Sola's two decades management of this networking served as a major impetus to INCAE's reputation building and fundraising.

With regard to the interpersonal relationship propelling INCAE-Harvard research collaboration, this has been nurtured over the years by a number of INCAE professors who either trained at Harvard or completed graduate degree programs there. Through this exchange strong bonds were established between HBS professors such as George Cabot Lodge, Ray Goldberg, and Michael Porter and various INCAE faculty members, in some cases with the HBS professors serving as doctoral committee members for the INCAE professors. Numerous joint research projects resulted from these relationships, some instigated by Harvard and some by INCAE. And as several of these INCAE faculty members went on to become rectors, these relationships extended to even higher levels.

The INCAE directory now lists over 50 professors, and its website claims that 43 percent of its faculty have doctorates from Harvard, MIT, or Wharton. This implies at least 20 Ivy League professors currently (not counting those that have already retired), which is impressive. It also implies that INCAE has been able to sustain recruitment and development of high-level faculty even after its initial batches of Harvard-trained professors have retired. This is important for INCAE to maintain as it assures more direct access to scholars at prestigious schools, continued possibilities for joint investigation, and solid grounding with regard to academic capacity, pedagogy, and methodology. The Harvard graduate education is embedded in INCAE and this is perhaps the most important legacy of the interpersonal relationship model to this partnership since it promises the sustainable continuation of a certain methodological approach to research even beyond the joint projects that may be inspired as a result.

Interestingly, in contrast to the Smith and Katz representation, the institutional affiliation here is of utmost importance as the Harvard name is undoubtedly a factor that has allowed for INCAE's leveraging of many other assets. Also, at least some of the interpersonal relationships did not endure with career move university changes; when Jeffrey Sachs left Harvard for Colombia University in 2002, for example, he left the INCAE relationships as well and did not pursue new research with the CLACDS counterparts with whom he had worked and co-authored publications in previous years.

Team Collaboration

The direct INCAE-Harvard interpersonal connection between individuals is also what has propelled years of team collaboration research between the two institutions and with other prominent global institutions. Among the first instances of this was the INCAE response to the 1972 Managua earthquake and the subsequent advisory council it set up to assist the Nicaraguan government with reconstruction. The Harvard connection and the ability to call on scholars in multiple disciplines for the different work and research required for rebuilding, along with the financial integrity implied by the Harvard relationship, enabled INCAE to assume the position it did and also obtain USAID funding for this effort. Other early team collaborations included an agribusiness program financed by the IDB and the Nicaraguan government, a development banking program also funded by IDB, and a family planning management program supported by the Ford Foundation (Strachan 2007).

Prominent team collaborations over the years since CLACDS was inaugurated include the CLACDS-HIID work with Central American governments and business leaders on the *Central American Agenda for the 21st Century* and the subsequent competitiveness projects spawned by the Agenda work; the CLACDS work with the WEF competitiveness index and its role in getting more developing countries represented in the index; the CLACDS-MIT Digital Nations research and development project; and the CLACDS involvement with governments, industry, and the World Trade Organization (WTO) and other international organizations in research and preparation for the Central American Free Trade Agreement (CAFTA) (Condo and Majano 2005). More recent CLACDS team collaborations include CAPSI, the initiative involving a large group of Central American private sector leaders working on border commerce, citizen security, and energy solutions, and the SPI Social Progress Index work sponsored by the Skoll, Avina, and Rockefeller foundations as well as Deloitte at Cisco.

As noted in the previous table, the team collaboration model has, indeed, helped INCAE to benefit from linking to important scholar networks for critical areas of study. It has also enabled INCAE to take on bigger and more complex projects and access international funding. Additionally, these collaborative endeavors have provided opportunities for experiential learning and capacity development for INCAE professors and students—and often for its partners as well. Even in its earlier years, without the base of academic talent and experience it has amassed to date, INCAE was able to contribute solid local and regional knowledge to a project. This attribute has continued to facilitate INCAE's academic growth and also forced it to stay relevant and current.

Over the years, the INCAE-CLACDS team collaboration research has expanded considerably beyond Harvard and USAID where it originated in the 1960s and 1970s, attracting funds and minds from organizations and institutions in all sectors. As the initial interpersonal Harvard links become more distant, however, with many of the founding scholars now retired, the challenge for INCAE will be to retain its connection to Harvard and other top universities and organizations to continue its tradition of team collaborations for regional development.

Corporate Partnership

Corporate partnership appears to be the least prevalent of the research collaboration models throughout INCAE's history, at least in the traditional sense of a single large corporate sponsor contracting a particular research objective. Nevertheless, much of the INCAE-Harvard research collaboration has contained elements associated with the corporate partnership model. Many, if not most, of the research projects have incorporated external financing and sought to advance group interests, increase market information, and promote competitiveness. The difference is that financial sponsorship has generally come from international organizations, governments, or composite groups of corporate enterprises. Additionally, the research goals have usually been broader than the aims of a single entity, of potential benefit to a wider group of participants, and usually focused on regional development objectives. The USAID, IDB, AVINA, and WEF affiliations, for instance, all demonstrate aspects of the corporate partnership paradigm, particularly in that they have all been consistent sources of external research funding for INCAE. Here, too, without the direct involvement of Harvard and USAID of the earlier years, INCAE has had to branch out, prove its added value to a wider audience, and continually attract new partners to finance innovative programming and research. This continues to be a challenge, especially for CLACDS, as it does for many institutions throughout the world.

MOTIVATION, OPERATIONALIZATION, AND CRITICAL SUCCESS FACTORS

Reviewing and analyzing the INCAE-Harvard research relationship as laid out in the previous sections, a number of observations can be made. Exploring the motivations for each institution to pursue such an alliance, objectives of learning, financing, and knowledge generation emerge as primary incentives for both Harvard and INCAE. For those associated with INCAE, the Harvard relationship has offered the opportunity to learn cutting-edge research methodology, become certified in it at the highest level, and apply it practically to a range of real-life regional development problems. It also imparted from the beginning implicit accreditation (and status) by association, which facilitated access to international funding and joint research opportunities. In the case of Harvard, while a presidential mandate and national technical assistance funding provided the initial reasons for embarking on the INCAE adventure, as time went on, the connection with INCAE offered a natural laboratory for experimenting with the application of existing theories and also access to professionals with in-depth local knowledge in areas previously unexplored or sparsely documented. When these conditions matched well with the academic pursuits of particular faculty members, specific research was propelled and nurtured to the benefit of both sides of the North-South equation. In recent years, there appears to be less of this direct interaction than in prior periods. Hopefully for INCAE and CLACDS, this relationship has propelled the development of a substantial enough base for the pattern to replicate with other research partners in a similar dynamic.

Regarding the operationalization of this relationship, much of it has been based on informal connections as opposed to official protocols or contracts. Certain joint research projects or programs with particular goals sponsored by international organizations have, of course, had their associated contracts, budgets, and timeframes. But more of the INCAE-Harvard relationship, as noted earlier, has been built on less formalized, interpersonal linkages. It began with a phone call and a letter from President Kennedy to HBS and has continued for decades, more often than not, through the direct but informal academic relationships established between scholars in both places. These alliances have often been based on individual intellectual interests—like competitiveness, rural development, disaster risk reduction, trade, and social progress, for example—that have been timely and pertinent for both sides. Such informal collaborative structuring can be highly flexible and responsive, but it can also be ephemeral and unsustainable over time, especially if it is not attached to consistent and reliable funding.

Distinguishing the key success factors associated with this 50-year alliance is more complex than highlighting its corresponding motivations or operational mechanics. Success factors cover a far broader scope of elements affected by time, nature, leadership, external economic and political circumstances, money, and personalities, among other influences. Isolating the more critical among these is undeniably a subjective exercise, but based on recurring references in both documented literature and personal historical accounts, several points surface repeatedly that merit reiteration for their importance in bolstering this North-South affiliation. Other factors such as timing, politics, and luck have had pivotal effects in specific moments, as is the case with all endeavors, but the following five factors have been reliably consequential over time.

First: powerful champions. The INCAE-Harvard collaborative relationship has had high profile, heavy hitters behind it from the beginning and throughout. From President Kennedy, HBS Dean Baker, and Francisco de Sola at the outset to Central American presidents and business giants to professors like Porter and Sachs, benefactors like Stephan Schmidheiny, and organizations like WEF in more recent years, these endorsements count for a lot and have been able to mobilize action at various levels. They also provide positive public relations that attract additional supporters and lead to future opportunities.

Second: recognized academic capacity. INCAE took complete advantage of Harvard's educational offer to develop and recruit its own internal doctoral talent, which has paid enormous dividends in terms of research capacity and reputation. Added to this, INCAE intelligently accredited its programming with recognized international accreditation agencies. This is especially advantageous given the lack of this tendency in Latin American institutions and considerably adds to INCAE's academic credibility in all areas.

Third: strategic, multi-sectoral networking. By leveraging the Harvard connection and other important contacts, INCAE and CLACDS have developed active networks that cross sectors and include an array of useful and profitable international associations. These networks have provided strategic partners with varied contributions for numerous projects. They also reinforce INCAE's reputation for being a trusted platform for convening important players to discuss and research important regional issues.

Fourth: diversified fundraising and effective cost management. This North-South alliance has always depended upon a combination of international, regional, and national investment from a collection of organizations and individuals. The exact composition of this funding diversification has shifted over time, but its inclusive breadth has allowed for financing from multiple sources to be directed toward covering knowledge gaps. In combination with astute internal cost management—born of necessity since INCAE and CLACDS have always been operating in situations that force productive utilization of funds—this has allowed for research to assume some priority within the institution. This will also likely remain the biggest challenge for INCAE as time goes on.

Fifth: tropicalization. This collaboration has worked, in large part, because INCAE took steps early on to "tropicalize" the Harvard input and tailor it to the needs and issues of the region. The Harvard case-study methodology fostered an emphasis on combining theory with practice; INCAE applied this practicality concept not only to business development in the region but also to regional development in its entirety. This mixing of micro and macro and business and development was interesting for Harvard, too, as it served to connect HBS with HIID, the university's international development unit at the time, and add perspectives to the research of both disciplines. Tropicalization also allowed INCAE to turn crises (such as natural disaster, war, and market upheaval) into research opportunities. Almost from the beginning, INCAE seemed to recognize the need for it to become more than a school, for it to become instead "a major facilitator for problem solving in [the] region" (Strachan 2007, p. 112). By maintaining rigorous Harvard standards for academic prowess and directing this toward research on the region's most pressing development issues, INCAE has become a critical advisory partner to national and regional government bodies and international organizations.

CONCLUSION

Interpersonal relationships, teamwork collaborations, and corporate partnerships all play important parts in the INCAE-Harvard project. All three types of engagement models influence the motivations for working together and the dynamic's success factors and limitations. The interpersonal relationship as a catalyst for collaborations is probably the strongest impetus, particularly in the earlier years, and has been strengthened by the number of Central American scholars educated at Harvard who returned to INCAE to teach and research. These interpersonal links also laid the foundation for collaborative research teamwork, initially with Harvard and INCAE/CLACDS and then later with other internationally renowned institutions and INCAE/CLACDS as well. Throughout, corporate partnership has been critical, though "corporate" in this case assumes a broader dimension. It includes prominent business actors from both the USA and Latin America and also extends to major international organizations and foundations. These partnerships have been essential sources of financing and have driven portions of the INCAE/CLACDS research agenda and knowledge production.

In terms of achievement, there appears to be considerable substantiation for demonstrating that the INCAE-Harvard collaboration has been successful in making CLACDS a research center focused on real-world problems and solutions. And there is general agreement that CLACDS's work in combination with INCAE's academic programming has contributed to a shift in the mindset and mentality in the region, making for a more holistic conceptualization and analysis by leaders of the problems affecting Central America at all levels (Artavia 2015; INCAE 2014a; Strachan 2007). What is less clear is to what extent this has impacted change at the governmental and intergovernmental levels. Many of the same regional challenges addressed in the early years of CLACDS—regional competitiveness, integration, security, and trade—are still being discussed without noticeable legislative or operational advances. In contrast, national and regional business enterprises seem to have responded more quickly to utilize similar inputs for modernization and competitive advantage.

For the future, however, the INCAE-Harvard research dynamic is not as strong as it was and has not been for at least a decade, which means INCAE and CLACDS must use the foundation established to reinvent and innovate. This is already being done to a certain degree, but without the strong Harvard research support and AVINA financial support prevalent in CLACDS's first decade of operation, the scenario is more challenging. Several areas for research attention look promising. The national and regional monitoring CLACDS is doing for WEF and SPI is solid and growing in significance. This is a niche that could be strengthened and expanded, with regard to additional monitoring of a similar nature that could be done as well as the utilization of the data gathered for new applications. Regional private sector dialogues, like CAPSI, that can mobilize the private sector to push for national and regional policy change are important, too, particularly for the economic power they could wield. Specific sectors such as healthcare, energy, and environmental management are also interesting because of their importance as well as their connection with international funding possibilities. Finally, the new frontier of Cuba as it emerges on the world market holds significant potential. This is especially true since INCAE and CLACDS are in a better position to offer options for capacity development than most US or European institutions (Contreras 2015).

The INCAE-Harvard partnership over the past 50 years has contributed notably and positively to research ability and output in Central America. George Cabot Lodge asserts that INCAE is probably USAID's most successful project ever in the Americas (INCAE 2014b). And it may well be. How the foundation established over the past decades evolves to meet the challenges and conditions of the coming decades remains to be seen. This North-South alliance was formed initially as a result of very specific timing, politics, and personalities, but it has continued for half a century enduring a series of foreseeable and unforeseeable obstacles and has left in its wake a research tradition in Central America that is largely unparalleled. Regardless of what its future holds, the factors associated with its success have been remarkably effective to date and will hopefully serve to inspire others seeking to accomplish similar results.

Acknowledgments Several individuals were critical to developing this chapter. Immense appreciation is extended to these scholars for contributing their personal accounts, which add another dimension to the documented facts and figures of the INCAE-Harvard history: George Cabot Lodge (Professor Emeritus of Harvard Business School), Harry Strachan (Professor Emeritus and former Rector of INCAE), Roberto Artavia (former Rector of INCAE and founding Director of CLACDS), John Ickis (Dean of Faculty at INCAE), and Ana Maria Majano (Associate Director of CLACDS).

NOTE

1. The Gini index (or coefficient) is a measure of statistical dispersion generally used to quantify income inequality. A low Gini coefficient indicates a more equal distribution, with 0 equivalent to perfect equality, while a higher Gini coefficient indicates a more unequal distribution, with 1 equivalent to perfect inequality.

REFERENCES

Artavia, R. (2008). *Centroamérica 1982–2007: 25 Lecciones que Aprendí en INCAE* [*Central America 1982–2007: 25 Lessons I Learned in INCAE*]. San Jose: Latinoamérica Posible.

Artavia, R. (2015). *Stephan Schmidheiny y su Legado para América Latina, 1984–2014* [*Stephan Scmidheiny and his Legacy for Latin America*] (pp 131–149). Bilanz: VIVA Trust.

Association to Advance Collegiate Schools of Business (AACSB). (2011). *International.* Spotlight: Business Schools and Ethics/Sustainability–INCAE Business School.

Barahona, J. C., Doryan, E., Sachs, J., & Larrain, F. (1999). *Facing Natural Disasters in a Vulnerable Region: Hurricane Mitch in Central America (Lessons learned).* Working Paper for INCAE/CLACDS-Harvard Institute for International Development.

Condo, A., & Majano, A. (2005). La Competitividad y el Desarrollo de la Región, el Enfoque de CLACDS [Competitiveness and the Development of the Region, the Focus of CLACDS]. *En Resumen* special edition – INCAE 40th Anniversary.

Contreras, C. (2015, September 16). Alberto Trejos: Espero que los Centroamericanos Avancemos en como Invertir en Cuba. *Estrategia y Negocios*. Available online at http://www.estrategiaynegocios.net/lasclavesdeldia/880668-330/alberto-trejos-espero-que-los-centroamericanos-avancemos-en-c%C3%B3mo-invertir-en-cuba. Accessed 29 Sep 2015.

Harvard Business School (HBS). (2014). Harvard Business School News. *INCAE Observes 50th Anniversary at Celebration at Harvard Business School*. Available online at http://www.hbs.edu/news/releases/Pages/incae-50th-celebration.aspx. Accessed 4 May 2015.

INCAE Business School. (2014a). *Memoria Anual 2014: INCAE 50 Aniversario [Annual Report 2014: INCAE 50th Anniversary]*. Available online at http://www.incae.edu/images/descargables/AcercaDe/incae_anuario_2014.pdf. Accessed 1 June 2015.

INCAE Business School. (2014b). *The INCAE Project*. Available online at https://www.youtube.com/watch?v=V9ZMGgC0oEc. Accessed 15 Aug 2015.

INCAE Business School. (2015a). *History of INCAE – Accreditations and Rankings*. Available online at http://conocimiento.incae.edu/EN/biblioteca/recursos-servicios/historia-incae/acreditaciones-rankings.php. Accessed 10 Aug 2015.

INCAE Business School. (2015b). *Why INCAE?* Available online at http://www.incae.edu/en/why-incae.html. Accessed 1 Aug 2015.

INCAE Business School. (2015c). *The ABC Guide*. Available online at http://www.incae.edu/en/master-programs/mba-costa-rica.php#compare-3. Accessed 20 Aug 2015.

INCAE Business School – Centro Latinoamericano para la Competitividad y el Desarrollo Sostenible (INCAE-CLACDS). (2015). Available online at http://www.incae.edu/es/clacds. Accessed 10 Mar 2015.

Jenkins, M., Esquivel, G., & Larrain, F. B. (1998). Export Processing Zones in Central America. HIID Central America Project Series – Development Discussion Paper No. 646.

Lodge, G. C. (1999, Fall). The Birth of INCAE (1963–1965): A View from Harvard. *ReVista Harvard Review of Latin America*.

Partnership for Educational Revitalization in the Americas (PREAL). (2007). *A Lot to Do: A Report Card on Education in Central America and the Dominican Republic*. Washington, DC: PREAL Task Force on Education Reform in Central America.

Pratt, L. (2000). *Rethinking the Private Sector-Environment Relationship in Latin America*. Background Paper for the Seminar on the "New Vision for Sustainability: Private Sector and the Environment" IDB/IIC Annual Meeting of the Board of Governors in New Orleans, Louisiana, March 25, 2000.

Smith, D., & Katz, J. S. (2000). *Collaborative Approaches to Research*. A joint project with the Higher Education Policy Unit (HEPU), University of Leeds and Science Policy Research Unit (SPRU) University of Sussex. Available online at http://users.sussex.ac.uk/~sylvank/pubs/collc.pdf. Accessed 15 Aug 2015.

Social Progress Imperative (SPI). *About – Origins*. Available online at http://www.socialprogressimperative.org/about/origins. Accessed 10 Sep 2015.

Solis, L. E. (2014, March). 50 Years Illuminating Latin America. *INCAE Alumni Magazine* (3).

Strachan, H. W. (2007). *INCAE Memories 1970–1982*. San Jose: Ediciones Guayacan.

Svenson, Nanette. (2012, September 23). R&D in Central America: Panorama and Prospects for International Cooperation. *Higher Education*, pp. 1–16.

Svenson, N. (2015). Central American Outliers: Leveraging International Cooperation for Research Productivity. In G. Gregorutti & J. E. Delgado (Eds.), *Private Universities in Latin America: Research and Innovation in the Knowledge Economy* (pp. 157–184). New York: Palgrave Macmillan.

United Nations Educational, Scientific and Cultural Organisation (UNESCO). (2007). *The State of Education in Latin America and the Caribbean: Guaranteeing Quality Education for All*. Santiago: UNESCO Regional Bureau of Education for Latin America and the Caribbean.

VIVA Trust. (2007). *AVINA-INCAE: A Partnership for Sustainable Development in Latin America*. Bilanz: VIVA Trust.

World Bank. (2005). *Central American Education Strategy: An Agenda for Action*. Washington, DC: World Bank.

World Bank. (2014). *World Development Indicators*. Available online at http://data.worldbank.org. Accessed 10 Aug 2015.

World Bank. (2015). *Data – Country and Lending Groups*. Available online at http://data.worldbank.org/about/country-and-lending-groups. Accessed 1 Sep 2015.

Yin, R. K. (2014). *Case Study Research: Design and Methods*. Los Angeles: Sage Publications.

CHAPTER 5

International Research Collaboration and Knowledge Production in Colombia: A Qualitative Network Analysis Approach

Clara I. Tascón

INTRODUCTION

International Research Collaboration (IRC) is a main enabler of knowledge production in the internationalization of higher education, and research universities are the primary vehicles for this endeavor (Altbach 2013). Research and scholarly collaborations (Knight 2004) enhance information exchange and knowledge building among universities that seek to find solutions for common problems in our interconnected world (de Wit 2010). Studying researchers' experiences in Colombia, this chapter focuses on what motivates academics in this country to engage in IRC, the challenges Colombian researchers face when collaborating internationally, and the extent to which these international research networks contribute to knowledge production in the country and beyond. These questions are purposively situated in a comparative study on IRC and

---

C. I. Tascón (✉)
Faculty of Education, Western University, London, ON, Canada

© The Author(s) 2018
G. Gregorutti, N. Svenson (eds.), *North-South University Research Partnerships in Latin America and the Caribbean*,
https://doi.org/10.1007/978-3-319-75364-5_5

knowledge production in two research networks tied to Colombia's public and private university systems. Findings about these two Colombian research networks are part of a larger research I focused on during the last four years (Tascón 2017).

Little of this type of investigation has been done, though some study was made of the 1991–2006 activity of one Colombian diaspora network (Meyer and Wattiaux 2006; Meyer 2001; Meyer et al. 1997; Tejada 2012). Studies regarding this group, the Colombian Network of Scientists and Engineers Abroad—Red Caldas (Red Colombiana de Científicos e Ingenieros en el Exterior, or Red Caldas, for its acronym in Spanish), provide information on the experiences of a highly skilled expatriate community and their corresponding knowledge ties across borders (Meyer and Wattiaux 2006). Still, a large research gap remains, especially with regard to the motivations, challenges, and contributions of IRC through current Colombian research networks (de Wit et al. 2005; Ordóñez-Matamoros 2008). Most existing research in this area involves quantitative data that counts co-publications and joint research projects from researchers in "centers" (universities in developed countries) and "peripheries" (universities in less developed countries) (Altbach 2007, 112). However, IRC entails numerous activities and different kinds of knowledge mobilization practices. Co-publication is only one factor in all of this and is not representative of the much richer IRC's involvement and processes. This international collaborative initiative represents a complex phenomenon influenced by local and global contexts of policies, practices, and rationales. It is also mobilized by various types of knowledge flows and networks (Appadurai 1990; Castells and Cardoso 2005) and made up of multiple actors (Smith 2001). IRC involves not only the production of journal articles, books, reports, and conference proceedings but also the processes in which the individuals in a research network participate. This includes different means for sharing and creating new knowledge and is underpinned by participating actors' relational dynamics, as well as their motivations and challenges.

This chapter begins with a brief overview of IRC and how it is typically measured and analyzed. It then introduces the concept of Social Networks Analysis (SNA) to illustrate the value of this approach from a qualitative perspective and its significance within the field of comparative and international education in relation to post-foundational ideas[1] and spatial thinking.[2] The chapter goes on to present two case studies that show how a diaspora network characterizes many of the dynamics of international research interconnections. SNA mapping of the two Colombian research networks reveals the networks' configurations and their particular international collaborative dynamics relative to participants' motivations, challenges, and knowledge production. Comparing and analyzing these two examples elucidate the contextual realities that shift the hegemonic view of IRC regarding North-South, center-periphery relationships. Examining these contextualized collaborative initiatives further helps to legitimate IRC knowledge production by going beyond the counting of co-publications and tracing and studying the nuances of these international practices, whereby researchers drive, exchange, and co-create new knowledge.

Brief Overview of IRC

The term "international research collaboration" is commonly used interchangeably with "international scientific collaboration," since research is seen as scientific investigation in academic terminology (Beaver 2001; Bukvova 2010; Sonnenwald 2007). Katz and Martin (1997) highlight two distinct perspectives for understanding research collaboration: (1) co-authorship, which has been the most tangible way to determine who publishes with whom and within which scientific communities, and (2) the less tangible, unmeasured, and taken-for-granted processes and practices of knowledge production in this collaborative endeavor. For the latter, scholars point out that IRC can take many forms, influenced by disciplinary or interdisciplinary practice, context, the reasons behind the collaboration, and the background of participating researchers (Bukvova 2010; Melin 2000; Morrison et al. 2003; Sonnenwald 2007). In addition, Sonnenwald (2007) emphasizes that different types of Information and Communication Technologies (ICT) used may also influence the forms that IRC can take. He cites as examples the contribution systems, virtual communities of practice, virtual learning communities, distributed research centers, and community infrastructure projects often associated with IRC (p. 660).

There are many reasons for embarking on a collaborative research project, and these may develop from an informal conversation between two individuals (Smith 2001) or through a social process with multiple participants involved. Factors influencing motivations include the need to share or obtain specific knowledge and skills from different researchers; a common interest in the research problem; access to resources; a desire for interdisciplinary and/or cross-cultural perspective and experience; pursuit of higher quality and/or productivity; and perceived prestige (Beaver 2001; Bukvova 2010; Sonnenwald 2007). Shin, Lee, and Kim (2013) highlight the broader view and understanding of a specific phenomenon that interdisciplinary IRC allows. Additionally, factors such as geographical proximity, common language, and historical ties (including colonial relationships) can facilitate or propel IRC (Wagner et al. 2001).

External and internal factors also affect IRC development (Zelnio 2013). External factors involve political, economic, and scientific driven forces that act upon the researchers or the relational contexts in which IRC takes place (Sonnenwald 2007). Globalization and ICT advances, for example, play a crucial role in knowledge mobilization and facilitation of local and global academic interconnections (Stier 2004). Internal factors, too, are important since they determine the structure of the research community within which the type of IRC and its processes and practices occur. These factors involve the characteristics of the research networks/scientific communities in relation to the social networks and personal characteristics of individuals working within them. Mutual respect, trust, and compatible working styles, specifically, have been identified as personal factors that contribute to IRC success (Wasser and Bresler 1996).

IRC Measurement and Analysis

Co-authorship, or co-publication of journal articles, has been the main bibliometric indicator for measuring and analyzing IRC. This indicator is created using databases of peer-reviewed articles across disciplines (e.g., Landry et al. 1996). The most complete of these databases are the ISI (Institute for Scientific Information) Web of Knowledge (WoK) and the Elsevier Scopus. However, as Smith and Katz (2000) point out, co-authorship is only a partial indicator of collaboration. The UNESCO Institute of Statistics (2005) discusses the advantages and disadvantages of standard quantitative indicators such as the Science Citation Index (SCI), the Social Sciences Citation Index (SSCI), and the Arts & Humanities Citation Index (AHCI) (Frame and Carpenter 1979; Katz and Martin 1997). These measurements do provide numerical information on national or regional academic production, by discipline, along with certain data on the concentrations and kinds of academic connections existing between countries, research institutions, and even individual researchers. But these indicators are insufficient for measuring data from non-Anglophone countries for several reasons. First, there is a language bias. English is the standard language of international publication and many non-Anglophone and developing countries do not produce much in English and may lack resources for translation or editing. Second, there is a thematic bias because research published in national journals that examine problems of national interest will often not be picked up or covered by the international journals since nationally oriented topics are frequently deemed too narrow for widespread appeal. Finally, there is a pure-science bias; coverage of the applied sciences, particularly the social and human sciences, is much less extensive and blinkered, meaning that various research and development (R&D) activities are excluded from these databases altogether. Additionally, co-authorship does not reflect other kinds of contributions provided by researchers in a network, like data collection, fieldwork support, data organization, verification and analysis, and information dissemination. Nor does it show what kinds of factors influence IRC, or what effect IRC has on research performance and knowledge production in local contexts (Ordóñez-Matamoros et al. 2010; Ordóñez-Matamoros 2008). There are numerous formal and informal connections through which IRC is linked and promoted, and many of these connections are not well identified or accounted for within the traditional academic indicator frameworks. Studies in Latin America, particularly in Colombia, note the glaring lack of complementary information on IRC in bibliometric databases (Meyer et al. 1995; Narvaez-Berthelemot et al. 1992; Ordóñez-Matamoros et al. 2010). Given the limits to the bibliometric approach, scholars have begun to use SNA to study IRC in combination with the quantitative input from bibliometric indicators (Shin et al. 2013; Wagner and Leydesdorff 2005). SNA researchers analyze IRC in more depth, using qualitative and mixed-methods approaches to explore the context and the network composition (Edwards 2010; Fuhse and Mützel 2011; Scott and Carrington 2011). This chapter illustrates how to use a qualitative SNA approach to analyze and compare two distinct research networks of IRC.

Qualitative SNA Approach

SNA is a methodological approach that helps to map the configuration of a network and the interconnections between its members. John Scott (2012) states that a network is a set of "points"—individuals or groups (p. 1)—interconnected by "lines," as the relations that connect each other (p. 1). Some scholars use the terms "nodes" and "ties" to mean individuals or groups and connections respectively (Borgatti and Halgin 2011; Pinheiro 2011; Scott and Carrington 2011). Nodes occupy different positions in a network according to their roles and they are connected by both direct and indirect links, which result in multiple nodes that are not always directly tied to each other. Direct links indicate strong ties, which involve overlapping relationships between people due to their similarities, knowledge, and expertise in a specific field. Indirect links represent weak ties that can include more distant relations as a possible source of novel ideas that have not yet circulated in a set of strong ties (Granovetter 1973). SNA studies all types of information about the relations of the network members (nodes), focusing on the ties or connections between the nodes rather than the members/nodes themselves. This differentiates SNA from data analysis. Although individual attributes—such as level of education, conferences attended, research conducted, and papers published—are important, other aspects may be even more influential (Pinheiro 2011). How individuals share their ideas and compile their works, as well as how their institutions coordinate their respective agendas, tend to carry more weight than individuals' skills, talents, and initiatives. This focus is reflected in the study presented in this chapter.

Also important to highlight is the fact that networks are open systems and thus able to expand without limits (Castells 1996, 470). Scientific and scholarly networks are characterized by interactions among co-authors and other colleagues (White 2011) that span a variety of different kinds of research activities. Castells and Cardoso (2005) suggest the notion of horizontal and vertical channels of communication in the network society. These channels of communication align with flows of knowledge, policy, and practice that help illustrate a notion of space that surpasses the institutional and national orders and that depicts different connections and ties between network members worldwide. This perspective contributes to the analysis of the two Colombian cases in this chapter where vertical channels of communication at the institutional level co-exist with internationally horizontal ones among members in the same network. Using SNA from a qualitative perspective to map the research networks configurations and their types of interconnections then helps to better understand the relational context within which IRC's practices operate. The following section presents a brief overview of recent studies and background on Colombian IRC before introducing the two cases involved in this study.

IRC in Colombia

Colombia is an emerging country with a rapidly improving scientific and technological capacity (Ordóñez-Matamoros et al. 2010; Ordóñez-Matamoros 2008), and IRC is an important contributor to the country's internationalization process. Ordóñez-Matamoros (2008) examines the effects of IRC on research performance focusing on knowledge production and research network ability to add to local knowledge in Colombia. His exhaustive mixed-methods study using SNA shows both the research productivity measured by co-authorship, certain characteristics of IRC as evidenced by the participation of foreign researchers in local networks, and the dependency of these local networks on foreign funding for R&D. Furthermore, his study points to some of the benefits and challenges (aspirations and tensions) of this complex international practice. Most scholars studying IRC in Colombia argue that it has had a direct and positive impact on journal articles in the country, with figures for co-authorship (as measured in the SCI) steadily rising over the last 20 years (Meyer et al. 1995; Narvaez-Berthelemot et al. 1992; Ordóñez-Matamoros et al. 2010). However, these scholars also highlight how co-authorship figures exclude substantial information on other bibliographic products, and how little is known about the determinants, characteristics, processes, and impacts of IRC in Colombia.

With the purpose of better understanding Colombian scholars' participation in IRC, it is important to take into consideration the national research database system created by the Administrative Department of Science, Technology, and Innovation (Departamento Administrativo de Ciencia, Tecnología e Innovación, or COLCIENCIAS for its acronym in Spanish). This database system registers active researchers and research groups from public and private universities and other research institutions, as well as their research projects by areas of knowledge (COLCIENCIAS 2018). In addition, COLCIENCIAS leads, guides, and coordinates Colombia's national policy on science, technology, and innovation. Colombia's research development is characterized by a relatively strong institutional foundation. However, this country spends a very low percentage of its GDP (0.23%) on knowledge production in basic and applied research including natural sciences and social sciences, arts, and humanities (World Bank 2016). This, in turn, leads to disturbing results for universities and scholars trying to engage in IRC.

IRC in Colombia has been influenced by national researchers' relationships with former professors or colleagues from abroad. These Colombian researchers maintain their affiliations and stay connected to international research networks for purposes of co-authoring journal articles, attending international conferences, and participating in local and regional research projects. These researchers usually speak a second language, which allows them to co-author and participate actively in IRC (Ordóñez-Matamoros 2008). Because international research funding is critical for Colombia, the participation of foreign researchers in national research teams is often tied to international agencies' interests and not always to Colombia's. Nevertheless, this funding does finance projects that would otherwise likely not be implemented. Ordóñez-Matamoros (2008) draws attention to this phenomenon as a predicament since what may be important in terms of scientific achievement for a developed country may not be a research priority for an emerging country. Still, he also notes that even issues that are not national priorities in a given moment may provide important contributions for the future. This is often an issue in IRC with countries from the North and has pushed local researchers and institutions to look toward other research partners in the South. To this end, international research networks have recently formed among countries in Latin America. An example of such a network is the Society of Universities Montevideo Group (Asociación de Universidades Grupo Montevideo), which advocates for IRC and faculty mobility (Knobel et al. 2013). Similar linkages facilitating IRC in terms of communications and even financial agreements can also be found among the Iberoamerican countries, though North-South issues may still present obstacles even if linguistic and cultural issues do not. The changing dynamic from North-South to South-South collaborations opens up new venues within which to embrace similar contextual realities, related problems, and common solutions.

Analysing Two Colombian Research Networks

As indicated at the beginning of the chapter, a qualitative SNA approach is employed here to map two Colombian research networks and answer the guiding questions regarding their motivations, challenges, and knowledge production in IRC. SNA mapping of these two networks helps to identify (1) their configurations in terms of a space that crosses international borders and is made up of interconnections among different university actors and (2) their dynamics in terms of activities that connect network members in relation to their motivations, challenges, and knowledge production. To this end, initial sub-questions asked are the following: Who are the members involved in these two Colombian networks? Is there a centralized relationship among any of the members? Are there horizontal flows that allow for and foster knowledge sharing and creation among network members? What types of activities link the different network members?

Research Methods

The study presented in this chapter draws upon data gathered from 14 semi-structured interviews with key participants associated with the two research networks studied. These research networks were located through their websites in connection with their respective private and public universities. Participants of these research networks were selected, taking into consideration that they participate actively in research as indicated by the COLCIENCIAS database. They included seven participants from each network: two staff members (one in charge of the international office and one in charge of the research office), two professors, and three students or alumni, which constitute the majority of members. All participants were active in their respective networks for at least two years. Anonymity is maintained throughout the chapter in reference to individuals and the research networks as a whole. The two research networks were selected purposively taking into consideration their connections to a public and a private university system and the fact that they both work in areas related to Colombian pre-Hispanic studies. The two directly linked institutions of the networks are research-intensive universities with high levels of interest and involvement in internationalization processes and IRC. A public and a private institution were chosen given the significant distinctions between private and public universities in Colombia. The public university depends entirely on state funding and regulation. The private university, though also regulated by the state, is self-financed through student tuition and particular sponsorships. Another difference between the two higher education systems refers to the sabbatical leave appointed to scholars in the public university, which is not the case for scholars in the private one. The findings from the study of these two research networks are presented as case studies for comparison.

From a network analysis perspective, the cases analyzed here are not framed as official partnerships under international agreements, as there are no formal agreements between the members of these research networks, either nationally or internationally. Rather, Zingerli's (2010) more general concept of partnership as a means for structuring any kind of human and institutional relations is utilized here, as opposed to the concept of partnership under official institutional agreements. The type of IRC portrayed in these two cases is defined by the different scholarly activities of the participating members. These research networks, as they appear in Figs. 5.1 and 5.2, were configured according to participants' descriptions of ties, roles, and activities of the different members. The following sections discuss the configurations along with the kinds of activities the networks engage in and their knowledge production as a result of IRC.

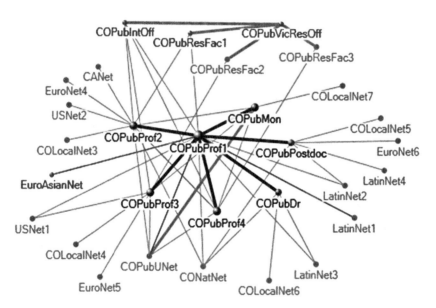

Fig. 5.1 Colombia Public Research Network—COPubResNet. (Direct members (nodes) of the COPubResNet: COPubProf1 (Coordinator of the network), COPubProf2, COPubProf3, COPubProf4, COPubPostdoc, COPubDr, COPubMon. Indirect members (nodes) of the COPubResNet: COPubResFac1, COPubIntOff, COPubVicResOff, and other research networks such as EuroAsianNet, COPubUNet, CONatNet, LatinNet1, and so on)

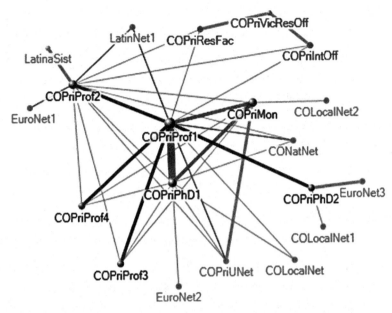

Fig. 5.2 Colombian Private Research Network—COPriResNet. (Direct members (nodes) of the COPriResNet: COPriProf1, COPriProf2, COPriProf3, COPriProf4, COPriPhD1, COPriPhD2, COPriMon. Indirect members (nodes) of the COPriResNet: COPriResFac, COPriVicResOff, COPriIntOff, and other research networks such as COPriUNet, CONatNet, EuroNet1, LatinNet1, and so on)

Findings

The two Colombian research networks show distinct configurations based on the members (nodes) involved and the types of interconnections among them. The SNA maps (Figs. 5.1 and 5.2) emerged from the information provided by the interviewees of each network. Specific codes identify each research network and the nodes within.[3] Figure 5.1 depicts the research network tied to the public university (Colombian Public Research Network—COPubResNet) and Fig. 5.2 shows the one tied to the private university (Colombian Private Research Network—COPriResNet). The nodes are represented by codes that correspond to the private or public status of the university and the individual's status (professor, student, alumni, staff, or another network). Of note, the two Colombian research networks studied are not connected to each other in any way.

As mentioned above, the interview data provided the information on the roles and connections among the different actors of the networks that allowed for a mapping of their configurations. Using SNA as a tool, participants were asked to identify the members of the networks, the types of ties (strong or weak), their roles, their channels of communication in terms of knowledge and policy, and the research activities in which these members engage and collaborate, as well as their distinct research projects and publications. Tables 5.1 and 5.2 present the codification of the nodes (members) and their descriptors.

Network Configuration and Activity

Regarding configuration, both of the Colombian networks discussed here are characterized by internal centrality for the network coordination, as depicted by the larger central circle corresponding to COPubProf1 and COPriProf1 in Figs. 5.1 and 5.2, respectively. A single professor in each of these networks is connected to most of the members and facilitates the communication among them. These professors are central actors, leaders that coordinate discussions and different collaborative activities of the research networks. This type of configuration helps keep all network members informed on and connected to the different IRC activities and opportunities at both individual and institutional levels. As a result, a variety of knowledge and policy flows (Appadurai 1990) circulates through these research networks, where the centrality of the coordination makes it easier to establish and achieve network commitments and goals. In both cases, the local professors have co-authored several publications with professors abroad. Members of the two research networks also maintain other connections with different international networks, as shown in Figs. 5.1 and 5.2. Another similar characteristic between COPubResNet and COPriResNet is that several of their permanent members are current or former students who have studied abroad and maintain close relationships with COPubProf1 and COPriProf1. As Meyer (2001) mentions, these professor-alumni relationships serve to form a diaspora network that acts as a primary driver of international connections for researchers in Colombia. At the same time, professors and alumni in both research networks also maintain close relationships with former professors-colleagues abroad. On the other hand, there is a subtle difference between the two Colombian research networks leadership's dynamics. Particularly in the COPriResNet, the coordinator (COPriProf1) shares his leadership with a

INTERNATIONAL RESEARCH COLLABORATION AND KNOWLEDGE... 99

Table 5.1 Colombian Public Research Network (COPubResNet), node codes and descriptors

Code/node	Descriptor
COPubProf1	Network Coordinator (Professor—Archaeology and Museum director)
COPubProf2	Professor—Musicology
COPubProf3	Professor—Geophysics
COPubProf4	Professor—Ethnomusicology
COPubProf5	Professor—Biology
COPubPostdoc	Postdoc/Alumni—Paleontology (in Mexican University)
COPubDr	Doctor/Alumni—Archaeology (in other Colombian University)
COPubMon	Student-monitor-Art Designer
COPubResFac1	Research Office Faculty of Integrated Arts
COPubIntOff	International Office
COPubVicResOff	Main Research Office
EuroAsianNet	EuroAsian network mostly from Russia connected to COPubProf1
COPubUNet	University network which includes students and other professors
CONatNet	National network related to cultural heritage
LatinNet1	A global network named *Americanists* which connects researchers across the world
LatinNet2	Mexican researchers
LatinNet3	Argentinean researchers
USNet1	US network connected to Prof3
EuroNet4	EU connected to Prof2
CANet	Canadian network connected to Prof2
USNet2	US network connected to Prof1 (Funding for publications)
COLocalNet3	Local network connected to Prof2
COLocalNet4	Local network connected to Prof3
EuroNet5	German network connected to Prof3
COPubResFac2	Research Office Faculty of Physics
COPubResFac3	Research Office Faculty of History
EuroNet6	Italian network connected to COPubPostdoc
LatinNet4	South American network connected to COPubPostdoc
COLocalNet5	Local network connected to Postdoc
COLocalNet6	Local network connected to Dr.
COLocalNet7	Local network connected to Monitor

graduate student (COPriPhD1) who has been directly involved since the establishment of the network.

SNA helps illustrate how the activities and roles that link the different network members reflect their direct and indirect participation in knowledge production. The "direct" members are the professors, students, and alumni who are involved in various IRC practices such as the discussion of ideas from

Table 5.2 Colombian Private Research Network (COPriResNet), node codes and descriptors

Code/node	Descriptor
COPriProf1	Network Coordinator—Professor Anthropology and Archaeology
COPriProf2	Professor—Anthropology and History
COPriProf3	Professor—Anthropology
COPriProf4	Professor—Anthropology
COPriPhD1	PhD student in Anthropology (same university)
COPriPhD2	Colombian PhD student in Spain who returned to do and internship in cultural heritage in this Colombian university
COPriMon	Student—Monitor—Music and Anthropology
COPriResFac	Research Office Faculty of Social Sciences
COPriVicResOff	Main Research Office
COPriIntOff	International office
COPriUNet	University network which includes students and other professors
CONatNet	National network related to cultural heritage
COLocalNet	Local network connected to COPubProf1 and COPriPhD1
LatinNet1	A global network named *Americanists* which connects researchers across the world
EuroNet1	French network connected to COPriProf2
EuroNet2	Italian network connected to COPriPhD1
COLocalNet1	Local network connected to COPriPhD2
EuroNet3	Spanish network connected to COPriPhD2

different perspectives to come up with collaborative research projects, co-editing and production of bulletins, co-supervision of doctoral work, and co-publications. Practices of these direct members represent strong connective ties within the IRC (Granovetter 1973). The "indirect" members tend to be the university staff and external actors, also researchers from international networks, who temporarily participate in or support the research network. Practices of these indirect members represent weak but often important ties (Granovetter 1973). The network tied to a public university (COPubResNet) is a relatively small group (Fig. 5.1). It involves eight (8) permanent direct members including professors, students, and alumni. The coordinator of this network, Professor 1 (COPubProf1), is a scholar with a vast research trajectory who earned his doctoral degree abroad. He has maintained strong connections with professors in the university where he obtained his PhD through its international research network (EuroAsianNet) and engages in frequent communications with them on research being conducted in both home and foreign universities. The network tied to a private university (COPriResNet) is also small (Fig. 5.2) and entails a lower connective density. It comprises seven (7) permanent direct members, all of them professors or students. Similar to the public case, the coordinator of this research network, Professor 1 (COPriProf1), also obtained his doctoral degree overseas.

Alongside the leadership provided by the head professors, staff nodes play an important role in supporting and facilitating IRC processes at the institutional level in both research networks. Additional connections involve professors and networks in other countries or regions as weak ties (indicated by the coding LatinNet, EuroNet, etc.), but which represent meaningful contributions to knowledge production through the provision of access to conferences and other international academic events, as well as student research internship opportunities. Granovetter (1973) emphasized the value of these "weak" ties, which, though less direct and more distant, are critical for bringing new and different information and perspectives to the research network dynamics.

The IRC activities identified in these two networks are similar with regard to the routine work carried out by the international researchers. This includes such tasks as exchange of information, bibliographic content and advice, supervisory support to students, and co-publication of papers and articles. Differences in the networks' IRC activities relate more to their particular projects, corresponding knowledge production, and the contextual realities, which dictate the specific topics of research determined by the Colombian researchers. Examples of the different types of IRC knowledge production associated with each of these networks help to illustrate this. COPriResNet (Fig. 5.2), for instance, produces a quarterly Web bulletin where different local and international scholars participate by sending in drafts of their work to be published. The theme of each issue revolves around research topics of mutual interest to national and international researchers and serves to foster fruitful discussions between scholars. Recently, the network published a symposium compendium that included material from different local and international authors and encouraged a series of important discussions related to cultural heritage. This type of IRC knowledge production demonstrates how results may extend beyond co-publication to include the processes in which these researchers are involved and the work being done on other research topics as well. COPubResNet (Fig. 5.1), on the other hand, manages an archaeological museum that serves and connects diverse local and international researchers through varied projects and co-publications related to pre-Hispanic Colombian studies. Due to the significance of the museum's archaeological pieces and innovative methods for studying local soil and artifacts, this network attracts and connects scholars from a number of countries that are interested in these and similar pursuits. There is also an interdisciplinary aspect in the COPubResNet, which includes a physicist, a musician, a historian, three archaeologists, and a graphic designer, contributing to a broader IRC view on the research topic (Shin et al. 2013). These distinct examples of IRC interaction and activity in the networks represent how SNA can be instrumental for capturing a broader range of collaborative knowledge exchange and production—both internationally and locally.

DISCUSSION

The closeness of permanent members in each of the networks is built on trust and largely from direct connections resulting from the formation of active research groups registered in COLCIENCIAS. Each research network is involved in multiple projects that link two or more members internationally. This also demonstrates the two research networks' success with horizontal channels of communication (Castells and Cardoso 2005) among their members, which allow for discussions of ongoing and potential future research, as well as exchange of knowledge, bibliographic sources, data, and other resources. This style of mutual communication is established from professor to professor, professor to student, and student to student as explained by different members of both research networks during their interviews. This direct two-way communication has succeeded in building trust among members and forming long-lasting relationships in both cases for nearly a decade.

Motivations

Professors' motivations for conducting IRC in the public and private university networks are similar. In both cases, IRC is seen as a way to exchange knowledge and discuss research issues that represent mutual interests and transcend national borders. For instance, the coordinator of the research network tied to the private university noted, "the bulletin produced facilitates discussions on cultural heritage among researchers internationally and creates potential for future collaboration" (COPriProf1-002).[4] Likewise, the coordinator of the research network tied to a public university stated, "our network relationships have allowed us to organize an international seminar of Eurasian museums at the university that serves as a basis for discussions of similar research problems related to archaeological artefacts and other topics" (COPubProf1-011). Moreover, the institutions involved are open to sharing in-kind resources with each other, which, in turn, can contribute to common research projects. For example, COPubProf1 emphasized that "when international researchers come to visit, we have discussion sessions that center around various of the archaeological pieces from the museum that serve as the foundation for other potential joint research projects" (COPubProf1-011). The private university counterpart likewise pointed out, "our quarterly bulletin provides an open invitation for discussions on current research topics for international scholars who want to participate" (COPriProf1-002). This bulletin appears on the research network's website, where it is also possible to identify the different participating international authors who are contributing to knowledge production. In this way, international, diaspora, and Colombian national scholarship is connected through this IRC space.

Professors and students in both research networks also assert that IRC offers an opportunity for students to discover new ideas and practices and become more open-minded and innovative. For instance, one professor in the public university network stated, "having the opportunity to share their research interest with other scholars internationally, students start to see and value the work that they do here at the university from other perspectives" (COPubProf3-013). Also, Colombian scholars are able to bring their own local perspectives to these IRC discussions for inclusion in the international discourse. A public university professor claimed, "we believe that our research has to focus on our own cultural heritage, has to have a social commitment, and has to recover our history and identity—then we have substantive knowledge to offer other researchers internationally" (COPubProf1-011). In all cases, the different IRC activities and interconnections provide a fruitful space for knowledge production that motivates Colombian scholars and universities to pursue joint projects, become more innovative, and develop broader perspectives. Directors of the research and international offices in both the public and private universities also refer to similar motivations for conducting IRC. They note that joining with foreign institutions contributes to Colombian universities' visibility and prestige. The international office interviewee said that "not only is IRC a means to financial resources, it also constitutes positive recognition of the Colombian institute, which is sometimes even more necessary" (COPubIntOff-019). Likewise one of the private university main research office participants added that "IRC allows universities to embrace projects that respond to Colombian realities" (COPriVicResOff-007). There is a strong belief that Colombian universities and research deserve and require more international visibility and recognition, and IRC seems to offer a way to advance in this direction.

Challenges

Both Colombian research networks explored here also face significant challenges as they cope with limited financial resources for IRC. Although the Colombian public university is a research-intensive institution, one participating professor referred to the fact that "funding opportunities at the institutional level are generally restricted to local projects and do not provide resources for professors or students to travel to meetings abroad" (COPubProf2-010). Since Colombian scholars have very limited support for conferences, this participant asserted, "we often pay for the majority of our travel expenses" (COPubProf2-010). In addition, according to the interviewee from the international office in the public university "governmental support for IRC in social sciences and humanities is much less than it is for natural and health sciences, engineering, and technology" (COPubIntOff-019). This is further complicated by the fact that Colombian governmental regulations and procedures for IRC funding lack clarity and only provide limited applications; professors in both universities found these limitations challenging (COPriProf2-010; COPubProf1-011). Staff and professors in both research networks further note that funding from foreign institutions is becoming scarcer and that few institutions favor long-term IRC projects. Generally, "funding from foreign institutions lasts a maximum of one to two years" stated participant from the Research Office in the Faculty of Social Sciences at the private university (COPriResFac-001), which means that research projects requiring long-term development and implementation are seldom funded. Adding to this, a professor in the private university stated, "the time allocated for research is concentrated between academic semesters as opposed to during the school year, which complicates engaging in IRC with foreign counterparts" (COPriProf2-010). Professors and students in both research networks found limitations to expand their IRC with their peers since both COPriResNet and COPubResNet lack funding to run their projects. As stated by the coordinator of the research network tied to the private university, "we do not receive funding from the Faculty. We do receive in-kind support and dedicate our own time to make it work...this is the magic of our effort" (COPriProf1-002). Likewise, the coordinator of the research network tied to the public university affirmed, "What we do in IRC is not funded by the university. We have the museum, our lab and brochures and some logistic support for events. We have to apply for grants to the Ministry of Culture and other agencies" (COPubProf1-011).

In addition to local factors that affect the research networks' dynamics, international policy flows, and higher education rankings—usually defined in northern countries—are also often imposed by Colombian governmental institutions as external indicators to qualify local researchers' work and publications. The interviewee from the main research office at the public university mentioned, "COLCIENCIAS indicators push researchers to publish in Q1 and Q2 journals[5] that are registered in ISI and SCOPUS databases" (COPubVicResOff-018). Syncing with international indicators becomes particularly challenging for researchers in the social sciences and humanities as their "research often responds to local realities that are difficult to relate to foreign contexts or priorities" stated professor 1 at the public university (COPubProf1-011). As a result, both national and international IRC policies can present challenges for professors and students in both research networks. A former public university student who is now part of the COPubResNet and pursuing post-doctoral work in Mexico (COPubPostdoc) stated, "my colleagues and I always have trouble publishing in US journals...they reject Latin American work...we have found that European journals are more neutral and willing to review research from Latin American researchers" (COPubPostdoc-017). This type of international policy, which pushes researchers to publish in specific international journals, also ends up getting adopted in Colombian national policy on knowledge production and becomes even more problematic for scholars. Although staff members in the public research network recognize the Colombian government's advances and support, they also emphasize there is much yet to be done. For instance, the director of the international office in the public university argued, "the government must depoliticize research matters with regard to the way in which decisions are made and let universities set their own IRC budgets and procedures" (COPubIntOff-019). IRC knowledge production processes and decisions are still enmeshed in international policy and financial flows and this requires research network members to be acutely aware of these limitations. Both national and external factors and actors influence the processes of IRC knowledge production, often creating unintended barriers for all researchers.

Research Networks and Knowledge Production

Notwithstanding the significant challenges these professors, students, and staff members face, participants believe that being engaged in these research networks increasingly contributes to knowledge production in Colombia. Scholars in both of the networks examined report research practices that are more intensive and connected to an updated, international perspective. One professor in the private university network stated, "the regular bulletin produced by this group and uploaded to the university website is becoming more international through its connections with other research networks worldwide and has become a higher quality publication over time" (COPriProf1-002). One professor in the public university noticed, "this research network provides the opportunity to meet with international peers and engage in interesting discussions to share academic solutions, or knowledge, or bibliography" (COPubProf2-012). University staff, too, consider these initiatives important and provide critical support to facilitate IRC—often maintaining official international relationships with different universities and processing corresponding IRC paperwork and agreements. According to the interview data, the international office directors in both the private and the public universities play similar roles regarding this support to faculty members and students and to their knowledge production (COPubIntOff-019 and COPriIntOff-007). The public university interviewee in the international office stated "we know that filling out research grant applications to foreign agencies requires a lot of time and understanding of different codes and formats. Our office provides this support" (COPubIntOff-019). Similarly, the interviewee of the research office in the private university declared "what is usually a barrier to applying to research foreign convocations is the amount of documents, signatures and administrative requirements that professors have to collect. We help them with this paperwork" (COPriResFac-001). Professors and students in both networks organize a number of local events that include professors from foreign universities and that require significant administrative support. Fliers, brochures, follow-up reports, and online links of these events are all part of the process. To this end, both the international office in the public and the private universities provide support with some basic funding and any advice professors and students may need. These events generally involve two-to-three-week seminars and other meetings to discuss research interests and mutual projects. The experience of being connected with these research networks allows students to access broader learning and generate more sophisticated knowledge products. They establish contact with foreign professors, share their learning experiences and research projects, access broader bibliography, and explore new research venues—all of which contribute to improved results. A student monitor in the public university pointed out

> When visiting Mexican archaeologists came few months ago, they worked with our professor (COPubPorfl) analyzing and comparing archaeological pieces in our museum. This allowed for us, as students, to see how studies are being done here and also hear foreign researchers talk about similar studies that are being done in their own countries. (COPubMon-014)

This kind of opportunity also helps to establish further relationships with other institutions in meaningful ways. One professor in the public university (COPubProf3) highlighted the importance of "being connected with other museums in different countries that also have pre-Colombian archaeological collections which are studied in multiple projects by international scholars" (COPubProf3-013). This works in reverse as well. Colombian professors often mobilize new knowledge and share mutual research interests and projects with foreign scholars. One of the public network professors mentioned "an extended relationship with scholars in Mexico that includes a series of bilateral visits between the two countries and extensive information sharing and discussion on academic topics of common interest" (COPubProfl-011). ICT advances serve to support these interconnections with foreign professors and students abroad. The diaspora network in both COPubResNet and COPriResNet also plays a crucial role in IRC. This driver is observable in the configurations of the two research networks presented above. In COPubResNet, a post-doctoral student in Mexico who obtained his degree in the Colombian public university is still a member of the research network. A Colombian PhD who obtained his degree in Argentina and works in another public university is also a member of the research network since the lead professor in the public university co-supervised his doctoral research. In COPriResNet, a Colombian doctoral student in Spain returned for an internship in the private university in Colombia and has been a member of the research network all along, even prior to starting his doctoral program in Spain. Several researchers who participate in the network's bulletin are doctoral students studying abroad who maintain close ties with this research network in spite of the distance. These Colombian researchers abroad preserve their relationships with former colleagues and contribute to knowledge production in Colombia as well as elsewhere. These IRC network examples illustrate many ways of collaborating internationally through activities and research practices that contribute in different ways to the individual network members and to the public and private universities of which they form a part.

Conclusion

IRC in the two Colombian research networks studied here is a challenging initiative entwined in a web of knowledge and policy flows. There are different national and international actors involved in mediation and decision-making, as well as economic and political matters that affect the work being done. Although Colombian scholars in these two research networks cope with considerable financial limitations and often cumbersome international policies, they continue to pursue intensive research agendas nurtured by knowledge flows from both national and international perspectives. There are significant factors that motivate these researchers to continue working on IRC. The positive international attention for developing projects focused on realities in Colombia is one such incentive. The Colombian historical, anthropological, and political scenario lends itself to a range of interesting and groundbreaking research possibilities for national, regional, and international scholars. Permanent interconnections through diaspora networks are other key resources for IRC. These linkages serve to establish and maintain two-way communications with scholars abroad, which subsequently allow for the blending of local and global perspectives in research projects. They facilitate cross-border sharing of knowledge, experiences, bibliographies, and other resources, and they promote co-publications. Much of the research and exchange established through IRC begins with informal communications between researchers in conferences abroad, between professors and students in other countries, or between colleagues at national academic events. ICT helps considerably in preserving these connections and in linking databases from different institutions; technology is now an essential means toward the end of building long-lasting IRC ties. Through continued connections and shared experiences, respect and trust grow among network members and their relationships are strengthened. This, in turn, allows for further connections with other global scholars and networks.

On the downside of IRC, the introduction of international policies for the assessment of national researchers' work and publications can create tensions. The utilization of international rankings and indicators for the qualification of research and publication in Colombia deserves further analysis. While these measures add quantitative dimension and may promote higher quality results, they may also lack certain qualitative substance. Furthermore, Colombian universities require greater allocation of resources, less restrictive procedures, and clearer operational mechanisms for facilitating IRC if they are to be engaged in long-lasting international projects on equal footing with global counterparts. Issues such as these must be addressed for IRC in Colombia to continue to advance in a healthy and productive manner for all parties.

SNA has served as a valuable research method for mapping the connections in IRC practices of two research networks in Colombia. Using a nonlinear approach allowed for a deeper exploration and description of the various interconnections of IRC, not only those of the researchers themselves but also those of other actors and networks involved. This tool also helped to illustrate how the links among research network members respond to their individual motivations and the challenges they have to overcome. By looking at IRC's nuanced processes, SNA shed light on a number of factors, overt and subtle, that combine to affect knowledge exchange and production in the IRC setting. As a final remark, the information presented in this chapter does not attempt to capture all types of interrelations, characteristics, and histories within these two Colombian research networks. Rather, it contributes an added dimension for studying some of the motivations and challenges that mobilize these Colombian academics' IRC involvement as well as the varied effects of such interconnections. The ultimate goal of analyzing these research networks is to provide a more complex depiction of the local and global knowledge and policy flows at work in IRC and provide insights for further analysis of knowledge production in comparative and international higher education.

NOTES

1. The term post-foundational includes post-modern, post-structural, and post-colonial thinking in comparative and international education (Ninnes and Mehta 2004). It breaks down the assumption of universal knowledge from the modern era, the Enlightenment, associated to positivist thought. It entails a pluralistic view to understanding social phenomenon, knowledge, and ways of knowing.

2. Spatial thinking draws upon concepts and theories associated with the "spatial turn" (Robertson 2010; Warf and Arias 2009). It shifts the notion of space not only as an object but also as a social phenomenon constructed by interrelations (Harvey 2006; Lefebvre 1991; Massey 2005; Soja 1996). Space is an open, complex system made by different flows and networks (Appadurai 1990; Castells and Cardoso 2005).
3. Research networks and their members (nodes) are marked with distinct codes: CO—Colombia; Pub—Public University; Pri—Private university; Res—Research; Net—Network; Int—International; Off—Office; Vic—Vice; Fac—Faculty; Postdoc—Post-doctoral scholar; Prof—Professor. Number indicates the sequence number, for example, Prof1, Prof2.
4. Direct quotes from interviews reflect the node's code. Numbers indicate a recording number, for example, COPubProf1-002.
5. The Journal Citation Reports by Thomson Reuters provides rankings of science and social science journals every year according to the Impact Factor (IF) data registered in ISI and Scopus. Rankings are categorized by Quartile Scores: Q1 represents the top 25% of the IF distribution, Q2 for middle-high position (between top 50% and top 25%), Q3 middle-low position (top 75% to top 50%), and Q4 the lowest position (bottom 25% of the IF distribution) (retrieved from Research Assessment, http://researchassessment.fbk.eu/quartile_score).

REFERENCES

Altbach, P. G. (2007). Peripheries and Centers: Research Universities in Developing Countries. *Higher Education Management and Policy, 19*(2), 111–134. https://doi.org/10.1787/hemp-v19art13-en.

Altbach, P. G. (2013). Advancing the National and Global Knowledge Economy: The Role of Research Universities in Developing Countries. *Studies in Higher Education, 38*(3), 316–330. https://doi.org/10.1080/03075079.2013.773605.

Appadurai, A. (1990). Disjuncture and Difference in the Global Cultural Economy. *Public Culture, 2*(2), 1–23.

Beaver, D. D. (2001). Reflections on Scientific Collaboration (and its Study): Past, Present, and Future. *Scientometrics, 52*(3), 365–377. http://journals1.scholarsportal.info.proxy1.lib.uwo.ca/pdf/01389130/v52i0003/365_roscisppaf.xml.

Borgatti, S. P., & Halgin, D. S. (2011). On Network Theory. *Organization Science, 22*(5), 1168–1181. https://doi.org/10.1287/orsc.1110.0641.

Bukvova, H. (2010). Studying Research Collaboration: A Literature Review. *Sprouts: Working Papers in Information Systems 10*(3), 1–17. https://www.researchgate.net/profile/Helena_Bukvova/publication/200629645_

INTERNATIONAL RESEARCH COLLABORATION AND KNOWLEDGE... 111

Studying_Research_Collaboration_A_Literature_Review/ links/0fcfd50d30e026bcc8000000.pdf

Castells, M. (1996). *The Rise of the Network Society. The Information Age: Economy, Society and Culture* (Vol. 1). Malden: Blackwell Publishers Ltd.

Castells, M., & Cardoso, G. (Eds.). (2005). *The Network Society: From Knowledge to Policy.* Washington, DC: Johns Hopkins Center for Transatlantic Relations.

Colombian Institute for the Development of Science and Technology – COLCIENCIAS. (2018). *About Colciencias.* Retrieved from: http://www.colciencias.gov.co

de Wit, H. (2010, December). Internationalisation of Higher Education in Europe and Its Assessments, Trends and Issues. *NVAO Nederlands-Vlaamse Accreditatieorganisatie.* http://www.cinda.cl/wp-content/uploads/2014/09/De-Wit-Internationalisation-of-Higher-Education-in-Europe.pdf

de Wit, H., Jaramillo, I. C., Gacel-Ávila, J., & Knight, J. Eds. (2005). Higher Education in Latin America: The International Dimension. *The World Bank.* http://siteresources.worldbank.org/EXTLACREGTOPEDUCATION/Resources/Higher_Ed_in_LAC_Intnal_Dimension.pdf

Edwards, G. (2010). *Mixed-Method Approaches to Social Network Analysis.* National Centre for Research Methods Review Paper. Economic and Social Research Council (ESRC). http://eprints.ncrm.ac.uk/842/1/Social_Network_analysis_Edwards.pdf

Frame, J. D., & Carpenter, M. P. (1979). International Research Collaboration. *Social Studies of Science, 9*(4), 481–497. https://doi.org/10.1177/030631277900900405.

Fuhse, J., & Mützel, S. (2011). Tackling Connections, Structure, and Meaning in Networks: Quantitative and Qualitative Methods in Sociological Network Research. *Quality & Quantity, 45,* 1067–1089. https://doi.org/10.1007/s11135-011-9492-3.

Granovetter, M. S. (1973). The Strength of Weak Ties. *American Journal of Sociology, 78*(6), 1360–1380. http://www.jstor.org/stable/2776392.

Harvey, D. (2006). Space as a Keyword. In N. Castree & Derek (Eds.), *David Harvey a Critical Reader* (pp. 270–293). Oxford: Blackwell Publishing Ltd.

Katz, J. S., & Martin, B. R. (1997). What is Research Collaboration? *Research Policy, 26*(1), 1–18. http://journals1.scholarsportal.info.proxy1.lib.uwo.ca/pdf/00487333/v26i0001/1_wirc.xml

Knight, J. (2004). Internationalization Remodeled: Definition, Approaches, and Rationales. *Journal of Studies in International Education, 8*(1), 5–31. https://doi.org/10.1177/1028315303260832.

Knobel, M., Simões, T. P., & Cruz, C. H. d. B. (2013). International Collaborations Between Research Universities: Experiences and Best Practices. *Studies in Higher Education, 38*(3), 405–424. https://doi.org/10.1080/03075079.2013.773793.

Landry, R., Traore, N., & Godin, B. (1996). An Econometric Analysis of the Effect of Collaboration on Academic Research Productivity. *Higher Education, 32*(3), 283–301. https://doi.org/10.1007/BF00138868.

Lefebvre, H. (1991). *The Production of Space.* Oxford: Blackwell Publishing Ltd.

Massey, D. (2005). *For Space.* London: SAGE.

Melin, G. (2000). Pragmatism and Self-Organization. Research Collaboration on the Individual Level. *Research Policy, 29,* 31–40. http://journals1.scholarsportal.info.proxy1.lib.uwo.ca/pdf/00487333/v29i0001/31_pas.xml

Meyer, J.-B. (2001). Networks Approach Versus Brain Drain: Lessons from the Diaspora. *International Migration, 39*(5), 91–110. https://doi.org/10.1111/1468-2435.00173.

Meyer, J.-B., & Wattiaux, J. P. (2006). Diaspora Knowledge Networks: Vanishing Doubts and Increasing Evidence. *International Journal of Multicultural Societies, 8*(1): 4–24. http://unesdoc.unesco.org/images/0014/001490/149086e.pdf#149125

Meyer, J.-B., Charum, J., Granés, J., & Chatelin, Y. M. (1995). Is It Opened or Closed? Colombian Science on the Move. *Scientometrics, 34*(1), 73–86. https://doi.org/10.1007/BF02019174.

Meyer, J.-B., Charum, J., Bernal, D., Gaillard, J., Granés, J., Leon, J., Montenegro, A., Morales, A., Murcia, C., Narvaez-Berthelemot, N., Parrado, L. S., & Schlemmer, B. (1997). Turning Brain Drain into Brain Gain: The Colombian Experience of the Diaspora Option. *Science, Technology & Society, 2*(2), 286–315. https://doi.org/10.1177/097172189700200205.

Morrison, P. S., Dobbie, G., & McDonald, F. J. (2003). Research Collaboration Among University Scientists. *Higher Education Research & Development, 22*(3), 275–296. https://doi.org/10.1080/0729436032000145149.

Narvaez-Berthelemot, N., Frigoletto, L., & Miquel, J.-F. (1992). International Scientific Collaboration in Latin America. *Scientometrics, 24*(3), 373–392. https://doi.org/10.1007/BF02051036.

Ninnes, P., & Mehta, S. (2004). *Re-imagining Comparative Education: Postfoundational Ideas and Applications for Critical Times.* New York: RoutledgeFalmer.

Ordóñez-Matamoros, G. (2008). *International Research Collaboration, Research Team Performance, and Scientific and Technological Capabilities in Colombia: A Bottom-Up Perspective.* PhD diss., Georgia State University. http://digitalarchive.gsu.edu/pmap_diss/18/

Ordóñez-Matamoros, G., Cozzens, S. E., & Garcia-Luque, M. (2010). International Co-authorship and Research Team Performance in Colombia. *Review of Policy Research, 27*(4), 415–431. https://doi.org/10.1111/j.1541-1338.2010.00449.x.

Pinheiro, C. A. R. (2011). *Social Network Analysis in Telecommunications.* Hoboken: John Wiley & Sons Inc.

Robertson, S. (2010). Spatializing the Sociology of Education: Stand-Points, Entry-Points, Vantage-Points. In M. W. Apple, S. J. Ball, & L. A. Gandin (Eds.), *The Routledge International Handbook of Sociology of Education* (pp. 15–27). London: Routledge.

Scott, J. (2012). *What Is Social Network Analysis?* London: Bloomsbury.

Scott, J., & Carrington, P. J. (Eds.). (2011). *The SAGE Handbook of Social Network Analysis.* London: Sage Publications Ltd.

Shin, J. C., Lee, S. J., & Kim, Y. (2013). Research Collaboration Across Higher Education Systems: Maturity, Language Use, and Regional Differences. *Studies in Higher Education, 38*(3), 425–440. https://doi.org/10.1080/03075079. 2013.774585.

Smith, D. (2001). Collaborative Research: Policy and the Management of Knowledge Creation in UK Universities. *Higher Education Quarterly, 55*(2), 131–157. https://doi.org/10.1111/1468-2273.00179.

Smith, D., & Katz, J. S. 2000. University of Leeds, Higher Education Policy Unit, University of Sussex, Science Policy Research Unit. *Collaborative Approaches to Research: Final Report.* Leeds: University of Leeds, Higher Education Policy Unit. http://users.sussex.ac.uk/~sylvank/pubs/collc.pdf

Soja, E. W. (1996). *Postmodern Geographies: The Reassertion of Space in Critical Social Theory.* London: Verso.

Sonnenwald, D. H. (2007). Scientific Collaboration. *Annual Review of Information Science and Technology, 41*(1), 643–681. https://doi.org/10.1002/aris.2007. 1440410121.

Stier, J. (2004). Taking a Critical Stance Towards Internationalization Ideologies in Higher Education: Idealism, Instrumentalism, and Educationalism. *Globalization, Societies and Education, 21*(1), 1–28. https://doi.org/10.1080/ 1476772042000177069.

Tascón, C. I. (2017). *Knowledge Production in International Research Collaboration: A Comparative Study of Canadian and Colombian Research Networks.* PhD diss., Western University, Electronic Thesis and Dissertation Repository. 4711. https://ir.lib.uwo.ca/etd/4711

Tejada, G. (2012). Mobility, Knowledge and Cooperation: Scientific Diaspora as Agents of Development. *Migration and Development, 10*(18), 59–92.

United Nations Educational, Scientific and Cultural Organization — UNESCO Institute for Statistics (UIS). (2005, September). What do Bibliometric Indicators Tell Us about World Scientific Output? *UIS Bulletin on Science and Technology Statistics,* Issue No. 2. http://unescoscience.blogspot.ca/2005_12_01_archive. html

Wagner, C. S., & Leydesdorff, L. (2005). Network Structure, Self-Organization, and the Growth of International Collaboration in Science. *Research Policy, 34,* 1608–1618. https://doi.org/10.1016/j.respol.2005.08.002.

Wagner, C. S., Brahmakulam, I., Jackson, B., Wong, A., & Yoda, T. (2001, March). *Science and Technology Collaboration: Building Capacity in Developing Countries.* Report Prepared for the World Bank: Science and Technology Policy Institute. http://www.rand.org/content/dam/rand/pubs/monograph_reports/2005/MR1357.0.pdf

Warf, B., & Arias, S. (2009). *The Spatial Turn.* London: Routledge.

Wasser, J. D., & Bresler, L. (1996). Working in the Interpretive Zone: Conceptualizing Collaborations in Qualitative Research Teams. *Educational Researcher, 25*(5), 5–15. https://doi.org/10.3102/0013189X025005005.

White, H. D. (2011). Scientific and Scholarly Networks. In J. Scott & P. J. Carrington (Eds.), *The SAGE Handbook of Social Network Analysis* (pp. 271–285). Los Angeles: SAGE.

World Bank. (2016). Research and Development Expenditure (% of GDP). *Data.* http://data.worldbank.org/indicator/GB.XPD.RSDV.GD.ZS

Zelnio, R. (2013). *A Complexity Approach to Evaluating National Scientific Systems Through International Scientific Collaborations.* PhD diss., George Mason University, Archival Repository Service. http://hdl.handle.net/1920/8272

Zingerli, C. (2010). A Sociology of International Research Partnerships for Sustainable Development. *European Journal of Development Research, 22*(2), 217–233. https://doi.org/10.1057/ejdr.2010.1.

CHAPTER 6

The Political Economy of Legal Knowledge in Action: Collaborative Projects in the Americas

Daniel Bonilla Maldonado and Colin Crawford

Introduction

Legal knowledge is a commodity; therefore, it may be understood as a product that is generated, exchanged, and used in specific contexts, following certain rules. Like any commodity, it is produced neither in a vacuum nor in a chaotic fashion. This set of rules and principles that shape the production of legal knowledge constitutes its political economy (Rubio

---

An early version of this research was presented at the Law School of the National Autonomous University of Mexico at the conference "Aproximaciones Postcoloniales del Derecho Internacional en América Latina" in June 2015. Professor Crawford's participation was generously supported by a grant from the Tulane University Stone Center for Latin American Studies.

D. B. Maldonado (✉)
Faculty of Law, Universidad de los Andes, Bogota, Colombia

C. Crawford
Louis D. Brandeis School of Law, University of Louisville, Louisville, KY, USA

© The Author(s) 2018
G. Gregorutti, N. Svenson (eds.), *North-South University Research Partnerships in Latin America and the Caribbean,*
https://doi.org/10.1007/978-3-319-75364-5_6

and Baert 2012) and comprises the conditions of possibility for its generation, circulation, and application. Thus, the political economy of legal knowledge determines which objects are worthy of study, which contexts are most valuable, and which procedures are acceptable for original legal knowledge production. The political economy of legal knowledge also dictates the direction its exchange should take—whether North-South or West-East, to cite two possibilities—and affirms who shall possess the capacity to create original legal knowledge.

This economy of legal knowledge is constituted by two models that coexist in cognitive dissonance in the modern political and legal imagination (Bonilla 2015), namely the free market model of legal ideas and the colonial model of legal knowledge production (Bonilla 2015). The first model represents the normative component of the political economy of legal knowledge; it offers the ideas that should, theoretically, guide the creation, exchange, and use of legal knowledge. This model evaluates legal knowledge according to norms like its utility for the stability or prosperity of a political community, its explanatory or analytical value, or the extent to which its production occurred through a meritocratic process. The second model, in contrast, provides the set of rules and principles that determine how we typically respond to the specific commodity that is legal knowledge. The colonial model is configured by a set of oppositions, including mimesis/autopoiesis,[1] universal/local knowledge, and appropriate/inappropriate languages for legal knowledge expression. These oppositions, in turn, determine the value given to legal products created and circulated within and among political communities (Bonilla 2015).

The political economy of legal knowledge is powerful not merely because of its rules and principles but also by the virtue of the type of legal subject it constructs (Bonilla 2015). The two models imagine specific types of subjects of legal knowledge, which contribute to the creation and shaping of the identities of persons and communities. Once these ways of imagining the legal subject are internalized, individuals and collectivities use them to describe themselves and, implicitly or explicitly, they are converted into the conceptual lenses through which we describe, examine, and act toward legal knowledge. The force of the political economy of legal knowledge is discernible, too, in the constructions of time and space in which legal subjects move (Bonilla 2015). Each of the models offers its own notion of history and conceptual geography.

These models do more than describe and analyze the macro-dynamics of the production, exchange, and application of legal ideas and practices.

They also help explain the micro-dynamics that constitute daily life in this social sphere. An examination of the political economy of legal knowledge thus contributes to the understanding of routine practices that determine how we create, exchange, and use it.

This chapter pursues this last objective. It creates a dialogue between the macro and micro, connecting the conceptual apparatus of the political economy of legal knowledge with collaborative practices for the creation of legal thought that advance particular legal subjects over others. The chapter therefore is an exercise in the cultural analysis of law (Kahn 1999) and its end is both descriptive and analytical. It makes use of the conceptual tools offered by the models to understand collaborative practices in the creation of legal thought as they play out in the legal academies of the global North and South (Mickelson 2009), and demonstrates how collaborative practices are characterized by a relation typically involving a dominant North and a subordinate South. The chapter also offers a set of general normative criteria to guide subjects committed to truly collaborative processes for legal thought construction, so has an additional normative objective of contributing to the creation of a new model for the political economy of legal knowledge distinct from both the free market and colonial models. The normative criteria offered are but first steps in this process, providing only general elements for the new model, but directly concerned with furthering epistemic justice[2] (Fricker 2007).

The chapter, more specifically, examines collaborative projects realized by its authors for over a decade to explore the reach and limitations of the dominant models of the political economy of legal knowledge. It documents, through several case studies, how the authors sought to create critical, reciprocally beneficial, and dynamic academic programming for US and Latin American scholars and students. A central aim of this programming was to promote joint academic research. The activities in the cases are varied, including individual academic exchanges and visits, trainings for legal and other professionals, student learning opportunities in clinical and simulated court competitions, applied learning seminars, and research projects and publications. This chapter surveys the success and challenges of these activities, which we refer to as "South-North Partnerships" (SNPs) (Bonilla 2013b) and focuses on four examples in which the authors worked directly to explore the arguments outlined above on the political economy of legal knowledge.

The chapter proceeds in three parts. The first, analytically considers the political economy of legal knowledge, describing the free market and colonial models for the production of legal knowledge and offering some alternative normative principles using examples from our SNPs. The second part builds upon this and is both descriptive and reflective, presenting four SNP examples that illustrate the challenges posed for the creation of truly collaborative legal knowledge production processes. It identifies common challenges in these endeavors, from surmounting organizational issues like language and conflicting academic calendars, and shows how the dynamics of the political economy of legal knowledge played out in the SNPs described. It also highlights ways to equalize these relationships and create SNPs geared toward truly collaborative legal knowledge production. The third part offers conclusions and recommendations.

THE POLITICAL ECONOMY OF LEGAL KNOWLEDGE

The political economy of legal knowledge is constituted by discourses and practices that determine how legal knowledge is produced, exchanged, and used (Clark 1998). These rules, principles, and activities determine the conceptual architecture that articulates normative horizons for producing, exchanging, and applying legal knowledge (Kahn 1999), which enables and circumscribes thought and action. It defines the range of actions considered possible and valuable, providing conceptual tools and practices within the colonial and free market models introduced above.

The Colonial Model

The colonial model creates two interdependent subjects: the metropolis[3] and colonial (Bonilla 2015). Their identities depend upon each other and are determined by the place they inhabit and race with which the model imagines them. The metropolis subject is identified with the Global North, imagined as white; the colonial subject is identified with the Global South, imagined as non-white. The metropolis is understood as an individual with the ability to create original legal knowledge, a true subject of legal knowledge and rights. By contrast, the colonial is a legal barbarian, a mere object of rights with the ability to reproduce and disseminate legal knowledge created elsewhere. The metropolis has a legal history and narrative that gives meaning to his work and identity. His is a story that merits study. The colonial has no history worth telling or studying (Morris and Spivak 2010).

The conceptual space inhabited by these subjects is also binary: the South and North, respectively (Bonilla 2015, 43–44). These global categories refer to the unequal distribution of power in the creation, exchange, and use of legal knowledge, not to a static material geography. At the same time, these categories overlap with the unequal distribution of political, economic, cultural, and military power among members of the international community. The colonial model imagines the North as a rich context for the production of legal knowledge and the South as a poor one.

The conceptual space the colonial model imagines is also unidirectional. Exchanges of legal knowledge follow a single route: North to South. The diverse political communities of the world have similar needs. However, the legal products that might satisfy them, according to the colonial model, can only be created in the North, the sole source of legal products worth exporting.

The concept of time in the colonial model is linear but finite (Bonilla 2015), with the metropolis located at the end of history. It has overcome all stages that lead to a strong, stable legal system and transformed itself into a robust context for original legal knowledge creation. Time for the colony, conversely, is inextricably linked to metropolis time—its future ideal. The past of the colony is something to be overcome; its present is a constant effort to conquer another stage on the way to the end of history.

The concepts of subject, space, and time that articulate the colonial model presuppose four oppositions: mimesis/autopoiesis; local /universal knowledge; culture/law; and suitable/unfit language for legal knowledge (Bonilla 2015, 44–49). The first conceptual opposition reaffirms the North as the locale for legal knowledge production suitable for global export, while the South is the space for reproduction, dissemination, and local application of the legal knowledge created by the North. The second conceptual opposition particularizes the legal knowledge produced in the South that cannot be severed from the context in which it was created and is thus unsuitable for export. In contrast, legal knowledge of the North is held to possess universal character, able to travel freely across borders, and applicable anywhere. The third conceptual opposition assumes that law can and should have an organic relationship with culture, with each culture creating its own law that reflects its ethos. The colonial model, therefore, claims the North constitutes a robust context for legal knowledge production because it contains the cultural prerequisites necessary to reach an elevated stage of legal development, whereas the cultures of the South do not have the necessary characteristics to generate original legal knowledge and practice as they are still "primitive," pre-modern cultures.

The fourth conceptual opposition assumes the dominant languages of the North, notably English, are particularly efficient vehicles for articulating high-quality, original legal knowledge. English, the dominant legal language, is the default language for legal academic dialogues. Seminars and higher-quality international publications are (and it is believed should be) done in English, which is understood to be precise, clear, and direct—capable of articulating and containing legal ideas. This implies that languages of the South, such as Spanish, are defective vessels for transporting legal ideas: dark, pompous, imprecise, and ambiguous. Consequently, the legal scholar who speaks no English is relegated to the margins of legal discussions, condemned to remain in a provincial corner.

The language variable merits special consideration because it is often accompanied by judgments about the quality of legal knowledge production in different regions—in our case, the US and Latin American legal academies. In this way, the language variable—and the skepticism generated if one is not fluent in English—interacts with the third, cultural element mentioned to the detriment of the Latin American legal academic. This variable cuts across our SNPs.

For example, in the US legal academy, being a Colombian law professor with English as a second language is very different from being a US professor with Spanish as a second language in Latin America. The US professor's status easily opens doors for organizing fieldwork or events with senior Latin American government officials, while the Latin professor—with comparable qualifications and status—finds it harder to achieve similar objectives in the USA. This emphasizes how in Latin America, simply being a US-based law professor, little matter the university of origin or quality of academic production, carries notable academic and social capital automatically according the US professor status as a serious actor. This is not necessarily so for a Colombian law professor in the USA. Rather, the isolationism and exceptionalism characterizing much of US academic life require the Latin academic to constantly overcome negative assumptions about quality and ability.

Language and membership in particular academic communities also create challenges for publication in some of the SNPs described earlier. A book or journal issue including contributions from Latin American academics is often viewed negatively by Northern publishers. If accepted, editors frequently insist on translations of sources prior to publication to assure correctness of citation and argument. Conversely, Latin American publishers usually accept full responsibility for working with English and other foreign-language sources as a necessary cost of publication. This detail illustrates the imbalance—and cost in financial and human terms—at the core of the political economy of legal knowledge production. More generally, publishers in the Americas usually have different reactions to work of US and Latin scholars. US publishers typically give manuscripts by Latin American law professors a cold or, at best, lukewarm reception, while Latin American editorial houses react warmly to books or articles by US legal academics. These views might change after the pieces are read, but publishers' a priori attitudes create unjustified obstacles for Latin legal scholars and unmerited flexibility for US scholars.

Finally, we have consistently encountered three attitudes that epitomize the concept of subject undergirding the colonial model. The first is the condescending attitude of some US law professors regarding Latin American legal production and scholars, in which Latin researchers are categorized as academic players who will disseminate—rather than generate—legal knowledge. The second attitude observed is a tendency of some Latin scholars to internalize and naturalize the colonial rules and principles, accepting their "less-than-ness" as a price to be paid for participating in international networks and academic publications. The third attitude actually works to the benefit of the colonial legal subject, who may be prized for his or her "exotic-ness." The colonial model does not always disfavor the South; sometimes belonging to the Latin American legal academy opens spaces typically unavailable to US law professors. For example, an outsider to Global North academia belonging to an elite Global South university can open channels with elite Northern academic institutions or individuals that would be difficult for faculty at less elite US institutions, demonstrating that a Latin scholar may simultaneously constitute the "other" and also a member of the international academic elite.

The Free Market Model

By contrast, the free market of legal ideas model posits an autonomous rational subject able to generate and exchange legal knowledge (Bonilla 2015). Since all individuals are potential creators of legal knowledge, the model commits to equality, in principle, with the only legitimate differences between subjects being those linked with talent, discipline, and hard work. The model is bound to principles intertwined with modern, enlightened values: truth, utility, and meritocracy. The most valuable legal products and subjects are those that capture the truth as completely and accurately as possible, regardless of the interpretation used to define this elusive concept. The strongest subjects of knowledge and more robust legal products are those that allow the political community to fulfill objectives of stability, justice, and prosperity. Legal products successful in the marketplace of ideas are presumed to result from the systematic, creative, and continuous work of individuals (Bonilla 2015).

The concept of space created by this model is a globalized and multidirectional one (Bonilla 2015). Its abstract subject of knowledge can create quality products anywhere with the material conditions characterizing the space responsible for enhancing or limiting this capability. The material conditions are also a function of individual and collective decisions, a result of individual autonomy. Similarly, the exchange of legal knowledge on abstract subjects can take any direction. The free market model does not predetermine the geographical orientation of trade; there is not, a priori, a single political community that monopolizes quality legal knowledge production. Instead, the direction the exchange of legal knowledge takes is determined by the needs of political communities and the quality of legal products each offers.

The concept of time that constitutes the free market model is linear but infinite (Bonilla 2015). Legal knowledge results from interactions between reason and will (Kahn 1999). Thus, its subject is immersed in an infinite process of knowledge generation. Reason should guide individuals toward legal products that are as close to truth as possible or as useful for realizing polity aims as possible. However, reason is not the sole criteria for determining value. The best legal product reason produces cannot be considered valid without the consent of the sovereign, those with the power to create law. And this may change over time with shifting political and social circumstances that require new legal products. Reason and will engage in a constant and infinite dialogue within the free market model.

This model conditions how we articulate and explain our joint SNPs. Our conversations and reflections describe the seminars, courses, and publications in terms of our work to achieve what we believe to be valuable political and epistemological aims. Yet these descriptions and analyses obscure variables like nationality, class, or language that are central components of our identities as subjects of legal knowledge. The influence of this model also drives the conception of our academic products as a consequence of the agreements we reach freely guided by reason. These ideas, generally implicit and not always clearly organized, often subjugate the geopolitics of legal knowledge.

Sometimes the direction our academic exchanges take, North-South or South-North, is in direct relation to the type of product we want to create or circumstances limiting the processes needed for its creation, such as the economic resources of or conditions imposed by sponsoring universities. Legal products are thus interpreted as a consequence of will and the scarcity of resources that influence actors in the global market of legal ideas. The free market model, therefore, obscures the role of certain variables related with factors that make us individual, flesh-and-bone legal academics rather than the capabilities we have as abstract subjects of legal knowledge.

Alternative Principles

Both models described above have weaknesses. The free market model can neither account for power imbalances determining the dynamics of creation, exchange, and use of legal knowledge nor explain how these imbalances intersect with economic, political, military, and cultural inequalities. For example, it cannot justify why legal transplants usually move North-South (Esquirol 2008 84–86), why authoritative interpreters of modern constitutionalism are predominantly Northern (Esquirol 2003), or why legal products created in the South are marginalized in the global legal conversation (Esquirol 2013). The colonial model's main weaknesses are that it homogenizes a reality full of nuance and contrast and creates a hierarchy between the legal academies of North and South that obscures the understanding of diversity of actors, practices, and quality in either context. The result is predominantly subordination of the South by the North, with the free market model generally pushed to the side, favored rhetorically but little practiced.

It is challenging to disentangle the reasons for this hierarchical relationship. We identify five arguments that help explain (not justify) it (Bonilla 2013a): (1) formalism of Global South legal systems[4] (Pérez Perdomo 2006); (2) treatment of Global South legal systems as iterations or reproductions of Northern "parent" legal systems (de Sousa Santos 1995); (3) failure to develop strong Global South legal identities given the influence of US law in content and practice (Domingo and Sieder 2001; Murillo 2005); (4) weakly developed Global South academic communities (Bonilla 2013a); and (5) provincialism of Global North legal agents (Mattei 1998).

This is not to overlook the Global South tendency to commit implicitly and explicitly to legal formalism, or deny the weaknesses created by excessive dependence on European and US law, legal models, and academic institutions (Esquirol 2008). As a result, the identities and self-esteem of Global South legal agents may appear fragile to both locals and foreigners. Additionally, the US tendency to endorse alternately isolationist and exceptionalist positions inhibits mutually productive interactions, as does the Western European tendency of selective opening to the outside, such that joint work is promoted only between those considered peers, namely North American and other European legal agents.

Formalism is not the only concept and practice that forms Latin legal awareness. Various oppositional strains of thought, from methodological positivism to critical legal studies, natural law, the free school of law, and legal postmodernism (Gomes and Singer 2001; Huneeus et al. 2010; Menski 2006), have had significant traction in Latin America and other Global South regions, reflecting eagerness for models and paradigms to order the legal complexity in these regions, which the dominant political economy of legal knowledge is unable to capture. This has led to an articulation of spaces for intellectual resistance to dominant models and for emancipation of new ideas in opposition to the geopolitics of legal knowledge, as, for example, by Third World Approaches to International Law (TWAIL) (Makau 2000) or postcolonial (Alpana 2008; Ruskola 2002) and critical comparative legal studies (Esquirol 2008, 2013). The dominant interpretation of the political economy of legal knowledge is incapable of recognizing Global South contributions to the international law dialogue, the strengths of certain legal research nodes in the South, or Global North institutions and individuals open to working with the "other" through horizontal exchanges of legal discourse and practice.

In our work, we have tried to avoid the descriptive and practical weaknesses of the two models discussed above by applying three principles to our joint SNPs. These principles were not clearly articulated from the start but rather evolved over time. First, we strove for mutual recognition, taking into account our strengths and weaknesses as academics and people, and also acknowledging that we belong to different national legal communities operating within a global system that tends not to endorse an equality principle in the abstract or acknowledge the inequality underlying postcolonial relations. Second, we worked to achieve consensus, building our SNPs by mutual agreement in all respects and at every stage of the collaboration. Third, we prioritized the SNPs' academic objectives over purposes of personal and institutional professional development. In the following section, we explain the links between these three principles and recently organized SNPs. We also show more precisely how the dominant political economy of legal knowledge has influenced our work.

THE POLITICAL ECONOMY OF LEGAL KNOWLEDGE AND OUR SNPS

The political economy of legal knowledge relies on continuous interaction between structure and subject. Actors inside this structure may view it uncritically, internalizing its rules, principles, and activities and reproducing the structure, consciously or not. Others may view the structure critically and try to question or transform it. The SNPs described here were shaped by the political economy of legal knowledge and comprise initiatives determined by a set of discourses and practices constituted by the two models, free market and colonial, composing most of our legal imagination. The two models, implicitly or explicitly, determine relevant aspects of how we articulate and execute our projects and coexist, in cognitive dissonance, within our juridical imagination. Nevertheless, we worked to distance ourselves from how these models dictate academic design and implementation and sought to construct an alternative narrative and practical path. We did this by applying the three principles described above: (1) mutual recognition; (2) construction of rules for the formation and implementation of our initiatives by consensus; and (3) conviction that the political and academic aims of our projects should be prioritized over professional development aims. This was not always easy. Conflicts between the demands of the dominant conceptual structure and the modest, alternative principles often generated internal and external disputes without simple resolutions.

This section details some of our joint activities over the past decade and offers critical reflections. In our analyses, we also describe the planning and preparation stages, stressing the structure and physical arrangements of the conferences, which often shape the nature of the interactions, including the intercultural and cross-national dynamics. Before turning to particular examples, however, it is useful to distinguish our efforts from those of many others. We believe they are distinct in at least four respects. First, we worked to create international encounters; therefore, most events have a strong comparative focus. Second, we often sought to reject the norm of English language-dominant encounters. Third, we coordinated events that demonstrated a commitment to geographic diversity. Fourth, we created events and activities that foster discussion across disciplines. While many pay lip service to the importance of interdisciplinary learning, there are few who actually undertake it. Thus, we endeavored to commit to the equality value embodied in the free market model on the assumption that all individuals may be capable of creating, using, and exchanging legal knowledge. We further assumed all individuals may be able to contribute to legal knowledge production in a permanent way that is both linear and infinite, without acknowledging the hierarchy of location.

To clarify, we are not fully committed to the free market model, but have been influenced by the values it defends. We recognize the importance of ideals like meritocracy and utility, but find problematic the absence of "power" as an analytical category within this model. Moreover, we aim to reject the colonial model by virtue of our attempted embrace of all local products, production, and particularity as possible expressions of universalizable and exchangeable legal knowledge. Nevertheless, the structural components of the political economy of legal knowledge are sufficiently powerful that even conscious efforts to resist their influence are moderately successful at best.

SNP 1: Central America and Caribbean Legal Pedagogy

This first SNP was a US government-funded effort to improve Central American and Caribbean professionals' legal pedagogy capacity. It implicitly valued what US-trained academics would bring to their counterparts elsewhere, so it was difficult to avoid the colonial model; what was being shared to improve local capacity was the legal knowledge largely generated and used in the North. As a result, the free market model, too, was largely absent. The emphasis was clearly on replicating a historical pattern of North-South knowledge transfer. We were required to deliver classes and moderate discussions aimed to produce law and policy teaching materials useful and appropriate for Central American and Caribbean law classrooms. The participants were faculty and researchers from universities in three Central American and one Caribbean country. All sessions were delivered in Spanish, the native language of all participants except the Project Director and one US-based instructor. The promised deliverables (classes and discussions) were completed and by that measure the project was successful.

What we wish to highlight here, however, are matters related to the political economy of legal knowledge production. Financing for this project came entirely from the US government and its underlying purpose was compliance with a multi-lateral trade treaty. The project instrument was capacity development of academics in the region for responding to the consequences of increased trade. This meant the project was conceived as a vehicle to bring mostly US-based professionals to the region for imparting knowledge. Regarding salient features of the colonial model discussed earlier, this SNP revealed strongly the dynamics of subject, time, and space. The subject was Latin American legal academics, placed in a subordinate position to receive the original legal knowledge produced in the USA—a rather typical unilateral knowledge transfer. With respect to time, the SNP underscored the notion of a North-led movement of continual progress in the North-dominated legal knowledge production. In this context, the knowledge produced in the North and disseminated in South was aimed at promoting the objectives of a free trade treaty that had economic prosperity and regional cooperation as central goals, under the guiding hand of the metropolis. The concept of space in this SNP exhibited similar characteristics: North-based legal experts arrived in Latin American-South space to direct the discussion and debate. And the participation and engagement of the Southern participants affirmed this dynamic. Southern participants made significant time commitments to act as recipients of Northern legal knowledge, attending a series of ten one-week seminars over three years. Again, mostly US-based academics were the authors and designers of the project—illustrating how even those wishing to break the dominant models are often bound and influenced by them.

We endeavored to break this dynamic by including in the seminars interactive exercises that invited participants to share examples of legal knowledge from their countries, an attempt to promote ownership in some of the proceedings and a role in determining content. We tried to conduct the sessions, whenever possible, in a rectangular format as an explicit rejection of a hierarchical colonial teacher-student arrangement that elevates Northern participants. But the basic design of the SNP made it difficult to overcome fully the inherent power imbalance in its execution. Additionally, the event's framing choices implicitly reflected colonial assumptions that impede true collaboration.

In part, some of our dissatisfaction with how the dominant political economy of legal knowledge imposes itself in SNPs like the project described above drove us to organize more focused events where established personal and professional relations would redirect the tendency to adopt default behaviors and practices characterized by the dominant models. A second SNP, designed in part as a response to some of the above-mentioned concerns, provides our next example.

SNP 2: US-Latin American Debate on the Social Function of Property

This SNP consisted of a semi-closed seminar format (the public was allowed to attend and observe but not participate) with 15–20 participants. Organizers concentrated on the physical arrangement of space to permit a focused dialogue and a rectangular table was chosen to promote discussion among participants. It was decided in advance for convenience that the working language would be English, which privileged the universalist values of the dominant models of the political economy of legal knowledge. The event was held in New York and all participants spoke fluent English, although many were from Latin America and the topic, the social function of property, was one with little traction in the US legal academy but extensive attention outside US borders.[5] Nonetheless, this initiative presented fewer of the concerns noted in SNP 1. First, all participants were trained in the same discipline (law) with shared interest in a particular legal topic. Second, all participants had a high command of English. Third, the topic was extremely focused, so the participants were all speaking the same academic language, which facilitated a robust and nuanced discussion. The participants were familiar with the same literature and global debates surrounding the issue. As a result, the conference came as close as we have experienced to expressing the meritocratic intellectual aims of the free market of ideas model. All parties were treated as potential agents of creation and diffusion of legal knowledge (equal subjects), engaged in a reasoned and purposeful debate (not limited in time or considered a priori more or less valuable), with the objective of sharing legal knowledge that could be replicated freely in different contexts (not limited in space).

Fourth, the group was assembled by invitation. A South American and a North American law professor equally shared organizational responsibilities. This equality of responsibility expressed the importance of mutuality and transparency that work to recalibrate the often unequal norms of legal knowledge production. In this case, the fact that most participants had a relatively sophisticated understanding of the theme, in combination with the organizers' commitment to create a respectfully critical tone, helped promote a unique spirit throughout. Event organization was guided by the principles of mutual recognition and consensus on the rules directing it. This was true despite the fact that event financing, including transportation costs for some non-US participants, came entirely from a US source. Fifth, most participants submitted paper drafts in advance, were asked to read the drafts prior to the event, and were each assigned a specific commentator role. This process helped maximize understanding and communication among the participants.

This example suggests that focus on and commitment to creating a platform devoid of subordination (explicit or implicit) is key to fruitful SNPs. Even in this case, though, organizers decided to use English as the default language, in spite of its not being the first language of the majority of participants. This was largely because of an advance commitment to publish the papers involved by one of the US university's journals and the tendency among US academic legal publishing for all sources to be translated into English. Consequently, while the event was characterized by fewer of the power imbalances created by the dominant political economy of legal knowledge, the publication process that followed was not.

In short, some of the same subject, time, and space features imposed by the dominant models of the political economy of legal knowledge were observed. First, the topic of the seminar was one first articulated by a French scholar in lectures delivered in Argentina in the early twentieth century. Thus, the seminar itself reified the tendency to look to the North for original ideas to be applied elsewhere, including in countries we now refer to as the South. So in some sense, the mega-subject of our seminar was Latin American law dependency upon and subordination to European-generated legal knowledge. Second, this SNP reflected the cognitive dissonance noted above that coexists in our minds and experiences with the dominant models. With respect to space and time, this SNP aspired to free market model values celebrating a linear and infinite notion of time as it built upon the progress of earlier thinkers. The physical space of the seminar also expressed the values of time, utility, and equality with its internal setup and format, and individual subjects were treated as equal players differentiated only by the degree and quality of their participation and work produced.

SNP 3: Discussion of Urban Development, Law, and Policy in the Americas

A third SNP presents a longer-term, field-focused seminar format with 10–15 mostly junior scholars and senior graduate students convened in a major city to study a theme related to urban development and regional/global social justice, law, and policy. From the outset, we organized activities with the express purpose of overturning many of the usual assumptions. By not insisting on a default model, some of the field seminars evolved implicitly and explicitly to reject central features of both the free market and colonial models. Interestingly, though, this departure from the dominant norm was not always the result of deliberate structuring; it sometimes came about rather unintentionally and sometimes not at all, as discussed later in the chapter.

The seminars in question all lasted a week. Participants were provided with a substantial packet of daily readings (in both English and Spanish or Portuguese) to prepare for each day's session, which began with a 60–90-minute academic lecture on the seminar theme, followed by a field excursion related to the lecture. At the end of the day, the entire group reconvened to discuss the day's activities and develop individual research projects and related publications.

Five such events were held over the course of four years: one in Central America, three in South America, and one in the USA. The first event in Central America consisted of mostly US-based law professors and students, was conducted mainly in English with translation as necessary, and demonstrated many characteristics of the free market model of the political economy of legal knowledge production. As with SNP 2, the free market ideal was served by all participants being US-based, speaking the same language and sharing similar progressive political views. The group arrived to Central America, received information on legal and policy knowledge produced and utilized in the region, and engaged the speakers in a discussion. Thus, regarding the characteristics of subject, space, and time, the parties started on equal footing to hold a reasoned, purposeful debate and produce legal knowledge that, theoretically, could be useful in Latin

THE POLITICAL ECONOMY OF LEGAL KNOWLEDGE IN ACTION... 131

America and elsewhere. Nevertheless, the SNP's execution in accord with free market model principles was somewhat compromised by practical concerns, as English was again the working language for most activities, though a majority of the US-based participants spoke Spanish. When lectures were delivered by speakers who did not speak English, there was staggered translation (as opposed to costly simultaneous translation with professional translators, sound booths, and headsets) with a group member translating portions of the lecture and often summarizing original content. Problems arose on several occasions when the conversation continued in Spanish without translation. The consternation of some English-speaking US professors was palpable, which contrasted markedly with similar situations involving Latin professionals in the USA at events with Spanish-speaking participants and no option for translation. As indicated above, the colonial model privileges one form of communication (English), even when the event takes place in a Global South space. The free market model is quietly and not so politely ushered to the side.

The implications of this example are subtle but important. The reaction described above reflects the values embedded in a legal imagination that creates expectations for communication in the dominant global language. "Everyone" in academic circles is expected to speak some English, even where English is not the primary language. We suggest also that the choice to use English is more insidious—an assertion of the dominant political economy of legal knowledge. By objecting to the choice of local communication rather than the "universalizing" default option, one tends to endorse the universalizing values presumed to be achievable by expression in the default language.

What alternatives might exist for the political economy of legal knowledge? One possibility would be to commit to a habit that undertook to learn something of the local language prior to engaging a legal culture in the space where it exists. Since no mode of communication can be truly universal without at least a general understanding of local communication, one cannot properly grasp the successes, challenges, and limitations of any single legal imagination. This is recognized in the deep connection between language and cognition (Lakoff and Johnson 2003) and in practice would signify committing to a pluralist rather than universalist principle, acknowledging the subject, time, and space limitations of any model of legal knowledge production.

Another important point in this Central American SNP relates to the balance between North and South scholars. In Central America, the participants consisted entirely of US-based scholars, which sometimes resulted in behavior characteristic of the dominant colonial model and suggested a visit to the colony. For instance, one field trip involved a tour of the country's most important national agency and primary foreign-income generator. Several of the US-based participants arrived to leave for the tour clad in tee shirts, shorts, and flip flops and objected when asked to change to more appropriate professional attire. It is unlikely any law professor would attempt to visit a US government agency dressed in shorts; the colonial subject was not accorded equal respect.

Similar observations can be offered for time and space elements. With respect to time, Central American laws were discussed as particularized, temporary, and underdeveloped local responses to global pressures and changes, not as contributions to a global body of legal knowledge. This was true of space also since these discussions allowed Northern professors to return content with their belief in the solidity of their system, having generously shared their legal knowledge with the colonial subject in situ. At the same time, the discussions in this SNP were characterized by a spirit of a free market exchange of legal ideas, with invitations for scholarly contributions in English from the Central American speakers and collaborators.[6] This serves to underscore the initial point made that the two dominant models of the political economy of legal knowledge tend to coexist in cognitive dissonance, often within the same initiative or event.

SNP 4: *Moot Court in Latin America*

The fourth and final SNP is an international, multi-institutional, student-focused initiative: a Moot Court Competition developed in collaboration with colleagues from a prominent Brazilian law school. Moot court competitions are academic activities where groups of law students represent litigants in a simulated trial, with law professors and other legal professionals acting as judges. This kind of competition is common in US law schools, so this effort did represent a kind of legal transplant and borrowing of a model developed largely in the English-speaking world, a move replete with the challenges and implications associated with legal transplants (Graziadei 2009). Nonetheless, we tried to use the experience to shift thinking and practices observable in the dominant models.

Three institutions in different countries with different languages undertook to establish this competition for several reasons. First, because of Moot Court success in the USA, exporting the concept to Latin America seemed to offer a number of opportunities, especially given the increasing importance of multi-national tribunals and the development of law students' oral advocacy skills. Second, most such competitions are held outside of Latin America, so developing a Moot Court program that would rotate among sponsoring Latin American institutions presented a means for broadening the participant base beyond the USA. Third, such competitions are mostly held in English, so developing Moot Court in other languages offered another way to broaden institutional and student participation—and on a level playing field. Even Latin American students, who have developed strong English language skills, are generally at a disadvantage when forced to debate in a non-native language; this difficulty is mitigated when students are allowed to write and argue in their native language. Fourth, establishing Moot Court in Latin America presented an opportunity to showcase the importance of sustainable development law, an emerging area of international law with considerable social, economic, political, and environmental implications. By these measures, the competition was a success. In its first year, 2011, held in Rio de Janeiro, 12 teams competed from three countries and Puerto Rico. In 2015, the event included 21 teams from nine countries (including Germany and India) and Puerto Rico. The increased interest appears to vindicate decisions to hold these events in Latin America, in multiple languages, and focused on sustainable development law (this was the catalyst for the Indian team's enrollment).

Nonetheless, this event faced significant challenges. First, there were financial limitations. In the USA, team enrollment fees are often $1000 or more. As this would preclude many Latin American teams from participating, we began with far lower fees and more support from host institutions, though this ultimately presented a challenge to event sustainability.[7] In addition, the cost of simultaneous translation is high. Second, simultaneous translation presents other concerns as words and phrases, particularly technical ones, may be dropped or poorly understood. Judges can interrupt and ask questions before participants with headphones have heard the full translation. Less time to form arguments diminishes competitive advantage. Over the four years of competitions, multiple complaints about this have surfaced. Third, there were differences of legal academic culture to address. For instance, Moot Court in Latin America often includes faculty coaching on input and preparation, while this is almost never the case in the USA and this created some tension. Fourth, styles of argumentation differ by culture, which can foster implicit biases depending on where a competition is held. Argument and oral presentation in the civil law tradition typically begins in a highly formal manner, focusing first on the legal theory and hierarchy of legal sources that defend a position. By contrast, common-law training encourages students to be discursive with a propensity to focus on illustrative examples. These cultural differences can create difficulties. Fifth, multi-lingual events constantly require extra effort—in terms of translation, interpretation, and time commitment.

The real costs—human and financial—associated with reshaping the political economy of legal knowledge are high, but so are the benefits. The Moot Court event was influenced by the free market model, yet it was also free of some of this model's weaknesses. Specifically, although the transplanted model came from the North, the shape it took on in the South was distinct. In addition, perhaps because students were writing and arguing in their native languages, they tended to cite opinions and decisions from national and regional courts, which worked against the traditional intellectual dominance of Northern sources. Holding events outside the USA also appeared to shift the value placed on common-law reasoning and presentation styles. In only one of the four years of the competition did an English-speaking team rank in the top two, which effectively served to elevate Spanish and Portuguese to the level of universalizing, collaborative languages in this context and raise the value of Southern legal sources (Wilson 2013). This event successfully used collaborative work to reshape the political economy of legal knowledge and its subsequent production. At the same time, however, the concerns described above also highlight the need to advance these efforts with the greatest possible transparency and respect for differences.

Of all the SNPs discussed, this Moot Court experience was perhaps the most balanced regarding event politics and economics, as a result of the collaborators' shared vision and common objectives. Solutions sought respected different organizational and institutional cultures as well as financial realities. Contributions to the required financial and human resources for the event were shared equally by all three national sponsors. This SNP proved the exception rather than the rule in our experience, in part perhaps because the greater Latin American economic participation ended up dictating working language and performance patterns. Finances, however, were not the only determinant. Shifting language and culture bases also worked to upturn traditional notions that the default, "universalist" language should form the basis for legal knowledge creation. This example suggests that "universalism" is ultimately a matter of perspective.

THE POLITICAL ECONOMY OF LEGAL KNOWLEDGE IN ACTION... 135

That this occurred in the context of a relatively new area of legal study may also have helped subtly to shift the nature of the discussion. Language shapes the way we think and form ideas (Boroditsky 2009). To create legal texts for study and argument in one language therefore, inevitably, shapes how concepts are formed. To translate texts for common use and application from their original languages serves to redirect the way legal ideas are framed. This was the objective of the Latin American Moot Court SNP, and in this sense it was a success.

ANALYTICAL AND PRACTICAL LESSONS LEARNED

Our experiences reveal the extent to which the dominant models of the political economy of legal knowledge impede Latin American contributions to legal research and dialogue on a global scale. Nonetheless, we have learned that a concerted effort to resist the dominant models can yield results, in at least four respects. First, small tactical steps help erode the power of models that dominate the legal imagination. For example, a deliberate preference for a language other than English can slowly change the way people imagine and analyze the law. Not only does such a step represent an explicit rejection of the colonial model, it also demonstrates that the universalizing and infinite time features of the free market model can find expression in different languages.

Second, focused efforts to treat seriously notable creations of legal knowledge outside the Global North can promote knowledge transfer that rejects the usual trade routes. This helps recalibrate dominant structures and modes of law creation, application, and use. To this end, we worked to draw from relevant Latin American and other Global South examples wherever possible, and by example prompt others to do likewise. This included discussion of the Mexican concept of "social right" (Müller 1997) (Carroza 2006), the Brazilian notion of the "right to the city" (City Statute 2001), and Colombian contributions that favor the expansion of basic human rights by means of the nation's distinctive form of *tutela* action[8] (Iturralde 2013). Similarly, we sought to emphasize the importance of centers of investigative strength in Latin America, like the National Autonomous University of Mexico and the University of the Andes in Colombia, which often surpasses that of many Global North peers.

A third and related point demonstrated by the collaborations described here is the need to take law seriously *ab inicio*, from the outset, wherever and whenever created. This is to commit to a form of global legal pluralism. Earlier we argued that the dominant models of the political economy of legal knowledge tend to elevate Global North legal production and view productions of the Global South as products of a parochial or highly localized (and therefore not replicable) political and social culture, or expressions of failed and/or corrupt states (Bonilla 2013a, Esquirol 2008). Changing social and political perceptions is not easy or quick. But new legal production from different spaces and circumstances as a means to solving the challenges of an increasingly connected world is essential. And it offers potential for producing more analytical and practical tools for scholars and students in both the North and South.

Finally, our experience suggests the continued importance of adhering to the three principles of successful SNPs we stressed throughout this chapter: (1) mutual respect and acknowledgment of difference, (2) commitment to building consensus, and (3) recognition of the need to design activities that balance academic and political aims with differing and often conflicting professional advancement requirements. As indicated, these principles were not articulated clearly from the start. Rather, they evolved, representing a rationalization of our practices and political commitments over time. We do not imply that our commitment to these principles indicates consistent application or operationalization of them; many times we failed in this regard. We do suggest that by working to observe these principles to the greatest possible extent, we try to prevent legitimate career advancement objectives from compelling acceptance of rules imposed by dominant models of legal knowledge production. In the process, we pave the way for the construction of alternative models of legal knowledge production.

As our narrative also demonstrates, the political economy of legal knowledge makes it difficult to implement many of the measures described. For example, with shifting the default language choice to recognize that language goes beyond communication and encompasses structures and modes of thought that influence how ideas are conceived (Lakoff and Johnson 2003), the reality is that this is not always practical. Similarly, to describe and acknowledge legal innovations and contributions from the Global South may be easier said than done for at least two reasons. First, serious costs in time and effort for translation and explanation are incurred. Second, the dominant model of legal knowledge production, namely the colonial model, is vertical in structure and by its nature inhibits horizontal exchanges of legal knowledge and practices. Small roadblocks can interfere with a concerted effort to shift the dominant models.

In our work we have tried to get away from descriptive and policy weaknesses present in both prevailing models of legal knowledge production. Gradually, our experience suggests, careful structuring of new forms of academic collaboration help shift the contexts for legal knowledge creation and thus the forms that are created, applied, and used. It is our hope that continued adherence to shared principles and conscious collaboration to achieve them as precisely as possible is what will allow for cooperative work and improved academic collaborations in the Americas and elsewhere.

CONCLUSIONS

All told, the political economy of legal knowledge dominates the production, circulation, and use of legal knowledge. The colonial and free market models of legal ideas control the ways the modern liberal imagination describes, analyzes, evaluates, and acts with respect to legal knowledge; they do so explicitly and implicitly. Our collaborative academic activities of the past decade were, in part and inevitably, concrete expressions of the dominant models governing the political economy of legal knowledge. They also demonstrate an effort to escape the centripetal force these models impose. In this respect they represent modest efforts, incomplete and only partially successful, to create horizontal relationships between North and South legal academies. Hopefully, these general contributions toward the construction of a pluralist political economy of legal knowledge will lead to new ways of imagining law, sharing the fruits of different legal imaginations, and collaborating with respect and deliberation to create, apply, and use law in diverse global contexts.

NOTES

1. These philosophical terms, both from the ancient Greek, translate as "imitation" or "reproduction" and "self-design so as to be self-sustaining," respectively. This conceptual opposition, mimesis/autopoiesis, describes the contents of the colonial legal systems as representations of the legal systems of the metropolis. The mimetic colony is the space where the original knowledge emerging in the autopoietic metropolis is disseminated and applied locally.

2. This field reflects upon the connections and tensions between epistemology and justice. More precisely, it examines the links between knowledge, knowers, and ethics.
3. For the sense in which we use "metropolis" in opposition to "colonial," see Jennifer Anne Boittin, *Colonial Metropolis: The Urban Grounds of Anti-Imperialism and Feminism in Interwar Paris* (University of Nebraska: Lincoln, 2015).
4. The concept of formalist law identifies the legal system with legislation; considers the law to be comprehensive, coherent, and closed; indicates that it alone is able to provide the answers to all problems that arise in a political community; and, in extreme versions, equates formal validity with justice. This concept of law is intertwined with a classical interpretation of liberal democracy that promotes a radical separation of the branches of government.
5. Namely the "social function of property." In English, see Duguit (1919).
6. In the end, no such contributions were received.
7. The 2016 sponsor, based in the USA, canceled the event due to insufficient US enrollments, which the institution had hoped would underwrite the participation of non-US teams.
8. The Colombian *tutela* is a writ (a form of legal request) available to citizens to secure fundamental constitutional rights.

REFERENCES

Alpana, R. (2008). Postcolonial Theory and Law: A Critical Introduction. *Adelaide Law Review, 29*(1/2), 315–357.

Bonilla, D. (2013a). Introduction. In D. Bonilla (Ed.), *Constitutionalism of the Global South: The Three Activist Courts of India, South Africa and Colombia* (pp. 1–40). Cambridge: Cambridge University Press.

Bonilla, D. (2013b). Legal Clinics in the Global North and South: Between Equality and Subordination. *Yale Human Rights & Development Law Journal, 16*(1), 176.

Bonilla, D. (2015). La Economía Política del Conocimiento Jurídico [The Political Economy of Legal Knowledge]. *Brazilian Journal of Empirical Legal Studies, 2*(1), 26–59.

Boroditsky, L. (2009). How Does Our Language Shape the Way We Think? In M. Brockman (Ed.), *What's Next? Dispatches on the Future of Science* (pp. 116–129). New York: Random House.

Carroza, P. (2006). La Perspectiva Histórica del Aporte Latinoamericano al Concepto de los Derechos Económicos, Sociales y Culturales. [The Historical Perspective of the Latinamerican Contribution to the Concept of Economic, Social and Cultural Rights]. In A. E. Yamin (Ed.), *Derechos Económicos, Sociales*

THE POLITICAL ECONOMY OF LEGAL KNOWLEDGE IN ACTION... 139

y Culturales en América Latina: Del Inventivo a la Herramienta [*Economic, Social and Cultural Rights in Latin America: From Conception to Tool*] (pp. 43–62). Mexico: Plaza y Valdez Editores.

City Statute: Law No. 10.257 of 10 July 2001. The standard English-language version was published by Cities Alliance and [Brazilian] Ministry of Cities (São Paulo, 2010) and is available at citiesalliance.org

Clark, B. S. (1998). *Political Economy: A Comparative Approach* (pp. 18–20). New York: Greenwood Publishing.

de Sousa Santos, B. (1995). Three Metaphors for a New Conception of Law: The Frontier, the Baroque and the South. *Law & Society Review, 29*(4), 569–584.

Domingo, P., & Sieder, R. (Eds.). (2001). *Rule of Law in Latin America: The International Promotion of Judicial Reform.* London: Institute of Latin American Studies.

Duguit, L. (1919). *Law in the Modern State.* London: George, Allen & Unwin.

Esquirol, J. L. (2003). Continuing Fictions of Latin American Law. *Florida Law Review, 55*, 41–114.

Esquirol, J. L. (2008). The Failed Law of Latin America. *American Journal of Comparative Law, 56*, 75–123.

Esquirol, J. L. (2013). Legal Latin Americanism. *Yale Human Rights and Development Law Journal, 16*, 145–170.

Fricker, M. (2007). *Epistemic Justice.* New York: Oxford University Press.

Gomes, M., & Singer, H. (2001). Sociology of Law in Brazil: A Critical Approach. *The American Sociologist, 32*, 10–25.

Graziadei, M. (2009). Legal Transplants and the Frontiers of Legal Knowledge. *Theoretical Inquiries in Law, 10*(2), 723–743.

Huneeus, A., Couso, J., & Sieder, R. (2010). Cultures of Legality: Judicialization and Political Activism in Contemporary Latin America. In J. Couso, A. Huneeus, & R. Sieder (Eds.), *Cultures of Legality. Justicialization and Political Activism in Latin America.* Cambridge: Cambridge University Press.

Iturralde, M. (2013). Access to Constitutional Justice in Colombia: Opportunities and Challenges for Social and Political Change. In *Constitutionalism of the Global South: The Three Activist Courts of India, South Africa and Colombia* (pp. 361–400). Cambridge: Cambridge University Press.

Kahn, P. (1999). *The Cultural Study of Law.* Chicago: University of Chicago Press.

Lakoff, G., & Johnson, M. (2003). *Metaphors We Live By.* Chicago: University of Chicago Press.

Makau, M.. (2000). What Is TWAIL? *American Society of International Law, Proceedings of the 94th Annual Meeting, 30*, 31–39.

Mattei, U. (1998). An Opportunity Not to Be Missed: The Future of Comparative Law in the United States. *American Journal of Comparative Law, 48*, 709–718.

Menski, W. (2006). *Comparative Law in Global Context, the Legal Systems of Asia and Africa.* Cambridge: Cambridge University Press.

Mickelson, K. (2009). Beyond a Politics of the Possible? South-North Relations and Climate Justice. *Melbourne Journal of International Law, 10,* 411–423.

Morris, R., & Spivak, G. (2010). *Can the Subaltern Speak?* Columbia University Press.

Müller, L. T. D. (1997). Derechos Económicos, Sociales y Culturales: Aportación de México [Social, Economic and Cultural Rights: Mexico's Contribution]. *Boletín Mexicano de Derecho Comparado, 88,* 79–92.

Murillo, M. V. (2005). Partisanship Amidst Convergence: The Politics of Labor Reform in Latin America. *Comparative Politics, 37*(4), 441–458.

Pérez-Perdomo, R. (2006). Rule of Law and Lawyers in Latin American. *Annals of the American Academy of Political and Social Science, 603,* 179–191.

Rubio, F., & Baert, P. (Eds.). (2012). *The Politics of Knowledge.* London: Routledge.

Ruskola, T. (2002). Legal Orientalism. *Michigan Law Review, 101*(1), 79–234.

Wilson, M. J. (2013). Improving the Process: Transnational Litigation and the Application of Private Foreign Law in US Courts. *New York University Journal of International Law & Politics, 45,* 1111–1150.

CHAPTER 7

Small Fish in a Big Pond: Internationalization and Research Collaboration in Bolivia and Paraguay

Jorge Enrique Delgado

INTRODUCTION

As globalization and academic markets expand worldwide, higher education systems, and particularly universities, are experiencing increasing pressures to participate in innovation initiatives and develop their research capacity and productivity to be competitive (Delgado 2015). The usual discourses about Latin America and the Caribbean in this regard point out the region's modest though growing achievements. However, Latin America is not a homogeneous region and it is commonly described based on the analyses of the largest and most studied countries. Small countries such as Paraguay and Bolivia have not been much studied. The purpose of this chapter is to analyze the ways university researchers from Bolivia and Paraguay have found to participate in international research

J. E. Delgado (✉)
University of Pittsburgh, Pittsburgh, PA, USA

Pontificia Universidad Javeriana, Bogota, Colombia

© The Author(s) 2018   141
G. Gregorutti, N. Svenson (eds.), *North-South University Research Partnerships in Latin America and the Caribbean*,
https://doi.org/10.1007/978-3-319-75364-5_7

collaborations (Delgado and Weidman 2012). The argument is that even though capacity, size of research, and research outcomes from these countries are small, there are some international collaboration initiatives showing progress and promising accomplishments. However, more efforts at the government level are necessary to create the conditions to develop research, promote economic development, and use international collaboration to achieve these.

Data collection for this chapter took place in three stages. The first step consisted of reviews of different data sources and repositories that provided general indicators on economics, higher education, and science and technology, and specific information about scientific journals. The second phase included a close inspection of journal repositories to identify trends and characteristics of international collaboration through participation of experts in journal editorial boards and researchers in article co-authorship. The third stage aimed to identify examples or experiences of successful international collaborations between researchers in Bolivia and Paraguay and counterparts in institutions abroad such as universities, research centers, government agencies, non-governmental organizations (NGOs), and even private enterprises. This was the most challenging part of the project since it took time to identify those experiences. The strategies to find them involved networking, snowballing, website reviews, and journal inspections. At the end, the cases included in this chapter came from different sources.

The chapter is developed in seven sections. The first section portrays the countries through demographic, economic, and research and development (R&D) indicators. It uses data mainly from the Iberic-American and Inter-American Network of Science and Technology Indicators (RICYT: *Red de Indicadores de Ciencia y Tecnología—Iberoamericana e Interamericana*) and the World Bank, and compares them with Brazil (the largest economy, most populated country, and one of the most developed nations in terms of science, technology, and innovation (STI) in the region) and the whole Latin America and Caribbean. Using the same sources, the second section analyzes science and technology capacity and general outputs of Bolivia and Paraguay. It includes indicators about human capital (researchers), scientific output (patents and articles published in mainstream journals), and knowledge transference (high-technology exports). The third section describes the higher education systems of Bolivia and Paraguay and how they are articulated to the national STI systems. The latter serves as a preamble to the analysis of internationalization through the publication of scientific journals in regional repositories in the fourth section (Delgado 2010, 2011; Delgado Troncoso 2011; Delgado and Fischman 2014). That section looks at the participation of international scholars in editorial/scientific boards/committees of Bolivian and Paraguayan journals, which is a part of indexation criteria that have been promoted globally and through regional bibliographic analysis services, such as Latindex, SciELO, and RedALyC, which were created in the last two decades (Delgado 2014). The fifth section reviews international co-authorship in articles published by journals from the SciELO Bolivian and Paraguayan collections. The sixth section presents four cases of innovation through international collaboration, two from Bolivia and two from Paraguay. The last section discusses the strategies and challenges to obtain data, analyzes the findings of this chapter, and provides some recommendations for countries like Bolivia and Paraguay to look for international collaborations to promote the development of their STI systems (Delgado 2011).

General Demographic, Economic, and R&D Indicators

Bolivia

Bolivia is a land-locked country located in South America. In 2013, this country had a population of 10.67 million inhabitants, which was 1/18th the size of Brazil (201 million) and 1/57th of the Latin American and Caribbean region (607.93 million) (RICYT 2013h). In terms of economy, Bolivia had a GDP of US$30.6 billion in 2013 (in current US dollars). It was 1/78th of Brazil (US$2.4 trillion) and 1/203rd of Latin America (US$6.2 trillion) (RICYT 2013f). Data from 2009 show that Bolivia spent US$27.41 million on R&D (0.15 percent of GDP), which contrasts with Brazil that spent US$ 29.6 billion (1.23 percent of GDP) in 2012. Latin America spent in 2013, on average, 0.76 percent of GDP (RICYT 2013e, i). The World Bank defines R&D as public and private cash and capital expenditures on systematically conducted creative work to increase knowledge, including knowledge about humanity, culture, and society, as well as new ways to apply knowledge. R&D encompasses basic and applied research and experimental development (The World Bank 2015b).

Paraguay

Paraguay is also a South American land-locked country. Paraguay had 6.7 million inhabitants in 2013, that is, 1/30th of the population of Brazil and about 1/90th of Latin America and the Caribbean (RICYT 2013h).

Regarding the total value of goods and services produced, in 2013, Paraguay had a GDP of US$29.8 billion, which was 1/80th of Brazil and 1/208th of Latin America (RICYT 2013f). In 2012, Paraguay spent US$21.68 million in R&D (0.08 percent of GDP) (RICYT 2013e, i).

SCIENCE AND INNOVATION CAPACITY AND OUTPUT

STI sectors worldwide have been gaining relevance as key actors for national economic development. However, the emphasis has changed in recent decades from capacity building to R&D investment and productivity measures (Aguirre-Bastos and Gupta 2009; Delgado 2011, 2014, 2015). The previous section provided general comparative demographic, economic, and R&D indicators of Bolivia and Paraguay. This section creates a profile of both countries based on one capacity indicator, researchers, and three productivity or output indicators: patents, high-technology exports, and journal articles in mainstream journals.

Researchers

The World Bank recognizes researchers working in research and development as those professionals who design or generate new knowledge, products, processes, methods, or systems and manage their projects. Doctoral students working on research and development are included in this group (The World Bank 2015c). The number of researchers in science and technology in Bolivia was 1746 in 2010, which represents 0.045 percent of the labor force. In 2012, there were 1550 researchers in Paraguay (0.053 percent of the workforce). Those indicators contrast with Brazil whose researchers represented 0.251 percent of the workers in 2010 (170,209 researchers) (RICYT 2013l, m), that is, around five times the proportion of either Bolivia or Paraguay. Regarding the distribution of researchers by field of science, in 2010 Bolivia had the largest percentage in the natural sciences (25.4 percent) and the lowest in the humanities (5.66 percent). Considering that research in engineering is not particularly one of the largest research fields in Latin America, it is interesting that 21.31 percent of researchers in Bolivia are in engineering. In Paraguay, in 2009, the highest proportion of researchers was in the social sciences (24.62 percent), followed by agricultural sciences (22.13 percent). The lowest percentage of researchers was in the humanities (10.44 percent) (RICYT 2013j). Furthermore, the scientific capacity of a country has also been associated with the level of qualification of its researchers. It is assumed that the higher the number of researchers with graduate degrees, particularly doctorates, the higher the expected involvement in research projects and their research productivity. In this regard, in 2010, Bolivia reported that 11.19 percent of its researchers had doctoral degrees and 31.01 percent had masters. In 2011, Paraguay had a distribution like Bolivia: 13.79 percent doctors and 28.13 percent masters. In contrast, Brazil, a country that created a strong infrastructure to develop its STI system, which includes the development of doctoral programs, had in 2010, 35.42 percent researchers with doctorates and 44.28 percent with master degrees (RICYT 2013k).

Patents

Patent applications are intended to protect the rights of owners of inventions. They are filed worldwide through the Patent Cooperation Treaty or at national agencies (The World Bank 2015a). The most current data available in the RICYT database show that in 2001, Bolivia submitted 300 patent applications by residents and non-residents. The same year, Paraguay submitted 261 and 451 in 2013. In contrast, Brazil had 21,618 submissions in 2001 and 34,049 in 2013 (RICYT 2013g). All the patents from Bolivia came from non-residents.

High-Technology Exports

Another way to analyze a country's STI outputs is through the products of scientific activities that are used or transferred to the society, for instance, the productive sector. One of the indicators generally used to identify internationalization could be exports of high-technology products, which are highly intensive R&D products from the aerospace, computers, pharmaceutical, scientific instruments, and electric machinery industries. In 2013, nine percent of Bolivia's exports of manufactured products were high-technology products. The amount of these exports was US$44.1 million (in current US dollars). Paraguay's exports of high-technology products (US$57.1 million) represented seven percent of all manufactured products exported. In contrast, Brazil exported US$8.4 billion of high-technology products, which is 10 percent of the exports of manufactured products (World Bank 2015d, e).

146   J. E. DELGADO

Journal Articles

In 2013, authors from Bolivia published 57 journal articles that were indexed by CAB International (agricultural sciences). Paraguay had 40. In contrast, Brazilian authors published 20,054 articles in those disciplines (RICYT 2013b). In the field of medicine, Bolivia had in 2013 49 journal articles indexed by Medline, Paraguay had 62, and Brazil had 19,052 (RICYT 2013c). The indicators are similar for articles in the biological sciences indexed by BIOSIS. Bolivia had 73, Paraguay 89, and Brazil 19,057 (RICYT 2013a). In general, in all the scientific fields, the proportion of contributions of Bolivia and Paraguay is like the specific fields presented here. The general Collection of the Web of Science that includes the Science Citation Index showed 283 articles from Bolivia, 186 from Paraguay, and 44,530 from Brazil in 2013 (RICYT 2013d). These indicators represent in part the size of mainstream science of these countries but not the real size of their science or their actual impact on national, regional, or international science.

The next section describes the structure of higher education and STI systems in Bolivia and Paraguay. It identifies the main higher education institutions (HEIs) and public policies and programs to promote research. The section ends by identifying the HEIs that are included in some international university rankings. The latter information was used as a basis to find experiences of international research collaboration.

HIGHER EDUCATION AND THE RESEARCH ENDEAVOR

Bolivian Systems of Higher Education and STI

The Bolivian higher education system is made up of 16 public universities located in the cities of Beni, Chuquisaca, Cochabamba, La Paz, Oruro, Potosí, Santa Cruz, and Tarija. Among them, Major University of San Simón (UMSS: *Universidad Mayor de San Simón* in Cochabamba), Major University of San Andres (UMSA: *Universidad Mayor de San Andrés* in La Paz), Autonomous University Juan Misael Saracho (UAJMS: *Universidad Autónoma Juan Misael Saracho* in Tarija), and Autonomous University of Beni José Ballivián (UABJB: *Universidad Autónoma del Beni José Ballivián* in Beni) are some of the most prestigious nationwide and have some research developments. There are also 34 private universities throughout the national territory. Bolivian Catholic University San Pablo (UCBSP: *Universidad Católica Boliviana San Pablo* with campuses in La Paz, Cochabamba, Santa Cruz, and Tarija) and Private University of the Valley (Univalle: *Universidad Privada del Valle* with campuses in Cochabamba, La Paz, Sucre, and Trinidad) are also institutions with good reputation and do research (Plurinational State of Bolivia 2011).

The Bolivian higher education and science and technology sectors are regulated/governed by the Ministry of Education, which consists of four Vice Ministries: Regular Education, Alternative and Special Education, Higher Education for Professional Formation, and Science and Technology (Plurinational State of Bolivia, Ministry of Education 2016). The Vice Ministry of Science and Technology is divided into two departments: communication and information technologies (DCIT) and science and technology (DST). DCIT provides technical support and promotes technology development. DST oversees the Bolivian innovation system (through the development of innovation platforms and national research networks), the system for access to scientific information (through access to regional virtual libraries such as SciELO, Latindex, and RedALyC, and more global ones such as EBSCO and Cochrane, but there is not mention of access to the most comprehensive databases, Web of Science and Scopus), and the student scientific Olympiads. DST has promoted the development of national networks in the following strategic fields: food, biodiversity, forests, science communication and culture, energy, technology-based startups, nuclear, earth observation, paleontology, hydric resources, environment rehabilitation, local wisdom and ancestral knowledge, and communication and information technologies. DST lists in its website several researchers and universities and centers that are considered research institutions, which include UMSA (with units such as Higher Institute of Bolivian Studies, Chemical Research Institute, and Industrial Research Institute), UCBSP (Tarija academic unit, socioeconomic research laboratory, etc.), UMSS (gypsum research unit, child-mother unit, nutrition program, microbiology program, genetics and molecular biology program, geotechnics laboratory, etc.), and UAJMS (food laboratory, bromate laboratory, hydric resources institute, etc.), among other. In 2016, Bolivia launched the third version of the Plurinational Science and Technology Award in different strategic fields but is limited to Bolivian researchers affiliated to universities, research centers, foundations, NGOs, and/or corporations. It does not mention international collaborations (Plurinational State of Bolivia, Vice Ministry of Science and Technology 2016).

148   J. E. DELGADO

In its National Science and Technology Plan (2013), the Bolivian government recognizes as the two main challenges to develop the STI sector the lack of connection between academia and research along with a poor response to social and productive needs, and the distance of societal sectors from knowledge and technological advances. The plan emphasizes the formation of human resources as a fundamental axis of the STI policy. However, the Plan does not mention international collaborations or participation of international actors, other than Bolivian researchers attending international events. This may show the emphasis of the current government in strengthening the national sovereignty (Plurinational State of Bolivia, Ministry of Education 2013).

Paraguayan Higher Education and STI Systems

Founded in 1889, the National University of Asuncion (UNA: *Universidad Nacional de Asunción*) was the only university in Paraguay until 1960, when the government charted the Catholic University "Our Lady of Asuncion" (UCNSA: *Universidad Católica "Nuestra Señora de la Asunción"*). After the country returned to democracy, a massive creation of HEIs, mainly private, took place. Currently, there are 54 universities, of which 8 are public and 46 are private (González 2012; Morínigo Alcaraz 2013; National Agency for Higher Education Evaluation and Accreditation 2016). The most prestigious universities in Paraguay are UNA and UCNSA. Other institutions include Northern University (*Universidad del Norte*), Polytechnic and Artistic University of Paraguay (*Universidad Politécnica y Artística del Paraguay*), Autonomous University of Asunción (UAA: *Universidad Autónoma de Asunción*), and Autonomous University of Paraguay (*Universidad Autónoma del Paraguay*). In 2011, 303,539 students were enrolled in HEIs in Paraguay, distributed 81 percent in private and 19 percent in public institutions (Morínigo Alcaraz 2013). In addition, there are 37 higher institutes (*institutos superiores*).

The Ministry of Education and Culture (MEC) of Paraguay oversees the whole education system. However, MEC's strategic plans for 2020 and 2024 have focused mainly on basic education in areas such as education access and completion, curriculum development, teacher training, quality, citizen participation, efficiency and efficacy, and articulation of the system's levels/actors. Regarding higher education, the 2024 Plan established five areas of action: degree regulation, validation of degrees obtained abroad, curriculum standardization in some disciplines, promotion of research in education, and scholarships for graduate study abroad (Republic of Paraguay, MEC 2016).

Higher education in Paraguay is part of the National Education System as established by the General Education Law No. 1264 of 21 April 1998. Among HEIs, public and private universities are considered autonomous to establish governance bodies and academic structures. Likewise, the Law establishes that HEIs' mission includes teaching, research, and service. Universities were initially regulated by Law of Universities No. 136 of 29 March 1993 (Republic of Paraguay 2003; UNA 2012), which was replaced by Law No. 4995 of 9 May 2013. The latter defines types of HEIs, quality assurance mechanisms, and kinds of services provided by the HEIs, including research. Law 4995 also creates the National Council of Higher Education that consists of representatives from UNA, UCNSA, other HEIs and agencies, and the National Council of Higher Education (CONACYT: *Consejo Nacional de Ciencia y Tecnología*). Besides establishing research as a mission of higher education institutions and the rights and responsibilities of professors and researchers, Law 4995 does not further address it.

On the other side, the Paraguayan system of STI is coordinated through CONACYT. Law No. 2279 of 7 November of 2003, which modified the General Law of Science and Technology No. 1028 of 1997, provides the legal framework for the STI system (García Riart 2013; Republic of Paraguay 2013). CONACYT has four main programs: Prociencia, planned to strengthen research and technology capacities; the Technological Development, Innovation and Conformity Assessment Project in Paraguay (Proyecto Desarrollo Tecnológico, Innovación y Evaluación de Conformidad Paraguay, DETEIC), whose aim is to increase competitiveness through technology, innovation, and evaluation; the Support Program for the Development of Science, Technology and Innovation in Paraguay (Programa de Apoyo al Desarrollo de la Ciencia, Tecnología e Innovación Paraguay, PROCIT), intended to provide research funding, develop graduate programs, and provide scholarships; and the National Incentive Program for Researchers in Paraguay (Programa Nacional de Incentivo a los Investigadores Paraguay, PRONII), which creates incentives for research productivity (Republic of Paraguay, CONACYT 2016). CONACYT's website does not mention policy or strategies to promote internationalization or international research collaboration. Even though research is considered fundamental for economic development and is included in CONACYT's programs, research funding seems to be unclear, as pointed out by authors like Pedro González (2012).

The next three sections show the results of the attempt to portray international research collaborations in Paraguay and Bolivia. They start with an inspection of the composition of editorial boards/committees of journals included in SciELO. The following section looks at co-authorships

150   J. E. DELGADO

and how international research collaboration could be identified. The third section presents two cases from Bolivia and two from Paraguay of how international collaborations take place in both countries.

Internationalization as Seen Through Bolivian and Paraguayan Scientific Journals

With the purpose of building inventories of publications and increasing regional capacity, and as a response to international disparities in access to mainstream scientific journals and bibliographic information services, three regional indexes and/or open access journal repositories were created from the late 1990s to early 2000s: Latindex, SciELO, and RedALyC (Aguado et al. 2008; Alperín et al. 2011; Cetto et al. 2010; Delgado 2011; Meneghini and Packer 2008). The regional and national journal evaluation systems that have emerged since the early 1990s in Latin America have used worldwide accepted criteria. A group of measures include internationalization as proportion of members of editorial boards and scientific committees, authors, and peer reviewers external to the institutions where the journals are originated. An interesting characteristic of Latin American journals is the tendency to be published mainly by university academic units (Delgado 2010, 2014, 2015; Delgado-Troncoso and Fischman 2014). Therefore, the internationalization criteria were considered appropriate to explore international collaborations for this chapter.

This section analyzes internationalization of journals included in the Paraguayan and Bolivian chapters of SciELO through the composition of their governing and/or advisory bodies. Each journal has a unique management structure. First, there are different names for the bodies that govern and/or advise journals: council, committee, or board. Second, some journals distinguish between national and international or institutional and external collaborators. In addition, journals may have one or more bodies and call them editorial, scientific, or advisory. Since there is not a description of the roles of the members of each body, the analysis focuses only on the country of origin and/or institutional affiliation.

Internationalization of SciELO Bolivian Journals: Editorial and Scientific Boards

SciELO Bolivia is led by UMSA, the Program for Strategic Research in Bolivia, UCBSP, the Bolivian Association of Biomedical Journal Editors, and the Vice Ministry of Science and Technology. On 18 December 2015,

SciELO Bolivia had 16 active journals. One of them appeared as inactive, but its collection was up to date (Table 7.1) (SciELO Bolivia 2015).

International collaboration in editorial/scientific boards/committees varies among the 16 journals of SciELO Bolivia. Four journals do not list in their websites member affiliation/country of their editorial/scientific boards (*Revista Científica Ciencia Médica, Revista de la Sociedad Boliviana de Pediatría, Revista Médica La Paz,* and *T'inkazos*). One journal only has Bolivian members (*Gaceta Médica Boliviana*). Eight journals have board members from a combination of Latin American (Argentina, Brazil, Mexico, Chile, Peru, Ecuador, and Cuba), North American (US), European (Spain, Italy, France, UK, Germany, Belgium, and Sweden), and/or Asian (Japan) countries. The countries with the highest representation in SciELO Bolivia journal boards are Argentina, Spain, and the US. One journal, *Revista Integra Educativa,* only has board members from the Latin American and Caribbean Pedagogical Institute (Cuba), while two journals only have members from outside Latin America. They are the law journal *Iuris Tantum* with members from the Autonomous University Gabriel René Moreno (UAGRM: *Universidad Autónoma Gabriel René Moreno*) and Santa Cruz de la Sierra Private University (Bolivia) and the University of Valencia (Spain). The other journal is *Revista Ciencia y Cultura* whose collaborators are from the US (Loyola University New Orleans and University of Michigan) and Japan (National Museum of Entomology) (SciELO Bolivia 2015).

An interesting case of international collaboration is *Revista Latinoamericana de Desarrollo Económico*. This journal was co-founded by a group of organizations that includes UCBSP, the Bolivian Academy of Economic Sciences (ABCE: *Academia Boliviana de Ciencias Económicas*), the German Society for International Cooperation (*Deutsche Gesellschaft für Internationale Zusammenarbeit*), the US Agency for international Development (USAID), the World Council of Credit Unions, the Kiel Institute for the World Economy (Germany), the KFW Bank for Development (Germany), and the Development Bank of Latin America (CAF, former *Corporación Andina de Fomento*). This journal has an editorial committee with five members from UCBSP (two), ABCE (one), the University of Chile (one), and the London Metropolitan University (one). There is also an international editorial board with 21 members from organizations and universities from Belgium, Bolivia, Chile, Ecuador, England, Germany, and the US (SciELO Bolivia 2015).

152   J. E. DELGADO

Table 7.1   Journals in SciELO Bolivia, December 2015

Journal title	Publisher	City	Field	Year created
Ecología en Bolivia Revista del Instituto de Ecología	UMSA, Institute for Ecology	La Paz	Ecology	1982
Gaceta Médica Boliviana	UMSS, School of Medicine	Cochabamba	Medicine, medical specialties	1943
Iuris Tantum. Revista Boliviana de Derecho	Iuris Tantum Foundation	Santa Cruz	Bolivian law	2011
Journal of the Selva Andina Research Society	Selva Andina Research Society, Department of Biochemical and Microbiological Teaching and Research; UCBSP; and Peasant Carmen Pampa Academic Unit Foundation	La Paz	Entomology, basic and environmental microbiology, parasitology, biochemistry, nutrition, biotechnology, phytochemistry, and public health	2008
Punto Cero	UCBSP, Social Communication Sciences Undergraduate Program	Cochabamba	Communication and culture	1994
Revista Boliviana de Física	UMSA, Physics Research Institute; Bolivian Society of Physics	La Paz	Physics	1995
Revista Boliviana de Química	UMSA, Institute for Chemical Research	La Paz	Chemistry	1977
Revista Ciencia y Cultura	UCBSP	La Paz	Culture, science, and art in Bolivia	1997
Revista Científica Ciencia Médica	UMSS, School of Medicine	Cochabamba	Health sciences, medical specialties	1998
Revista de la Sociedad Boliviana de Pediatría	Bolivian Society of Pediatrics	Sucre	Pediatric medicine	1977
Revista Integra Educativa	International Institute for Integration of the Andres Bello Agreement (Instituto Internacional de Integración del Convenio Andrés Bello)	La Paz	Education	2008

(*continued*)

SMALL FISH IN A BIG POND: INTERNATIONALIZATION AND RESEARCH...   153

Table 7.1   (continued)

Journal title	Publisher	City	Field	Year created
Revista Latinoamericana de Desarrollo Económico	UCBSP, Institute for Socioeconomic Research	La Paz	Economics	2003
Revista Médica La Paz (formerly, Archivos del Hospital La Paz)	Medical College of La Paz	La Paz	Medicine	1994
Revista Perspectivas	UCBSP, Department of Business, Economics, and Finance (Regional Academic Unit of Cochabamba)	Cochabamba	Business and economics	1990
T'inkazos. Revista Boliviana de Ciencias Sociales	Foundation for Strategic Research in Bolivia (Fundación para la Investigación Estratégica en Bolivia)	La Paz	Social sciences and humanities	1998
Ajayu. Órgano de Difusión Científica del Departamento de Psicología UCBSP	UCBSP, Department of Psychology	La Paz	Psychology	2002

Internationalization of SciELO Paraguayan Journals

SciELO Paraguay is managed by the Institute for Health Science Research of UNA. The Paraguayan collection in SciELO is newer and less developed than its Bolivian counterpart. On 23 December 2015, SciELO Paraguay had eight active and two inactive journals (SciELO Paraguay 2015) Table 7.2 includes the active journals.

Among the eight journals in the Paraguayan collection of SciELO, one publication, *Anales de la Facultad de Ciencias Médicas*, has the explicit goal of publishing UNA faculty and students' research. This means that the primary intention is not to pursue external/international leadership or content. The editorial council of this journal, however, consists of 15 members, 11 from UNA and 4 from other Paraguayan institutions. In this case, there is collaboration external to the institution but at the local level (SciELO Paraguay 2015).

154   J. E. DELGADO

Table 7.2   Journals in SciELO Paraguay, December 2015

Journal title	Publisher	City	Field	Year created
Anales de la Facultad de Ciencias Médicas	UNA, School of Medical Sciences	Asunción	Medical sciences (emphasis on medicine and surgery, medical instrumentation, kinesiology and physical therapy, and nursing)	1968
Cirugía Paraguaya	Paraguayan Surgery Society	Asunción	Surgery	1977
Compendio de Ciencias Veterinarias	UNA, School of Veterinary Sciences	San Lorenzo	Veterinary sciences	2005
Del Nacional	National Hospital of Itauguá	Itauguá	Public health	2009
Investigación Agraria	UNA, School of Agricultural Sciences	San Lorenzo	Agriculture and forests	1996
Memorias del Instituto de Investigaciones en Ciencias de la Salud	UNA, Institute for Research in the Health Sciences	San Lorenzo	Health	2005
Pediatría	Paraguayan Society of Pediatrics	Asunción	Pediatrics	1971
Revista Internacional de Investigación en Ciencias Sociales	UAA	Asunción	Education, business, law, communication, and sociology	2005

The other seven journals had members from Latin American countries (Argentina, Chile, Mexico, Uruguay, Brazil, Colombia, Venezuela, and Costa Rica) in their editorial/scientific committees/boards. Only three journals, *Cirugía Paraguaya*, *Compendio de Ciencias Veterinarias*, and *Revista Internacional de Investigación en Ciencias Sociales*, had board members beyond Latin America, from Spain. *Cirugía Paraguaya* also had a board member from France. The countries more represented among these journals were Argentina, Chile, Spain, and Mexico (SciELO Paraguay 2015).

When comparing journals from Bolivia and Paraguay in SciELO, it is interesting to notice that Bolivian journals are more developed than Paraguayans regarding exogamy and international affiliations of their editorial/scientific board/committee members. Those affiliations could be related to institutions overseas where faculty, editors, and/or university authorities studied or where citizens from these countries study and/or work. On the other side, it cannot be inferred from this description the actual function that those board memberships have within the journals. Therefore, other factors should be considered when analyzing the amount and quality of international collaboration.

INTERNATIONAL CO-AUTHORSHIP

Another strategy used to find experiences or examples of international collaboration between researchers from Bolivian/Paraguayan HEIs and researchers from other organizations abroad was the identification of co-authorships among journal articles. With that aim, the tables of content of all the issues published in 2014 and 2015 by Paraguayan and Bolivian journals in the SciELO collections were reviewed. During the time data were collected for this chapter, there was not a Paraguayan chapter in RedALyC and the Bolivian journals in RedALyC were also included in SciELO. Thus, it was decided to work only with data from SciELO, even though RedALyC has a feature that shows international co-authorship by country.

International Co-authorship in Bolivian SciELO Journals

Of the 16 active journals published in SciELO Bolivia by January 2016, six included articles that suggested international co-authorship: *Ecología en Bolivia, Punto Cero, Revista Boliviana de Física, Revista de la Sociedad Boliviana de Pediatría, Revista Latinoamericana de Desarrollo Económico,* and *Ajayu*. The latter five journals published one or two articles with international co-authorship in the period analyzed. Among those journals, Bolivian researchers represented institutions like UCBSP, UMSA, and the Bolivian Private University (UPB: *Universidad Privada Boliviana*). On the other side, international authors were affiliated to institutions such as the University of Tarapacá (Chile), the University of Chile, Catholic University of Maule (Chile), Simon Bolivar University (Venezuela), the Centre for Environmental Epidemiology Research (Spain), and the University of Granada (Spain).

The case of *Ecología en Bolivia. Revista del Instituto de Ecología* was productive because it published ten articles between 2014 and 2015 that show international collaborations. Most of those articles indicate the existence of a consolidated international research group working in the field of environmental studies. These findings were useful to identify a project that is described in detail in the next section of this chapter.

Another inter-institutional study in the field of environmental studies was published in volume 26 of *Revista Boliviana de Física*, in 2015. The title is "Set to Work of a new Climate Monitoring Station in the Central Andes of Bolivia: The Gaw/Chacaltaya Station." The authors of this article are affiliated to the following institutions: UMSA, *Laboratoire de Glaciologie et Geophysique de l'Environnement* (France), *Observatoire des Sciences de l'Univers* (France), *Laboratoire de Météorologie Physique* (France), *Laboratoire des Sciences du Climat et de l'Environnement* (France), *Leibniz Institute for Tropospheric Research* (Germany), *Stockholm University* (Sweden), Institute of Atmospheric Sciences and Climate (Italy), National Aeronautics and Space Administration (US), IRD, and *Institut Pierre Simon Laplace* (France). In addition, other two inter-institutional environmental studies were published in volume 22 of *Revista Latinoamericana de Desarrollo Económico* in 2014. The titles are "Environmental and Socio-Economic Consequences of Forest Carbon Payments in Bolivia: Results of the OSIRIS-Bolivia Model" and "Social Impact of Climate Change in Bolivia: A Municipal-Level Analysis of the Effects of Climate Change on Life Expectancy, Consumption, and Inequality." The authors of both articles represent UPB, the Bolivian Institute for Advanced Studies in Development, the Bolivian office of the NGO Conservation International, the Center for Global Development (US), the University of California San Diego (US), and the Inter-American Development Bank.

International Co-authorship in Paraguayan SciELO Journals

In the case of Paraguay, the strategy to look for international research collaborations using journals published in SciELO did not give the same result as Bolivia. Among the eight journals of SciELO Paraguay only three published articles with international co-authorship. *Compendio de Ciencias Veterinarias* published in 2014 (volume 4) the article titled "Using Statistical Correlation for the Morphometric Study of Beef Cattle: Case Pampa Chaqueño," whose authors were affiliated to UNA and the Federal University of Paraiba (Brazil). *Investigación Agraria* published in 2014 (volume 16) two articles with international co-authorship. The first one was "Pyriproxyfen and Diflubenzuron Effects on the Reproduction of *Nezara viridula* (L.) [Hemiptera: Pentatomidae]" with authors from the State University of Londrina (Brazil) and UNA. The second article was "Water Erosion and Loss of Sediment, Water and Chemical Elements during Rainfall Events in two Rural Watersheds," whose authors were affiliated to UNA, the Federal University of Parana (Brazil), the Federal University of Santa Maria (Brazil), and the Federal Technological University of Parana (Brazil). In volume 17 of 2015, there was an article, "Effect of Different Temperatures on Physiological Quality of Sesame Seeds," whose authors belonged to the National Institute for Forestry, Agriculture, and Livestock Research (Mexico) and UNA. There were also two articles with international co-authorship published by *Memorias del Instituto de Investigaciones en Ciencias de la Salud*: "Abnormal Atrial Endocardial Electrograms in Aging Patients with Idiopathic Paroxysmal Atrial Fibrillation" (2014) with authors from UNA and the Nagasaki University School of Medicine (Japan); and "Enteroparasites Frequency in Children of the First Cycle of Basic Education Of Public Schools in Ciudad del Este, Paraguay" (2015), whose authors were affiliated to the National University of the East, Catholic University of Our lady of Asuncion, and State University of Western Parana (Brazil).

As it can be noticed, there were not trends regarding institutions or topics among Paraguayan journals in SciELO suggestive of international collaboration initiatives. The only observations were that the collaborations came from the fields of biology and health, and mainly with researchers in Latin American institutions. The strategy to find international initiatives focused on biology studies. The search in databases showed some results in zoology, which are represented in the case described in the next section.

CASES OF INNOVATION THROUGH INTERNATIONAL COLLABORATION

This section depicts some cases of international collaboration involving researchers and/or HEIs from Bolivia and Paraguay and those from other countries in Latin America or other continents. The cases cover different disciplines and show different types of collaborations.

Bolivian Think Tank Ciudadanía *(Citizenship): Political Analysis, Public Opinion, and Human Development*

Ciudadanía, Social Studies and Public Action Community, is a not-for-profit research center located in Cochabamba, Bolivia. *Ciudadanía* was founded in 2004 with the goal of generating socially relevant knowledge and promoting dialogue and social action to improve the quality of life of communities that suffer from any type of exclusion (Ciudadanía, Constitution 2015b). Projects include public opinion analysis, public action, and promotion of citizenship. Its founder and director is a political scientist who works with a pool of scholars/researchers and collaborates with partner institutions region wide and beyond.

Ciudadanía is a partner of the Latin American Public Opinion Project (LAPOP), a consortium of academic institutions originated at Vanderbilt University from the US with the purpose of conducting public opinion surveys throughout the Americas. One of LAPOP's projects, the *AmericasBarometer* survey, covers 28 countries and analyzes individual attitudes, evaluations, and experiences (Latin American Public Opinion Project—LAPOP, Home 2015b). International donors and partners of LAPOP include USAID, the Inter-American Development Bank, the National Council for Scientific and Technological Development (CNPq) of Brazil, Princeton University from the US, the Swedish International Development Cooperation Agency, Laval University and York University from Canada, and Kellogg Institute for International Studies (LAPOP, Donors and Partners 2015a), but the national surveys are basically funded locally. Another NGO, the Information and Resource Center for Development, is the partner of LAPOP in Paraguay (LAPOP, Country Partners 2015c).

Besides LAPOP, *Ciudadanía* works in collaboration with several Bolivian, Latin American, and international organizations. Bolivian partners consist of the University Center for Higher Studies at UMSS, Coordination of Women (*Coordinadora de la Mujer*—for women rights), the Program for Strategic Research in Bolivia (PIEB: *Programa de Investigación Estratégica en Bolivia*), the Bolivian Center for Multidisciplinary Research (CEBEM: *Centro Boliviano de Investigación Multidisciplinaria*), the Center for Studies on Economic and Social Reality (CERES: *Centro de Estudios de la Realidad Económica y Social*), and the news outlet *Los Tiempos* (http://www.lostiempos.com/) (Coordination of Women 2015; CEBEM 2016; CERES 2016; PIEB 2016). *Ciudadanía* has a partner in Latin America, the Peruvian NGO Manuela Ramos that focuses on women rights (Manuela Ramos 2015).

International partnerships involve organizations in a combination and wide range of fields such as family farming and microfinance (Belgian NGO Sos Faim), women rights (Netherlands/Canadian *Conexión Fondo de Emancipación*, Danish *Alianza Libres sin Violencia*), human rights, housing advocacy, and rural development (Swedish We Effect), natural resources and environment (Helvetas Swiss Intercooperation), democratic participation (Swedish *Institute for Democracy and Electoral Assistance—IDEA*), and sustainable development (United Nations Development Program—UNDP) (Alliance Free from Violence 2015; Connection Emancipation Fund 2015; Helvetas Bolivia 2016; IDEA 2016; Sos Faim 2015; UNDP 2016; We Effect 2016).

Another area in which *Ciudadanía* has been involved in collaborations is the publication of books and didactic and research material. The think tank has published some of them locally with the UMSS and other with CERES and Los Tiempos. Recent publications are *Migration and Citizenship in Bolivia in the Latin American Context, State of the Question* (Roman 2012), *Cochabamba: Equality, Identity, and Citizenship* (Vargas Villazón 2015), *Studies in the Metropolitan Axis* (Laserna 2015), *Cochabamba: Politics, Rights, and Daily Life* (Laserna 2014), and *Living in the Cities. Experiences and Perceptions in the Bolivian Metropolitan Axis* (Moreno Moreno 2016). There are also some publications with international partners, such as, *Political Participation and Leadership of Indigenous Women in Latin America. Case Study: Bolivia* with UNDP (Roman 2008) and the learning guide *The Secret of Co-Responsible Care* with We Effect (Ciudadanía and We Effect 2015).

Ciudadanía has served as an incubator of innovation. In 2011, it became a for-profit enterprise. Its director conceptually developed a software called Android Data Gathering System (Adgys) to conduct individual public opinion surveys and analyses (Ciudadanía, Adgys System 2015a). Adgys is commercialized as a private initiative and has been used in Mexico, Paraguay, and Central American countries. Adgys helps reduce surveying costs, employs a geographic information system (neighborhood, block, and home), applies randomized sampling, and allows differentiating between good and bad samples.

In short, *Ciudadanía* is an example of organization that serves as an articulator of a network of government, not-for-profit and for-profit national and international partners. Even though not-for-profit organizations are among *Ciudadanía*'s main allies, local and international universities, particularly research centers, are key partners of this think tank: The University Center for higher Studies at UMSS, CEBEM, and CERES at the national level, as well as Vanderbilt University and the Institute of Latin American Studies of Stockholm University internationally. Their participation focuses on the different areas of study that *Ciudadanía* carries out.

BIO-ICE and BIO-THAW: Biodiversity and Ecosystems in Bolivian Tropical Andean Highlands

The UMSA Institute of Ecology works in collaboration with the IRD to study the patterns of distribution of plants and invertebrates in the high tropical Andes to understand the impact of environmental changes (acceleration of glacial retreat) on biodiversity (Quenta et al. 2016). The responses of species and communities of organisms to those changes have been almost unknown. The BIO-ICE (Biodiversity in Bolivian Glaciers) program started in 2012 and includes sites in the regions of Tuni Condoriri, Sajama, and Apolobamba. Besides UNSA and IRD, BIO-ICE counts with the participation of researchers from other universities such as Copenhagen, Bordeaux, UMSS, and UAGRM (IRD 2016a).

A central pillar of BIO-ICE is the study of colonization of newly deglazed surfaces in sites located in Charquini, Zongo, and Chacaltaya. A specific BIO-ICE program is BIO-THAW (Tropical High Andean Wetlands), which measures the consequences of glacial melting on the functioning of high-altitude wetlands (*bofedales*) in terms of biodiversity and productivity for livestock (indicators: flow, chemical properties, turbidity, and temperature). In the study of responses of invertebrates and plants in alpine tropical environments, the program looks at the creation of organic soils, which will initiate the plant succession and the development of microfauna and macrofauna of the soil, and have a stabilizing role for the entire ecosystem, to regulate water resources. At the same time, the project gradually implements in situ experimental manipulations to test the effect of a limited number of environmental variables on the dynamics of biodiversity. In short, BIO-THAW studies glacier changes and water run-off inputs to wetlands, biodiversity, and land management practices. The BIO-THAW program also takes place in Ecuador (IRD 2016a, b).

BIO-THAW is a multidisciplinary project that involves scientists (anthropologists, sociologists, glaciologists, ecologists, experts in agent-based modeling), resource managers, NGOs (such as ALTAGRO and PROINPA),[1] and indigenous communities. In 2013, more than 53 reports and articles (in Bolivian and international journals) were published because of studies carried out within the BIO-THAW program (IRD 2016b).

Inter-institutional Research Collaboration on Fauna in Paraguay

Paraguay is considered a highly biodiverse country. Research on Paraguayan fauna (mammals, birds, fish, insects, reptiles, and amphibians) seeks to create detailed inventories of existing species and advocate for their conservation. The content of inventories is made available to the public through repositories of publications, documentaries, images, and sounds. The main repository is called *Fauna Paraguay*[2] and is published by the National Museum of Natural History of Paraguay (NMNHP), which is affiliated to the Secretary of Environment of Paraguay (2016). *Fauna Paraguay* is part of the National Biological Inventory and includes reports since 1981. Besides the NMNHP, other national and international organizations work in collaboration on fauna studies. They include NGOs such as *Guyra Paraguay*[3] (2017) and *Para La Tierra*[4] (2017); other government agencies like CONACYT's Institute for Biological Research; national and international HEIs like UNA (Biology Department), the University of New Mexico, and Texas A&M University (Department of Wildlife and Fisheries Sciences); and international agencies such as the Smithsonian Institute and the World-Wide Fund for Nature (Cabral and Weiler 2014; Cacciali et al. 2013; Motte et al. 2009).

Among the several publications on Paraguayan amphibians and reptiles, there is an extensive special report that well exemplifies the result of collaborations between actors from Paraguayan and international institutions. The report is titled, "The Reptiles of Paraguay: Literature, Distribution, and an Annotated Taxonomic Checklist," and was published by the Museum of Southwestern Biology of the University of New Mexico in June 2016. Well-known experts representing some of the organizations mentioned above co-author the report (Cacciali et al. 2016). Interesting to emphasize here is how collaborations involve universities but also other types of organizations like NGOs.

UNA: International Collaborations in Higher Education and Research

As it was indicated before, UNA is the main university of Paraguay. This multi-campus institution has campuses/locations in 21 cities, 12 schools (law and social sciences, medicine, engineering, economics, dentistry, chemistry, philosophy, agriculture, veterinary medicine, architecture, design and art, polytechnic, and natural sciences), three institutes (Dr. Andrés Barbero, Social Work, and Health Sciences Research), a business incubator, and an experimental high school. In 2013, UNA's total student enrollment was 50,048, of which 228 were doctoral students. The total graduate enrollment was 3055. UNA offers 267 academic programs, of which 12 are doctoral programs, 68 masters, and 92 specializations (mainly in education—43.5 percent, followed by social sciences and law, health sciences and social services, engineering and construction, services, agriculture, natural sciences, and the humanities). UNA allocates 5 percent of its annual budget (US$263 million) to research. Of UNA's 8369 faculty members, 61 (0.73 percent) are full-time researchers/professors. A search through UNA's website showed a list of 16 international academic networks in which the university participates, as well as 79 national and 113 international collaboration agreements signed with other institutions (UNA, President Office, Planning and Development Department 2014b, c). A search for details of the characteristics and achievements of those agreements only showed a few results. Most of those agreements were carried out with other South American institutions and focus on the development of education and research capacities (UNA n.d.).

One of the institutes, Dr. Andrés Barbero's of health sciences (nursing and obstetrics), enumerated several agreements with other UNA academic units, national organizations, government agencies, and international universities. In one of the projects, UNA partnered with the San Martin de Porres University from Peru to design a competency-based curriculum in gynecology and obstetrics. Another project is a research agreement with the University of Chile's School of Medicine to develop research capacity and evaluate midwifery services (UNA n.d.). Another institute, UNA's Health Science Research Institute (2012), has also signed several agreements with institutions within the South American region. They are about general collaborations between UNA and the National University of Northeastern Argentina and the University of Sao Paulo (academic mobility of students and faculty). Those agreements include collaborations in teaching, research, and service, but there is no mention of specific projects developed under the terms of those agreements. In addition, a UNA report indicates that the university participated in a study on information and communication technologies titled, "Long-Distance Teaching among Iberic-American Universities: Basic Characteristics of the Teaching-Learning Process – Learning and Use of Information and Communication Technologies (ICTs)" [*"La Enseñanza a distancia en universidades iberoamericanas: características básicas del proceso enseñanza – aprendizaje y la utilización de las tecnologías de información y comunicación (TIC)"*]. This study is carried out by a researcher from the State University of the Grand River of the South from Brazil. The purpose was to describe the perception of students and professors from Spain, Brazil, Paraguay, and Portugal about the teaching-learning processes in different fields regarding distance education and ICTs. 235 participants from UNA responded an electronic survey. It is unclear what the role of the university was beyond taking the survey (UNA, President Office, Planning and Development Department 2014a). Even though the agreements retrieved from UNA's websites do not involve specific and innovative research projects, it is interesting how international collaboration takes place between South American institutions.

DISCUSSION AND RECOMMENDATIONS

The chapter argues that even though capacity, size of research, and research outcomes in Bolivia and Paraguay are minor, there are some initiatives through international collaboration that show some progress and promising accomplishments. However, more efforts at the government level are necessary to create the conditions to develop research, promote economic development, and use international collaboration to achieve these objectives. Even though general demographic, economic, higher education, and STI indicators of both countries, as well as their share and contribution to Latin America science seem to be similar, there are differences that show more development of Bolivian research than of Paraguayan. This was observed in the number of universities included in international rankings, the characteristics of SciELO and RedALyC collections (there was not a Paraguayan chapter in RedALyC by the time data were collected for this project), and the composition of editorial/scientific boards and international collaboration as evidenced by co-authorships in SciELO journal articles. In addition, finding exemplary cases of international collaboration was challenging for both countries, but, in the end, the quality of Bolivian cases was higher than that of Paraguayan.

The goal of this book is to present case studies of North-South university research partnerships in Latin America and the Caribbean to illustrate how collaborative efforts have produced significant knowledge transfer (in both directions), increased research productivity and scope, and contributed to the strengthening of the participating institutions. An interesting initial observation is that two cases portrayed in this chapter show collaborations in which the main actor is not a university but an NGO (*Ciudadanía* in Bolivia) or a decentralized government institute (the NMNHP). There was also a clear partnership between an international research center (IRD from France) and a Bolivian University (UMSA, Institute of Ecology). A second observation is that participants in these projects included university professors/researchers, as well as actors representing research centers, international cooperation/assistance agencies, international organizations, national government agencies and institutions, NGOs, and community organizations. One of the cases, BIO-ICE/BIO-THAW, is a multinational project with sites in Bolivia and Ecuador.

Three of the projects had products that were transferred to society. First, *Ciudadanía* developed software that originated a spin-off that sells services to conduct public opinion surveys throughout Latin America. Second, BIO-ICE/BIO-THAW serves as a monitor of climate change and documents land management practices in the high Andes. The results of this partnership include several journals articles. Third, in the case of research on Paraguayan fauna, there are two examples of knowledge transfer. One is the repository *Fauna Paraguay* that makes content (documents, images, and sounds) available to all audiences through a website. The other one is the report published by the University of New Mexico in collaboration with the NMNHP and other institutions.

Regarding the geography of collaborations, *Ciudadanía*, BIO-ICE/BIO-THAW, and the research on Paraguayan fauna show North-South and even North-South-South collaborations. However, it is interesting to note that collaborations listed by UNA's Dr. Andrés Barbero and Health Sciences Research Institutes (2012) are predominantly South-South. Moreover, the emphasis of these collaborations was less research than education administration (curriculum development, student/faculty mobility, and program/service evaluation).

Information about the Bolivian and Paraguayan journals was collected mainly from SciELO. The analysis of the composition of editorial/scientific boards/committees showed internationalization. This could be expected since the inclusion of journals in the regional and more global bibliographic information services and indexes requires such internationalization, which is usually referred as exogamy. However, the actual work or contribution of international members to journal boards and committees cannot be determined from the analysis conducted here. They could just be reflective of internationalization on paper, so further study would be necessary to clarify this. The analysis of co-authorship in journal articles showed more interesting results. It allowed for the identification of the BIO-ICE/BIO-THAW program in Bolivia and even other multi-institutional collaborations.

Even though research productivity of Bolivia and Paraguay is minor in the global and the Latin American contexts, it was interesting to find more development in Bolivia than in Paraguay. This was evident in the institutions included in the university rankings analyzed and those where SciELO journals are published. Bolivian universities included UMSA, UMSS, and UCBSP, among others, while Paraguay was basically represented by UNA. The case of UNA is understandable since this was the only university in the country until 1960 when the Catholic University was founded. The main focus of UNA has traditionally been teaching over research (Cummings et al. 1993; Fogel 1994; Ministry of Education and Culture of Paraguay 1998).

In conclusion, the analysis of the composition of scientific/editorial boards/committees of Bolivian and Paraguayan journals and co-authorships of articles published in Bolivian and Paraguayan journals in SciELO was useful to identify examples of international collaborations. Those strategies plus networking and website reviews allowed for identifying some interesting experiences of North-South and even South-South collaborations that involved actors from different types of organizations and institutions. Likewise, other studies on international collaborations through publications should include the challenges and decisions to publish in English, Spanish, and/or Portuguese. It was interesting also to see how some of the cases portrayed have generated knowledge that has been transferred to society. Bolivia seems to be more developed than Paraguay regarding research productivity and collaborations, but this observation requires further study. Finally, both countries need to increase funding and support for research, probably targeting specific areas, to have greater impact on their national societies, the region, and the world.

Acknowledgments The author is grateful to Daniel Moreno, founder and director of the think tank *Ciudadanía*, for conceding an interview; Jill Perry, education professor at the University of Pittsburgh for sharing her contacts and books on Paraguay; Gustavo Gregorutti and Nanette Svenson, editors of this book for their feedback and patience.

166   J. E. DELGADO

NOTES

1. Agriculture Alternative (Anternativas Agropecuarias, ALTAGRO) and Andean Products Promotion and Research Foundation (Fundación Promoción e Investigación de Productos Andinos, Bolivia, PROINPA).
2. For information, see http://www.faunaparaguay.com/updates.html
3. More information available at: http://guyra.org.py
4. More information available at: http://www.paralatierra.org

REFERENCES

Aguado, L. E., Salazar, R. R., Oropeza, G. G., & Zúñiga, M. F. (2008). Redalyc: una Alternativa a las Asimetrías en la Distribución del Conocimiento Científico [RedALyC: An Alternative to Scientific Knowledge Distribution Asymmetries]. *Ciencia, Docencia y Tecnología, XIX*(37), 11–30.

Aguirre-Bastos, C., & Gupta, M. P. (2009). Science, Technology and Innovation Policies in Latin America: ¿Do They Work? *Interciencia, 34*(12), 865–872.

Alliance Free from Violence [Alianza Libres sin Violencia]. (2015). *Who Are We?* [*¿Quiénes somos?*]. La Paz: Alianza Libres sin Violencia. Available at: http://alianzalibressinviolencia.org/

Alperín, J. P., Fischman, G., & Willinsky, J. (2011). Scholarly Communication Strategies in Latin America's Research-Intensive Universities. *Liinc em Revista, 4*(2), 172–185. Available at: http://www.ibict.br/liinc

Bolivia, H. (2016). *Quienes somos* [*Who Are We*]. La Paz: Helvetas Swiss Intercooperation. Available at: https://bolivia.helvetas.org/helvetas_bolivia/

Bolivian Center for Multidisciplinary Research [CEBEM: Centro Boliviano de Investigación Multidisciplinaria]. (2016). *Who Are We?* [*¿Quiénes somos?*]. La Paz: CEBEM. Available at: http://cebem.org/?page_id=614

Cabral, H., & Weiler, A. (2014, May). Commented List of Reptiles from the Zoological Collection of the School of Natural and Exact Sciences of Asunción, Paraguay [Lista comentada de los reptiles de la Colección Zoológica de la Facultad de Ciencias Exactas y Naturales de Asunción, Paraguay]. *Cuadernos de Herpetología, 28*(1), 19–28.

Cacciali, P., Smith, P., Källberg, A., Pheasey, H., & Atkinson, K. (2013). Reptilia, Squamata, Serpentes, *Lygophis Paucidens* Hoge, 1052: First Records for Paraguay. *Check List, 9*(1), 131–132. Available at: http://www.checklist.org. br/getpdf?NGD201-12

Cacciali, P., Scott, N. J., Ortiz, A. L. A., Fitzgerald, L. A., & Smith, P. (2016, June 25). *The Reptiles of Paraguay: Literature, Distribution, and an Annotated Taxonomic Checklist.* Special Report No. 11. Albuquerque: University of New Mexico, Museum of Southwestern Biology.

Center for Studies on Economic and Social Reality [CERES: Centro de Estudios de la Realidad Económica y Social]. (2016). *Institutional Information [Infor. Institucional]*. Cochabamba: CERES. Available at: http://www.ceresbolivia. org/informacion-institucional-2

Cetto, A. M., Gamboa, J. O. A., & González, S. C. (2010). Ibero-American Systems for the Dissemination of Scholarly Journals: A Contribution to Public Knowledge Worldwide. *Scholarly and Research Communication 1*(1) 010104. Available at: http://www.src-online.ca/index.php/src/issue/current

Ciudadanía. (2015a). *Adgys System (Sistema Adgys)*. Cochabamba: Ciudadanía. Available online at: http://www.ciudadaniabolivia.org/es/node/334

Ciudadanía. (2015b). *Constitution (Constitución)*. Cochabamba: Ciudadanía. Available online at: http://ciudadaniabolivia.org/es/node/113

Ciudadanía, We Effect. (2015). *The Secret of Co-responsible Care* [El Secreto del Cuidado Corresponsable]. Learning Guide. Cochabamba: Ciudadanía, We Effect. Available at: http://www.ciudadaniabolivia.org/es/node/598

Connection Emancipation Fund [Conexión Fondo de Emancipación]. (2015). *Who Are We? [¿Quiénes somos?]*. La Paz: Conexión Fondo de Emancipación. Available at: http://www.conexion.org.bo/seccion/Quines-Somos-.html

Coordination of Women [Coordinadora de la Mujer]. (2015). *Who Are We? [¿Quiénes somos?]*. La Paz: Coordinadora de la Mujer. Available at: http://www.coordinadoradelamujer.org.bo/web/index.php/qsomos/mostrar/id/1

Cummings, W., Galeano, L., & Rivelli, D. (1993). Higher Education [Educación Superior]. In F. Reimers (Ed.), *Analysis of the Education System in Paraguay. Policy Recommendations and Strategies for Reform [Análisis del Sistema Educativo en el Paraguay. Sugerencias de política and estrategia para su reforma]* (pp. 245–304). Asunción: Harvard institute for International Development/ Centro Paraguayo de Estudios Sociológicos.

Delgado, J. E. (2010). Trends in the Publication of Refereed Journals in Spanish- and Portuguese-Speaking Latin America. *Comparative & International Higher Education, 2*, 43–49.

Delgado, J. E. (2011). University Research in Latin America and the United States: Evolution, Roles, and Challenges. *International Studies in Education, 12*, 76–91.

Delgado, J. E. (2014). Scientific Journals of Universities of Chile, Colombia, and Venezuela: Actors and Roles. *Education Policy Analysis Archives, 22*(34). https://doi.org/10.14507/epaa.v22n34.2014.

Delgado, J. E. (2015). Latin American Private Universities in the Context of Competition and Research Productivity. In G. Gregorutti & J. E. Delgado (Eds.), *Private Universities in Latin America: Research and Innovation in the Knowledge Economy* (pp. 27–49). New York: Palgrave Macmillan.

Delgado, J. E., & Weidman, J. C. (2012). Latin American and Caribbean Countries in the Global Quest for World Class Academic Recognition: An Analysis of

168   J. E. DELGADO

Publications in Scopus and the Science Citation Index Between 1990 and 2010. *Excellence in Higher Education, 3,* 111–121. https://doi.org/10.5195/ehe.2012.73.

Delgado Troncoso, J. (2011). Role of Open Access in the Emergence and Consolidation of Refereed Journals in Latin America and the Caribbean. *Revista Educación Superior y Sociedad (UNESCO-IESALC), 16*(2).

Delgado-Troncoso, J. E., & Fischman, G. E. (2014). The Future of Latin American Academic Journals. In B. Cope & A. Phillips (Eds.), *The Future of the Academic Journal* (2nd ed., pp. 370–400). Oxford: Chandos.

Fogel, R. (1994). *Science and Technology in Paraguay. Socio-Environmental Impact [La ciencia y la tecnología en Paraguay. Su impacto socio-ambiental].* Asunción: Centro de Estudios Rurales Interdisciplinarios.

García Riart, J. (2013). Institutional Configuration of the Paraguayan Higher Education System [Configuración Institucional del Sistema de Educación Superior Paraguayo]. In M. Rivarola (Ed.), *University Higher Education and Its Regulatory Framework [Educación Superior Universitaria y su Marco Regulatorio]* (pp. 8–23). Asunción: USAID, Semillas para la Democracia.

González, P. G. (2012, September 2). Situation and Proposals for Higher Education in Paraguay [Situación y Propuestas para la Educación Superior en Paraguay]. *ABC Color.* Available at: http://www.abc.com.py/edicion-impresa/suplementos/cultural/situacion-y-propuestas-para-la-educacion-superior-en-paraguay-445310.html

Guyra Paraguay. (2017). *Who We Are [Quiénes somos].* Asunción: Guyra Paraguay. Available at: http://guyra.org.py/institucional/quienes-somos/

Iberic-American and Inter-American Network of Science and Technology Indicators (RICYT): [Red de Indicadores de Ciencia y Tecnología—Iberoamericana e Interamericana]. (2013a). *Articles in BIOSIS [Artículos en BIOSIS].* Buenos Aires: RICYT. Available online at: http://db.ricyt.org/query/AR,BB,BO,BR,CL,CO,CR,CU,DO,EC,ES,GT,GY,HN,HT,JM,MX,NI,PA,PE,PT,PY,SV,TT,UY,VE,AL,IB,TL/1990%2C2013/CBIOSIS

Iberic-American and Inter-American Network of Science and Technology Indicators (RICYT). (2013b). *Articles in CAB International [Artículos en CAB Internacional].* Buenos Aires: RICYT. Available online at: http://db.ricyt.org/query/AR,BB,BO,BR,CL,CO,CR,CU,DO,EC,ES,GT,GY,HN,HT,JM,MX,NI,PA,PE,PT,PY,SV,TT,UY,VE,AL,IB,TL/1990%2C2013/CCAB

Iberic-American and Inter-American Network of Science and Technology Indicators (RICYT). (2013c). *Articles in Medline [Artículos en Medline].* Buenos Aires: RICYT. Available online at: http://db.ricyt.org/query/AR,BB,BO,BR,CL,CO,CR,CU,DO,EC,ES,GT,GY,HN,HT,JM,MX,NI,PA,PE,PT,PY,SV,TT,UY,VE,AL,IB,TL/1990%2C2013/CMEDLINE

Iberic-American and Inter-American Network of Science and Technology Indicators (RICYT). (2013d). *Articles in SCI [Artículos en SCI].* Buenos Aires:

SMALL FISH IN A BIG POND: INTERNATIONALIZATION AND RESEARCH... 169

RICYT. Available online at: http://db.ricyt.org/query/AR,BB,BO,BR,CA,CL, CO,CR,CU,DO,EC,ES,GT,GY,HN,HT,JM,MX,NI,PA,PE,PT,PY,SV,TT,US, UY,VE,AL,IB,TL/1990%2C2013/CSCI

Iberic-American and Inter-American Network of Science and Technology Indicators (RICYT). (2013e). *Expenditure on Research and Development as a Percentage of GDP [Gasto en investigación y desarrollo como porcentaje del PIB]*. Buenos Aires: RICYT. Available online at: http://db.ricyt.org/query/AR,BO, BR,CA,CL,CO,CR,CU,EC,ES,GT,HN,JM,MX,NI,PA,PE,PR,PT,PY,SV,TT, US,UY,VE,AL,IB/1990%2C2013/GASTOxPBI

Iberic-American and Inter-American Network of Science and Technology Indicators (RICYT). (2013f). *Gross Domestic Product in Dollars [Producto interno bruto en dólares]*. Buenos Aires: RICYT. Available online at: http:// db.ricyt.org/query/AR,BB,BO,BR,CA,CL,CO,CR,CU,DO,EC,ES,GT,GY, HN,HT,JM,MX,NI,PA,PE,PR,PT,PY,SV,TT,US,UY,VE,AL,IB/1990 %2C2013/PBIUSD

Iberic-American and Inter-American Network of Science and Technology Indicators (RICYT). (2013g). *Patent Applications—Resident and Non-resident [Solicitudes de patentes—residentes y No Residents]*. Buenos Aires: RICYT. Available online at: http://db.ricyt.org/query/AR,BO,BR,CA,CL, CO,CR,CU,DO,EC,ES,GT,HN,HT,JM,MX,NI,PA,PE,PT,PY,SV,TT,US, UY,VE,AL,IB/1990%2C2013/CPATSOL

Iberic-American and Inter-American Network of Science and Technology Indicators (RICYT). (2013h). *Population [Población]*. Buenos Aires: RICYT. Available online at: http://db.ricyt.org/query/AR,BB,BO,BR,CA, CL,CO,CR,CU,DO,EC,ES,GT,GY,HN,HT,JM,MX,NI,PA,PE,PR,PT,PY, SV,TT,US,UY,VE,AL,IB/1990%2C2013/CPOBLA

Iberic-American and Inter-American Network of Science and Technology Indicators (RICYT). (2013i). *Research and Development Expenditure [Gasto en investigación y desarrollo]*. Buenos Aires: RICYT. Available online at: http:// db.ricyt.org/query/AR,BO,BR,CA,CL,CO,CR,CU,EC,ES,GT,HN,JM,MX, NI,PA,PE,PR,PT,PY,SV,TT,US,UY,VE,AL,IB/1990%2C2013/GASTOUSD

Iberic-American and Inter-American Network of Science and Technology Indicators (RICYT). (2013j). *Researchers by Field of Science [Investigadores por campo científico]*. Buenos Aires: RICYT. Available online at: http://db.ricyt. org/query/AR,BO,CL,CO,CR,EC,GT,MX,PA,PT,PY,SV,TT,UY,VE/1990 %2C2013/INVESTPFDISCPER

Iberic-American and Inter-American Network of Science and Technology Indicators (RICYT). (2013k). *Researchers by Highest Qualification Level [Investigadores por más alto nivel de calificación]*. Buenos Aires: RICYT. Available online at: http://db.ricyt.org/query/AR,BO,BR,CL,CO,CR,EC,GT,PA,PT, PY,SV,TT,UY,VE/1990%2C2013/INVESTPFNIVELPE

Iberic-American and Inter-American Network of Science and Technology Indicators (RICYT). (2013l). *Researchers Per 1000 Labor Force [Investigadores por cada 1000 trabajadores]*. Buenos Aires: RICYT. Available online at: http://db.ricyt.org/query/AR,BO,BR,CA,CL,CO,CR,CU,EC,ES,GT,HN,MX,NI,PA,PE,PR,PT,PY,SV,TT,US,UY,VE,AL,IB/1990%2C2013/CINVPEA

Iberic-American and Inter-American Network of Science and Technology Indicators (RICYT). (2013m). *S&T Personnel–Headcount [Personal en C&T—recuento]*. Buenos Aires: RICYT. Available online at: http://db.ricyt.org/query/AR,BO,BR,CL,CO,CR,CU,EC,ES,GT,HN,MX,NI,PA,PE,PR,PT,PY,SV,TT,UY,VE,AL,IB/1990%2C2013/CPERSOPF

Institute for Democracy and Electoral Assistance (IDEA). (2016). *Bolivia: Context*. Stockholm: IDEA. Available at: http://www.idea.int/americas/bolivia/bolivia-context.cfm

Latin American Public Opinion Project (LAPOP). (2015a). *Donors and Partners*. Nashville: Vanderbilt University. Available online at: http://www.vanderbilt.edu/lapop/sustaining-donors.php

LAPOP. (2015b). *Home*. Nashville: Vanderbilt University. Available online at: http://www.vanderbilt.edu/lapop/index.php

LAPOP. (2015c). *Country Partners*. Nashville: Vanderbilt University. Available online at: http://www.vanderbilt.edu/lapop/partners.php

Laserna, R. (Compilator). (2014). *Cochabamba: Politics, Rights, and Daily Life [Cochabamba: Política, Derechos y Vida Cotidiana]*. Cochabamba: Ciudadanía, CERES, Los Tiempos. Available at: http://www.ciudadaniabolivia.org/es/node/422

Laserna, R. (Compilator). (2015). *Studies in the Metropolitan Axis [Estudios en el Eje Metropolitano]*. Cochabamba: Ciudadanía, CERES, Los Tiempos. Available at: http://www.ciudadaniabolivia.org/es/node/453

Meneghini, R., & Packer, A. (2008). Is There Science Beyond English? Initiatives to Increase the Quality and Visibility of Non-English Publications Might Help to Break Down Language Barriers in Scientific Communication. *EMBO Reports 8*(2), 112–116. Available at: https://doi.org/10.1038/sj.embor.7400906.

Ministry of Education and Culture (MEC), Advisory Council for Educational Reform. (1998). *Advances of the Educational Reform. Perspectives, Strategies, and Policies of Paraguayan Education [Avances de la reforma educativa. Perspectivas, estrategias y políticas de la educación paraguaya]*. Asunción: MEC.

Moreno Moreno, D. E. (Compilator). (2016). *Living in the Cities. Experiences and Perceptions in the Bolivian Metropolitan Axis [Vivir en las Ciudades. Experiencas y Percepciones en el eje metropolitano de Bolivia]*. Cochabamba: Ciudadanía, CERES, Los Tiempos. Available at: http://www.ciudadaniabolivia.org/es/node/605

Morínigo Alcaraz, J. N. (2013). University Education in Education System of Paraguay [La Educación Universitaria en el Sistema Educativo del Paraguay] (pp. 24–31). In M. Rivarola (Ed.), *University Higher Education and Its Regulatory Framework* [*Educación Superior Universitaria y su Marco Regulatorio*] (pp. 8–23). Asunción: USAID, Semillas para la Democracia.

Motte, M., Núñez, K., Cacciali, P., Brusquetti, F., Scott, N., & Aquino, A. L. (2009). Categorization of the Conservation Status of Amphibians and Reptiles of Paraguay [Categorización del Estado de Conservación de los Anfibios y Reptiles de Paraguay]. *Cuadernos de Herpetología, 23*(1), 5–18.

National Agency for Higher Education Evaluation and Accreditation [ANEAES: *Agencia Nacional de Evaluación y Acreditación de la Educación Superior*]. (2016). *List of Legally Approved Public and Private Universities* [*Nómina de Universidades del Sector Oficial y Privado con Marco Legal de Aprobación para su Funcionamiento*]. Asunción: ANEAES. Available at: http://www.aneaes.gov.py/aneaes/index.php/ct-menu-item-31

National Museum of Natural History of Paraguay (NMNHP). (2016). *Fauna Paraguay* [Repository]. Asunción: NMNHP. Available at: http://www.faunaparaguay.com

National University of Asunción (UNA). (2012). *Higher Education in Paraguay* [*Educación Superior en Paraguay*]. Asunción: UNA. Available at: http://www.una.py/index.php/unidades-academicas/evaluacion-y-acreditacion/519-educacion-superior-en-paraguay

National University of Asunción (UNA), Health Sciences Research Institute. (2012). *Current Agreements* [*Convenios y acuerdos vigentes*]. Asunción: UNA. Available at: http://www.iics.una.py/index.php?view=article&id=135%3Aconvenios&tmpl=component&print=1&layout=default&page=&option=com_content&Itemid=133

National University of Asuncion (UNA), President Office, Planning and Development Department. (2014a). *Management Report 2004–2013* [*Informe de gestión 2004–2013*]. Asunción: UNA.

National University of Asuncion (UNA), President Office, Planning and Development Department. (2014b). *Paraguay in Numbers. Year 2013* [*Paraguay – en cifras. Año 2013*]. Asunción: UNA.

National University of Asuncion (UNA), President Office, Planning and Development Department. (2014c). *Statistical Yearbook 2013* [*Anuario estadístico 2013*]. Asunción: UNA.

National University of Asunción [UNA: Universidad Nacional de Asunción], Dr. Andrés Barbero Institute. (n.d.). *Record of Signed Agreements* [*Ficha de convenios firmados*]. Asunción: UNA.

Para La Tierra. (2017). *Home*. Asuncion: Para La Tierra. Available at: http://www.paralatierra.org/index.html

Plurinational State of Bolivia. (2011). *List of Public and Private Universities in Bolivia* [*Listado de Universidades Públicas y Privadas en Bolivia*]. La Paz: Agency for the Development of Information Society in Bolivia. Available at: https://bolivia.gob.bo/index4.html

Plurinational State of Bolivia, Ministry of Education. (2013). *National Science, Technology, and Innovation Plan* [*Plan Nacional de Ciencia, Tecnología e Innovación*]. La Paz: Ministry of Education.

Plurinational State of Bolivia, Ministry of Education. (2016). *Home* [Internet]. La Paz: Ministry of Education. Available at: http://www.minedu.gob.bo/

Plurinational State of Bolivia, Vice Ministry of Science and Technology. (2016). *Home* [Internet]. La Paz: Vice Ministry of Science and Technology. Available at: http://www.cienciaytecnologia.gob.bo/

Program for Strategic Research in Bolivia [Programa de Investigación Estratégica en Bolivia]. (2016). PIEB. La Paz: PIEB. Available at: http://www.pieb.org/pieb_pieb.php

Quenta, E., Molina-Rodríguez, J., Gonzales, K., Rebaudo, F., Casas, J., Jacobsen, D., & September, O. D. (2016). Direct and Indirect Effects on Aquatic Biodiversity in High Andean Peatlands. *Global Change Biology, 22*(9), 3196–3205. https://doi.org/10.1111/gcb.13310.

Ramos, M. (2015). *Who Are We?* [*¿Quiénes somos?*]. Lima: Manuela Ramos. Available at: http://www.manuela.org.pe/

Republic of Paraguay. (2003, November 7). Law No. 2279: General Law of Science and Technology.

Republic of Paraguay. (2013, May 9). Law No. 4995: Law of Universities.

Republic of Paraguay, Ministry of Education and Culture. (2016). *Description of Institutional Policy* [*Descripción de la Política Institucional*]. Asunción: Ministry of Education and Culture. Available at: http://www.mec.gov.py/cms?ref=296221-descripcion-de-la-politica-institucional

Republic of Paraguay, National Council of Science and Technology (CONACYT). (2016). *Programs and Projects* [*Proyectos y programas*]. Asunción: CONACYT. Available at: http://www.conacyt.gov.py/

Research Institute for Sustainable Development [IRD: *Institut de Recherche pour le Développement*]. (2016a). *Biodiversity and Climate Change in High Tropical Andean Ecosystems* [*Biodiversidasd y cambio climático en los ecosistemas de altura de los Andes tropicales*]. France: IRD. Available at: http://www.bolivia.ird.fr

Research Institute for Sustainable Development [IRD: *Institut de Recherche pour le Développement*]. (2016b). *Biodiversity and People Facing Climate Change in Tropical Highland Wetlands*. France: IRD. Available at: http://www.biothaw.ird.fr

Román, O. (2008). *Political Participation and Leadership of Indigenous Women in Latin America. Case Study: Bolivia* [*Participación Política y Liderazgo de Mujeres Indígenas en América Latina. Estudio de Caso: Bolivia*]. Cochabamba: Ciudadanía, UNDP. Available at: http://www.ciudadaniabolivia.org/es/node/274

Román, O. (2012). *Migration and Citizenship in Bolivia in the Latin American Context, State of the Question [Migración y Ciudadanía en Bolivia en el Contexto Latinoamericano. Estado de la Cuestión]*. Cochabamba: UMSS, Ciudadanía. Available at: http://www.ciudadaniabolivia.org/es/node/284

Scientific Electronic Library Online SciELO Bolivia. (2015). *Library Collection*. La Paz: Ministry of Education, Vice Ministry of Science and Technology. Available online at: http://www.scielo.org.bo/scielo.php?script=sci_alphabetic&lng=en&nrm=iso

Scientific Electronic Library Online SciELO Paraguay. (2015). *Library Collection*. Asuncion: National University of Asuncion. Available online at: http://scielo.iics.una.py/scielo.php?script=sci_alphabetic&lng=es&nrm=iso

Sos Faim. (2015). *Family Farming in Bolivia*. Brussels: Sos Faim. Available at: https://www.sosfaim.org/be/en/nos-actions/en-amerique-latine/bolivie/

The World Bank. (2015a). *Data. Patent Applications, Nonresidents*. Washington, DC: World Bank Group. Available online at: http://data.worldbank.org/indicator/IP.PAT.NRES/countries

The World Bank. (2015b). *Data. Research and Development Expenditure (% of GDP)*. Washington, DC: World Bank. Available online at: http://data.worldbank.org/indicator/GB.XPD.RSDV.GD.ZS/countries

The World Bank. (2015c). *Data. Researchers in R&D (Per Million People)*. Washington, DC: World Bank. Available online at: http://data.worldbank.org/indicator/SP.POP.SCIE.RD.P6/countries

The World Bank. (2015d). *Data. High-Technology Exports (Current US$)*. Washington, DC: World Bank. Available online at: http://data.worldbank.org/indicator/TX.VAL.TECH.CD/countries

The World Bank. (2015e). *Data. High-Technology Exports (% of Manufactured Exports)*. Washington, DC: World Bank. Available online at: http://data.worldbank.org/indicator/TX.VAL.TECH.MF.ZS/countries

United Nations Development Programme (PNUD: Programa de las Naciones Unidas para el Desarrollo). (2016). *UNDP in Bolivia [PNUD in Bolivia]*. La Paz: PNUD. Available at: http://www.bo.undp.org/content/bolivia/es/home.html

Vargas Villazón, G. (Compilator). (2015). *Cochabamba: Equality, Identity, and Citizenship [Cochabamba: Igualdad, Identidad y Ciudadanía]*. Cochabamba: Ciudadanía, CERES, Los Tiempos. Available at: http://www.ciudadaniabolivia.org/es/node/548

We Effect, Swedish Cooperation Center. (2016). *We Effect in Bolivia*. Guatemala City: We Effect, Regional Office for Latin America. Available at: http://www.weeffect.org/es/donde-trabajamos/regional/bolivia/

CHAPTER 8

Comparing Urban Mobility and the Energy Transition in France, USA, and Brazil: From Research Collaboration to Institutional Partnerships

J. Kent Fitzsimons, Guy Tapie, Patrice Godier, and Cristina de Araújo Lima

INTRODUCTION

Study topics that concern global challenges require a novel kind of research that adapts the conventional model of case-study comparison to provide a transnational understanding of their scope (Hassenteufel 2005). This is the case for the energy sector and sustainability, linked as they are through the problem of climate change. At the same time, urban development, in which energy use is an important parameter, is eminently tied to local

---

J. Kent Fitzsimons (✉) • G. Tapie • P. Godier
PAVE Research Laboratory, Bordeaux National School of Architecture and Landscape Architecture, Bordeaux, France

C. de Araújo Lima
Department of Architecture and Urban Planning, Federal University of Parana, Curitiba, Brazil

© The Author(s) 2018   175
G. Gregorutti, N. Svenson (eds.), *North-South University Research Partnerships in Latin America and the Caribbean*,
https://doi.org/10.1007/978-3-319-75364-5_8

conditions, whether they be geographical, historical, political, or cultural (Ruano 1999; Vigour 2005). Research on the manner in which the energy transition is affecting urban growth and city life, for example, would therefore have to keep one proverbial foot on the ground and another in the supranational sphere, through case studies compared along new lines (Bardet and Helliun 2010; Donzelot 2003; Dureau and Levy 2007; Erhenberg 2010; Pinderhughes 2004). This chapter will discuss one such research project that was carried out through a collaboration between teams located in Brazil, France, and the USA.

The international research collaboration discussed here was initiated to respond to a call for proposals for a research program co-organized by the Ministry of Culture and Communication and the Ministry of Ecology in France in 2011. The program, called "*Ignis Mutat Res* (IMR): Looking at Architecture, the City and the Landscape through the Prism of Energy," aimed to improve the understanding of the complex relationship between contemporary lifestyles and energy considerations, as mediated by human environments at different scales. Requirements were that research teams associate expertise from the spatial design disciplines (architecture, urbanism, landscape architecture, and territorial planning) with competencies from the different kinds of scientific disciplines: exact, social, human, and environmental. Projects were encouraged to include collaboration with relevant public and private entities, as well as educational components that would be clearly identifiable parts of a master's or PhD curriculum.

The French urban research center PAVE (*Profession Architecture, Ville, Environnement*)—housed at the Bordeaux National School of Architecture and Landscape Architecture (*Ecole Nationale Supérieure d'Architecture et de Paysage de Bordeaux*, EnsapBx)—responded to the Call for Proposals (CFP) by proposing an international comparative study of the effects of changing energy paradigms on mobility policy and practices in metropolitan areas. The goal was to put forward a comprehensive and multicultural study in order to acquire a more advanced understanding of the phenomenon. The call for proposals did not mention the need for international teams. However, in a historic context where the world economy requires energy from multiple sources and when climate change induces lifestyle changes everywhere, especially in high resource-consumption environments like cities, it seemed a global view of the research topic, spanning national or even continental borders, would be appropriate if not necessary (Beck 2001; Jonas [1979] 1991; Lévy 2010). This attitude also resonated with the signals that had been sent by the 1992 Earth Summit (United Nations Conference on Environment and Development, UNCED) in Rio de Janeiro and its resultant Agenda 21 action plan, which stimulated a desire to share projects with partners in other social, cultural, political, and economic contexts and, as a consequence, to develop a better grasp of global phenomena (Rodrigues 2005; UNCED 1993).

Prior encounters among professors and scholars from different countries were the basis for composing a team including members from three institutions: EnsapBx, which acted as the coordinating body; the University of Cincinnati (UC) in the USA, through its School of Architecture and Interior Design and School of Planning; and the Federal University of Paraná in Curitiba, Brazil (UFPR), through its Department of Architecture and Urbanism. Indeed, a professor from UFPR had spent time at EnsapBx during her post-doctoral work and on another occasion met a professor from UC during a workshop in Curitiba. The triangulation was reinforced by another coincidence: the principal investigator at PAVE knew a different UC professor from their respective prior teaching positions in Paris. These existing relationships were, of course, conditioned by common areas of expertise, lending substance to the team's composition.

The team aimed to study the impact of changing energy paradigms on urban mobility by comparing three cities that were experiencing metropolitan growth, where each city would represent a particular context with regard to culture, politics, geography, and resources.[1] The resulting proposal, "Sustainable Metropolitan Areas and Mobility Facing a New Energy Paradigm: Cincinnati (USA); Curitiba (Brazil); Bordeaux (France)," was retained as one of eight (out of twenty-nine) research projects to be financed over a two-year period. Research began in November 2011, and the final report was submitted in November 2013.

This chapter describes and analyzes the experience of conducting research with a team whose members come from three different countries and contexts. Reflecting on this experience allows for identifying the key factors that contributed to the positive results of the partnership. It also sheds light on the factors that functioned as obstacles or limits during the research program, and that perhaps prevented an even more satisfying outcome. These positive and negative factors may be put into perspective by exploring the reasons that members volunteered to embark on this rather daunting adventure. This chapter therefore explains the motivations for participating in the partnership, before discussing the limiting factors and obstacles encountered, and finally presents the key factors that led to the project's success. Following this discussion, it offers some final thoughts and conclusions. First, however, we will provide information about the research methodology as well as an overview of the results.

RESEARCH METHODOLOGY

The choice for an international comparison was part of a general growing awareness of global energy stakes stimulated by supranational as well as more local summits, international regulation, climate plans at different levels of government, and, of course, the controversies that ensue with each of these (Banister 2005). This awareness is emerging, as the power relations between public policy and popular action are undergoing significant transformation in many countries (Godier and Tapie 1997; Rifkin 2011). Since energy transition, as well as urban growth, pose problems and challenges for multiple levels of government, it seemed appropriate to probe these phenomena by adopting a global vision grounded in three contrasting contexts, a trio perceived as providing a minimum of complexity for comparison. Prior teaching and research relationships oriented the choice toward a European, a North American, and a South American case.

The project proposed to study case cities rather than attempt broad generalizations about urban processes in each country. In contrast to a macro-level global study, the contextualization of the research question in specific urban areas allowed for grasping local dynamics (national and infra-national) and identifying each case's singularities, while also raising common points in the different urban conditions (Le Néchet 2011; Newman and Kenworthy 1999). Among these last, the consolidation of a human- and world-consciousness signals a new state of societies and their relationship to different territorial dimensions. This is due in part to the circulation of academics and experts, as well as to more open information systems. The research partnership would therefore also participate in conjugating local and global awareness.

Case studies are fundamental for comparative research on urban production processes. However, this method risks sacrificing each case's specificity in the search to define models or reach a level of generalized knowledge. On the other hand, the case study has heuristic value because it incorporates national or global characteristics. For selecting the study cases, we therefore chose to privilege a city's demonstrative capacity as a determining parameter over the application of principles such as representativeness (of an ostensible national identity), statistical comparability (population size, land area), or morphological comparability (geographic situation, building typologies and density), which would have been very difficult to implement for practical reasons (financial means, knowledge of the sites, local contacts). The challenge then lay in selecting cases that would be demonstrative without necessarily being either homologous or "typical." For example, while the three selected cities differ in their demographic and geographic characteristics, each is the major metropolitan center for its region.

Regarding general organization, the research project was structured in four parts. The first step was to organize local teams based on disciplines and competencies. The team in Bordeaux was composed of sociologists and architects with an interest in the social sciences, while the Brazilian team in Curitiba included architects and planners as well as transport engineers, and the American team in Cincinnati consisted of architects and urban designers and planners. This disciplinary asymmetry meant that each researcher would have to apply their particular viewpoint to all three cities, rather than work only on their local situation. The second step involved scheduling research seminars, stages of data collection, discussion periods, and production of the final report over the two-year project period. The third step was to conduct seminars (involving researchers, professionals, and officials) and workshops (for students and teachers) in each city, first in Bordeaux, then in Cincinnati, and finally in Curitiba. This phase included producing a mid-term report between the events in Cincinnati and Curitiba for a review by the national program's scientific committee. The fourth and last phase consisted of preparing the final report and presenting the results during the comprehensive program seminar in Paris in November 2013.

As suggested above, the protocol required that each of the three partner institutions host a weeklong event to gather the international team in the cities under study. Each city event included two main components: a research seminar and a pedagogical workshop. These meetings assembled professors, researchers, and, when possible, undergraduate and graduate students from each participating research structure. Each seminar included data collection, analysis and debates, and interviews with experts, public officials and managers, and local stakeholders. Field visits undertaken with local experts and community members provided familiarity with the different urban contexts; these were of particular interest for foreign team members. This fieldwork increased awareness of each city's unique physical, environmental, social, and cultural conditions by revealing the specificities of social interactions between different groups in each city, whether related to power struggles and racial strife, or to social, political, economic, and cultural factors. Close contact with the field thus resulted in more precise definitions of the categories of data and information under study. Awareness of how these superficially nonspatial phenomena may influence the urban layout and spatial practices, particularly with regard to metropolitan functions such as mobility, allowed for a better assessment of the three cases, and also placed each local condition within a broader perspective.

For the research project's conceptual structure, the team developed an ambitious analytical model (which in retrospect exceeded the means of the research program) that identified three levels of governance whose impact on mobility could be observed: the supranational level, the national level, and the local (metropolitan) level. This allowed the group to tease out how international policies weigh on mobility practices and policies at the metropolitan level, how each national political system, industrial apparatus, and culture impacts local realities, and how each metropolitan condition is unique yet also shares policies and projects with other large cities. The analytical model furthermore employed three axes to characterize mobility cultures and the effects of the energy variable in each metropolitan area: metropolitan experience, which explored the effects of mobility policies and projects on spatial perception and practices; urban form and territorial structure, which involved studying changes in the physical organization of urban habitat in response to consequences of energy consumption such as climate change; and governance and decision-making processes, in particular representations of the energy or ecological transition in political discourse and public policy. Finally, for each axis of the study, the model distinguished different dimensions specific to the data gathered. For example, the governance and policy-making axis produced results for three distinct dimensions: the territorial perimeters of action, the system of actors, and collective narratives. This triple framework—levels of governance, research axes, and dimensions—was progressively structured through debate among researchers, through fieldwork in the cities, and through the nature of the results.

Each axis of study was pursued jointly by team members residing in different cities, largely for the sake of disciplinary or interdisciplinary specificity: the governance axis, for example, brought together specialists in planning and sociology across national divides. For this reason, exchanges during the periods between seminar and workshop events were of capital importance. This was carried out mainly by electronic mail, but also by videoconference or telephone. In addition to these collaborations, each researcher produced a distinct contribution for the final report in order to render, at least partially, the specificity of different research cultures. Translation and assembly of these contributions were managed by PAVE in Bordeaux.

OVERVIEW OF RESEARCH RESULTS

The main findings of the research may be presented through the three study axes (Fitzsimons et al. 2013). Regarding governance and policy making, we identified highly different political systems with respect to the ability of different levels of government to act on infrastructure projects and mobility practices, as well as with respect to the continuity of articulations between those different levels. On the other hand, all three cities shared a propensity to use "storytelling" as a way of communicating about urban energy concerns and to produce guideline plans at different temporal horizons (e.g., 2025, 2030, 2050). Also, we found that the potential for local action in each case city, as well as its scope, is highly conditioned by its national government's energy, environmental, and industrial policies. Thus, France's nuclear industry, Brazil's biofuel policies, and the USA's refusal to sign the Kyoto protocol, for example, produce tangible effects at the municipal level, rendering simple comparison between cases impracticable. In the urban form axis, the most salient point was that the existing physical organization in each city, which may be understood as the combination of geographic features, infrastructure (in particular roadways), and buildings, creates path dependency that determines in great part the plausibility of major modifications such as residential densification, public transportation projects, or such planning policies as transit-oriented development. Finally, the emerging "metropolitan experience" of each city was found to share common traits with the two others when comparing how public transportation policies attempt to facilitate access to the urban area, but also to have unique articulations between active modes of transportation (walking, biking), personal motorized transportation (automobiles), and public transportation that distinguish it from the other cases.

The team's presentations at seminars organized by the funding institutions were well appreciated, judging from the program's scientific committee feedback. The final report was also singled out for its combination of quality academic and exploratory material. This allowed the team to successfully compete for subsequent support from the sponsoring institutions for transferring research results to a broader public and to teaching. For example, the team organized a round table discussion for the International Forum on the Renewable City held in parallel with the Solar Decathlon Europe competition exhibition in Versailles, France, in July 2014. PAVE also was awarded a special fund to have students in the professional architecture program at EnsapBx develop master's theses on subjects related to the study.

Independent of the research results themselves, the project produced multiple lasting effects. The local authorities, experts, and stakeholders who collaborated with the research team were content with the experience and have continued to cooperate with the higher education institutions for which the team members work. Also, EnsapBx (France) signed partnership agreements with both UFPR (Brazil) and UC (USA) during the research program, completing the triangulation among the three institutions (the latter two had an agreement before research began). This has resulted in healthy interinstitutional dynamics in the form of student exchanges at the professional program level and a joint PhD candidate (EnsapBx and UFPR), annual research seminars for UC master's and PhD students at EnsapBx, and a research fellowship for one of the UC team members at the Université de Bordeaux.

In sum, the research project produced quality scientific research in line with different disciplinary standards, as well as lasting interuniversity relationships and improved relations between higher education and research institutions and their social, economic, and political environments. The following sections will describe the motivations that lay behind forming an international partnership for the research project, the obstacles and limits encountered during the collaboration, and the major factors we perceive as having contributed to its success.

Motivations for International Collaboration

When identifying the conditions that favor research productivity in a partnership, it is important to consider the level and nature of motivation for those involved. Ferraz (2013) has proposed a model in which five motivational factors are at play: money, security, learning, recognition, and self-realization. These categories are useful for analyzing the dynamics in the *Ignis Mutat Res* research program partnership. Money and security were not the motivating factors: no financial gain was at stake, and there was no particular opportunity or risk regarding employment for the researchers involved, as all participated under the auspices of their employer institutions and maintained their positions in their respective hierarchies. The combined promise of learning, self-realization, and recognition, on the other hand, was a significant motivating factor for each member. The detail of this composite motivating factor can be presented through two main objectives: the prospect of knowledge production in a comparative, multidisciplinary context; and personal and professional growth.

Knowledge Production in a Comparative, Multidisciplinary Context

A Logical Evolution
PAVE's initiative to propose an international study lay in a long-standing tradition of comparison in the human sciences, which the Bordeaux research center had applied in previous studies. Since the mid-1980s, recourse to international comparison in France has become increasingly frequent, to the point of becoming a right of passage for many researchers. More than a passing trend, this demand can be explained by the need to consider a new scale of relationships to explain many socio-political and economic processes that condition the evolution of human settlements and the lifestyles associated with them. A number of phenomena favor comparative study: changes in the form of governance at the state and international level, population movements, geopolitical dynamics, an interdependent and globalized economy, increased density of exchanges among individuals and groups due to communication networks, mobility (professional, educational, cultural), and the opening of societies and their spaces beyond the borders inherited from their nation-states. These trends have introduced a transnational perspective into analytical models, no longer limited solely to strict comparison between multiple national or regional units (Hassenteufel 2005).

Indeed, the current enthusiasm for international comparison may be explained by a change in its very nature. International comparison is no longer simply a method for revealing spatial and social phenomena. It addresses issues that transcend municipal or national borders, in terms of transnational logic that explains current societal dynamics and in particular how they conceive of urban and regional space. Comparison today goes beyond confronting one national profile with another in order to evaluate similarities and differences. It consists of changing perspectives in order to reconceptualize phenomena, processes, and practices (Dupré et al. 2003). This kind of comparison is increasingly frequent among doctoral students and young researchers.

PAVE's work has developed its capacity for comparative analysis over several years. Various studies focused on the production of the built environment using a combination of concepts (analysis of urban and regional means of action; professions and stakeholders in the planning processes) and objects (architectural and urban projects, sustainable development policies, housing, mobility) (Godier 2001, 2003; Tapie 2000, 2003, 2005). The integration of national and supranational dynamics broadened interpretative models by placing observations in multiple configurations and at numerous scales. Initially, PAVE undertook comparison among countries in Europe with similar levels of development, with the objective of comparing several architectural and urban production systems in the mid-1990s, when European unification called for the uniformization of practices (Biau et al. 1998; Chadoin et al. 2000; Godier and Tapie 1997); then, after 2005, between countries highly differentiated in terms of culture, politics, and economics (France and Thailand) to measure the impact of sustainable development on planning policies (Parin et al. 2008).

The *Ignis mutat res* call for proposals was seized as an opportunity for PAVE to further develop its comparative model by undertaking international research on somewhat similar yet nonetheless contrasting countries: France, the USA, and Brazil. This new phase would allow the center's approach to evolve from juxtaposing France's specificity against that of other countries, to a broader comprehension of transnational dynamics (Tapie et al. 2014, p. 4). PAVE considered that, in the field of urban analysis, the dissemination of cases from numerous countries and urban areas— through benchmarking, showcasing emblematic experiments and exemplary projects, and circulation of experts and ideas at conferences, seminars, and colloquiums subsequently indexed in electronic distribution networks—is a necessary development for providing material from which authorities and experts may draw. In this context, concepts, urban theories, forms of government, and systems of territorial production are all incorporated as interactive points of reference. For PAVE members, then, comparative observation had a history of several years of stimulating work, so the sense that this program fit into a broader trajectory was a significant driving force for the coordinating team.

Cultural Difference as a Methodological Device

For all research participants, working in a transnational team was seen as an opportunity to improve the understanding of the research subject as a whole. The value of this opportunity appeared in a triple perspective. First, with regard to the analysis of the subject in light of increasing energy constraints. As team members were from different societies, three different sets of experiences with and knowledge on energy and mobility would come together. Viewpoints on the political, technical, societal, and ecological aspects of nuclear energy or biofuels, for example, vary greatly between France and Brazil. The three national subgroups that composed the research team shared the desire to imagine a better future, yet each represented a different energy culture and phase of development.

The second perspective concerned the matter of bias in research. The analysis of each city's local conditions by experienced "non-resident" researchers provided by the IMR partnership was perceived as a way to access an expanded scrutiny free from local biases, whether conscious or unconscious. From the Brazilian standpoint, this opportunity would shed new light on the case of Curitiba, as its experience in contemporary urbanism—and, in particular, the creation of the Bus Rapid Transit (BRT) system—had already been subject to media to coverage and research at home and abroad since the 1980s (Figueiredo and Lamounier 1996; Goodman et al. 2006; Gruber 2012; Gunderson 2014; McKibben 2005; Menezes 1996; Pinderhughes 2004; Ruano 1999).

The third perspective regarded methodological exchange more generally. All researchers on the team had some degree of interest in learning about other methodologies and research techniques. The proposed team's pluridisciplinarity was seen as an opportunity to discuss common and familiar practices as well as new methodologies and trends in scientific endeavors, and to access a more comprehensive view of the issues studied.

Places, Cases, and People

Participating in the partnership represented an opportunity to expand horizons by gaining knowledge of other urban areas in a privileged way, in particular through specialists' presentations of local conditions, "in situ" visits, and interviews with relevant local actors and stakeholders. Participation in an international partnership with well-connected institutions can allow for this kind of experience more easily than can visits as an isolated researcher. Such rich field experience was perceived as an opportunity for capacity development and for expanding the knowledge network of the researchers and research centers involved.

Informal Benchmarking

Another motivating factor for joining the partnership and comparing the three situations was an interest in being able to situate one's own city and study area through a kind of informal benchmarking practice. For instance, would the innovations in Curitiba from the 1980s and 1990s appear precocious when compared to urban areas in Europe and the USA with more complex systems and experienced public management? Is the current French model of urban development truly more virtuous than those in other countries? Researchers perceived the international research project as an opportunity to better evaluate the discourse on one's home city through its confrontation with discourses on realities in other countries.

Personal and Professional Growth

Interest in one's own benefits also plays a role in embarking on a challenging project. In the case of the IMR proposal, the academic dimension defined in great part the kinds of returns expected. These concerned professional considerations above and beyond the research methods or content themselves.

Professional Development

In Brazil, a university professor's participation in a research project in partnership with academic institutions from abroad is a factor for increasing the classification of a *stricto* sensu graduate program (master's and doctorate).[2] The evaluation of such programs in Brazil is performed by an entity of the federal government, under the Ministry of Education (MEC), called the Higher Education Personnel Improvement Coordinator (*Coordenação de Aperfeiçoamento de Pessoal de Nível Superior, Capes*).[3] *Capes* establishes evaluation criteria such as the scientific publication ranking system "Qualis," in which the author of a scientific article accumulates points for his or her program, in proportion to the publishing journal's ranking. It also evaluates the published books based on criteria detailed in the "Roadmap for classification of books." International cooperation is a prominent item in the list of *Capes* actions that motivate teachers, researchers, and graduate students to work in partnerships, exchanges, and traineeships, which are means for greater openness to study and research in other countries. Brazilian graduate professors, therefore, have an interest in participating in international partnerships in order to contribute to a better ranking for their graduate programs, beyond the investment in their own scientific development. This is also a factor of recognition on the institution's part for the researcher's commitment to a collective enterprise.

International Group Collaboration and Disciplinary Diversity
Collaborating in an international research group represents a double challenge for the participants, as it concerns work at both the personal level and the team level. For the IMR project, working with new foreign scientific partners, under strict deadlines, with a somewhat limited budget, and without an adjustment period was a daunting prospect. As team members came from different national and academic cultures, there were different worldviews, expectations, and conceptions of scientific work, all of which could be challenging to the coordination of results. Countering these potential deterrents was each volunteer's predilection for confronting a form of otherness that enables the development of new skills, reconsideration of opinions and knowledge, and acceptance of uncertainty. Articulating simultaneously between disciplines and between cultures would require specific intellectual and interpersonal skills from each team member, in addition to those related to the usual relationship management needed for group work. Furthermore, the project's international dimension would require that some strongly held opinions, even when based on prior scientific study, be reconsidered in light of new encounters at home and abroad. Finally, the prospect of an unusually complex research process incorporating unknown variables that would surely require changes in the program along the way attracted the kind of academic partner who thrives on risk, or who in any case was up for a change from more predictable projects. The very nature of the project favored self-selection of researchers by provoking a particular motivational factor in people interested in personal growth through a challenging international encounter.

OBSTACLES AND LIMITS

The multiple obstacles and limitations that arose during the development of the partnership may be divided into three main categories: (1) those related to compatibility and comparability, in particular with regard to data; (2) those concerning communication and exchange, where language and distance were determining factors; and (3) those linked to institutional input and in particular, the securing and allocating of additional resources needed for the main program.

Data Compatibility, Availability, and Processing

The search for relevant data for the three countries revealed the existence of certain common global information, but also the lack of specific data within countries and the difficulty of comparing data across borders. Governance practices at the global level have done much to increase data uniformity and legibility. The United Nations Organization and its commissions (forums) and satellites, the Organisation for Economic Co-operation and Development (OECD), the World Bank, and various intelligence agencies (e.g., the Central Intelligence Agency) have all been instrumental in these efforts. Also, international policies regarding, for example, the Carbon Trade Exchange or greenhouse gas reduction have pushed countries to produce unprecedented databases that are accessible and relatively homogeneous (on energy production and consumption, and greenhouse gas emissions, among other indicators). Indeed, the "Greenhouse Gas Inventory" by country is based on common statistical categories and is thus a political tool for international negotiations and for public opinion, as well as a useful metric for research. This data is generally produced by national statistics agencies, guaranteeing their reliability, at least for countries that dispose of such resources. However, their data is generally global, regional, or national, and only rarely local, thus constituting a limitation for those studying specific territories within a given country.

Even when comparable data from different countries is available, using it can be difficult. Measuring systems differ from one country to another (gallons vs. liters, miles vs. kilometers, and dollars vs. euros, for instance), as do methods for aggregate reporting (access to source files is rare and, when it is possible, processing them is complex). Variables regarding behavior, practices, or opinions often prove to be heterogeneous. The racial or ethnic characteristics that are common in the USA and in Brazil are officially inapplicable in France. Regarding mobility, vehicle categories differ from one country to another. The same applies for certain details about housing, family composition, or even social class, with Brazil distinguishing itself from the American and European contexts. Diachronic analysis is even more difficult, as the timeframes for surveys vary depending on the country, while the categories and scales used may evolve over time. Aligning government data relative to the population, to behavioral aspects, to attitudes, and over the range of spatial scales studied (from the neighborhood to the metropolitan area) can be complicated. Also, the use of different methodologies for surveying mobility practices among citizens made it difficult to homogenize statistics across the board: authorities in Cincinnati employed a novel method using real-time geo-tracking and personal log books, while a comparable study in Bordeaux still relied on questionnaire-based interviews.

Regarding the governance and public policy research axis, statistics from the three countries rarely covered the same territorial perimeters: while the reference point *de rigueur* in France is the municipality (commune), in the USA, it is the county, and in Brazil, the principal criterion for measuring metropolitanization is the distinction between urban and rural territories, independent of administrative limitations. As a consequence, the organization of public transit systems in Bordeaux, Curitiba, and Cincinnati are only partially analogous, and household surveys—precious data for lining up supply and demand—diverge. Such surveys are nonexistent at the desired metropolitan scale in Brazil, or difficult to acquire for political reasons; in Cincinnati, for example, privacy constraints on a data set held by one US team member greatly limited its use and sharing, which was a disappointment given its large scale and fine granularity. In Brazil, public agencies that held relevant data about transport and energy did not always allow for its consultation. In general, comparing federal states with other constitutional entities proved a daunting task.

Processing these differences consumed valuable time and energy, without necessarily producing satisfying results. The lack of sufficient financial resources for collecting more primary data and performing advanced analysis thus proved to be an obstacle.

Communication and Exchange

As an international team involving three linguistic communities, communication and exchange naturally posed a particular challenge. This is a common problem for many international research groups and collaborative projects (Tress et al. 2005). For the IMR project, defining the common work language took time, and the issue was only resolved toward the end of the first phase. Still, the solution was complex: while French was the official language for report submissions and for the program seminars in Paris, English was used as a bridge language for written exchanges and live discussions. However, as some team members were fluent in neither French nor English, exchanges between certain research pairs was very limited; this was particularly true of some France/Brazil combinations for which English could not serve as a lingua franca. Also, as the coordinating team in France took responsibility for giving coherence to the final report, much time was necessary for translating English contributions and improving French versions drafted by Brazilian team members.

Physical distance between research participants was also clearly an obstacle. While digital communication facilitated many tasks, there were two roles that it could not fulfill. First, despite the use of recent advances in videoconferencing, real face-to-face exchange remained the most productive for brainstorming, clarifying ideas, and building consensus about key issues. Indeed, the seminars attended by the most team members were the most productive. Second, digital communication proved insufficient for curtailing the "out of sight, out of mind" phenomenon: it was difficult to respect the objective of exchanges at strict, regular intervals, and applying pressure on collaborators to meet deadlines was harder without physical presence.

The Challenges of Complementary Institutional Resources

The French government's call for proposals represented a unique opportunity during a serious global economic crisis that was affecting all three countries involved in the response, although with different specific local manifestations. The program's financial envelope therefore represented very welcome means for enabling significant research activities. However, in order to fully develop the research program, additional funding sources were also necessary. This proved to be a challenge given the particular context at each home institution, especially in France and Brazil. The team in Curitiba would have liked to benefit from the services of a public agency planning technician assigned to the project, but this was ultimately not possible. Also, technical expertise for such tasks as mapping, information processing, editing, graphic design, text revision, translation, and maintenance would have resulted in a better synthetic three-country database, and thus a smoother research process. One consequence of the difficulty in funding these tasks was that overburdened professors had trouble devoting the necessary time to the project (Lima and Lima-Filho 2009).

In contrast, the team in Cincinnati managed to mobilize complementary university resources. As the director of an independently financed community design center housed by the university, one of the team members was able to mobilize human and material resources, in particular for spatial analysis involving intensive graphic production. The other American team members applied for and obtained a university stimulus grant

("UC Forward") for pedagogical innovation, which allowed master's and PhD students to travel to France for intensive teaching weeks that drew on and fed the research in progress. These funding successes highlighted interesting differences between the models of higher education and research in Brazil, France, and the USA.

Despite these obstacles and constraints, the team succeeded in concluding the partnership with a report that received very satisfactory reviews by the organizers. This may be attributed to the conditions discussed in this chapter's final section on key success factors.

KEY SUCCESS FACTORS

The partnership's satisfactory output was the result of a fortuitous combination of hard work and specific work conditions, in which different key factors were determinant. Overall, the most important factors are organized here into three categories: (a) organizational; (b) methodological; and (c) attitudinal.

Organizational Factors

The principal investigator was highly invested in the project, in part because it was his first time in that capacity. Much care was thus taken in corresponding with individual city teams or team members regarding content. Still, the PI's proactive organization, control, and guidance were most tangible during the city seminars. The physical distance between city teams explains in part the relative absence of firm global coordination and direction between seminars.

The program funding was used primarily to finance travel for team members to attend the research seminars in each of the three cities, as well the general program seminars organized by the funding institutions in Paris. As far as personal availability allowed, each participant could therefore travel to both other cities in the study, and to Paris. Additionally, each city team was allotted a budget to cover local seminar expenses such as transport, facility use, and peripheral events. Overall, the equitable distribution of financial resources was perceived as a sign that the collaboration was indeed horizontal in nature, and contributed to good relations among team members.

A form of decentralized management also contributed to the program's success. At a local level, each city team made efforts to establish or foster collaborations and partnerships with a variety of stakeholders or experts. This occurred in different ways and with varying intensities: cooperation through the release of data, availability for interviews, guided visits, and participation in technical meetings and seminars. Most of the time, this involved cooperation with local public institutions, but there was also some cooperation with individual social actors linked to issues such as the protection of public transit users or of bicycle users. This decentralized management of partnerships was perhaps a factor in securing all external cooperation without cost.

Methodological Factors

The IMR research partnership brought together sociologists, engineers, architects, and urban designers and planners and provided the opportunity to exchange knowledge, methods, and research content. Aided in part by each researcher's prior experience with such practices, the project put the theoretical concepts of interdisciplinarity and multidisciplinarity into practice, which has become increasingly common since the end of the twentieth century (Besselaar and Heimeriks 2001). Although individual contributions to the final report respected the conventions of their authors' disciplinary affiliations, their elaboration benefitted from a rich interdisciplinary context.

Overall, five modes relative to the core concept of the disciplines were employed: disciplinary, interdisciplinary, multidisciplinary, transdisciplinary, and participatory to borrow the classification articulated by Tress, Tress, and Fry (2005).[4] As Choi and Pak (2006) argue, interdisciplinary practices generally allow more interaction than multidisciplinary practices: while "multidisciplinarity draws on knowledge from different disciplines but stays within their boundaries," "[i]nterdisciplinarity analyzes, synthesizes and harmonizes links between disciplines into a coordinate and coherent whole" (351). In this project, interdisciplinarity occurred principally during the seminars, when team members exchanged information on common research objects from different disciplinary perspectives. This was enhanced by the willingness for each member to read texts from fields different from his or her own (sometimes in a foreign language). Online communication also occasioned and facilitated disciplinary exchange (email, video conference). The result was an enlarged and diversified view of the issues at hand, which stimulated each participant's work.

Another methodological factor that contributed significantly to the project's success was the organization of three weeklong events that were held during the two-year project, each of which took place in one of the partner cities: Bordeaux, Cincinnati, and Curitiba. As described earlier, each event included a research seminar and a pedagogical component. All three times, the research seminar included the same three tasks: identification of comparative theoretical themes; completion of group interviews with stakeholders related to the projects under study (about ten interlocutors in each city); and visits to the "field" in order to experience and measure the spatial characteristics of the metropolitan entities and their projects. The first task occasioned intense interaction among team members from France, Brazil, and the USA. The latter two tasks allowed each national group to establish close contact with people and places from the two other countries. This constituted a veritable learning experience for visiting researchers, who were sensitized to unfamiliar ways of thinking and being, in particular by physically "sensing" different metropolitan spatial realities during the field trips.

Attitudinal Factors

Each team member's attitude toward to the project, fellow team members, and the partner cultures was a determining factor in ensuring smooth project elaboration and completion. Sustaining epistemological objectivity while not stifling a subjective intellectual disposition conducive to discovery requires special efforts when working across multiple countries. Comparison carries the risk of value judgments regarding the "best system" or the relative efficiency of different public policies (Tocqueville 1986 [1835]). While it may be tempting to list failures on one side and successes on the other, the objective of such a study is to characterize and to explain different systems. Comparison therefore navigates between value judgment and objective analysis, with latent cultural-centrism making it more difficult to stay the latter course. In our study, it would have been easy to decry American environmental ineffectiveness in view of automobile use, to denounce Brazil's policies supporting personal vehicle production and purchase, or to commend European virtue for its efforts to counter climate change. Due to a shared awareness of these pitfalls, team members managed to find a productive balance between subjectivity and objectivity when dealing with cultural and societal factors bearing on the study topic.

Another attitudinal factor that contributed to satisfactory project completion and outcomes was the gender neutrality in all interactions. Among the nine members of the core team (three from each country, not counting students, junior researchers, or stakeholders), four (44%) were women. According to UNESCO figures based on 2014 data, only 30% of the world's researchers are women (UNESCO 2015), and this proportion is higher in Brazil, where it reaches 50% (Melo and Rodrigues 2006; Veiga 2006). This participation by women in the IMR partnership was fully egalitarian, with no traces of prejudice or segregation, which constituted an ideal working environment and major factor in the work's success.

DISCUSSION

Practical Considerations

Based on our experience, we observe that the unprecedented access to documentary, bibliographical, statistical, and qualitative data and information, thanks to digitization and enhanced virtual or conventional exchange networks, has both positive and negative consequences. The multiplication of databases and their interactivity have created favorable conditions for international comparison. Similarly, the proliferation of personal and institutional websites is clearly beneficial to researchers, as they provide resources for information or material for empirical studies. However, harmonizing the data coming from different countries and types of sources proved to be a daunting and time-consuming task. In the future, the team would better weigh the advantages and disadvantages of information access and exercise more discrimination to ensure more efficient processing and analysis.

We also observe that, despite the rapid development of powerful communication tools, co-presence is still an important factor in implementing a team research program. The most important methodological discovery was the protocol developed for the city seminars. Gathering team members from all three participant countries for one week in each of the case cities proved highly productive on many levels. The seminars afforded precious contact time among researchers for coordinating objectives, methods, data, and interdisciplinary relations. Being together, even for a limited amount of time, was rather efficient for working out structural and content issues, as well as for exercising a form of "peer pressure" with regard to production schedules. Furthermore, these events allowed each scholar to meet a variety of stakeholders in each urban context under study and to develop an understanding of the cases through first-hand experience. It proved very productive for researchers to observe onsite the urban phenomena in question, with respect to the spatial dimensions and also the structure and composition of social and political realities. This is perhaps truer for studies connected to practices in urban space than for other research topics. We would also mention that the itinerant seminar protocol allowed team members to interact with students at partner institutions. As a whole, this protocol will be developed for use in future projects, with improvements brought to the general scheduling and specific agenda of each seminar. Such co-presence raises budget and time considerations, especially when the team and the study sites straddle three continents. This parameter can now be incorporated in a more informed manner in the budgets and schedules of future proposals.

If the city seminars were generally very satisfactory, the area requiring the greatest improvement is communication among team member in the intervals. This could be achieved through implementing a more powerful and efficient virtual platform, as well as through programming more—and more focused—conference calls.

A final practical consideration concerns the required complementary funding sources. This was complicated in the case presented here, as the institutional structures contrasted significantly between the three countries. While the University of Cincinnati could provide special project funding on a competitive basis (US$30,000) and mobilize a specific study center's human and material resources, the Bordeaux team only secured a small supplementary grant (6000 euros) from the main funding source (Ministry of Culture and Communication) and relied for the rest on in-kind resources from local governments and professionals in the form of expertise and data. The latter model also held true for the Brazilian team, which was not able to secure additional funding beyond in-kind resources. The differences in these complementary resources, compounded by their decentralized management and incomparable calendars, created problems and hampered coordination and efficiency.

General Considerations

In addition to knowledge of the physical aspects of cities in France, the USA, and Brazil, particular social and cultural conditions pertaining to spatial practices and resource consumption were also observed. Acquiring that kind of understanding was a valuable experience and represented an opportunity to verify in the field the existence of common human conditions in all three locations. Each city presents a distinct physical space (geography, climate, ecosystem) and sociology (society, economy, politics, culture). But attention to the research program's fundamental question—human needs in relation to urban issues and mobility—showed strong similarities among the urban communities with similar levels of development, as far as human factors are concerned.

Related to this, the research protocol that consisted of international comparison undertaken by a multinational and multidisciplinary team embodied the need to conceptualize urban challenges that are necessarily localized in relation to global dynamics. The requirement that each researcher study all three cities through the lens of a common theme in collaboration with team members from the two other countries brought all participants to assimilate the broad research question about urbanization and energy considerations as a transnational concern. This was enhanced by the physical encounter with foreign lands. At the same time, one's knowledge of one's more familiar local terrain was improved thanks to the detour through faraway places. Thus, each participant experienced conceptual de-territorialization and re-territorialization during the program. Beyond the spatial extension that each team member acquired, the cultural encounter amounted to the acquisition of access to a broader citizenship without the loss of one's original identity. This can be related to the weakening of the territorial boundaries of nation-states and the progression of globalization since the late twentieth century. Geographer Rogerio Haesbaert (2003) suggests that

> the territory is at the same time a resource or an instrument of power and a value [...]—a value that goes beyond the simple use or exchange value, extending to a symbolic value, with identity and existential components. This perspective breaks down the division between "political territory" (a redundant adjective) and "identity territory" that some authors propose, by seizing the territory as both a political resource and an identity strategy. (p. 15)

In this light, the de-territorialization and subsequent re-territorialization experienced by each team member appeared to work against local essentialisms that can hinder the needed changes in policies and practices, and toward a strategic re-politicization of the issues under study (energy, the right to the city) through their global contextualization. For example, the research contributed to questioning a certain myth regarding the North-South relationship, whereby metropolises from the South would hold the monopoly on grave urban paradoxes. In general, the research experience reproduced, at the scale of each team member, the evolution in comparative studies described at the beginning of the chapter: the environmental, ecological, and political aspects of urbanization in different places must be studied in parallel not for the sake of hierarchical comparison, but rather precisely because they are necessarily linked to global systems, processes, and risks, and not solely to local matters.

CONCLUSION

Our research on urbanization through the double lens of mobility and energy considerations studied three cities in three countries at a time of rapid globalization driven by the growing importance of regional and international policies. It was also a period of unexpected changes in the energy sector due to geopolitical events as well as industrial developments. Indeed, the price of oil dropped drastically midway through the research program, notably because the USA announced that it would be energy independent at a horizon of 20 years, thanks to the exploitation of unconventional fossil fuels. These developments underscored the degree to which local urban issues were tied to supranational economic and political dynamics, and reinforced the team's choice to embark on an ambitious multidisciplinary and international study.

Some of the difficulties encountered involve parameters that can be better controlled in future collaborations, such as improved articulation between the intense city seminar moments and the more dissipated intermediate periods. Others, however, are beyond the team's control, such as the highly contrasting structures of higher education and research funding in the three countries; in such cases, improved functioning will require thinking "outside the box," as harmonizing the systems is not a plausible objective. As the motivational threshold for this project was rather high and thus attracted participants with a certain drive, overcoming such difficulties in the future is a realistic goal. This is corroborated by the IMR project's key success factors, which encompass inventive organization, methodological audacity, and flexible attitudes toward situations and partners.

The research results, as presented at the general program seminars as well as in the final report, were well received by the Ministry officials responsible for the program. The collaboration produced abundant material pertaining to evolutions in urban lifestyles, urban form, and policy-making processes in the light of metropolitan growth and energy considerations, specifically with regards to mobility. Furthermore, lasting relationships have been established among the three institutions involved, in the form of partnership agreements that encompass both research and pedagogical activities. Team members thus continue to interact across national borders, in particular, for organizing research proposals, teaching events, and publishing projects.

NOTES

1. Urban mobility in this context refers to the general phenomenon by which people and goods move about urban environments, meaning cities and their surrounding areas of influence. While the term mobility concerns transportation in its practical and measurable dimensions, it aims to grasp these within the broader social and cultural fields that influence citizens' desires, expectations, and efforts regarding their access to different areas and resources in the city, as well as to goods (see Cresswell 2011; Massot 2010; Orfeuil 2010; Sheller and Urry 2006).
2. Regarding post-graduate studies, the education system in Brazil distinguishes between *lato* sensu degrees, which concern specializations and are not a basis for subsequent research career, and *stricto* sensu degrees, including research masters, doctoral degrees, and post-doctoral research, which prepare for academic work.
3. More information in Portuguese available online at: http://www.capes.gov. br/avaliacao/sobre-a-avaliacao
4. For these authors, disciplinary projects take place within the bounds of a single, currently recognized academic discipline; multidisciplinary studies as projects that involve several different academic disciplines researching one theme or problem but with multiple disciplinary goals; participants exchange knowledge, but do not aim to cross subject boundaries to create new knowledge and theory; participatory studies as projects that involve academic researchers and nonacademic participants working together to solve a problem; interdisciplinary studies as projects that involve several unrelated academic disciplines in a way that forces them to cross subject boundaries to create new knowledge and theory and solve a common research goal; transdisciplinary studies as projects that both integrate academic researchers from different unrelated disciplines and nonacademic participant and combines interdisciplinarity with a participatory approach (Tress et al. 2005).

REFERENCES

Banister, D. (2005). *Unsustainable Transport: City Transport in the New Century.* London: Taylor and Francis.

Bardet, F., & Helluin, J.-J. (2010). Comparer les Performances des Villes. Le Programme des Indicateurs Pour les Villes du Monde de la Banque Mondiale [Comparing City Performance: The World Bank's Program for World City Indicators]. *Revue Française de Socio-Économie, 5*(1), 83–102.

Beck, U. (2001). *La Société du Risque. Sur la Voie d'une Autre Modernité* [*Risk Society: The Path of Another Modernity*]. Paris: Aubier.

Biau, V., Godier, P., & Haumont, B. (1998). Métiers de l'Architecture et Position des Architectes en Europe : Une Approche Comparative [Practices in Architecture and the Positioning of Architects in Europe: A Comparative Approach]. In M. Bonnet (Ed.), *L'Elaboration des Projets Architecturaux et Urbains en Europe* V. 3 "Les Pratiques de l'Architecture". Paris: PUCA.

Chadoin, O., Godier, P., & Tapie, G. (2000). *Du Politique à l'Œuvre. Bilbao, Bordeaux, Bercy, San Sébastian. Systèmes et Acteurs des Grands Projets Urbains et Architecturaux* [*From Policy to Project. Bilbao, Bordeaux, Bercy and San Sebastian. Systems and Actors in Major Urban and Architectural Projects*]. La Tour d'Aigues: Editions de l'Aube.

Choi, B. C. K., & Pak, A. W. P. (2006). Multidisciplinarity, Interdisciplinarity and Transdisciplinarity in Health Research, Services, Education and Policy: 1. Definitions, Objectives, and Evidence of Effectiveness. *Clinical & Investigative Medicine, 29*(6), 351–364.

Cresswell, T. (2011). Mobilities I: Catching Up. *Progress in Human Geography, 35*(4), 550–558.

de Melo, H. P., & Rodrigues, L. (2006). *Pioneiras da Ciência no Brasil.* [*Women Science Pioneers in Brazil*]. Rio de Janeiro: SPBC.

de Tocqueville, A. (1986 [1835]). *De la Démocratie en Amérique* [*Democracy in America*] (vol. 1). Paris: Gallimard.

Donzelot, J. (2003). *Faire Société. La Politique de la Ville aux Etats-Unis et en France* [*Making Society: Urban Policy in the USA and in France*]. Paris: Seuil.

Dupré, M., Jacob, A., Lallement, M., Lefèvre, G., & Spurk, J. (2003). Les Comparaisons Internationales: Intérêt et Actualité d'une Stratégie de Recherche [International Comparison: A Research Strategy's Topicality]. In M. Lallement & J. Spurk (Eds.), *Stratégies de la Comparaison Internationale.* Paris: Presses du CNRS.

Dureau, F., & Levy, J.-P. (2007). Villes et Mobilités au Nord et au Sud: la Construction d'une Problématique Commune [Cities and Mobility in the North and in the South: Building a Common Problematics]. *Autrepart, 1*(41), 135–148.

Erhenberg, A. (2010). *La Société du Malaise* [*The Uneasy Society*]. Paris: Odile Jacob.

Ferraz, E. (2013). *Seja a Pessoa Certa no Lugar Certo* [*Be the Right Person in the Right Place*]. São Paulo: Gente.

Figueiredo, R., & Lamounier B. (1996). *As Cidades que Dão Certo* [*Cities That Work*]. Brasilia: MH Comunicação.

Fitzsimons, J. K., de Andrade Pereira, M., de Araújo Lima, C., Chifos, C., Gerbeaud, F., Godier, P., Schmid, A. L., Russell, F., Tapie, G., & Williamson, R. (2013). *Métropoles et Mobilités Durables à l'Epreuve d'un Nouveau Paradigme Energétique; Bordeaux – France, Cincinnati – Etats unis, Curitiba – Brésil* [Sustainable Metropolitan Areas and Mobility Facing a New Energy Paradigm: Bordeaux, France, Cincinnati, USA, and Curitiba, Brazil]. Final Report for Research Program *Ignis Mutat Res: Looking at Architecture, the City and the Landscape Through the Prism of Energy*, Bureau de la Recherche Architecturale Urbaine et Paysagère, Ministère de la Culture et de la Communication, France [Office of Architectural, Urban and Landscape Research, Ministry of Culture and Communication, France].

Godier, P. (2001). Coordination et Coopération dans les Grands Projets Urbains et Architecturaux en France et en Espagne [Coordination and Cooperation in Major Urban and Architectural Projects in France and Spain]. In *Cahiers Ramau* 2, May. Paris: Éditions de La Villette.

Godier, P. (2003). Du Projet à la Coordination : Parcours d'un Architecte Urbaniste 'Coordonnateur' [From Project to Coordination: The Career Path of a 'Coordinator' Architect-Planner]. In *Cahiers Ramau* 3, October. Paris: Éditions de la Villette.

Godier, P., & Tapie, G. (1997). *L'Elaboration des Projets Architecturaux et Urbains en Europe: Acteurs et Projets* (1) [*The Elaboration of Architectural and Urban Projects in Europe: Actors and Projets* (1)]. Paris: PUCA-CSTB.

Goodman, J., Laube, M., & Schwenk, J. (2006, Winter). Curitiba's Bus System is a Model for Rapid Transit. *Race, Poverty and Environment.* (2005/2006): 75–76. http://www.reimaginerpe.org/files/25.Curitiba.pdf. Accessed 16 Jan 2015.

Gruber, S. (2012). Learning From Curitiba. The Successes and Failures of an Early Instance of Urban Acupuncture. *Urban Transit*, 72–73. www.ifa.de/fileadmin/pdf/kunst/poc-gruber_en.pdf. Accessed 10 Jan 2015.

Gunderson, D. (2014). The Curitiba Experiment. *Planning Required. Boise State Community and Regional Planning Student Blog.* https://boiseplanning.wordpress.com/2014/04/28/the-curitiba-experiment. Accessed 16 Jan 2015.

Haesbaert, R. (2003). Da Desterritorialização à Multiterritorialidade [From De-territorialization to Multi-territoriality]. *Boletim Gaúcho de Geografica, 29*, 11–24. http://seer.ufrgs.br/bgg/article/view/38739/26249. Accessed 18 Jan 2015.

Hassenteufel, P. (2005). De la Comparaison Internationale à la Comparaison Transnationale [From International Comparison to Transnational Comparison]. *Revue Française de Science Politique, 55*, 113–132.

Jonas, H. ([1979]1991). *Le Principe de Responsabilité [The Responsibility Principle]*. Paris: Flammarion.

Le Néchet, F. (2011, May 18). Consommation d'Energie et Mobilité Quotidienne Selon la Configuration des Densités dans 34 Villes Européennes [*Urban Spatial Structure, Daily Mobility and Energy Consumption: A Study of 34 European Cities*]. *Cybergeo: European Journal of Geography, Systèmes, Modélisation, Géostatistiques.*

Lévy, J. (2010). Le Développement Urbain Durable entre Consensus et Controverse [Sustainable Urban Development, Between Consensus and Controversy]. *L'Information Géographique, 74*(3), 39–50.

Lima, M. F. E. M., & Lima-Filho, D. O. (2009). Condições de Trabalho e Saúde do/a Professor/a Universitário/a [The Working Conditions and Health of the University Professor]. *Ciências & Cognição, 14*(3), 62–82.

Massot, M.-H. (2010). *Mobilités et Modes de Vie Métropolitains. Les Intelligences du Quotidien [Metropolitan Mobility and Lifestyles. Everyday Intelligence]*. Paris: L'Oeil d'Or.

McKibben, B. (2005, November 8). Curitiba: A Global Model For Development. *CommonDreams.* http://www.commondreams.org/cgi-bin/print.cgi?file=/views05/1108-33.htm. Accessed 15 Jan 2015.

Menezes, C. L. (1996). *Desenvolvimento Urbano e Meio Ambiente: A Experiência de Curitiba [Urban Development and the Environment: The Curitiba Experiment]*. Campinas: Papirus.

Newman, P., & Kenworthy, J. (1999). *Sustainability and Cities: Overcoming Automobile Dependence.* Washington, DC: Island Press.

Orfeuil, J.-P. (2010, December 27). La Mobilité, Nouvelle Question Sociale? [Mobility, a Novel Social Question?]. *SociologieS.* http://sociologies.revues.org/3321. Accessed 7 Nov 2016.

Parin, C., Tapie, G., Gerbeaud, F., & Malignon, C. (2008). *Développement Durable Territorial, une Comparaison Franco-Thaïlandaise [Sustainable Territorial Development: A Franco-Thai Comparison]*. Final report, D2RT PUCA 2005–2008, PUCA, MEDAD.

Pinderhughes, R. (2004). *Alternative Urban Futures. Planning for Sustainable Development in Cities Throughout the World.* Lanham: Rowman & Littlefield.

Rifkin, J. (2011). *The Third Industrial Revolution; How Lateral Power is Transforming Energy, the Economy, and the World.* New York: Palgrave Macmillan.

Rodrigues, A. M. (2005, December). Problemática Ambiental – Agenda Política. Espaço, Território, Classes Sociais [Environmental Problematics as Political Agenda. Space, Territory, Social Class]. *Boletim Paulista de Geografia. Perspectiva Crítica, 83*, 91–110.

Ruano, M. (1999). *Eco-urbanism – Sustainable Human Settlements: 60 Case Studies*. Editorial Barcelona: Gustavo Gili.

Sheller, M., & Urry, J. (2006). The New Mobilities Paradigm. *Environment and Planning A, 38*(2), 207–226.

Tapie, G. (2000). *Architectes: Mutations d'une Profession* [*The Architect: Changes in a Profession*]. Paris: L'Harmattan.

Tapie, G. (2003). *Les Professions de la Maîtrise d'Œuvre : Architectes, Ingénierie, Economistes de la Construction* [*The Construction Professions: Architects, Engineers, Quantity Surveyors*]. Paris: La documentation Française.

Tapie, G. (2005). *Maison Individuelle, Architecture, Urbanité* [*The Single-Family House, Architecture and Urbanity*]. La Tour d'Aigues: Editions de l'aube.

Tapie, G., Kent Fitzsimons, J., & Godier, P. (2014). *Comparer la Fabrication de la Ville: Rigueur Méthodologique et Imagination Sociologique* [*Comparing City Building: Methodological Rigor and Sociological Imagination*]. 13p. (Unpublished).

Tress, B., Tress, G., & Fry, G. (2005). Defining Integrative Research Concepts and Process of Knowledge Production. In B. Tress, G. Tress, G. Fry, & P. Opdam (Eds.), *From Landscape Research to Landscape Planning: Aspects of Integration, Education and Application*. Dordrecht: Springer. http://atlas.uniscape.eu/allegati/02_tress.pdf. Accessed 19 Jan 2015.

United Nations Conference on Environment and Development [UNCED]. (1993). *Agenda 21: Programme of Action for Sustainable Development; Rio Declaration on Environment and Development; Statement of Forest Principles: The Final Text of Agreements Negotiated by Governments at the United Nations Conference on Environment and Development (UNCED), 3–14 June 1992, Rio de Janeiro, Brazil. Chapter 38: International Institutional Arrangements.* New York: United Nations Department of Public Information.

United Nations Educational, Scientific and Cultural Organization [UNESCO]. (2015). Women in Science. *UNESCO Institute for Statistics Fact Sheet* N. 34. http://www.uis.unesco.org/ScienceTechnology/Pages/gender-and-science.aspx

van den Besselaar, P., & Heimeriks, G. (2001, July 16–20). Disciplinary, Multidisciplinary, Interdisciplinary. Concepts and Indicators. Proceedings of the 8th International Conference on Scientometrics and Infometrics-ISSI2001. Sydney, Australia, 705–716. http://heimeriks.net/2002issi.pdf. Accessed 19 Jan 2015.

Veiga, A. M. (2006). Mulheres e Ciência: Uma História Necessária [Women and Science: a necessary history]. *Estudos Feministas*. Florianopolis, *14* (3): 819–820.

Vigour, C. (2005). *La Comparaison dans les Sciences Sociales. Pratiques et Méthodes* [*Comparison in the Social Sciences. Practices and Methods*]. Paris: La Découverte.

CHAPTER 9

International Partnerships for Collaborative Research in Argentinian Universities

Ángela Corengia, Ana García de Fanelli, Marcelo Rabossi, and Dante J. Salto

INTRODUCTION

Although several universities in Latin America have made noteworthy strides in scientific production, research is largely seen as an activity relegated to the developed world. The region shows considerable variability regarding levels of research productivity and not all countries have been able to redirect their universities from mainly teaching to also increasing

---

Á. Corengia (✉)
National Institute of Public Administration (INAP), Ministry of Modernization, Buenos Aires, Argentina

A. García de Fanelli
National Scientific and Technical Research Council (CONICET) – Center for the Study of State and Society (CEDES), Buenos Aires, Argentina

M. Rabossi
School of Government, Torcuato di Tella University, Buenos Aires, Argentina

D. J. Salto
Institute of Humanities, National University of Cordoba, Cordoba, Argentina

© The Author(s) 2018
G. Gregorutti, N. Svenson (eds.), *North-South University Research Partnerships in Latin America and the Caribbean*,
https://doi.org/10.1007/978-3-319-75364-5_9

knowledge production (Altbach and Balan 2007). Pursuing external funding for research is another of the problems many universities face. Within this context, university partnerships with top institutions from industrialized countries may be paramount for advancing national research and development (R&D) (Ynalvez and Shrum 2011).

The evolving knowledge society requires international cooperation at the scientific level to produce relevant research in critical areas. Collaboration in key areas tends to enhance results, improve academic performance, and develop human resources in critical ways. In Argentina, according to the National Scientific and Technical Research Council (*Consejo Nacional de Investigaciones Científicas y Técnicas*—CONICET), about 40 percent of all research production within the agency is the result of international collaboration. Key partners involve research centers in the United States (US), Spain, and Brazil (CONICET 2015a).

Due to the relevance of research partnerships between different countries, this chapter is set to analyze the benefits and limitations yielded by the association of two universities in Argentina with prestigious research centers in Europe and the US. This research centers on the motivations, strengths, and barriers faced by international North-South cooperation. The study may be framed in three main questions: (1) What motivates collaboration among researchers from different countries at an international level? (2) What barriers and limitations do these projects face in developing the partnerships? (3) What are the results of those interactions? This study helps to bridge current gaps in the study of research partnerships in three ways. First, it blends three distinct but related bodies of relevant literature on (1) research collaboration, (2) international development (North-South collaboration), and (3) organizational studies of higher education. Second, it approaches the issue in both public and private sector institutions, and within each sector in two different fields of study, chemistry and medicine. Third, it focuses on research partnerships designed for knowledge production and the strengthening of research capacity.

This chapter has five sections. The first presents the theoretical framework and discusses the existing research on (international) research collaborations. The second gives an overview of the core public policies for promoting international collaborations in Argentina. The third introduces the questions guiding the inquiry and the methodology used for the research. The fourth section presents the key findings of the case studies. And the fifth section concludes with a discussion of the findings and some of the major issues encountered in the North-South partnerships studied.

International Research Collaborations: Key Concepts and Definitions

Cross-border research partnerships represent a long-standing tradition in academia (Gaillard and Arvanitis 2013). These collaborations (North-South and South-South partnerships) form the cornerstone of the internationalization of higher education institutions. Increasingly they have become common practice, with researchers formally or informally partnering with colleagues who share similar interests and building upon their mutual strengths with perceived benefits for both sides (Gaillard 1994). Strikingly, though, research on the internationalization of higher education tends to overlook the study of international research collaboration (Kehm and Teichler 2007); related topics usually deal only with institutionally led endeavors rather than with those developed through individual relationships among researchers.

Additionally, science and technology fields have dominated most of the studies on collaboration, utilizing a variety of methodological approaches but limited theoretical frameworks. The most frequently used methodology is quantitative bibliometric counting of international and national co-authorship (Bozeman et al. 2013; Katz and Martin 1997). Tracking research collaboration through co-authorship has been the preferred approach historically; because of this method's visibility, verifiability, stability over time, and ease of traceability, it is simpler to employ than, for example, an analysis of the impact of an international collaboration (Katz and Martin 1997). Although co-authorship is a default way to measure research association, it is far from a comprehensive proxy. Bozeman, Fay, and Slade (2013) note that various types of collaboration do not involve publication of results but rather encompass other kinds of cooperation such as technology and software development or patent registration.

Studies beyond co-authorship analysis have tended to assess efficiencies gained through author collaboration, exploring the benefits and drawbacks of these types of relationships. A wide array of publications has provided strong evidence that collaboration tends to enhance productivity and provide overall positive effects for those involved. However, the same studies tend to overlook a number of important issues faced by those involved in the partnerships, including matters of ownership, sustainability, and the development of national research capacity (Bozeman et al. 2013).

Scientific cooperation includes a range of definitions. Bozeman, Fay, and Slade (2013) propose a broad characterization describing it as "social processes whereby human beings pool their human capital for the objective of producing knowledge" (p. 3). When addressing specific research partnerships, the definition is sometimes narrowed to "a form of interaction among producers of knowledge, allowing effective communication and exchange; sharing of skills, competencies and resources; working, generating and reporting findings together" (Ynalvez and Shrum 2011, p. 205). These definitions bring to the forefront the core features of such collaboration and the potential that may result for capacity building on both sides. Various rationales guide the interactions between the Northern and the Southern researchers, with different key motivations driving the partnerships.

Consistent with Hackett (2005) and Ynalvez and Shrum (2011), the operationalization of collaboration implies that parameters be set for each partner with regard to two necessary dimensions: first, the degree of participation in the collaborative activities, and second, the physical location(s) of the collaborators. Accordingly, our theoretical definition restricts the universe of collaboration to North-South bilateral partnerships and to those that take place in universities. In all cases, the relationships are based on active participation from both sides in the wide range of collaborative activities.

In a detailed review, Bozeman, Fay, and Slade (2013) trace the latest developments in research collaboration studies involving initiatives at the individual researcher level. These studies have examined the attributes of collaborators (e.g., gender, national origin, network ties, career stage) and the collaborative process (including, but not limited to, periodicity of interactions, management style, and task distribution, for example). Other publications (Cummings and Kiesler 2005; Fox and Mohapatra 2007; Siegel et al. 2003) have focused on the effects of various types of organizational features (e.g., center vs. department lead collaboration, resource provision and regulation). However, throughout these investigations, the primary concern is how different organizational schemes and attributes impact the efficacy of research cooperation, not necessarily the motivations and obstacles encountered from the researchers' point of view.

While research collaboration studies do not usually differentiate between national and international arrangements, another set of publications (Beerkens 2002; Gaillard 1994; Gaillard and Arvanitis 2013; Katz and Martin 1997; Ynalvez and Shrum 2011) does deal specifically with issues of cross-border, North-South research partnerships. Gaillard (1994) stresses that collaboration between developed and developing countries yields positive results, mostly in terms of capacity building and research productivity levels for the Southern partner. Nonetheless, differences between North-South partners become evident when prioritizing research topics. Studies show that researchers, in both developed and developing countries, collaborate when they both have strong mutual interests and something to gain from the association (Gaillard 1994; Gaillard and Arvanitis 2013). Among the various types of benefits offered, research collaborations can generate platforms for sharing and transferring knowledge, skills, and techniques; spur innovative ideas and contributions; and widen research networks (Katz and Martin 1997). Researchers may also use partnerships as a way to attract alternative sources of funding (Beerkens 2002). International development agencies in developed countries such as the German Academic Exchange Service (*Deutscher Akademischer Austausch Dienst*—DAAD-Germany) and the US Agency for International Development (USAID-US), among others, call for proposals to partner with developing countries. In those cases, both developed and developing countries benefit from an extra source of funding for their endeavors. This research builds on these inputs and focuses on best practices, inquiring about obstacles and solutions associated with North-South partnerships.

Ynalvez and Shrum (2011) provide several relevant insights related to partnership practices in developing countries. Their analysis focuses on the links between professional networks and publication productivity in the context of resource-constrained research institutions. Interestingly, this research finds that scientists are willing to engage in collaboration even in spite of coordination difficulties and without any measurable impact on their productivity. Evidence indicates that researchers may value the professional opportunities created through the established network and the extrinsic rewards involved, such as additional income in the form of honoraria and travel opportunities (Ynalvez and Shrum 2011). Motivation to engage in this type of academic practice is a major issue covered in several studies. On this point, Jeong, Choi, and Kim (2013) contend that international partnerships offer more potential for improved productivity and greater impact than similar arrangements at the domestic level, even though the international collaboration may entail a higher cost. Their empirical exploration shows that substantial financial and "attentional" resources[1] coupled with academic excellence, individual motivation, and active informal communication are all factors that contribute to the success of these efforts.

As a result of higher education scholars' limited study of research collaboration, university organizational dynamics have not been examined in much detail. Rather than research on collaboration, final reports toward sponsoring agencies tend to dominate the main publications on partnerships (Bradley 2007). This chapter integrates organizational dynamics into the study of research partnerships. Scholars have addressed motivations, benefits, and issues of research collaboration, but little has been documented on actual cases where North-South cooperation may, directly or indirectly, enhance various research indicators. The following section presents key science and innovation policies, critical to the understanding of the examined partnerships.

THE MACRO LEVEL: NATIONAL POLICIES TO PROMOTE INTERNATIONAL RESEARCH COLLABORATION

In 2012, Argentina spent 0.65 percent of its gross domestic product (GDP) on R&D, far below the investment levels registered in industrialized countries and even certain Latin American countries such as Brazil (1.16 percent), but still higher than most countries in the region (MINCYT 2014). By analyzing the composition of the expenditure by sector in 2012, 45.6 percent corresponds to CONICET and other public bodies,[2] 29.7 percent to public universities, 21.5 percent to business enterprises, 1.8 percent to nonprofit organizations, and only 1.5 percent to private universities (MINCYT 2014). CONICET among the national R&D actors stands out with responsibility for nearly half of the total 2012 investment and far more than that of the university or business sectors.

Founded in 1958, CONICET is a national institution under the Ministry of Science, Technology and Productive Innovation (*Ministerio de Ciencia, Tecnología e Innovación Productiva*—MINCYT). One of its main activities is its science research career development program. Through this program, CONICET finances full-time researchers and grants doctoral and postdoctoral scholarships at public and private universities. The majority of the 8508 CONICET researchers are also full-time or part-time professors at public and private universities (CONICET 2014).[3] This is important because it has helped boost the number of full-time faculty in the university sector. In 2012, full-time faculty at public universities represented only 10.9 percent of the total, or 20,000 faculty posts (SPU 2012).

With respect to full- and part-time researchers devoted to R&D activities in 2012, the majority were employed by public universities (48.9 percent), followed by other public research centers (34.7 percent), private sector firms (9.6 percent), private universities (5 percent), and nonprofit organizations (1.9 percent) (MINCYT 2014). When compared with the national economically active population, the total number of full-time equivalent positions at R&D institutions is higher in Argentina than in the rest of Latin America but lower than in industrialized countries (MINCYT 2014).

Argentina's scientific production, measured as the number of papers in the Science Citation Index (SCI), more than doubled from 4184 in 2001 to 9065 in 2012 (MINCYT 2002, 2014). In 2012, the most productive areas were physics, chemistry, and earth sciences (36.7 percent); life sciences (35.9 percent); agriculture, biology, and environment (26 percent); and clinical medicine (21.4 percent). Nevertheless, Argentina's portion of research output still represented only 0.57 percent of the total international productivity (MINCYT 2014).

As with SCI production, Argentina's international collaboration in science has also grown dramatically over the past decade. Evidence of this expansion is seen in the number of international co-authored papers that rose from 1745 in 2000 to 3565 in 2010. As a consequence, the relative weight of the country's scientific production with international collaboration also increased, representing 34.1 percent of the total scientific production in 2000 and 42.3 percent at the end of 2010 (Merlino-Santesteban 2013). Hence, international collaboration in the scientific domain appears to have contributed to enhancing national productivity.

In terms of international papers co-authored in 2012, Argentina's main counterpart was the US, followed by Spain.[4] Fig. 9.1 shows that between 2008 and 2012, scientific papers from international collaborations increased for all countries with which Argentina was engaged in cooperative research efforts.

Although some of this expansion likely results from individual researchers' personal contacts and the bonds developed during their doctoral and postdoctoral studies, CONICET and other agencies of the MINCYT have contributed considerably to the linkages formed between the national scientific community and its international peers, mainly through implementation of a series of competitive grants. MINCYT funding allocated to international collaboration activity more than doubled from almost US$4 million in 2009 to US$8 million in 2015 (MINCYT 2015a).[5]

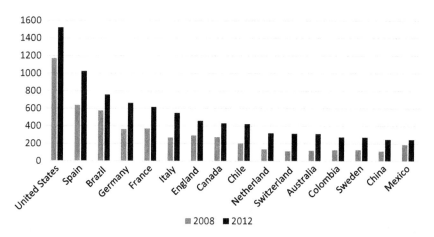

Fig. 9.1 Argentinian papers produced through international collaboration, by country, 2008–2012. (Source: MINCYT 2014)

Until 2015, CONICET's main cooperation modalities were the following: (1) visiting scholar programs, (2) bilateral cooperation, (3) international research groups, (4) international laboratory collaborations, and (5) international research center projects (CONICET 2015b). Regarding the first, visiting scholars promote contact among researchers and foster possibilities for exploring cooperation or developing joint research projects. CONICET provides Argentinian researchers with funds for travel expenses to counterpart countries or allocates grants to cover the travel expenses for international researchers coming to Argentina. The second modality, bilateral cooperation programs, allotted funding of ARS 50,000[6] for biannual projects with foreign institutions and of ARS 90,000[7] for triennial cooperation projects related to specific topics (MINCYT 2015b). The grants associated with the triennial cooperation projects varied according to the partner country and usually covered travel for researchers, doctoral, and postdoctoral fellows at the host institution, as well as supplies and minor equipment. The third modality identified, international research groups, consists of forming associations between researchers from national and foreign institutions to conduct joint projects, or train doctors and young researchers for a period of four years with the possibility of a two-year extension. Annual funding varies according to the number of groups, with an estimated budget in 2014 of about ARS 100,000[8] for each group to cover travel and supplies for researchers and fellows for up to six months per year at the counterpart institution (MINCYT 2015b). Counterpart funding generally comes from internal resources or third-party institutions. Collaboration with international laboratories, the fourth modality presented above, includes activity with research institutes that have at least one operating location in Argentina and one in another country. These associations seek to deepen and consolidate a pre-existing and fruitful scientific cooperation. To access this funding, the associated laboratories must demonstrate evidence of continuous collaboration and joint publications. Contributions by CONICET and the counterpart are generally similar and cover operating expenses, scientific exchanges, joint thesis supervision, seminars, and workshops. Finally, international research center projects are a cooperation modality comprised of units that are co-managed with international institutions. They are located in Argentina, nationally and internationally recognized in their disciplines, topics, or fields of study, and jointly supervised by CONICET and the international counterpart. One such example is the National Structural Biology and Neurobiology Center, which works with the Max Planck Society (Max-Planck-Gesellschaft—MPG) in Germany.

During the last decade, MINCYT, too, has implemented separate funding instruments for development of joint research projects, organization of international scientific events, creation of binational centers, and concession of training scholarships. The Argentinian Bureau for Enhancing Cooperation with the European Community (Oficina de Enlace Argentina—Unión Europea en Ciencia, Tecnología e Innovación, ABEST) is an example of output from the MINCYT efforts. ABEST is a platform designed to facilitate and improve scientific cooperation between Argentina and the European Community. It has a national and international support structure (France, Italy, Germany, and Spain), and an advisory board that includes representatives from institutions in each of these countries. In Argentina, it offers thematic national contacts for reporting on cooperation opportunities in priority areas for the country, counseling on the presentation of proposals, and a network of institutional centers that facilitate the flow and updating of information at the national level (MINCYT 2015b).

METHODOLOGY

This chapter uses a case study approach for examining North-South university partnership contributions to Argentinian R&D. The case study offers an effective tool for descriptive purposes and helps to structure a more accurate picture of the particular event under analysis (King et al. 1994). According to Yin (2014), "A case study is an empirical inquiry that investigates a contemporary phenomenon (the "case") in depth and within its real-world context, especially when the boundaries between phenomenon and context may not be clearly evident" (p. 16). With this in mind, our study considers the context of national R&D, focusing on the phenomenon of North-South research partnerships within Argentinian universities. Of particular interest are the national public policies and institutional arrangements that enable and support these partnerships along with the corresponding incentives (or motivations) and disincentives (or obstacles) for the scholars involved in these endeavors.

The two cases selected for presentation were chosen using the logic of a purposive sample, taking into account the positioning of Argentinian universities in the World and Latin American QS Rankings (QS World University Rankings 2014/15; QS University Ranking Latin America 2015). The QS data includes a set of indicators and different weights for each.[9] The University of Buenos Aires (*Universidad de Buenos Aires*— UBA, a public institution) is ranked first and the University Austral (*Universidad Austral*—UA, a private institution) is ranked second among Argentinian universities in the two QS data sets, respectively. Moreover, both universities also hold the first and second positions among Argentinian universities with regard to the research indicator "citations per faculty."

To select cases within UBA and Austral University, we chose those research units[10] specialized in fields with a greater number of SCOPUS Database publications. In the case of UBA, until 2015, 32 percent of SCOPUS publications came from the basic sciences (biochemistry, genetics and molecular biology, physics and astronomy, and chemistry). The research unit selected as a case study, the Institute of Chemical Physics of Materials, Environment and Energy (*Instituto de Química Física de los Materiales, Medio Ambiente y Energía*—INQUIMAE) registers the most publications in SCOPUS of all UBA-CONICET research institutes: 902 as of September 2015, followed by the Medical Research Institute Alfredo Lanani with 449 (SCOPUS 2015). In the case of UA, the research unit selected, the School of Biomedical Sciences (*Facultad de Ciencias Biomédicas*—FCB), represents 50 percent of the university's total publications in Scopus (medicine, biochemistry, genetics and molecular biology, and neuroscience) (SCOPUS 2015).

INQUIMAE was created in 1992 as part of the UBA through a grant from the German Federal Enterprise for International Cooperation

(*Deutsche Gesellschaftfür Technische Zusammenarbeit*—GTZ). It belongs to the Department of Inorganic, Analytical and Physical Chemistry at the UBA School of Natural and Exact Sciences. Since March 1999, it has worked under the administration of both UBA and CONICET. INQUIMAE is the direct result of a North-South university research partnership. Currently, it has exchange programs for chemistry students via the "Partnerships for International Research and Education" (PIRE-National Science Foundation), von Humbolt, Volkswagen, and the DAAD. INQUIMAE is also linked to the Max Planck Gesellschaft Institute and other universities in Europe and the US. Moreover, it is an associated center of excellence registered in the Third World Academy of Science (TWAS) and participates in the Seventh Framework Program of the European Community FP7 within the EURALSUR Coordination Action[11] and BIOMOLECTRONICS (Biomolecular Electronics and Electro-catalysis), a Marie Curie International Research Staff Exchange program.

INQUIMAE has 47 research staff members, 86 research assistants, 72 doctoral students and postdoctoral fellows, and 15 administrative staff members (INQUIMAE 2014). In terms of productivity, and according to the SCOPUS database (2015), the institute has published 902 scientific articles. Its scientific output also increased from 21 research papers in 1996 to 61 in 2014. INQUIMAE recorded 501 publications in Web of Science in 2008 and 1044 in the same database in 2013 with 13,686 citations (INQUIMAE 2015). The current goal of INQUIMAE is to promote applied research in materials, environment, energy, biophysical chemistry and nanotechnology to train young researchers and technicians.

In the School of Biomedical Sciences at UA we analyzed five groups within the FCB Area of Basic Research. These groups, together with the ones located in the Austral Teaching Hospital (*Hospital Universitario Austral*—HUA), constitute the recently established Translational Medicine Research Institute (*Instituto de Investigaciones de Medicina Traslacional*), operating under the administration of both FCB and CONICET since June 2015. The FCB Area of Basic Research comprises five groups with a staff of nine researchers from CONICET, one international researcher, four research students, and ten doctoral students and postdoctoral fellows. The publications through March 2015 total 142 (62 percent with international co-authors) and citations amount to 2279 (SCOPUS 2015). Publications increased from 49 (for the period

1999–2006) to 83 (for the period 2007–2015). Total numbers of publications and citations in SCOPUS (2015) for the UA through March 2015 are 681 and 6329, respectively.

Among the international institutions actively collaborating with the FCB groups analyzed is the Karolinska Institute (*Karolinska Institutet*—KI), a medical university in Stockholm (Sweden) and one of the world's largest. A committee of the KI appoints the laureates for the Nobel Prize in Physiology and Medicine. The collaboration between the FCB Gene Therapy group, established in 2004, and the following institutions is also significant: Center for Applied Medicine Research (*Centro de Investigación Médica Aplicada*—CIMA) and the Teaching Hospital of the University of Navarra (*Universidad de Navarra*), Spain; the University of Trieste, Italy; the University of North Carolina, US; the School of Medicine at Mount Sinai Hospital, US; and the Charité—School of Medicine of Berlin, Germany. Moreover, it is important to mention the continuous partnership between the FCB Liver Fibrosis group with the University of Pittsburgh and the University of Cincinnati in the US. Finally, since 2012, there has been an international collaboration between the Federal Ministry of Education and Research (*Bundes Ministerium für Bildung und Forschung*—BMBF) in Germany and the FCB Cellular and Molecular Medicine group.

The study of each case focuses on three analytical dimensions: (a) the factors at the macro and micro levels that have contributed to international research collaboration, (b) the obstacles and problems encountered during the implementation of the international partnership and, (c) the results achieved in terms of the number of papers published in peer-reviewed journals with international collaboration.

To collect data and information on each of these dimensions, we examined the internal institutional documents—such as research policies, web pages, annual research reports, research regulations, and international partnership policies—as well as public use files, including national government statistical data and the SCOPUS database. We also conducted 13 in-depth interviews with the directors and senior researchers of these units and with university officials responsible for R&D.[12] All interviews took place between November 2014 and March 2015. To analyze the data collected, information was organized according to the criteria presented in Table 9.1.

Table 9.1 Criteria and dimensions

Criteria	Dimensions
Overview	Date of establishment of the institute and its research groups
	Institute and research group staff and publications
	Research lines and major international partners
Main types of international partnerships	Type of partnership based on size; time frame; and scope of activities
	Type of partnership based on human resources; funding; infrastructure; or joint scientific output
Factors contributing to partnership establishment	Researchers' personal networks
	International collaboration policies developed by Europe or the US
	International collaboration policies developed by Argentina
Factors promoting partnerships	Prestige within the scientific community
	Research funding
	Increased potential for publication in top SCI journals
	Mobility of researchers nationally and internationally
	Scope of the research line and resource requirements
Partnership contributions to institute/research group consolidation	Increased scientific production in terms of patents and SCI publications
	Increased funding resources earmarked for research
	Attraction of young researchers, domestically and internationally
	Development of human resources through study abroad
	Cooperation with the business sector
Obstacles encountered in partnerships	Ad hoc nature of partnership
	Bureaucratic processes at university and/or CONICET levels
	Changes in international collaboration policies and financial status of developed nations

CASE STUDY FINDINGS

To sum up concisely the findings of this study: international scientific cooperation between the South and North is highly beneficial for the parties involved. Data culled from the interviews indicates that although personal ties in general dominate with regard to influencing the instigation and implementation of partnerships, state support is also critical for developing partnerships in both the public and private sectors. To illustrate, in 2011, nearly 44 percent of all funds invested in R&D were in the hands of public research centers, with public universities receiving 27 percent and private universities only 1.5 percent. Private enterprise and not-for-profit entities explain the rest (MINCYT 2014). These figures tend to confirm the need for public support in advancing complex research, particularly in the more expensive areas of scientific investigation. The following sections provide a synthesis of the main findings. Benefits as well as shortcomings of the cooperation are described in greater detail.

The *INQUIMAE* Case

In 1966, a coup d'état brought down the elected Argentinian government for the fifth time since 1930. The new military government was characterized by its strong repression of public universities. Given such a hostile environment, the Department of Chemistry at UBA, along with many others, became very isolated. Consequently, both the quality of its academic staff and the productivity of the faculty in terms of the number and relevance of their publications plummeted.

Argentina returned to a stable democracy in 1983.[13] One of the first educational initiatives of the new administration was to consolidate the nation's higher education system to better coordinate the future expansion of the sector. In order to rebuild what had been dismantled in terms of human and physical capital during the period between 1966 and 1983, the new Dean of the UBA School of Exact and Natural Sciences hired one of the most prestigious scholars in the country to rebuild the chemistry department. Changes aligned with the objective of regaining the university's former prestige began to be implemented in 1986. The idea was to improve not only the UBA Department of Chemistry but also the entire university system.

With limited resources and obsolete equipment, there was an obvious need for additional funds to modernize the department. The personal relationship between the Department Director at that time and an Argentinian researcher living in Germany was decisive for obtaining the necessary funding. Thus, more than a strategic desire to broaden the department's international reach, the creation of the INQUIMAE in 1992 came about as a spontaneous fundraising decision. The role played by UBA at the institutional level linking INQUIMAE and GTZ (the German Agency responsible for the donation that launched the institute) was less important. According to one interviewee, "UBA limited its role to backing the agreement, signing the contract, and more importantly, not interfering". Also, in the words of one senior researcher:

> Personal relationships are a key part of any agreement, but this doesn't mean that I have to know the other party personally; we may know each other through our respective publications, then, sometimes by chance, we meet at a conference, and say, 'Finally we meet in person!'

The personal relationship may be a rather distant one, but one based on a perception of mutual professional trust. The personal links involved for securing the contract between the two entities in this case played a fundamental role at the moment of finalizing the project. All six interviewees at INQUIMAE agreed with the conclusion that personal ties between researchers matter more for bringing about bilateral cooperation agreements than any measure promoted or implemented at the institutional level.

The initial funding from GTZ was not actually for research but rather for the establishment of what would become INQUIMAE and for the acquisition of modern equipment. The idea behind the donation, at least from the German perspective, was to promote applied research abroad and strengthen the links between research and Argentinian industry. GTZ made a donation of two million German Marks[14] to set up the institute, and UBA and CONICET provided for the operational expenditures and faculty salaries needed to run it. In short, this North-South partnership agreement was bilateral, triggered by a personal relationship between two colleagues who happened to be located in different countries. It was initially conceived of as a short-term project involving the donation of specific funds for the creation of an institute. However, given the success of the relationship, the association between the two partners continues to this day. Even more notably, it has opened doors for other international projects, with the GTZ association providing for INQUIMAE an important first step for developing collaborative agreements with other centers in the industrialized North. In bilateral partnerships, the role played by each country at the government level is also significant. Scientific cooperation policies followed by European nations, mainly those in Germany, France, and the UK, were more beneficial for Argentina than other collaborative agreements with the US, for instance. The latter only provided funds for travel but not for equipment and physical capital. Given UBA's need to create a research center from scratch, the European policy was far more appealing. As one senior researcher put it:

> Germany's well-developed policy for start-up projects does much to promote this type of bilateral agreement, which is highly beneficial because given that donations are tied to matching fund arrangements, the investment in scientific production ends up being double on the receiving end.

Following the creation of the National Agency for Science and Technology Promotion (*Agencia Nacional de Promoción Científica y Tecnológica*—ANPCYT) in the 1990s and MINCYT in 2007, researchers in Argentina are in a better position to obtain the financial support to back their scientific activities. All interviewees agreed that resources for acquisition of equipment are still scarce, but that things have improved over the last decade and funds for travel are now commonly available. As one director pointed out, "with the creation of the MINCYT in 2007, it is not only the prestigious INQUIMAE that gets financial support (and more currently than in previous years), but the whole research system in Argentina". This represents a considerable impetus to the generation of knowledge at the national level.

Benefits from partnerships are also mutual. One professor highlighted that "because of this association, Germany secures sales of state-of-the-art equipment not available in Argentina". Another researcher included that the partnership introduced "German culture" to Argentinian academia, which was seen as a positive, professionalizing force for scientific production. The recruitment of good researchers from Argentina is an added benefit received by the Northern partner. In an effort to thwart brain drain, INQUIMAE does not promote student exchange below the post-doctoral level. According to one senior researcher:

> postdoctoral students tend to return to their country of origin and not to stay as full-time researchers in developed countries, so we mainly promote postdoc academic exchanges in the form of short stays, three or six months, at different universities and public or private research centers.

In other words, the academic collaboration is mainly bilateral and primarily for the benefit of postdoctoral fellows and scholars. Still, overall, INQUIMAE gets the better part of the deal, particularly when we analyze collaboration at an organizational or individual level. According to one director, only a handful of researchers and students come to Argentina. He notes, "in general, it is an almost one-way flow, from South to North, but this dynamic allows us, as researchers, to have access to technology that is not available in Argentina". One of the INQUIMAE researchers who is currently part of a team working in France agreed. She emphasized that "by having access to top-notch equipment it is possible to carry out a project that in the absence of cutting-edge technology would end up being nothing more than a theoretical hypothesis". Another researcher remarked similarly, "a stint at a laboratory in Germany, France, the UK or US--countries that are at the forefront of scientific knowledge in the field of chemistry--is a major advantage for any researcher". Accessing funds for acquisition of the state-of-the-art equipment through international collaboration is another significant benefit for the partners in the South; "for advancing knowledge in the field of materials and inorganic chemistry, this is paramount", emphasized one of the interviewees. This type of equipment is prohibitively expensive, so gaining access to this sophisticated machinery without external help is a challenge.

Researchers at INQUIMAE agreed that international cooperation between the global South and the industrialized North is helpful for increasing productivity and mobility of researchers and students. Because this type of cooperation puts researchers in contact with scholars in centers of excellence elsewhere and allows those from the South use of infrastructure not available in their home country, this aids in upping the number of publications accepted in prestigious research journals. In spite of espoused double-blindness of peer reviews, it is possible to speculate that known researchers from well-established institutions in developed countries have better chances of publishing in reputed journals than unknown researchers from somewhat isolated centers in Latin America. Beyond having a relevant research paper, good communication and prior experience are paramount for getting a work published (Gould 2014). One researcher observed this issue is also affected by questions of scale and networking. He said that "while a US researcher may attend five or six international conferences a year, his or her counterpart at INQUIMAE goes to no more than one or two academic events". Thus, it is harder for Southern scholars to build strong networks for confronting the "publish or perish" dilemma. The same researcher noted that "it is easier to get cited in another publication if they know you personally, nothing replaces a personal contact, regardless of whether your work is available through the internet". The human factor plays a fundamental role.

Benefits outweigh obstacles in international collaboration, but there are some drawbacks, often associated with domestic problems. For example, inefficient bureaucracy at both institutional and governmental levels can prevent efficient financial management of projects and hinder scholar mobility. Some interviewees mentioned fluctuations in the economic situations of industrialized countries as an additional barrier to fluid movement of students and scholars. Many agree that commercial policies followed by Argentina, characterized by strong quantitative restrictions on imports and exchange rate volatility, have had a negative impact. In the words of one scholar, "because of bureaucratic obstacles, laboratory supplies can be stuck for a long time in customs". These import difficulties have also affected the acquisition of equipment and spare parts needed for laboratory repairs.

220   Á. CORENGIA ET AL.

The Case of the School of Biomedical Science at Austral University

The School of Biomedical Science (FCB) at Austral University (UA) was founded in 1996. From the beginning, research groups were established that have grown and consolidated over the years. As mentioned previously, this case analyzes five particular groups currently working under the FCB area of basic research.

Each group began its research activities at different times, with some of the current endeavors resulting as offshoots of previously existing groups. Each corresponds to a specific branch of research, all within the medical sciences. The first research group (neurosciences) began operation in 1997 in association with the Swedish KI. The director of this group had a personal relationship with KI even before coming to work at the FCB because he completed a postdoctoral fellowship there. This bilateral association continues still after nearly 20 years. Although this is a small team, it is very active with regard to research production and human capital training. As the director of the unit stated, "this cooperation has generated a kind of virtuous circle given the sustained performance of the Argentinian students, paving the way for future candidates as well". A close association between the director of the group and KI opens the door for potential research stints in Sweden and the completion of formal studies for Argentinian doctoral students.

Group 2 (cellular and molecular medicine) began in 1997, simultaneously with Group 1. It is also a small team made up of a director, a research assistant, and two doctoral fellows, four academics in total. Since 2012, the center has maintained a bilateral and international association with the German Federal Ministry of Education and Research (*Bundes Ministerium für Bildung und Forschung*—BMBF). The relationship began as the product of informal interaction between the director of Group 2 and a researcher at BMBF. Over time, this connection triggered a more formal cooperative agreement. The Argentinian and the German governments both played a critical role in the consolidation of the partnership. With funds from the MINCYT, together with resources provided by the German government, this unit put together the financial means to launch its international cooperation project. This partnership represents a case where interaction between the private sector and the state proved necessary, mainly to advance the transference of knowledge in a field as expensive as the medical sciences. Additionally, the government supported the project through the provision of human capital and funding. All four researchers in this group are part of CONICET, which also pays their salaries.

Although this international cooperation began as a three-year project, given the ensuing mutual benefits, both parties expect the association to continue.

In 2004, Group 3 (genetic therapy) began its research activities. In comparison to the other teams, it is a relatively large research unit in terms of academic human resources. Besides its director, it has three senior researchers, four doctoral fellows, and two undergraduate students from the School of Medicine of the same university. Except for the students, for whom the association to the group is part of their academic training as future medical doctors, and a fellow, the rest are CONICET researchers. Their affiliation means that most of them receive at least part of their salaries from public funding. The group's main international cooperation is with the Applied Medicine Research Center and University Clinic of the University of Navarra, Spain. Again, the link between the centers was the product of personal contacts, as the director of the unit is a University of Navarra graduate who completed his doctoral and postdoctoral education there. Group 3 has fostered other partnerships as well with research centers in the US, Italy, and Germany. In contrast to the previous groups, this unit has developed multilateral research cooperation.

Group 4 (chronic pain) began its activities in 2010. Thus, it is relatively new and a direct result of Group 1 as the director was originally part of that unit. While working in Group 1, the director obtained his PhD from the FCB at UA and after that, a second doctorate from KI, the Swedish institute associated with Group 1. Later on, he completed postdoctoral training at the University of Pittsburg (UP) and returned to Argentina as part of the Network of Argentinian Researchers and Scientists Abroad (*Red de Argentinos Investigadores y Científicos en el Exterior*—RAICES), a program sponsored by MINCYT aimed at repatriating scientists and researchers who wish to re-enter academia in Argentina. This group has developed partnership agreements with UP and also with KI and the University of Cincinnati (UC), all institutions directly linked to the director of this team. As with Group 3, the international cooperation is multilateral. With a total of four researchers and two undergraduate students, the Argentinian government, through CONICET, is also crucial for sustaining the operating expenditures of the group.

Group 5 is a recent creation. Its director (first part of Group 1 and then of Group 3), opened the hepatic fibrosis unit in 2014. This director is also a scientist repatriated through the RAICES program after obtaining his PhD at KI. This arrangement demonstrates vividly how bilateral cooperation between FCB and KI has been dynamic over time, as well as instrumental with the formation of high-quality human capital for Argentina.

Currently, this group works with KI as its main international partner. Once again, personal ties appear to be fundamental for consolidating a cooperative international collaboration.

What the UA FCB case shows is that the social capital or network of the researchers is the starting point that works to cohesively connect the South with the North. Similarly, personal links tend to consolidate bilateral or multilateral cooperation programs. Likewise, the role of the Argentinian government in helping to launch this private medical research center is also essential. MINCYT and CONICET both gave this research unit critical support for its establishment: the former through a program of "return subsidies" to help Argentinian researchers living abroad return to the country; the latter, by financing the salaries of the academics. Taking advantage of these public programs was key and an important part of UA's strategic vision. In this case, personal links between scholars together with UA institutional policies and the help of the Argentinian government coincided to give FCB its opportunity to become an international research unit.

International partnerships are formally encouraged in various sections of the UA Institutional Project (*Proyecto Institucional de la UA*). This is evident in all of the following official documents: (a) the UA Vision, under Section II.3, Founding Principles, paragraph n; (b) the UA By-laws, RM 126/09 version, Annex I, under Article 3: Main Functions of the University, paragraph g; (c) Research Policies; and (d) Policies on Institutional Relations, Section 5. The existence of both master and individual agreements between FCB and all international partners mentioned above shows that solid institutional policies underlie these international partnerships and provide for their foundation. Moreover, the interviewees stated they had received financial aid from internal UA grants, along with encouragement from FCB, for participating in research visits to the foreign institutions. A statement by the UA Vice President of Research is worth noting in this regard, as he explains that the most relevant partnerships usually come about after lengthier stays, which allow for closer ties to be developed, generating a greater likelihood of continued joint research efforts:

> Even though the importance of international partnerships is included in [UA's] Vision, By-laws and General Policies, if it weren't for our more proactive policy of encouraging people to go and pursue more extended research stays abroad—for doctoral and postdoctoral work--the general policy would not work. In this sense, research partnerships are essential to staying alive in the competitive world of research.

Also, as one of the research group directors put it, "Our group has survived in good measure thanks to its partnerships, given the difficulties that we sometimes have with obtaining funding." He added that joint partnerships offer:

> a chance to grow and a chance to survive, since our research fellows are able to carry out research abroad....cooperation means an exchange of people—a very meaningful one, indeed. When you travel abroad, there's a research infrastructure that we don't have here.

In sum, the benefits to FCB from international networking with top-notch centers from the global North are many. Among these, interviewees mentioned: better dynamics for mobility of researchers and fellows from the South to the North; greater job possibilities as academics; more funding for research and infrastructure; better opportunities for accessing sophisticated equipment not available in Argentina; potential for broadening the network of contacts for future projects; and increased opportunities for publishing in well-known and prestigious journals.

At the same time, these groups have faced a number of political and bureaucratic obstacles to keep the cooperation programs active and productive. As in the INQUIMAE case, Argentina's macroeconomic instability and exchange rate volatility makes it harder to acquire necessary laboratory equipment and supplies. As one scholar put it, "While in Sweden it takes four days to import an antibody reagent from the US, the same procedure can take four months in Argentina." Likewise, another interviewee remarked, "The dollar rate, inflation, and import restrictions are extremely important. They slow down your research immensely." Also, and in contrast to what happens in most advanced research centers in the industrialized world, FCB lacks a well-trained management support system to ease the administrative procedures involved in such collaborations. Tasks such as filling out the requisite documentation or obtaining the necessary background information for the corresponding paperwork, for example, can be daunting at times without adequate back office support.

As a means to summarizing the findings in terms of the output and international impact of both research centers, Table 9.2 presents their total number of publications and citations during the last five years, according to SCOPUS. What is clear from this data is that, on average, more than half the production (of both publications and citations) is the product of international partnerships.

Table 9.2 Number of publications and citations in relation to international collaboration at INQUIMAE and FCB, 2010–2014

	INQUIMAE	FCB	INQUIMAE	FCB	INQUIMAE	FCB	INQUIMAE	FCB	INQUIMAE	FCB
Year	2014		2013		2012		2011		2010	
Number of publications	66	12	72	8	71	11	69	11	74	9
Percentage of international co-authored publications	56.1	50.0	50.0	75.0	45.1	54.5	56.5	54.5	56.8	33.3
Number of citations[a]	77	8	272	33	398	53	649	96	972	161
Percentage of international co-authored citations	70.1	62.5	50.0	84.8	56.0	64.2	60.1	56.3	63.3	55.9

Source: SCOPUS (2015) and authors' calculations

[a]Refers to the number of citations a paper has received since its publication to March 2015. For example, INQUIMAE published 69 papers in 2011. These were cited 649 times from 2011 to March 2015

Based on the information collected, especially from interviews with researchers in the five FCB groups and the university's Vice Provost for Research, different motivations and dynamics surfaced when it came to deciding how to initiate North-South cooperation. Some of the groups started as a result of institutional support, at the university or national government level; others were more spontaneous and a consequence of personal ties among certain researchers involved. However, what became clear during the interviews is that as in the INQUIMAE case, the social capital of the researcher and his or her professional contacts are vital for initiating the relationship and keeping it alive over time. In short, the qualitative analysis of the interview data shows the importance of personal ties among researchers when deciding the kind of international cooperation to be fostered. It also supports the conclusion that partnerships with the industrialized North can be helpful for increasing the productivity of Southern research centers.

DISCUSSION AND CONCLUSIONS

The main objectives of this chapter were to determine what motivates international collaboration and inquire about the advantages, barriers, and limitations faced by those partnerships. Various motivations lead to the establishment of formal links with centers abroad. The results of this exploration match certain findings from previous studies. Motivation usually originates with individual contacts between researchers working in different centers (Bozeman et al. 2013). In the case of INQUIMAE, the development of the research center came about through funding from GTZ, a relationship initiated by the INQUIMAE director with a colleague from Germany. FCB follows a path similar to that of most of the research groups examined there, linked through bonds developed during postdoctoral academic training. As Bozeman, Fay, and Slade (2013) state, the sustainability of these partnerships is critical to the long-term success of international collaboration. Although individual connections spurred most of the partnerships analyzed in this study, the majority of them were subsequently structured to allow for continued work with their foreign counterparts, regardless of the involvement of the individuals initially responsible for the foundation of the cooperative alliances.

The findings presented here coincide with Ynalvez and Shrum (2011) expectation that in a resource-constrained context, such as that of the Argentinian universities, obtaining access to resources not available in the home country is a major motivation for establishing links abroad. Besides the personal ties with researchers abroad, most partnerships strategically involved collaborations with European universities that provided funding for infrastructure in addition to travel, beyond what US funding typically allows for. In all the cases analyzed, the science and technology agencies from the home country (Argentina), such as CONICET and MINCYT, have played a critical role in the funding of local research positions, doctoral and postdoctoral fellowships. Though crucial, this funding is neither the only nor even necessarily the major motivation for embarking on associations with international universities. Several interviewees mentioned how these international relationships brought added prestige to their research centers, strengthening both internal and external legitimization in the academic community. This finding is related to what Ynalvez and Shrum (2011) call extrinsic rewards.

Key advantages to the establishment of international collaborations in the cases examined here follow those reflected in the main literature on research partnerships (Gaillard 1994; Katz and Martin 1997). As the previous section of this chapter shows, researchers tend to value their cross-border associations as a means of increasing their productivity and the impact of the research they conduct beyond the local academic community. In some areas, such as with the medical sciences, publishing in international journals and participating in key conferences is the only way to stay current with the latest developments. Jeong, Choi, and Kim (2013) stress the importance of these benefits as essential reasons for seeking foreign partners. Counter to findings in previous studies (Gaillard and Arvanitis 2013), none of the interviewees in this study mentioned research priorities as an issue when partnering with Northern institutions. Although those differences may exist, they do not seem to be critical issues in these ventures.

This study also corroborates the importance of the influence that certain organizational features may have on the relative success of these endeavors (Cummings and Kiesler 2005; Fox and Mohapatra 2007; Siegel et al. 2003). Strong departmental leadership tends to increase the chances of partnership survival in the long run (Fox and Mohapatra 2007). In the case of INQUIMAE, interviewees highlighted that though the central offices of the university were instrumental in the formalities of signing agreements between two universities, the key to success was the local, departmental management of the specific partnership. To some extent, arrangements at the departmental level were seen as more productive and less bureaucratic than those at the university level. Other constraints mentioned were linked with economic stability and bureaucratic issues on both sides of the collaboration.

The findings signal a variety of implications, including policy recommendations at the organizational and governmental levels. The cases analyzed show that researchers' personal ties with colleagues abroad play a critical role in initiating partnerships. Policies promoting short-term mobility (at the doctoral and postdoctoral levels) between research centers can help generate vital networks. Despite the relevance of personal ties among researchers, organizational as well as governmental policies play a relevant role in creating sustainable partnerships that transcend small networks. For instance, through funding for human resources (principal researchers and collaborators), government agencies of science and technology contribute to offsetting costs not included in the external sponsorship. Furthermore, those structures may facilitate the application process to obtain grants and provide technical assistance to research teams. However, both governments and higher education institutions should be cautious about regulatory overreach, since it may inhibit the growth of those endeavors.

All in all, international research partnerships are quite diverse, and the types of arrangements explored span a variety of purposes with regard to knowledge production and intended outcomes. Despite this heterogeneity, governments and higher education institutions should take into account some common policy recommendations to promote more and better international partnerships. Regarding human resources, governmental agencies and institutions should expand postdoctoral fellowships, increase the number of international visiting researchers programs in partnerships with the existing cooperation agencies (e.g., Fulbright Commission, Campus France, DAAD), and continue funding full-time research positions for faculty members. Another set of policies should be directed toward reducing the bureaucratic limitations on imported equipment and material, and detecting and funding strategic areas for the development of science and research. The provision of funding and infrastructure is critical to the sustainability of international partnerships and it promotes the development of capacity in the "recipient" country, strengthening the overall relationships between partners. Capacity building implies a first stage of vertical, unidirectional assistance from a more developed research center to one with potential but lesser developed (economic and human) resources. These relationships evolve over time, however, and can transform into more horizontal exchanges between the partner institutions that provide for expansion of perspectives on both sides.

NOTES

1. Jeong, Choi, and Kim (2013) refer to attentional resources as the investment of team members in terms of commitment and time, including but not limited to the effort involved in finding appropriate partners, arranging long-distance travel for face-to-face meetings, among others.
2. For example, the National Atomic Energy Commission (*Comisión Nacional de Energía Atómica*—CNEA), the Armed Forces Scientific and Technological Research Institute (*Instituto de Investigaciones Científicas y Tecnológicas de las Fuerzas Armadas*—CITEFA), the National Space Activities Commission (*Comisión Nacional de Actividades Espaciales*—CONAE), the Agricultural Technology Institute (*Instituto de Tecnología Agrícola*—INTA), and the Industrial Technology Institute (*Instituto de Tecnología Industrial*—INTI).
3. Unfortunately, we do not have any information about the percentage of CONICET researchers employed by public and private universities as full- and part-time professors.
4. For a detailed analysis of the international scientific collaboration between Argentina and Spain during the 2000–2007 period, see De Filippo, Barrere, and Gómez (2010).
5. In Argentinian pesos, funds devoted to international collaboration grew from 14 million in 2008 to almost 73 million in 2015. We use the official exchange rate to convert Argentinian pesos to US dollars.
6. Around US$5800 according to the Argentinian official exchange rate in January 2015.
7. Around US$10,000 according to the Argentinian official exchange rate in January 2015.
8. Around US$11,600 according to the Argentinian official exchange rate in January 2015.
9. The indicators and weights in the QS World are Academic reputation (40 percent), Employer reputation (10 percent), Faculty Student (20 percent), International faculty (5 percent), International students (5 percent), and Citations per faculty (20 percent), and those in the QS Latin American ranking are: Academic reputation (30 percent), Employer reputation (20 percent), Faculty Student (10 percent), Papers per faculty (10 percent), Citations per paper (10 percent), Staff with PhD (10 percent), and Web impact (10 percent).
10. By "research unit", we refer to institutes within the schools that are responsible for research activity within a field of knowledge.
11. EURASUL is a Network in Advanced Materials and Nanomaterials of industrial interest, an academic network in advanced materials and nanomaterials of industrial interest between European and Latin American MERCOSUR countries.

INTERNATIONAL PARTNERSHIPS FOR COLLABORATIVE RESEARCH... 229

12. In INQUIMAE-UBA Case, we interviewed (1) Director of INQUIMAE and Senior Researcher CONICET-UBA (Molecular Electrochemistry), (2) the Emeritus Professor and Senior Researcher CONICET-UBA and former Director of INQUIMAE (Chemical Thermodynamics), (3) the Emeritus Professor and Senior Researcher CONICET-UBA (Coordination Chemistry), (4) Professor and Principal Researcher (CONICET-UBA) (Laboratory of Surfaces and Functional Materials), (5) Principal Investigator (CONICET) (Metastable systems, glasses, and super cooled liquids), (6) Principal Investigator (CONICET) (Organometallic, Bioinorganic and Supramolecular Chemistry), and (7) Secretary of Science and Technology-UBA.

In the case of the FCB Basic Research Area, Austral University, the following individuals were interviewed:

(1) Vice President of Research at UA 2013, former Research Director at UA since 2003; (2) Research Group 1 Director (Neurosciences), Former President at UA (2008–2013), former Vice President of Research at UA, former Dean of FCB at UA; (3) Research Group 2 Director (Cellular and Molecular Medicine); (4) Research Group 3 Director (Gene Therapy); (5) Research Group 4 Director 4 (Chronic Pain); and (6) Research Group 5 Director (Hepatic Fibrosis).

13. In 1976, for the sixth time during the twentieth century, a military junta overthrew a constitutional government (Floria and García Belsunce 1988). That was the last coup d'etat, which overthrew a civil government.

14. Around US$1.3 million.

REFERENCES

Altbach, P. G., & Balan, J. (Eds.). (2007). *World Class Worldwide: Transforming Research Universities in Asia and Latin America*. Baltimore: Johns Hopkins University Press.

Beerkens, E. (2002). International Inter-Organisational Arrangements in Higher Education: Towards a Typology. *Tertiary Education and Management, 8*, 297–314.

Bozeman, B., Fay, D., & Slade, C. P. (2013). Research Collaboration in Universities and Academic Entrepreneurship: The-State-of-the-Art. *The Journal of Technology Transfer, 38*(1), 1–67. https://doi.org/10.1007/s10961-012-9281-8.

Bradley, M. (2007). *North-South Research Partnerships: Challenges, Responses and Trends. A Literature Review and Annotated Bibliography*. Ottawa: International Development Research Center.

CONICET. (2014). Recursos Humanos [Human Resources]. *Consejo Nacional de Investigaciones Científicas Y Técnicas*. http://www.conicet.gov.ar/recursos-humanos/

CONICET. (2015a). El Dr. Salvarezza Participó de La Apertura de La FAPESP Week Buenos Aires [Dr. Salvarezza Participated in the Opening of the FAPESP Week Buenos Aires]. http://www.conicet.gov.ar/el-dr-salvarezza-participo-de-la-apertura-de-la-fapesp-week-buenos-aires/

CONICET. (2015b). International Cooperation. http://www.conicet.gov.ar/description/?lan=en

Cummings, J. N., & Kiesler, S. (2005). Collaborative Research Across Disciplinary and Organizational Boundaries. *Social Studies of Science, 35*(5), 703–722. https://doi.org/10.1177/0306312705055535.

De Filippo, D., Barrere, R., & Gómez, I. (2010). Características E Impacto de La Producción Científica En Colaboración Entre Argentina Y España [Scientific Collaboration Features and Impact in Argentina and Spain]. *Revista Iberoamericana de Ciencia Tecnología y Sociedad, 6*(16), 179–200.

Floria, C. A., & García Belsunce, C. A. (1988). *Historia política de la Argentina contemporánea, 1880–1983* [*Political history of the contemporary Argentina, 1880–1983*]. Madrid: Alianza Editorial.

Fox, M. F., & Mohapatra, S. (2007). Social-Organizational Characteristics of Work and Publication Productivity Among Academic Scientists in Doctoral-Granting Departments. *The Journal of Higher Education, 78*(5), 542–571.

Gaillard, J. (1994). North-South Research Partnership: Is Collaboration Possible Between Unequal Partners? *Knowledge and Policy, 7*(2), 31–63. https://doi.org/10.1007/BF02692761.

Gaillard, J., & Arvanitis, R. (2013). Science and Technology Collaboration Between Europe and Latin America: Towards a More Equal Partnership? In J. Gaillard & R. Arvanitis (Eds.), *Research Collaboration Between Europe and Latin America: Mapping and Understanding Partnership.* Paris: Archives Contemporaines.

Gould, J. (2014, November 3). How to Get Published in High-Impact Journals: Big Research and Better Writing. *Nature Jobs Blog.* http://blogs.nature.com/naturejobs/2014/11/03/how-to-get-published-in-high-impact-journals-big-research-and-better-writing/

Hackett, E. J. (2005). Introduction to the Special Guest-Edited Issue on Scientific Collaboration. *Social Studies of Science, 35*(5), 667–671. https://doi.org/10.1177/0306312705057569.

INQUIMAE. (2014). Annual Report. http://www.inquimae.fcen.uba.ar/investigacion_memoria.htm

INQUIMAE. (2015). Proyecto Institucional [Institutional Project]. Buenos Aires.

Jeong, S., Choi, J. Y., & Kim, J.-Y. (2013). On the Drivers of International Collaboration: The Impact of Informal Communication, Motivation, and Research Resources. *Science and Public Policy, 41*(4), 520–531. https://doi.org/10.1093/scipol/sct079.

Katz, J. S., & Martin, B. R. (1997). What Is Research Collaboration? *Research Policy, 26*(1), 1–18. https://doi.org/10.1016/S0048-7333(96)00917-1.

Kehm, B. M., & Teichler, U. (2007, September). Research on Internationalisation in Higher Education. *Journal of Studies in International Education, 11,* 260–273. https://doi.org/10.1177/1028315307303534.

King, G., Keohane, R., & Verba, S. (1994). *Designing Social Inquiry: Scientific Inference in Qualitative Research.* Princeton: Princeton University Press.

Merlino-Santesteban, C. (2013). *Producción Científica de Las Universidades Nacionales [Argentine Scientific Production at National Universities].* Buenos Aires: Centro Redes. http://www.centroredes.org.ar/files/documentos/Doc_Nro43.pdf

MINCYT. (2002). *Indicadores de Ciencia Y Tecnología. Argentina 2001 [2001 Science and Technology Indicators].* Buenos Aires: Ministerio de Ciencia, Tecnología, e Innovación Productiva. http://www.mincyt.gob.ar/indicadores/indicadores-de-ciencia-y-tecnologia-argentina-2012-10397

MINCYT. (2014). *Indicadores de Ciencia Y Tecnología. Argentina 2012 [2012 Science and Technology Indicators].* Buenos Aires: Ministerio de Ciencia, Tecnología, e Innovación Productiva. http://www.mincyt.gob.ar/indicadores/indicadores-de-ciencia-y-tecnologia-argentina-2012-10397.

MINCYT. (2015a). Email dated June 25, 2015.

MINCYT. (2015b). International Cooperation. http://www.conicet.gov.ar/description/?lan=en

QS Latin American University Ranking. (2015). http://www.topuniversities.com/university-rankings/latam-university-rankings/2015#sorting=rank+region=+country=350+faculty=+stars=false+search=.

QS World University Rankings. (2014/15). http://www.topuniversities.com/university-rankings/world-university-rankings/2014#sorting=rank+region=-349+country=350+faculty=+stars=false+search

SCOPUS. (2015). SCOPUS Database. http://www.scopus.com/

Siegel, D. S., Waldman, D., & Link, A. (2003). Assessing the Impact of Organizational Practices on the Relative Productivity of University Technology Transfer Offices: An Exploratory Study. *Research Policy, 32*(1), 27–48. https://doi.org/10.1016/S0048-7333(01)00196-2.

SPU. (2012). *Anuario de Estadísticas Universitarias 2012 [University Statistics Yearbook 2012].* Buenos Aires: Secretaría de Políticas Universitarias.

Yin, R. K. (2014). *Case Study Research: Design and Methods.* Los Angeles: Sage Publications.

Ynalvez, M. A., & Shrum, W. M. (2011). Professional Networks, Scientific Collaboration, and Publication Productivity in Resource-Constrained Research Institutions in a Developing Country. *Research Policy, 40*(2), 204–216. https://doi.org/10.1016/j.respol.2010.10.004.

CHAPTER 10

Collaborative Research by Chilean and North American Scholars: Precedents and Projections

Oscar Espinoza, Luis Eduardo González, and Noel F. McGinn

INTRODUCTION

Chile has long attracted researchers from other countries, including the United States. Its earlier history of political stability, highly diverse geography, flora and fauna, proximity to Antarctica, educational accomplishment, and welcoming culture appealed to a variety of scholars and researchers. Some of these early academic explorers may well have

---

O. Espinoza (✉)
Universidad de Playa Ancha, Santiago, Chile

L. E. González
Programa Interdisciplinario de Investigaciones en Educación (PIIE), Santiago, Chile

N. F. McGinn
Graduate School of Education, Harvard University, Boston, MA, USA

© The Author(s) 2018
G. Gregorutti, N. Svenson (eds.), *North-South University Research Partnerships in Latin America and the Caribbean*,
https://doi.org/10.1007/978-3-319-75364-5_10

233

established collaborative relationships with Chilean scholars, but little of this has been documented for historical record.

Beginning in 1948, Latin American scholars had sought to build a regional research network, not directly linked to North American institutions. Their ambition was to escape what they considered to be the "peripheral" or "dependent" status of Latin America. The center of this network was located in Chile, which served as a haven for intellectuals and academics fleeing instability in other Latin American and Caribbean (LAC) countries. Within a relatively short period, Chile became the headquarters for various intergovernmental and non-governmental organizations such as the United Nations Economic Confederation for Latin America and the Caribbean or ECLAC in 1948 (Comisión Económica para América Latina y el Caribe—CEPAL); the Latin American Faculty of Social Sciences in 1957 (Facultad Latinoamericana de Ciencias Sociales—FLACSO); the Latin American and Caribbean Center of Demography, also in 1957 (Centro Latinoamericano de Demografía—CELADE); the Latin American Institute for Economic and Social Planning in 1962 (Instituto Latinoamericano para la Planificación Económica y Social—ILPES); and the Latin American Council on the Social Sciences in 1967 (Consejo Latinoamericano de Ciencias Sociales—CLACSO). One early consequence of this congregation of academic and applied research talent was an upsurge of academic and intellectual collaboration independent of Northern universities (Beigel 2013). Their efforts included increased collaborative research and publication within the region (South-South), and this worked to counter, to some degree, the history of peripheral status. Leading economists such as Raul Prebisch (Argentina) and Celso Furtado (Brazil) promoted a new theory, which stated that economic development was determined principally by the structural relationships between countries. They argued the current underdevelopment of Latin America occurred because of its dependent relationship with the North (Love 2005) and that measures should be taken to rebalance this dynamic.

Around the same time, in 1953, the United States initiated a ten-year development program called Plan Chillán that sought to stimulate knowledge transfer from the US end. The program paired US agricultural extension agencies with their Chilean counterparts and aimed to improve farm production, housing, and transportation in three Chilean provinces. More than 100 Chilean technicians worked with agronomists, urban planners, economists, and veterinarians from US institutions. They worked on improvement of milk production, soil conservation, reforestation, and development of farm cooperatives. Agronomists from the University of California participated in the creation of a Faculty of Agronomy at the University of Concepción.

The first formal agreement between a Chilean and a US university was signed in 1963. The Chile-California Program, which linked the University of Chile with the University of California, was prompted by a request to the governor of California from President John Kennedy. This new program was featured as part of the Kennedy's call for an Alliance of Progress to achieve higher standards of living and freedom for all people of the Americas (Melillo 2016). Professors from the University of California worked with Chilean counterparts to improve the quality of fruits already grown in Chile and to introduce new varieties of fruits to the country. Some 50 Chilean students and professors studied and taught at the Davis campus of the University of California. Those who returned to Chile were known as the "Davis boys," a parallel to the "Chicago boys," who were trained in economics at the University of Chicago.

The Chile-California program was a major contributor to the development of modern agribusiness in Chile (Melillo 2016). On the other hand, although participants from both countries contributed to the success of the program, it was largely designed and managed by US scholars. As such, it has been criticized by Edmundo Fuenzalida as another instance of dependent development (cited in Melillo 2016, p. 163):

> Whatever the Convenio is able to create in the University of Chile in the area of science and technology lacks roots in the Chilean soil...Instead of producing a modern higher education institution capable of self-sustained growth, the Convenio contributed to the creation of a subsidiary of the international centers of higher education (particularly the University of California).

Nevertheless, collaborative and exchange relationships between Chilean and US universities increased over time and produced valuable results. In one such project, Harvard University, funded by the Ford Foundation in 1970, seconded a professor to assist with the establishment of an educational research center, the Interdisciplinary Program for Educational Research (Programa Interdisciplinario de Investigaciones en Educación—PIIE) under the sponsorship of the Pontifical Catholic University in Santiago. This center now operates independently of both the Catholic University and the US universities and is regarded as a leading source of quantitative research and analysis on the Chilean education system (Avalos 2008).

Collaboration was severely constrained for a period following the violent intrusion of a military dictatorship in Chile in September 1973. Chilean universities were taken over and governed by military officers; large numbers of researchers and professors fled Chile, some were imprisoned, and others were killed. Only a few US institutions continued to carry out studies in Chile. The effects of this interruption continued even after the re-establishment of democracy in 1989. Research collaboration between 1984 and 2007 (the most recent period for which data have been published) was significantly below that of other Latin American countries (Russell and Ainsworth 2014). Research in Chile declined from 13% to 8% of the total for the region (Russell and Ainsworth 2014, p. 55). During this same period (1984–2007), research production in the rest of the region expanded.

In recent years, international collaboration has contributed much to the increase in published research for the entire region. The rate of growth has been most marked in Chile and in other Latin American countries, which suffered similar dictatorial regimes (Russell and Ainsworth 2014). During the same period of time (1984–2007), Chilean authors tended to engage more with European scholars than North American as partners for collaboration. Although the United States as a single country by 1993 accounted for the largest share of internationally co-authored papers (46%), the combined 27 European countries represented 53% of the total collaboration with Chileans scholars (Russell and Ainsworth 2014). So, Europe, collectively, became Chile's largest international research collaborator. Some of the projects associated with these figures have a relatively long history. For example, beginning in the 1980s an international consortium of universities began a series of archeological studies of the ancient civilizations in the north of Chile (Lozano et al. 2014). Similarly, regional sustainable development has been the focus of a 20-year project between a Canadian and a Chilean university (Salas et al. 2006). International collaboration on land use studies, too, played a critical role to facilitate collaboration with Spanish and other Northern institutions (Becerril-Tinoco and Rogel-Salazar 2015). Also, within the same period of time, public health research in Chile grew enormously, teaming up with US and European institutions as well as with other Latin American universities (Kiemle Trindade 2006).

In sum, international research collaboration, both North-South and South-South, has a long history in Chile and Latin America. It continues to expand, both because of its contribution to knowledge and its positive impact on research among Latin American universities. The present study offers a more detailed look at the contributions and difficulties of collaboration efforts between Chilean and US institutions. Specifically, the chapter illustrates how partnerships between Chilean and US universities during the past five years have impacted the generation and transfer of knowledge, increased scholarly publication, and strengthened participating teams and institutions. We begin exploring some key concepts explaining collaboration and then review several illustrative cases. Following this, we analyze the data collected from a sample of researchers in Chilean universities known for their level of publication. We close with several recommendations for policies and practices to further improve gains from such collaboration.

COLLABORATION AND RESEARCH PUBLICATIONS

Reviews of North-South research collaboration studies point out a number of positive benefits from interuniversity relationships (Bradley 2007; Carbonnier and Kontinen 2014). Many publications indicate a correlation between levels of collaboration and gains in research-based knowledge (Ductor 2015; Jones et al. 2008; Ordoñez-Matamoros et al. 2010; Presmanes and Zumelzu 2003). The expansion of cross-institutional collaboration contributes to significant advances in scientific methodology (Jones et al. 2008). For example, collaborative research in economics not only shows more attention paid to specific findings and theory but also increased publication by individual researchers (Ductor 2015). Jointly authored Latin American articles on management published between 1990 and 2010 had more impact than those with single authors. Colombian university teams that collaborated with universities outside of Colombia increased their production of articles by almost 40% (Ordoñez-Matamoros et al. 2010). Research collaboration over time between Spanish and Chilean universities has also been accompanied by higher numbers of publications and researchers in both countries (Presmanes and Zumelzu 2003). One important example of international research collaboration's widespread beneficial effect is seen in how it has advanced the understanding of asthma in Chile, a serious public health problem (Boneberger et al. 2010).

Conditioning Factors in Research Collaboration

Research collaboration begins for many different reasons. Several possible scenarios include (1) a leading institution seeks collaborators with complementary areas of expertise; (2) researchers with limited resources in their own institutions look for new opportunities; (3) research entrepreneurs seek to expand their portfolios; (4) researchers seek partners to fund projects; and (5) external groups offer a project designed to generate knowledge on a specific topic of interest (Genuth et al. 2000). Given the multiple objectives for embarking on collaboration, approaches to implementation vary as well. The actual development of the project is mediated by numerous factors, some of which may not even be linked to the original objectives. Most importantly, participants on both sides must have incentives to engage and be willing and able to share their assets and capabilities.

A common theme of studies of international research cooperation is the complexity of the process. Participants learn most from each other when what each knows about the research topic is highly different. Complementary differences in the partners' topic-relevant knowledge and methodological skills increase the likelihood that the research will contribute to the field. This is defined as complementarity. The relationship between complementarity and gains from collaboration, however, is non-linear. Partners with different knowledge and skills may also use different methods and vocabulary. Very large differences in methods and vocabulary can make it difficult for partners to communicate and work together (Bjorkman et al. 2007).

The optimal level of complementarity depends on the compatibility of the participants. Collaboration is more likely to succeed when there is a good fit between institutions' goals, capabilities, and approaches (Universities UK 2008). Collaboration is further enhanced when researchers are able to work together harmoniously despite their differences. This compatibility is linked to at least five core elements, namely, (1) prior experience in research collaboration by at least one of the partners; (2) assignment to tasks based on prior experience; (3) free flow of research-relevant information and shared responsibility in data processing and analysis; (4) efficient distribution of tasks; and (5) use of technical tools and technology to streamline data and information management (Deiglmayr and Spada 2010; Meier et al. 2007). When one or both of the partners fall short in some of these practices, projects tend to fail; targets are not met; topics are not thoroughly explored; analysis is not sufficiently deep; some tasks are overlooked; and reporting is insufficient. Thus, complementarity and compatibility are equally necessary for successful partnering.

Complementarity The term "complementarity," as alluded to above, refers to the extent to which each participant in a relationship differs in ways that enrich the group's overall resources, skills, or knowledge for a particular project. These differences are found in the skills and knowledge of individuals, institutional structures, and processes, and even geographic, cultural, and economic characteristics of countries. These attributes can also be associated with age, gender, level of training, and research experience. Complementarity can be contrasted with duplication and replication. In a research situation, the higher the level of complementarity between participants, the greater the likelihood that the project will contribute to the expansion of knowledge (Beerkens and van der Wende 2007).

The expansion of knowledge attributable to research collaboration is also linked to the heterogeneity of collaborative relationships. The more meaningful variation there is in a research consortium, the more complementarity is likely to exist. This variability among partners may be a consequence of increased funding for research (Ubfal and Maffioli 2011), but some research shows that there is a threshold above which increased amounts have little effect (Clark and Llorens 2012).

Greater heterogeneity in collaborative research in the business administration field has been shown to improve research publication (Orozco and Villaveces 2015). A similar relationship is found in the biomedical field. All three levels of participants, that is, countries, institutions, and individuals can vary in many ways. Of the three, complementarity of individual participants is most highly related to research publication and to the indicator of the "impact" of a research report, or its frequency of citation by other researchers (Bordons et al. 2013). Internationally co-authored papers are cited most frequently, and their impact is greatest when at least one of the authors' countries invested heavily in the research and was active in its execution. In contrast, there is no relationship between which country leads the project and its eventual impact (Bordons et al. 2015).

Complementarity can exist at both international and regional levels. In Latin America and the Caribbean, increases in medical research publication and citations have been attributed more to the greater partnering within the region than outside the region (Chinchilla-Rodríguez et al. 2012). The authors conclude that this occurs because researchers within the region differ significantly from each other in skills and knowledge. Chinchilla-Rodriguez et al. (2012) conclude that overall research outputs would be enhanced by incentivizing both intraregional relationships and international initiatives.

Complementarity between researchers can also be found at the country level, independent of external relationships. Because the citation indices tend to under-report research publication within a given country, internationally authored papers receive more attention and can actually diminish recognition of national complementarity. To illustrate this point, the two Latin American countries that publish most on public health research (in Spanish) are Chile and Cuba, but public health research from other countries that involves North American collaborators (and is published in English) is more frequently cited in the North-dominated research literature (Chinchilla-Rodríguez et al. 2015). Most public health studies published in Chile are by national authors (i.e., without international collaboration) and include relatively few citations of research done in other countries of the region (Macias-Chapula 2010). In the absence of other studies that compare rates of publication in other disciplines, one can only speculate as to why the public health research field is more developed in Chile and Cuba than in other countries (and about why that research is not cited as frequently internationally). We are reminded, however, that "peripheral" status can persist despite significant internal development. This point is elaborated upon in the following section.

Compatibility A review of research on scientific synthesis (combining knowledge from two or more disciplines) concludes that large, diverse teams (likely to have higher complementarity) are more likely to advance new fields of understanding and also increase research publication. These outcomes are enhanced, however, when participants (and leaders) set clear rules and expectations, manage power relations, encourage diverse viewpoints, promote group cohesion, and simultaneously maintain order in discussion (Hampton and Parker 2011). In other words, collaboration is more effective when participants are "compatible" and rules of engagement are well defined.

The exercise of the skills of compatibility results in the formation of strong relationships among the members of the research project. The more a given individual is linked to other participants, the more s/he is said to be "embedded" in the research network. How deeply research participants are integrated in a network is related to the "quality," or impact, of their research output (as indicated by its frequency of citations) but not to its quantity (González-Brambila et al. 2013). Participants that "get along" with their colleagues and communicate frequently are more likely to be read by them. How scientists relate to each other influences the perceived importance of their work but not its completion. Some of these relationship skills can be acquired in the home country, others would depend on extended interactions with persons from other cultures. Researchers that have studied abroad or have foreign work experience develop communication and other skills that facilitate their incorporation into collaborative research efforts. Once returned to their home country, they are more likely (than those who have not been abroad) to publish internationally, and to publish in journals whose articles are more frequently cited even when their co-authors are not from other countries (Jonkers and Cruz-Castro 2013).

Although there is considerable diversity within any country, there appear to be national differences with regard to what elements of compatibility are most important. Researchers from the United States, the United Kingdom, the Netherlands, China, South Africa, and Chile were asked to describe the strategies they used to ensure that their research findings would influence policy (Pittman 2006). Those from the first three (Northern) countries emphasized most of the scientific legitimacy of their findings. To gain acceptance of their findings, they would call the attention of readers to their institutional sponsors, the professional qualifications of the researchers, and the prestige of the journal in which the research was published. The other set of researchers (from China, Chile, and South Africa) emphasized most the cultivation and optimization of personal relationships. They said they were more likely to promote their research through the intervention of representatives with personal ties to the intended audiences. In other words, compatibility in some countries is based primarily on shared technical or professional attributes, while in other countries personal relationships are more important (Pittman 2006).

Personal relationships are more likely to be of importance in countries characterized by economic and political instability. Using self-reports of researchers in India, Kenya, and Ghana, Ynalvez, Sooryamoorthy, Mbatia, Dzorgbo, Shrum, and Duque (2005) concluded that collaboration in those settings had no impact at all on publication:

> research collaboration presents a paradox for less-developed areas. The research institutions of sub-Saharan Africa for which collaboration has seemed to hold the greatest promise, are the least equipped to benefit, since the very conditions that problematize the relationship between collaboration and productivity also undermine the benefits of new information and

communication technologies. It is not collaboration, or collaboration alone, that causes research problems. It can also be attributed to poverty, corruption and family obligations--in short, the routine problems of everyday life in many less-developed regions. (p. 777)

If researchers in developing countries are more likely to form relationships on a personal (rather than a professional) basis, it can be expected that the use of technologies that facilitate communication with distant partners would increase their participation in projects that are more likely to be cited. One of those technologies is the Internet. Large international collaborative research projects are characterized both by high diversity and by high use of electronic communication. Local networks of researchers, however, make less use of e-mail, texting, or other digitally linked methods, relying instead on more telephone and face-to-face communication.

This is true also in Chile, where researchers in international projects use e-mail and skype or video conferences for communication abroad and rely on the Internet for access to research publications. But as Duque and others note, not all scientists in Chile experience the positive effects of international collaborative research. And sometimes even those who do may be doing so at the cost of developing local partnerships. A study of Internet use reports a negative correlation between the level of electronic communication within Chile and communication between Chile and other countries; in other words, Chilean researchers who use e-mail to communicate with the North send fewer messages to addresses in Chile and also make less use of the telephone for calls within Chile (Duque et al. 2009). Chilean researchers can be divided into two groups on the basis of their level of access to and facility with the Internet. One has links to networks in developed countries, and the other is composed of national researchers who participate only in regional collaboration networks. Although Internet accessibility may be more advanced in Chile than in neighboring countries, Duque et al. claim that it lags behind that which is prevalent in the developed countries (particularly the United States). There is a gap in access to data and primary sources between Chilean and US researchers due to the high cost of databases and different kinds of available sources. In fact, in Chile, only a few universities have access to a wide range of international databases. As a consequence, many Chilean researchers encounter obstacles in their research that could make them second-class participants in international collaborative projects. This may result in Chilean researchers playing only a "peripheral" role in collaborative projects, and in Chile being more of a mere supplier of data than a co-producer of new scientific knowledge. This would be a new form of South-North dependency. These same constraints on North-South communication may also explain why Chile and Cuba have developed their capacity for public health research (Duque et al. 2012; Kiemle Trindade 2006). It can be argued that faced with limited access to the North, public health researchers were obliged to develop national resources. To conclude, differences (in skills, knowledge, and technological access) of participants in research projects are most likely to increase the benefits of collaboration when partners are able to work well together.

METHODOLOGY

This chapter describes, from the perspective of Chilean participants, reasons for and benefits of international research collaboration.[1] This is a descriptive case study focusing on the relationships between Chilean and US researchers over the last five years. The findings presented here are based on a survey of collaborative research projects carried out by researchers from both countries between 2010 and 2014.

The population for this study was all collaborative research projects initiated since 2010 in 14 universities belonging to the Council of Rectors. These institutions were selected because of their prior record of publications. They include several large universities in the capital city of Santiago, as well as universities located in some of the provinces. They are among the oldest universities in Chile, receive most of the research funds allocated by the national government, and are favored by private foundations. As a consequence, almost all university-based research carried out in Chile occurs in one or more of these institutions.

Information about projects was obtained from university Vice Rectors (provosts) and directors of research and innovation. We asked them to list all research projects initiated within the last five years in collaboration with US institutions. Nine of the 14 universities contacted responded to the request for information. These included seven public and two private universities. The respondents identified a total of 79 collaborative projects begun since 2010. Of these, 37% (29) belong to the natural sciences (biology, chemistry, physics), 19% (15) to health sciences, 18% (14) to engineering, and 16% (13) to social sciences. Architecture and arts, economics and management, law, humanities, and education each have one project. Therefore, there were collaborative projects in all typical areas of knowledge that universities use to organize disciplines, but there was more concentration in natural sciences (see Table 10.1).

Table 10.1 Number of collaborative research projects by university and topic (2010–2015)

University	Agriculture	Architecture and arts	Natural sciences	Economy and management	Health sciences	Social sciences	Law	Humanities and education	Engineering and technology	Total
University 1	2	1	13	0	12	0	0	0	5	33
University 2	0	0	0	0	0	1	0	1	1	3
University 3	0	0	1	0	0	0	0	0	0	1
University 4	1	0	1	0	0	9	0	0	0	11
University 5	0	0	1	0	0	0	0	0	2	3
University 6	1	0	2	1	3	1	1	0	6	15
University 7	0	0	1	0	0	0	0	0	0	1
University 8	0	0	4	0	0	0	0	0	0	4
University 9	0	0	6	0	0	2	0	0	0	8
Total	4	1	29	1	15	13	1	1	14	79

Source: Elaboration by authors

The principal investigator listed for each of the 79 projects was also contacted and responses were obtained from 7 researchers involved in 11 projects: 5 in natural sciences, 4 in social sciences and 2 in engineering. No responses were obtained in the areas of health (15 projects) or agriculture (4 projects). Most of the projects were located in regional state universities. For each project, respondents filled out a 15-minute questionnaire prepared for the purposes of this study. The survey inquired about initiation, sponsorship, and financing of the project, qualifications, and institutional affiliations of the researchers, topic, and a brief description of methodology, findings, and an evaluation of the collaborative experience.

Five of these 11 projects were completed; 4 of them corresponded to the natural sciences. Six projects are still underway, of which three belong to the social sciences, two to engineering, and one to natural sciences. A majority (nine) of the projects are more in theoretical rather applied areas. The average duration of a project is three years.

SURVEY RESULTS

The results of the study refer to six relevant issues identified as important in published studies on collaboration: funding, participants, constraints, benefits, and impact of research collaboration between Chilean and US scholars. In order to maximize participation, we chose to not ask respondents to describe their motivations for seeking collaboration.

Funding

Seven of the 11 projects were funded by Chilean institutions, using competitive government grants from public organizations such as the National Commission for Scientific and Technological Research (Comisión Nacional de Investigación Científica y Tecnológica—CONICYT) and the National Fund for Science and Technology (Fondo Nacional de Ciencia y Tecnología—FONDECYT). In recent years, these two organizations have provided funding for scientific exchange and cooperation between research groups from different regions and countries, including resources for strengthening of research networks. The objective of this new program is to consolidate niches of research in different disciplines and to generate high-level investigation associated with an increase in scientific productivity (with incentives for publication in high-impact journals). US agencies and universities funded 4 of the 11 projects analyzed, while 2 projects obtained resources from both Chilean and US sources. The US funds were mainly concentrated in the area of basic sciences (three of four projects).

Among the reported projects, four had limited funding (less than US$50,000 for an average time frame of three years). On the other hand, three projects stated that they had external funding of close to US$300,000, which represents a significant figure for the development of applied research. Another three projects obtained resources ranging from US$100,000 to US$300,000. There is no obvious association between the amount awarded per project and their topics, length, or institution, except that projects corresponding to basic sciences, on average, received higher levels of funding than those in other knowledge areas.

Projects targeted different populations to disseminate their research results. Reports in physics and natural sciences were written in academic style using scientific jargon and published in academic journals whose audience was their scientific community. In contrast, the studies in the social sciences often were published in newspapers and popular magazines, aiming for a general audience. Their language and style were much more accessible to people with less academic training. Two of the studies surveyed published articles that were intended to be read by the business community (see Table 10.2 for more details).

Participants The 11 projects involved 33 scholars (including principal and co-investigators) of which 20 were Chilean. This results in an average of three researchers per project. In engineering, technology and social sciences, there is an average of 3.5 researchers per project, while in basic sciences, the average is somewhat lower at 2.4 (see Table 10.3). The number of Chilean researchers participating in the area of natural sciences (nine) is greater than that of US counterparts (three). In contrast, with other knowledge areas, the ratio of national-US researchers is very similar.

As reported in Table 10.3, all US researchers have doctoral degrees, while 70% of Chileans have doctorates. Among Chilean researchers, the largest concentration of scholars without doctoral studies was in the social sciences (55% of researchers had master's degrees only), whereas in basic sciences, only one of nine researchers involved did not have a doctorate.

COLLABORATIVE RESEARCH BY CHILEAN AND NORTH AMERICAN... 247

Table 10.2 Research reports by targeted population

		Area of knowledge			
Indicator	Categories—audience	Natural or basic sciences	Social sciences	Engineering and technology	Total
Target population	Scientific community	4		1	5
	Industry	2			2
	General population	2	4		6
	Services and government productive sector			1	1
	Ethnic groups		2		2
	Tourists	1	1		1
	NA				1

Table 10.3 Participating researchers, disciplines, and degree levels

Indicator	Categories	Knowledge area			Total
		Natural or basic sciences	Social sciences	Engineering and technology	
Number of researchers	Chilean	9 (45%)	7 (35%)	4 (20%)	20 (100%)
	US	3 (23%)	7 (54%)	3 (23%)	13 (100%)
	Subtotal	12 (36%)	14 (42%)	7 (22%)	33 (100%)
Chilean researchers' degrees	PhD	8 (58%)	3 (21%)	3 (21%)	14 (100%)
	Master	0 (0%)	4 (80%)	1 (20%)	5 (100%)
	Bachelor	1 (100%)			1 (100%)
	Subtotal	9 (45%)	7 (35%)	4 (20%)	20 (100%)
US researchers' degrees	PhD	3 (23%)	7 (54%)	3 (23%)	13 (100%)
	Total	12 (36%)	14 (42%)	7 (22%)	33 (100%)

Note: Researchers participating in more than one project are counted only once

Collaboration Facilitators The survey did not solicit information about motivations for collaboration in these specific projects. One can speculate, however, that there are two main motivations. The first is the maintenance of personal relationships. Many of the Chilean researchers studied in the United States, and some of the US scholars had been in Chile before the beginning of these projects. The collaborative research project is one way to continue existing relationships. The second possible facilitator is the pursuit of interests shared by the proposed collaboration partner. These include research objectives, publications, and expansion of networks, all of which are universally common motivations for collaborative projects, as mentioned in the preceding literature review.

Constraints to Collaboration The respondents reported that the main limitations to developing projects are administrative and management difficulties, which arise mainly at the institutional level. For example, inefficient management of funds and restrictions on the use of resources for activities not covered by institutional rules and protocols were among those most cited. In addition, respondents mentioned that it is sometimes difficult to find international contacts with similar interests. The initiative to carry out collaborative projects comes primarily from Chile. In only 1 of the 11 cases did the move toward collaboration rise out of an interinstitutional agreement.

Benefits from Collaboration The most frequently mentioned outcomes are collaborative publications in high-impact journals. Other benefits include the training and development of young researchers through postgraduate studies, thesis development, participation in scientific events (conferences and congresses), and initiation of new lines of research. Researchers in 8 (of 11) projects completed or nearing completion were highly satisfied with their experiences. They felt that all their goals had been met. The three remaining researchers indicated that their projects were recently initiated or at an intermediate stage of completion, so they opted not to respond. Similarly, all eight of the researchers with studies finished or nearly completed considered that the experience could be described as excellent. Good interpersonal relationships between US and Chilean researchers were considered a relevant factor for the achievement of the objectives. The respondents used phrases such as "the excellence of the research groups," "cooperation and good predisposition," "pre-existence of collaborative work," "highly motivated teams," and "the type of relationship between pairs," to describe their positive feelings. Another noteworthy contribution to collaboration was the congruence of interests between the teams. The researchers referred to a similarity of scientific capacity, common objectives, and joint work of a permanent nature as contributing factors. Also mentioned were methodological considerations such as the use of certain investigative techniques, the proper allocation of functions, the originality of the project, and the need to generate information on different units of analysis.

Impact of Collaboration Researchers associated positive impacts on institutions with opportunities for undergraduate and graduate students to expand their research skills and discipline knowledge. Equally important was learning English as the language that facilitated communication with researchers from Northern countries. Chilean researchers also emphasized the importance of their access to more complex and higher quality laboratories, as well as to cutting-edge technologies.

At a national level, North-South collaboration prompted improvements in the existing human capital. This type of venture, on one hand, encourages other teams of researchers to generate new projects applying to national and international competitive funding agencies. On the other hand, these experiences push teams that already received funds to continue seeking new resources for expanding their studies. At the international level, the impact of cooperative projects resulted in the generation and dissemination of new disciplinary knowledge through publications and participation in peer-reviewed conferences.

Limiting Factors Limited funding restricted the range of activities of some projects. In response to reduced project funding, researchers sought to lower costs by (1) recruiting young researchers and students as assistants and (2) promoting joint workshops and networking with other projects. These activities provided a corollary benefit of broader awareness for the research results among other groups with shared research interests or complementary skills. As mentioned above, several projects sought to reduce costs in various ways. A broader set of strategies could include (a) obtaining additional or complementary resources to finance travel expenses and laboratory aspects; (b) improving the management of resources; (c) setting objectives that are more feasible; (d) building stronger links between research partners in both hemispheres; (e) increasing the capacity for and interest in collaboration among regional universities; and (f) establishing policies for strengthening student mobility and involvement in international research collaboration.

Discussion

The results of this study are consistent with the reported findings from other countries and regions (Carbonnier and Kontinen 2014; de Filippo et al. 2009; Freshwater et al. 2006; Khor and Yu 2016). Collaboration with international institutions and researchers was seen as contributing to greater research productivity and publication and consequently positive for expanding ideas that would lead to new knowledge generation. International research collaboration should therefore be further encouraged and funded.

There are several reasons to exercise caution in using these results to inform research policy in Chile. These stem from the difficulty experienced in obtaining a sample of cases representative of Chilean collaborative projects. Not only is the sample essentially self-selected and relatively small, but intentionally restricted to projects linking Chile and the United States. We cannot be certain that collaboration with, say Canada, other countries in Latin America, or countries in Europe and Asia, would generate the same type and range of experiences. Perhaps research topics germane to Latin America would differ significantly from some of those of interest to scholars in countries outside the region. Regional differences (in economy, political structure, linguistic diversity, climate, natural resources, flora and fauna, health conditions, etc.) would in some cases dictate not only different research topics but also different methodologies for approaching similar problems.

In addition, collaboration with researchers from another Spanish-speaking country could engage the participation of a different cohort of Chileans (with less ability to speak, read, and write in English). Research suggests that the impact of collaboration on individual researchers varies as a function of their prior experience with the partner country, their ease of use of communication technologies commonly employed in the partner country, and cultural factors that shape relationships with others (Jonkers and Cruz-Castro 2013).

As we lack information about the experiences of those researchers who did not participate in the study, we cannot infer the impact of their exclusion. Conceivably, their experiences in collaboration could have been much different than those reported in our sample. We are limited, therefore, to confirming only that research collaboration between Chilean and US institutions and scholars can be a highly positive experience. Further study will build a more comprehensive sample and include a wider range of variables.

The one factor cited repeatedly as the obstacle to carrying out collaborative research projects was the lack of sufficient public and private funding resources. Because of this, universities wishing to support increased international research collaboration must make a concerted, creative, and proactive effort to do so. For instance, they could and should develop a broader range of institutional financial strategies such as grants and contracts to support joint projects; subsidies to allow academic and graduate student mobility; funds to participate in international research networks; and resources to promote international training at the graduate level with actions that include joint graduate programs, co-advising of doctoral students, and academic exchange programs to generate new research projects. In this pursuit, universities may also need to explore less traditional sources of financing at local, national, and international levels.

CONCLUSIONS

This chapter is an effort to expand the understanding of collaborative research in a country about which relatively little has been published. The findings indicate that a significant amount of collaborative research projects were carried out during the past five years (2010–2015) by universities included in the Council of Rectors of Chilean Universities (CRUCH). The number of collaborative projects identified in this study may underestimate the reality, as other initiatives may not have been reported directly to university vice presidents, directors of research, or offices of international relationships. Many projects that originate with individual researchers escape the attention of both government and university officials. In addition, as our experience in collecting data showed, some researchers were reluctant to talk about their projects and processes. We recommend, therefore, that the results of this present study be considered tentative.

The projects studied reveal considerable variation in level of training of researchers, particularly those from Chile. In part, this reflects the success of efforts by Chilean governments and their agencies to incorporate into research projects recent graduates and those still in training.

As noted throughout this chapter, Chilean scientists benefit in many ways from involvement in international collaborative research projects. First, they gain through access to more up-to-date equipment and technology difficult to acquire in Chile because of its cost. Second, they improve access to information, in the form of specialized libraries, databases, associations, and networks. Third, they benefit from the possibility of disseminating the results of research to a wider public through the publication and presentation of papers and books in English.

The collaborative experience allows US researchers to benefit as well. They come to know in greater depth the differences among developing countries. They gain access to ethnic groups with different cultural characteristics allowing for examination of both divergence across groups and potentially improved validity and representativeness through inclusion of broader and more varied populations and samples. Collaboration allows US scholars to compare experiences and models, and to publish in another language, which promotes wider dissemination and knowledge transfer. In addition, collaboration enables US researchers to experience the working conditions of researchers in less-developed countries. These conditions include limited material resources (e.g., lack of modern equipment and laboratories), organizational experience, and qualified personnel.

The study verified a significant number of recent and ongoing collaborative research projects involving Chilean and US scholars. It also identified a number of the conditions favorable for promoting such partnerships and also the types of constraints most likely to be faced by participants. The favorable conditions include (a) the interpersonal relationships developed between Chilean doctoral students and US researchers; (b) prior efforts developed to set up joint research projects; (c) motivations to collaborate based on common research goals in similar subjects; and (d) desire to expand the research field and its social impact. Among the difficulties are the following: (a) limited resources for joint research projects; (b) dissimilar formal training observed between Chileans and US research teams: (c) language constraints and (d) differences in access to up-to-date sources for data and information. In spite of the challenges, results of the joint research experiences show that both groups have benefited from the interaction. Interpersonal relationships are strengthened, knowledge is advanced, and participants declare themselves to be satisfied with the work done. These are reasons for universities, governments, and other entities in both North and South to invest in and facilitate opportunities for more collaborative research.

NOTE

1. This study is solely based on the information from Chilean researchers, even though the literature review includes perspectives of all participants in collaboration.

REFERENCES

Avalos, B. (2008, December). Individual and Institutional Partnerships: Some Experiences. *Norrag News, 41*, 103–104. http://www.norrag.org/en/publications/norrag-news/online-version/the-new-politics-of-partnership-peril-or-promise.html

Becerril-tinoco, Y., & Rogel-Salazar, R. (2015). Redes de Colaboración Científica en los Estudios Teritoriales [Collaborative Scientific Networks in Territorial Studies]. *EURE, 41*(123), 309–323. http://www.scielo.cl/pdf/eure/41n123/art13.pdfx

Beerkens, E., & van der Wende, M. (2007). The Paradox in International Cooperation: Institutionally Embedded Universities in a Global Environment. *Higher Education, 53*(1), 61–79.

Beigel, F. (2013). Centros y Perferias en la Circulación Internacional del Conocimiento [Centers and Peripheries in the International Movement of Knowledge]. *Nueva Sociedad, 245* (Mayo-Junio), 110–123. http://nuso.org/articulo/centros-y-periferias-en-la-circulacion-internacional-del-conocimiento/

Bjorkman, I., Stahl, G. K., & Vaara, E. (2007). Cultural Differences and Capability Transfer in Cross-Border Acquisitions: The Mediating Roles of Capability Complementarity, Absorptive Capacity, and Social Integration. *Journal of International Business Studies, 38*, 658–672. https://helda.helsinki.fi/bitstream/handle/10227/399/JIBS,?sequence=3

Boneberger, A., Radon, K., Baer, J., Kausel, L., Kabesch, M., Haider, D., Schierl, R., von Kries, R., & Calvorio, M. (2010). Asthma in Changing Environments-Chances and Challenges of International Research Collaborations Between South America and Europe-Study Protocol and Description of the Data Acquisition of a Case-Control-Study. *BMC Pulmonary Medicine, 10*(43), 1–8. http://bmc-pulmmed.biomedcentral.com/articles/10.1186/1471-2466-10-43

Bordons, M., Aparicio, J., & Costas, R. (2013). Heterogeneity of Collaboration and its Relationship with Research Impact in a Biomedical Field. *Scientometrics, 96*(2), 433–466. http://thirdworld.nl/heterogeneity-of-collaboration-and-its-relationship-with-research-impact-in-a-biomedical-field

Bordons, M., Gonzalo-Albo, B., & Aparicio, J. (2015). The Influence of R&D Intensity of Countries on the Impact of International Collaborative Research. *Scientometrics, 102*(2): 1385–1400. http://link.springer.com/article/10.1007%2Fs11192-014-1491-4#/page-1

Bradley, M. (2007). *North-South Research Partnerships: Challenges, Responses and Trends.* Ottawa: Canadian Partnerships Program, IDRC. https://idl-bnc.idrc.ca/dspace/bitstream/10625/36539/1/127716.pdf

Carbonnier, G., & Kontinen, T. (2014). *North-South Research Partnership: Academia Meets Development?* Bonn: European Association of Development Research and

Training Institutes (EADI). http://www.academia.edu/10338110/North-South_Research_Partnerships_Academia_Meets_Development

Chinchilla-Rodríguez, Z., Benavent-Perez, M., de Moya-Anegon, F., & Miguel, S. (2012). International Collaboration in Medical Research in Latin America and the Caribbean (2003–2007). *Journal of the American Society for Information Science and Technology, 63*(11), 2223–2238. http://digital.csic.es/bitstream/10261/63798/1/international_collaboration_latinamerica_medicine_arxiv.pdf

Chinchilla-Rodríguez, Z., Zacca-González, G., & Vargas-Quesada, B. (2015). Latin American Scientific Output in Public Health; Combined Analysis Using Bibliometric, Socioeconomic and Health Indicators. *Scientometrics, 102*(1), 609–628. http://digital.csic.es/bitstream/10261/108463/1/latin_american_scientific_output_public_health_preprint.pdf

Clark, B., & Llorens, J. (2012). Investments in Scientific Research: Examining the Funding Threshold Effects on Scientific Collaboration and Variation by Academic Discipline. *Policy Studies Journal, 40*(4), 698–729. https://www.researchgate.net/profile/Jared_Llorens/publications

de Filippo, D., Aparicio, J., & Gomez, I. (2009). *Measuring the Benefits of International Collaboration: A Case Study of the Relationship Between Latin-American and European Countries*. Rio de Janeiro: 12th International Conference on Scientometrics and Informetrics ISSI 2009, Conference paper. https://www.researchgate.net/publication/281100474

Deiglmayr, A., & Spada, H. (2010). Developing Adaptive Collaboration Support: The Example of an Effective Training for Collaborative Inferences. *Educational Psychology Review, 22*(1), 103–113. https://www.researchgate.net/publication/227283929_Developing_Adaptive_Collaboration_Support_The_Example_of_an_Effective_Training_for_Collaborative_Inferences

Ductor, L. (2015). Does Co-Authorship Lead to Higher Academic Productivity? *Oxford Bulletin of Economics and Statistics, 77*(3), 385–407. http://www.otago.ac.nz/economics/news/otago075947111111111111.pdf

Duque, R., Shrum, W., Barriga, O., & Henríquez, G. (2009). Internet Practice and Professional Networks in Chilean Science: Dependency or Progress? *Scientometrics, 81*(1), 239–263. http://worldsci.net/Duque_etal_2009_Science_Networks_Internet_Chile.pdf

Duque, R., Miller, P., Barriga, O., & Henríquez, G. (2012). Is Internet Use Associated with Reporting Fewer Problems in Collaboration? Evidence from the Scientific Community in Chile. *Science Communication, 34*(5), 642–678. https://www.researchgate.net/profile/Ricardo_Duque3/publication/258186575_Is_Internet_Use_Associated_With_Reporting_Fewer_Problems_in_Collaboration/links/54f5da910cf2ca5efefd3a56.pdf

Freshwater, D., Sherwood, G., & Drury, V. (2006). International Research Collaboration: Issues, Benefits and Challenges of the Global Network. *Journal of Research in Nursing, 11*(4), 295–303. https://www.researchgate.net/publication/230639996

Genuth, J., Chompalov, I., & Shrum, W. (2000). How Experiments Begin: The Formation of Scientific Collaborations. *Minerva, 38*(3), 311–348. https://www.researchgate.net/publication/226625032_How_Experiments_Begin_The_Formation_of_Scientific_Collaborations

González-Brambila, C., Veloso, F., & Krackhardt, D. (2013). The Impact of Network Embeddedness on Research Output. *Research Policy, 42*(9), 1555–1567. http://www.sciencedirect.com/science/article/pii/S0048733313001248

Hampton, S., & Parker, J. (2011). Collaboration and Productivity in Scientific Synthesis. *Bioscience, 61*(11), 900–910. http://www.umces.edu/sites/default/files/al/pdfs/Hampton%26Parker2011.pdf

Jones, B., Wuchty, S., & Uzzi, B. (2008). Multi-University Research Teams: Shifting Impact, Geography, and Stratification in Science. *Science, New Series, 322*(5905), 1259–1262. http://www.kellogg.northwestern.edu/faculty/uzzi/ftp/081121%20Multiuniversity%20teams%20Science%20WJ.and%20Uzzi.pdf

Jonkers, K., & Cruz-Castro, L. (2013). Research Upon Return: The Effect of International Mobility on Scientific Ties, Production and Impact. *Research Policy, 42*(8), 1366–1377. https://www.researchgate.net/publication/270814936_Research_upon_return_The_effect_of_international_mobility_on_scientific_ties_production_and_impact_Research_Policy_428_1366-1377

Khor, K., & Yu, L. (2016). Influence of International Collaboration on the Research Citation Impact of Young Universities. *Scientometrics, 107*, 1095–1110. https://www.semanticscholar.org/paper/Influence-of-International-Collaboration-on-the-Khor-Yu/24229e44ff29d078b3009ad0fd1cb56d79a1bc75/pdf

Kiemle Trindade, I. (2006). Scientific Research in Latin America: Collaborative Projects on Craniofacial Abnormalities. *Cleft Palate-Craniofacial Journal, 43*(6), 722–725. http://www.cpcjournal.org/doi/pdf/10.1597/05-124.

Love, J. L. (2005). The Rise and Decline of Economic Structuralism in Latin America: New Dimensions. *Latin American Research Review, 40*(3), 100–125. http://faculty.nps.edu/relooney/00_New_48.pdf

Lozano, S., Rodríguez, X.-P., & Arenas, A. (2014). Atapuerca: Evolution of Scientific Collaboration in a Large-Scale Research Infrastructure. *Scientometrics, 98*(2), 1505–1520. http://www.academia.edu/14514904/Atapuerca_Evolution_of_scientific_collaboration_in_an_emergent_large-scale_research_infrastructure

Macias-Chapula, C. (2010). Influence of Local and Regional Publications in the Production of Public Health Research Papers in Latin America. *Scientometrics, 84*(3), 703–716. https://www.researchgate.net/publication/220365263_Influence_of_local_and_regional_publications_in_the_production_of_public_health_research_papers_in_Latin_America

Meier, A., Spada, H., & Rummel, N. (2007). A Rating Scheme for Assessing the Quality of Computer Supported Collaboration Processes. *International Journal of Computer-Supported Collaborative Learning, 2*(1), 63–86. http://www.learnlab.org/research/wiki/images/a/a9/Meier_Rating_Scheme.pdf

Melillo, E. D. (2016). *Strangers on Familiar Soil; Re-discovering the Chile-California Connection.* New Haven: Yale University Press.

Ordoñez-Matamoros, H., Cozzens, S., & García, M. (2010). International Co-authorship and Research Team Performance in Colombia. *Review of Policy Research, 27*(4), 415–431. http://doc.utwente.nl/90277/1/ordonez%20international%20research%20collaboration%20dissertation.pdf

Orozco, L., & Villaveces, J. L. (2015). Heterogeneous Research Networks in Latin American Schools of Business Management. *Academia-Revista Latinoamericana de Administracion, 28*(1), 115–134. http://www.emeraldinsight.com/doi/abs/10.1108/ARLA-05-2013-0052?journalCode=arla

Pittman, P. (2006). Beyond the Sound of One Hand Clapping: Experiences in Six Countries Using Health Equity Research in Policy. *Journal of Health Politics, Policy and Law, 33*(1), 33–50. https://www.researchgate.net/publication/7291822_Beyond_the_Sound_of_One_Hand_Clapping_Experiences_in_Six_Countries_Using_Health_Equity_Research_in_Policy

Presmanes, B., & Zumelzu, E. (2003). Scientific Cooperation Between Chile and Spain: Joint Mainstream Publications (1991–2000). *Scientometrics, 58*(3), 547–558. https://www.researchgate.net/publication/220364371_Scientific_cooperation_between_Chile_and_Spain_Joint_mainstream_publications_1991-2000

Russell, J., & Ainsworth, S. (2014). Mapping S&T Collaboration Between Latin America and Europe: Bibliometric Analysis of Co-authorships (1984–2007). In J. Gaillard, & R. Arvanitis (Eds.), *Research Collaboration Between Europe and Latin America: Mapping and Understanding Partnership* (pp. 49–77). Paris: Editions des Archives Contemporaires. http://biblioteca.ibt.unam.mx/articulos/Russell_Ainsworth2014.pdf

Salas, S., Gauthier, D., & Diaz, P. (2006). Capacity-Building, Reach and Impact of Research on Sustainable Development for Chilean and Canadian Universities and the Communities They Serve. In Association of Colleges and Universities of Canada (Eds.), *Highlighting the Impacts of North-South Research Collaboration Among Canadian and Southern Higher Education Partners* (pp. 67–73). Ottawa: AUCC. https://idl-bnc.idrc.ca/dspace/handle/10625/32515?mode=full

Ubfal, D., & Maffioli, A. (2011). The Impact of Funding on Research Collaboration: Evidence from a Developing Country. *Research Policy, 40*(9), 1269–1279. http://idbdocs.iadb.org/wsdocs/getdocument.aspx?docnum=35383563

Universities UK. (2008). *International Research Collaboration: Opportunities for the UK Higher Education Sector.* London. https://globalhighered.files.wordpress.com/2008/08/uukreportmay2008.pdf

Ynalvez, M., Sooryamoorthy, R., Mbatia, P., Dzorgbo, D.-B., Shrum, W., & Duque, R. (2005). Collaboration Paradox: Scientific Productivity, the Internet and Problems of Research in Developing Areas. *Social Studies of Science, 35*(5), 755–785. http://worldsci.net/paradox.pdf

CHAPTER 11

Research Partnership Over Neocolonialism: Max Planck Society Policy in Latin America

Pedro Pineda and Bernhard Streitwieser

INTRODUCTION

The chapters in this book have examined how universities and institutes in Latin America have followed different policies to strengthen research linkages with their Northern counterparts over the last decades. The contributors and editors share a belief in the bidirectional benefits of North-South research cooperation and in this volume have set out to examine how these can be explored and described through specific case studies. Similar reflections can be historically traced to classic works on the sociology of science (Merton 1938, 1973, 1996; Ben-David 1960, 1977, 1991), as well as more contemporary studies on scientific inquiry from the sociology of higher education (Clark 1993, 1995, 1998) and international higher education studies (Altbach 1998a, b; Bernasconi 2007, 2011). The cases reported throughout this volume provide an updated and contextualized view of the

P. Pineda (✉)
International Centre for Higher Education Research (INCHER),
University of Kassel, Kassel, Germany

B. Streitwieser
Graduate School of Education and Human Development,
George Washington University, Washington, DC, USA

© The Author(s) 2018

G. Gregorutti, N. Svenson (eds.), *North-South University Research Partnerships in Latin America and the Caribbean*,
https://doi.org/10.1007/978-3-319-75364-5_11

259

North-South scientific cooperation in Latin America and the Caribbean. Each case shares experiences, observations, and recommendations for better institutionalization of research, by highlighting the significant role played by national higher education and science policy, stressing the role of university management in expanding opportunities, or drawing attention to the critical role of key individuals—or any combination of these factors.

The chapters of Tascón and Bonilla and Crawford also recognize outright some of the issues related to power struggles in Latin American universities with their efforts to build research cooperation. While these authors agree on the benefits of cooperation, they also discuss promising possibilities for decolonization that Tascón labels "post-foundational, post-colonial thinking" and Bonilla and Crawford refer to as the upending of the "colonial model." They offer a reflective debate on other studies of transnational research cooperation (Crossley and Tikly 2004; Gaillard 1994; Nguyen et al. 2009), that emerged in the 1980s (Conrad and Eckert 2007) and describe how some of these research partnerships entail cultural controls from the global North that correspond to former colonial power arrangements and can limit the evolution of these relationships.

From such a foundation, the resulting scientific cooperative relations may not always be fluid and bidirectional, as some of the chapters in this volume illustrate. But an expanding dynamic of research activities and publications that opens new opportunities for research networks can still be established, even under unequal relationships. This approach, in turn, seems to be grounded in certain critiques of decolonialization in the social sciences formulated by Latin American authors (Mignolo 2011; Quijano and Ennis 2000) that have influenced other fields, including comparative education (Takayama et al. 2017). These authors have extended this discussion to collaborative North-South research activities suggesting a tendency in some cases for Northern scholars to control the scientific dynamics and agenda of shared knowledge production, causing the interaction to take on a hierarchical nature, framed by broader social and economic structures, instead of a bidirectional cooperative spirit.

In this concluding chapter, we delve further into these theoretical reflections and attempt to answer a question of paramount importance for understanding North-South university research partnerships: how can these collaborations maximize aspects of egalitarian cooperation and minimize those of hierarchical neocolonial control? We incorporate an analysis of the work of the German Max Planck Society (MPS) and its corresponding Max Planck Institutes[1] (MPI) throughout Latin America, describing how policy instruments conceived of in the global North have led to the establishment of research partnerships that have benefited public and private universities and institutes in the global South primarily during the late 2000s. We start by considering the expandability of decolonial and standard approaches to understanding the dynamics of research partnerships. We then review the history of cooperation between Latin American and German scholars and introduce the Max Planck (MP) work being done in the region, highlighting the different instruments currently used to reinforce collaborative development. Furthermore, we describe which universities in which countries have adapted their research agendas through policies that serve to strengthen their academic environments. In the final section, we discuss why and how cooperation occurs based on our study of the MP collaborative dynamic.

Theoretical Approaches to North-South Research Cooperation

A functionalist approach to understanding research partnerships assumes that programmatic research builds capacity better than unstructured individual initiatives. Those supporting this view tend to explain differences by focusing on national science and higher education policy and/or university administrative capacity. For example, Baud (2002), using evidence from Dutch North-South cooperation experience, highlights the comparative advantage of structured programs in comparison to unconnected initiatives for capacity development and international networking. Alternatively, Zingerli (2010) discusses how individual possibilities to undertake research depend on institutional conditions that emerge in particular historical and social conditions.

In the context of Latin America, Pineda (2015a) makes a parallel connection to the earlier work of Ben-David (Ben-David 1960, 1977) on the United States. Pineda highlights the importance of the government's role in identifying and promoting science as a public good through a comparative policy analysis of Chilean and Colombian research productivity and its relationship with the stability of research funds. Ben-David had previously explained how research institutionalization needed the government to create conditions for competition between students and academics in order to gain access to long-term research funds. An historical US example of this was the congressional initiatives promoting the Land-Grant universities in 1862, which became critical drivers of subsequent entrepreneurial research activities in US universities (Thelin 2011).

Another view of research cooperation looks at the unequal relationships deriving from a history of European colonialism in different regions of the world where colonizers sought to establish their own power centers based on homeland models (Mignolo 2011). This Eurocentric type of relationship is still present, to a degree, in the hegemonic Northern knowledge production inherent in the hierarchical structures of certain collaborations (Quijano and Ennis 2000). More recent critiques (Gaillard 1994; Crossley and Tikly 2004; Nguyen et al. 2009) also argue that research partnerships may continue to enforce cultural controls from abroad, representing a form of neocolonialism. This inequity has been characterized as a relationship of dependency (Altbach 1998b) in which the partnership generally favors the North perpetuating its dominance over the South in the production of knowledge and technological goods. Within this perspective, many established relationships have roots going back to particular histories in which geography and language played crucial roles. A number of North-South research collaborations can be traced back to the end of colonization, as can those of countries that never had colonial holdings but sought collaborations with Southern partners.

A valid post-colonial view of research partnerships must therefore include a historical and contextual dimension that differentiates cases and types of collaborations. In one of the first papers adopting a neocolonial critique of research cooperation, Jacques Gaillard (1994) traced how the motivations of industrialized countries shifted from developmental assistance in the 1950 and 1960s to capacity building in later decades. Over this period, the value of creating mutually beneficial research partnerships became increasingly apparent to donor as well as recipient countries and collaborations began to migrate toward more democratic arrangements. Earlier forms of these relationships had skewed toward Northern control, in part due to dominant political and economic strategies and also because of the limited conditions in Latin American countries for undertaking research. Early concerns about Northern partners in connection with military and commercial exploitation, abuses of resources, and increased brain drain have given way over time to appreciation for legitimately beneficial research partnerships that add value to Southern-inspired initiatives (Mignolo 2011). Some new approaches to the topic (Mazzoleni and Nelson 2007) stress the potential advantages associated with nationals staying abroad and contributing to their home countries from afar, using the term "brain circulation," whereas others disagree, claiming that support from abroad is not compensatory (Lehr 2008). Though most concur that parameters of research cooperation agendas may have been initially propelled by the North, over time Southern scientists have come to choose and adapt these Northern policies for themselves to benefit their own needs and aspirations (Gaillard 1994).

Despite theoretical reflections that North-South collaborations have taken on a more egalitarian hue over time; however, gauging whether these research partnerships have truly achieved success in this regard remains open to debate. While various types of cooperative relations between partners of unequal footing may have come closer to finding the right balance of competence and good intentions by now, the jury is still out. To add to the literature, this chapter considers the MP activities throughout Latin America. We choose to study this case because its large-scale research agenda in different countries allows for a broader perspective on cooperation with multiple governments, universities, and research centers. Also, the particular focus on basic science at a time when the discursive emphasis is on innovation makes the Max Planck Society and its corresponding Max Planck Institutes an interesting example in Latin America. These Latin American MP activities are based on many small joint research projects and rooted in the long historical relationship of Europe, Germany, and Max Planck with the region.

HISTORY OF THE MAX PLANCK INSTITUTE IN LATIN AMERICA

The 1801 meeting of pioneering Prussian naturalist Alexander von Humboldt with local Spanish botanist José Celestino Mutis in Bogotá (Ordoñez 2008) can be seen as a prelude of future German-Latin scientific partnerships. Although the term "research partnership" would not be coined until the 1990s (Barrett et al. 2014), the interaction of these two precursors closely resembles much of the research cooperation occurring today, albeit on a different scale. Von Humboldt's travels to Latin America would later be viewed by the German colonial tradition as a form of peaceful conquest, in direct contrast with Spanish colonial occupiers (Conrad 2012). The illustrations shared by Mutis and von Humboldt through the Royal Botanical Expedition to New Granada became primary references of the time (Piedrahita 2004) and an early example of the generation of North-South collaborative research and knowledge. These early interactions between

European scientists and local thinkers give us an opportunity to reflect on both the effects of colonialism and the legacies of this type of cooperation.

Von Humboldt's voyages served to advance research in Latin America with local scientists, such as Francisco Zea and Francisco José de Caldas, who were able to advance their studies as a result (de Caldas 1808/1942). The scientific expeditions and the alliances formed were also central to the organized expansion of European societies in the region, and overtly described as scientific colonialism by German historian Sebastian Conrad (2012), as territorial domination became possible only through the knowledge gleaned about local culture, language, geography, and politics. Later influences from Europe were somewhat more bidirectional and helped to expanded local scientific inquiry through the transfer of new methods that arrived with visiting European researchers (Saldaña 2006). Inspired by this, governments in the region opened cultural institutions, such as botanical gardens and museums of natural history (Vessuri 1994), in a movement that would later propel universities and research institutions during the twentieth century (Palacios 2003). Since these earlier stages, European scientific activity in the Southern Cone has become increasingly sophisticated, as have their accompanying funding mechanisms.

Today, the post-war German research system is driven by universities and research institutes, the government—through the Federal Ministry of Education and Research (*Bundesministerium für Bildung und Forschung*) and the German Research Foundation (*Deutsche Forschungsgemeinschaft— DFG*)—and four independent scientific societies, one of which is the Max Planck Society for the Advancement of Science (*Max-Planck-Gesellschaft zur Förderung der Wissenschaften*). MP, founded in 1911 as the *Kaiser Wilhelm Society* and renamed in 1948 after the Nobel laureate, Max Planck (Vom Brocke 1996), conducts mainly basic research in the natural sciences, arts, and humanities, funded by both public and private resources.

In the second half of the twentieth century, the relationship between MP and Latin America involved a low level of cooperation with the region and was based primarily on an interest in exceptional research opportunities, as Latin America offered the kind of geographical, biological, and social diversity that inspired the earlier travels of Alexander von Humboldt (Max Planck Society 2017b). Scientific cooperation did not flourish during the so-called Latin American "lost decade" of the 1980s, with many countries of the region constrained by conservative fiscal policies that weakened scientific activities (Bulmer-Tomas 2003, 353) and concerns about brain drain (Vessuri 1994). The 1990s saw a resurgence of policy discourse on science and innovation, largely through its promotion by the OECD (1997) and other international organizations. Some universities redefined their societal role and institutionalized these new ideas by establishing research offices with vice-rectors (Pineda 2015b). These changes also affected academic careers, and scientists in university research centers began to develop stronger linkages with industry (Bozeman et al. 2015; Dietz and Bozeman 2005). With the end of the Cold War, research became more closely linked with economic competitiveness and relations with the defense industry diminished in both North and South (Krücken 2003). During the 2000s, one of the most stable research relationships between MP and Latin America began to crystalize through the establishment of the MP/CONICET Partner Institute in Biomedical Research in Buenos Aires (Max Planck Society 2017a). This institute was officially inaugurated in 2012 through the collaboration of Professor Florian Holsboer at the MPI of Psychiatry in Munich and Professor Eduardo Arzt in his role as External Scientific Member of the MPI of Psychiatry.

Today, MP collaboration with other countries in Latin America and elsewhere follows the research agenda set by the individual institutes. The goal of MP is to link with a nonprofit organization whose mission is to improve scientific knowledge for public good supporting emerging scientists that are pioneering new research methods. Eighty-three MPIs worldwide now house more than 22,000 scientists and technicians. The international character of their research activities is reflected in their scientific staff: 34% of their directors, 32% of their personnel, 72% of their postdoctoral researchers, and 54% of their doctoral students are all non-Germans (Max Planck Society 2016b). In 2015, more than 500 of the MPI's visiting researchers, doctoral students, and postdocs came from Latin America (Max Planck Society 2017b). Of the 5000 MP collaborative activities with partners around the world, 3200 have been undertaken with European countries, 890 with the United States and Canada, and 140 with Latin America.

INSTITUTIONALIZING COOPERATION

To strengthen research with the region, the MP Liaison Office for Latin America was established in Buenos Aires in 2013 to facilitate partnerships to support the 83 exiting MPIs in advancing scientific knowledge. The office identifies and promotes research projects developed with universities, research institutes and centers, governments and local scientific agencies. MP explains its strategic linkage to the region using the same logic as Alexander von Humboldt did 200 years ago: exceptional geographical conditions and biological and cultural diversity (2017b) with rigorous scientific partners.

MP institutionalizes cooperation using the following instruments: the MPIs, MP partner institutes and MP centers abroad, and independent research groups. A necessary condition for the establishment of institutes abroad is stable commitment and support from the host government for the research activities undertaken by the institute. Foreign MPIs follow general procedures set forth by MP and are similar in their governance structures to the German-based institutes. However, they have the autonomy to determine their own research priorities and set their own hiring criteria. According to the MP website, the purpose of its international cooperation is to increase its research portfolio, optimize cooperation opportunities in other countries, and attract top male and female scientists in the relevant countries to work at local MPIs (Max Planck Society 2017c). The 16 centers, in turn, are strategically located to facilitate cooperation of various MP programs, educational activities, and fund-raising activities.

MPI partner institutes and centers abroad are owned by foreign partners and linked with MPIs through cooperative agreements. Today, there are more than 50 MPI partner groups around the world that are involved with promoting postdoctoral stints at MPIs abroad and the development of research groups in their home countries with collaborative programs that operate for a period of five years within the Latin American university or research center. Tandem Groups (also called Independent Groups), offer another MP cooperation mechanisms that facilitate postdoc visits to the United States or Europe. Both opportunities are funded jointly by national and institutional sources. While these policies and operational procedures are publicly articulated, other ways MP works abroad are less explicit. For example, MP representatives advocate that to stay on the cutting edge in a globally competitive research environment, MPIs must promote early career PhDs and therefore considerable efforts are made to attract young scientists. To aid in this, MP has also established doctoral degrees in cooperation with various universities in Germany. Recent graduates in these programs are encouraged to work for some years at an MPI before they take their experience to other research centers and universities.

Directors of MPI research departments act autonomously in the development of their research programs. Each department is generally composed of several research groups, which include a number of postdocs and doctoral students. The governance structure is completely different from that of the universities and allows for a permanent inflow of fresh ideas and procedures. An often challenging characteristic of German universities for foreigners is the nature of their hierarchical structure, where the chair system continues to dominate and most activities are decided by a single professor who serves as long-term director of the research center. In the United States and Latin America, for example, the organizational hierarchy tends to be somewhat flatter and gives professors of equal status greater input into the broader institutional organizational structure and decision-making process (Bernasconi 2005). Perhaps for this reason, in part, only 6.1% of current university professors in Germany are foreign nationals (Neusel et al. 2014).

COOPERATION INSTRUMENTS IN LATIN AMERICA

The MPS report on activities in Latin America (2016a) discusses one MP partner institute, one partner laboratory, nine associated research groups, ten tandem research groups, three independent research groups, and two large research facilities involved with MP cooperation (Table 11.1). Overall, Argentina has the most robust cooperation in the region, followed by Chile, Colombia, and Brazil and Mexico, Uruguay, and Peru to a lesser degree. Mexico signed a cooperative MP agreement in 2015 with the National Council of Science and Technology (*Consejo Nacional de Ciencia y Tecnología*—CONACYT) and a program for postdoctoral researchers. Uruguay signed a cooperative MP agreement with the National Agency of Research and Innovation (*Agencia Nacional de*

Table 11.1 Development of Max Planck's partnerships with Latin America (2013–2015)

	Partner institutes and laboratories	*Partner groups*	*Tandem groups*	*Independent groups*	*Big research facilities*	*Number of research projects*
Brazil		3			1	39
Argentina	2	5		3		24
Chile		3	3		1	19
Mexico						18
Colombia			7			11
Uruguay						9
Perú		1				8
TOTAL	**2**	**12**	**10**	**3**	**2**	**128**

Investigación e Innovación—ANII). To date, no Central American country has engaged in MPI research partnerships, nor have Venezuela, Ecuador, or Bolivia, although young scientists from these countries have been trained in MPIs and participated in smaller MP-related research projects as well.

Cooperation typically develops bottom-up, starting with smaller projects, moving on to partner, tandem and independent research group projects, and culminating with partner institute and partner center initiatives, representing the highest degree of MP cooperation. The participating MPIs are located in Europe (four), and the United States (one). Cooperation at this level occurs in two Argentine institutes. The first of these is the Institute for Biomedical Research of Buenos Aires (*Instituto de Investigación en Biomedicina de Buenos Aires*—IBIOBA), a partner institute in cooperation with the National Council of Scientific and Technical Research (*Consejo Nacional de Investigaciones Científicas y Técnicas*—CONICET), Argentina's main scientific agency. The institute was officially established in 2007 after 20 years of joint research activities (Max Planck Society 2016a) and since 2012 is an internationally recognized research institute that also provides training for students and postdocs, as well as Argentinian scientists returning from abroad. The institute currently hosts 60 researchers working on diagnosis and treatment of illnesses. The second associated MP laboratory is located in Rosario. The MP Laboratory for Structural Biology, Chemistry and Molecular Biophysics in Rosario (*Laboratorio Max Planck de Biología Estructural, Química y Biofísica Molecular*—LMPbioR) was established in 2014 and today is recognized as a CONICET institute and linked with the MPI for Biophysical Chemistry in Göttingen. This associated laboratory supports a joint doctorate with the Universidad Nacional de Rosario and the University of Göttingen in molecular biosciences and biomedicine.

MPIs also have research facilities worldwide for studying special topics. In Brazil, for example, the MPI for chemistry established the Amazon Tall Tower Observatory (ATTO) for climate research in cooperation with Brazil's National Institute of Amazonian Research (Instituto Nacional de Pesquisas da Amazônia—INPA) (Andreae et al. 2015). In Chile, in the early 1990s, the MPI for radio astronomy established the Atacama Pathfinder Experiment (APEX) telescope as a pathfinder experiment for the international Atacama Large Millimeter Array (ALMA) telescope in the Atacama Desert. Today, MPI and Chilean scientists are cooperating on other different big telescope projects operated by ESO.

Table 11.2 Max Planck Research Groups currently operating in Latin America

Country	Type	Institute/university	MPI	Research area
Argentina	Partner	Instituto de Agrobiotecnología del Litoral (IAL)	MPI for Developmental Biology	ARN silencing on plant biology
	Partner	Instituto de Nanosistemas of the Universidad Nacional de General San Martín	MPI for Intelligent Systems	Nanoelectronics for cellular interfaces
	Partner	Fundación Instituto Leloir (FIL)	MPI for Plant Breeding Research	Transcriptional control of vegetal development
	Partner	Facultad de Ciencias Exactas y Naturales of the Universidad de Buenos Aires	MPI of Molecular Physiology	Functional microscopy of cancer biology
Brazil	Partner	Laboratório Nacional de Ciência e Tecnologia do Bioetanol (CTBE)	MPI of Molecular Plant Physiology	Regulation of plant growth and biomass
		Centro Brasileiro de Pesquisas Físicas (CBPF)	The Fritz Haber Institute	Artificial photosynthesis and superficial sciences
		Departamento de Biología Vegetal de la Universidade Federal de Viçosa	MPI of Molecular Plant Physiology	Plant metabolomics
Chile	Partner	Departamento de Biología of the Universidad de la Serena	MPU in Chemical Ecology	Plant resistance to pathogens
	Partner			
	Tandem	Pontificia Universidad Católica de Chile	MPI for Extraterrestrial Physics	Galactic centers
	Tandem	Universidad de Valparaíso	MPI for Astronomy	Evolution of circumstellar disks
		Universidad de Valparaíso	Max Planck Florida Institute for Neuroscience	Experimental and computer neuroscience
Colombia	Tandem	Universidad Nacional (Bogotá)	MPI for Infection Biology	Mucosal immunology
		Universidad de Antioquia (Medellin)	MPI for Infection Biology	Mosquito reproductive biology
		Tropic infectious deceases		Biophysics of tropical diseases Nano bioengineering
		Universidad de los Andes	MPI for Medical Research and	Computational biophysics
		Chemistry and Computational Biology	MPI for Intelligent Systems MPI for Developmental Biology	Computational and microbial ecology
		Universidad de los Andes Transformations in public rights	MPI for Comparative Public Law and International Law	Public Latin-American right: Towards a new esperanto
Peru	Partner	Pontificia Universidad Católica del Perú	MPI for Chemical Ecology	Monitoring of vegetal defensive response

The MPS 2016 Latin American brochure (2016a) presents seven partners and three research groups, detailed in Table 11.2.

The strongest cooperation in terms of joint research activity is with Argentina, followed by Chile and Colombia. According to MPS representatives, cooperation in Latin America has grown considerably in the last several years, particularly because of increased interest from universities and funding institutions. Top-tier young researchers are coming back to Latin America to build research groups in cooperation with MPIs. These groups get established in the universities that offer the most supportive research environment, which includes connections with internationally recognized scientific partners. MP activities in Latin America are also branching into a variety of new fields, some of which go beyond the natural sciences, as with the Universidad de los Andes in Colombia, where a research group is looking at the rapid transformation of legal reform in Latin America.

Links between Latin American researchers and their MP counterparts continue to be actively formed and are generally considered in the region to be relatively prestigious affiliations. However, there have also been examples of conflict between researchers of different nationalities. Salary discrepancies between Germans and foreign nationals were an issue of concern before MP reformed its remuneration policy for PhD students (Pain 2015) and ultimately led to a 2008 law suit. This prompted a system-wide survey conducted by the doctoral students' network that found international students received less compensation than German students. The same study also found that 7–8% of Asian and African students reported significant problems of xenophobia. While such discrepancies are sometimes difficult to study empirically, inquiry is constantly needed to better understand and adapt specific elements of the professional and personal relationships between research institutes and researchers. Knowing more about the intricacies involved in equitable academic status between counterparts and definitions of transparency and meritocracy within these relationships also helps further the discourse on critiques in the neocolonial literature.

Discussion

MP Latin American research cooperation is based on the Northern side, through a programmatic regional office, two international cooperation facilities, two partner institutes and laboratories, and more than 20 research groups affiliated in some way with an institute. All of these configurations work to facilitate access to high-level training, equipment, and experience for Latin American researchers in pursuit of the expansion of local knowledge. The MP initiatives and results support Baud's (2002) claims that programmatic research agendas, represented in this case by a prestigious Northern scientific society, foster better capacity-building opportunities than do unstructured individual initiatives.

On the Latin American side, public and private universities and institutes with varying profiles seek and develop joint international research collaborations based on policies that serve to advance their own scientific agendas. However, the utility of those activities—and the training and access they can provide—ultimately also depends on the degree of national government support that they enjoy. Not all universities and research centers benefit from such a situation. The universities currently carrying out MP research agendas are clearly visible in their countries because of a national research tradition that was instrumental in initially attracting interest from the MPI. The fact that these universities have attained success within such environments is also related to their own systems for institutionalization and organization of research.

Along these lines of thought, Gaillard's (1994) emphasis on facilitating collaboration and cooperation between individual scientists can be seen as a key principle for building long-term partnerships. Exchanges allow opportunities for dialogue between academics and for furthering the perspectives of both hemispheres. Scientific cooperation is foremost a joint activity among researchers that in the case of MPI are represented by the leaders of each group. Scientific cooperation depends on the two partners' motivation to work together through both formal and informal communications (Jeong et al. 2013; Ynalvez and Shrum 2011). A common feature that MP cooperating partners share, regardless of their public or private status and research profiles, is their ability to attract both scientists with previous links to German research institutes and new researchers coming from within the MP family of institutes.

The case of MPI international research cooperation, therefore, somewhat challenges the rhetoric that overestimates the capacities of university management to institutionalize research without having broader institutional frameworks in place to offer long-term stability and support for scientific exploration. This view is often put forth by authors who view universities as corporations that can identify and copy best practices, regardless of the cultural and historical context. Rather, the MP activity in

Latin America highlights the importance of both the governmental support needed for large-scale international scientific cooperation as well as the internal organizational academic interactions that lie at the heart of each partnership. Certain common university policies promoting academic environments that are cooperation-friendly indirectly contribute to the foundations necessary for research partnerships. For instance, the establishment of a research mission and office, innovation offices, and a meritocratic system for the allocation of resources, factor heavily into an institution's research profile, as described by Pineda (2015b). These practices and policies send internal and external messages about the perceived importance of research activity. Along with these discursive and structural supports, tangible instruments such as internal funding mechanisms and competitive salaries for attracting scholars with linkages or capacities to build partnerships with international scientists may also explain MP institutional partner selection and successful cooperation. In short, policy instruments for promoting research create inertia for laying the foundations of research partnerships. The best preparation for building successful international research collaborations is to foster an enriched academic and intellectual atmosphere at home.

Lastly, a decolonial perspective would conclude that the research activities analyzed here are, indeed, situated inside larger Northern research agendas, which can, subsequently lead to diminished influence of Southern peers with regard to the approaches and topics emphasized in the international collaboration. Although both partners benefit from the research agendas and the exchange of ideas in their different modalities of cooperation, often the main focus of the research agenda is established by MPI, the Northern researcher in this case. Much of the MP collaboration funding also comes from the North, perpetuating a clear Southern research dependency relationship, as many other scholars have discussed and analyzed (Altbach 1998b; Crossley and Tikly 2004; Nguyen et al. 2009). In this vein, the dynamics behind the research topics selected are more likely to be guided by the transfer of research cultures, paradigms, and approaches, as neocolonial perspectives claim (Crossley 2012).

Decolonial perspectives are useful for reflecting on this kind of potential imbalance and for maintaining the different identities of agents (Conrad and Eckert 2007); in this case, the researchers located in different parts of the world. The collaborations of MP in Latin America, however, show that not all forms of cultural exchange and research partnership fit neatly into a broad category of neocolonial-style relationships. Different forms of cooperation can emerge irrespective of macrohistorical processes.

CONCLUSION

In this chapter, we have examined North-South research collaboration and some of the theory behind it, taking the MP activity in Latin America as a case study. This case provided a paradigmatic platform from which to simultaneously analyze different countries in the region and the research areas in which they are engaged with the MP. The extent to which the university instruments highlighted here can help build successful networks should not be overestimated. MP cooperation occurs exclusively in countries with governments that actively support their university sectors by providing funding not only to establish institutes but also to ensure their sustainability and productivity over the long term. Following the line of argument promoted by Ben-David (Ben-David 1960, 1977), the role of the government is to promote Southern universities and research institutes by guaranteeing a long-term perspective that combines doctoral education, funding for basic and applied projects granted on a competitive basis, and stable funding for research infrastructure in the most capable research centers. This helps to explain the difference between Southern universities and research centers that do and do not achieve successful implementation of stable research agendas and development of cooperative partnerships with Northern counterparts.

The specific MP case and its emphasis on basic research draws attention to the importance of analyzing the role of the State in the research development context. Inviting a Northern center or partner can contribute to advancing local research, but mostly when the proper infrastructure and supports for universities are already in place. Future studies should continue exploring how research partnerships develop as has been done in this edited volume—particularly with a view to isolating the multitude of relevant organizational, institutional, and infrastructural factors at every level and examining patterns in and among successful cases. MP activities in Latin America have been clearly beneficial to both parties and cannot be portrayed as a neocolonial abuse of emerging territories——although North-South imbalances do still exist and continue to influence the structure and implementation of the research collaborations. Transformative evolutionary processes, especially those involving learning and knowledge production, will necessarily involve a number of gray areas regarding timing and strength of paradigm and power shifts. Little of this type of iterative change is black-and-white or before-and-after. Future work in this area should continue to dissect and unpack North-South research collaboration processes in different places with these lessons in mind and always with an understanding of the relevant historical dimension, as we have attempted to do here. Both North and South have much to gain, individually and collectively, by continuing to seek out and develop meaningful research partnerships. Whatever academia can do to further these efforts with instructive analytical documentation of comparative experience will be useful for governments, institutions, and scientists everywhere.

NOTE

1. The Max Planck Society operates through dozens of Max Planck Institutes and facilities worldwide that conduct basic research in the areas of the natural sciences, life sciences, social sciences, and humanities.

REFERENCES

Altbach, P. G. (1998a). *Comparative Higher Education: Knowledge, the University, and Development.* Greenwich: Ablex Publishing Corporation.

Altbach, P. G. (1998b). The University as Center and Periphery. In P. G. Altbach (Ed.), *Comparative Higher Education: Knowledge, the University, and Development* (pp. 19–36). Westport: Ablex Publishing.

Andreae, M. O., Acevedo, O. C., Araùjo, A., Artaxo, P., Barbosa, C. G. G., Barbosa, H. M. J., Brito, J., Carbone, S., Chi, X., Cintra, B. B. L., da Silva, N. F., Dias, N. L., Dias-Júnior, C. Q., Ditas, F., Ditz, R., Godoi, A. F. L., Godoi, R. H. M., Heimann, M., Hoffmann, T., Kesselmeier, J., Könemann, T., Krüger, M. L., Lavric, J. V., Manzi, A. O., Lopes, A. P., Martins, D. L., Mikhailov, E. F., Moran-Zuloaga, D., Nelson, B. W., Nölscher, A. C., Santos Nogueira, D., Piedade, M. T. F., Pöhlker, C., Pöschl, U., Quesada, C. A., Rizzo, L. V., Ro, C. U., Ruckteschler, N., Sá, L. D. A., de Oliveira Sá, M., Sales, C. B., dos Santos, R. M. N., Saturno, J., Schöngart, J., Sörgel, M., de Souza, C. M., de Souza, R. A. F., Su, H., Targhetta, N., Tóta, J., Trebs, I., Trumbore, S., van Eijck, A., Walter, D., Wang, Z., Weber, B., Williams, J., Winderlich, J., Wittmann, F., Wolff, S., & Yáñez-Serrano, A. M. (2015). The Amazon Tall Tower Observatory (ATTO): Overview of Pilot Measurements on Ecosystem Ecology, Meteorology, Trace Gases, and Aerosols. *Atmospheric Chemistry and Physics, 15*(18), 10723–10776. https://doi.org/10.5194/acp-15-10723-2015.

Barrett, A. M., Crossley, M. W., & Fon, P. T. (2014). North-south Research Partnerships in Higher Education: Perspectives from South and North. In B. Streitwieser (Ed.), *Internationalization of Higher Education and Global Mobility*. Oxford: Symposium Books.

Baud, I. (2002). North-South Partnerships in Development Research: An Institutional Approach. *International Journal of Technology Management and Sustainable Development, 1*(3), 153–170. https://doi.org/10.1386/ijtm.1.3.153.

Ben-David, J. (1960). Scientific Productivity and Academic Organization in Nineteenth-Century Medicine. *American Sociological Review, 25*(6), 828–843.

Ben-David, J. (1977). *Centers of Learning: Britain, France, Germany, United States*. New York: McGraw-Hill.

Ben-David, J. (1991). *Scientific Growth: Essays on the Social Organization and Ethos of Science*. Oxford: University of California Press.

Bernasconi, A. (2005). University Entrepreneurship in a Developing Country: The Case of the P. Universidad Católica de Chile, 1985–2000. *Higher Education, 50*(2), 247–274.

Bernasconi, A. (2007). Are There Research Universities in Chile? In P. G. Altbach & J. Balán (Eds.), *Transforming Research Universities in Asia and Latin America* (pp. 234–259). Baltimore: The John Hopkins University Press.

Bernasconi, A. (2011). Private and Public Pathways to World-Class Research Universities: The Case of Chile. In *The Road to Academic Excellence: The Making of World-Class Research Universities* (pp. 229–259). Washington, DC: The World Bank.

Bozeman, B., Rimes, H., & Youtie, J. (2015). The Evolving State-of-the-Art in Technology Transfer Research: Revisiting the Contingent Effectiveness Model. *Research Policy, 44*(1), 34–49. https://doi.org/10.1016/j.respol.2014.06.008.

Bulmer-Tomas, V. (2003). *The Economic History of Latin America Since Independence*. Cambridge: Cambridge University Press.

Clark, B. R. (1993). *The Research Foundations of Graduate Education: Germany, Britain, France, United States, Japan*. Los Angeles: University of California Press.

Clark, B. R. (1995). *Places of Inquiry: Research and Advanced Education in Modern Universities*. London: University of California Press.

Clark, B. R. (1998). *Creating Entrepreneurial Universities: Organizational Pathways of Transformation*. Oxford: International Association of Universities and Elsevier Science Ltd.

Conrad, S. (2012). *German Colonialism: A Short History*. Cambridge: Cambridge University Press.

Conrad, S., & Eckert, A. (2007). Globalgeschichte, Globalisierung, multiple Modernen: Zur Geschichtsschreibung der modernen Welt [Global History,

Globalization, Multiple Modernities: Towards the Global Description of the Modern World]. In S. Conrad, A. Eckert, & U. Freitag (Eds.), *Globalgeschichte: Theorien, Ansätze, Themen* [*Global History: Theories, Approaches, Topics*] (pp. 7–52). Frankfurt/New York: Campus Verlag.

Crossley, M. (2012). Comparative Education and Research Capacity Building: Reflections on International Transfer and the Significance of Context. *Journal of International Comparative Education, 1*(1), 4–12. https://doi.org/10.14425/00.36.36.

Crossley, M., & Tikly, L. (2004). Postcolonial Perspectives and Comparative and International Research in Education: A Critical Introduction. *Comparative Education, 40*(2), 147–156. https://doi.org/10.1080/0305006042000231329.

de Caldas, F. J. (1808/1942). *Semanario del Nuevo Reino de Granada*. Bogotá: Editorial Kelly.

Dietz, J. S., & Bozeman, B. (2005). Academic Careers, Patents, and Productivity: Industry Experience as Scientific and Technical Human Capital. *Research Policy, 34*(3), 349–367. https://doi.org/10.1016/j.respol.2005.01.008.

Gaillard, J. F. (1994). North-South Research Partnership: Is Collaboration Possible Between Unequal Partners? *Knowledge and Policy, 7*(2), 31–63. https://doi.org/10.1007/bf02692761.

Jeong, S., Choi, J. Y., & Kim, J.-Y. (2013). On the Drivers of International Collaboration: The Impact of Informal Communication, Motivation, and Research Resources. *Science and Public Policy, 41*(4), 520–531. https://doi.org/10.1093/scipol/sct079.

Krücken, G. (2003). Learning the 'New, New Thing': On the Role of Path Dependency. *Higher Education, 46*(3), 315–339.

Lehr, S. (2008). Ethical Dilemmas in Individual and Collective Rights-Based Approaches to Tertiary Education Scholarships: The Cases of Canada and Cuba. *Comparative Education, 44*(4), 425–444. https://doi.org/10.1080/03050060802481454.

Max Planck Society. (2016a). Cooperación científica con América Latina. https://www.mpg.de/10832876/Brochure_America_Latina_2016_WEB.pdf. Accessed 15 Apr 2017.

Max Planck Society. (2016b). International – Facts and Figures. https://www.mpg.de/international/facts_figures. Accessed 15 Apr 2017.

Max Planck Society. (2017a). CONICET-MPG Partner Institute Buenos Aires. https://www.mpg.de/7468700/Partner-Institute_Buenos-Aires. Accessed 15 Apr 2017.

Max Planck Society. (2017b). Cooperation with Latin America. https://www.mpg.de/7468478/Latin-America. Accessed 15 Apr 2017.

Max Planck Society. (2017c). Max Planck Institutes Abroad. https://www.mpg.de/272329/Max_Planck_Institutes_abroad. Accessed 15 Apr 2017.

Mazzoleni, R., & Nelson, R. R. (2007). Public Research Institutions and Economic Catch-Up. *Research Policy, 36*(10), 1512–1528. https://doi.org/10.1016/j.respol.2007.06.007.

Merton, R. K. (1938). Science, Technology and Society in Seventeenth Century England. *Osiris, 4,* 360–632.

Merton, R. K. (1973). The Normative Structure of Science. In R. K. Merton (Ed.), *The Sociology of Science: Theoretical and Empirical Investigations* (pp. 267–280). Chicago: University of Chicago Press.

Merton, R. K. (1996). *On Social Structure and Science.* Chicago: The University of Chicago Press.

Mignolo, W. D. (2011). *The Darker Side of Western Modernity: Global Futures, Decolonial Options (Latin America Otherwise).* Durham: Duke University Press.

Neusel, A., Wolter, A., Engel, O., Kriszio, M., & Weichert, D. (2014). *Internationale Mobilität und Professur: Karriereverläufe und Karrierebedingungen von Internationalen Professorinnen und Professoren an Hochschulen in Berlin und Hessen* [*International Mobility and Professorship: Carriers Paths and Carrier Conditions for International Professors in Universities in Berlin and Hessen*]. Berlin: Bundesministerium für Bildung und Forschung.

Nguyen, P.-M., Elliott, J. G., Terlouw, C., & Pilot, A. (2009). Neocolonialism in Education: Cooperative Learning in an Asian Context. *Comparative Education, 45*(1), 109–130. https://doi.org/10.1080/03050060802661428.

Ordoñez, S. (2008). Aspectos Geológicos del Viaje por Iberoamérica (1799–1804) de Alexander von Humboldt [Geographical Aspects of Alexander von Humboldt's Voyage Through Iberoamerica (1799–1804)]. In *Alexander von Humboldt: Estancia en España y Viaje Americano* [*Alexander von Humboldt: Visit in Spain and American Travel*] (pp. 177–200). Madrid: Consejo Superior de Investigaciones Científicas [National Council of Scientific Research].

Organization for Economic Cooperation and Development. (1997). *National Innovation Systems.* Paris: OECD.

Pain, E. (2015). Max Planck Society Unveils €50 Million Support Plan for Young Scientists. http://www.sciencemag.org/news/2015/03/max-planck-society-unveils-50-million-support-plan-young-scientists. Accessed 12 Apr 2017.

Palacios, M. (2003). *Entre la Legitimidad y la Violencia: Colombia 1875–1994* [*Between Legitimacy and Violence: Colombia 1875–1994*]. Bogotá: Editorial Norma.

Piedrahita, S. (2004). *La Escuela de Ciencias Naturales de la Universidad Nacional.* Bogotá: Facultad de Ciencias Humanas.

Pineda, P. (2015a). Institutional Frameworks and Scientific Productivity in Chile and Colombia 1950–2012. In G. Gregorrutti & J. E. Delgado (Eds.), *Private Universities in Latin America: Research and Innovation in the Knowledge Economy* (pp. 79–106). New York: Palgrave Macmillan.

Pineda, P. (2015b). *The Entrepreneurial Research University in Latin America: Global and Local Models in Chile and Colombia, 1950–2015*. New York: Palgrave Macmillan.

Quijano, A., & Ennis, M. (2000). Coloniality of Power, Eurocentrism and Latin America. *Nepantla: Views from South, 1*(3), 533–580.

Saldaña, J. J. (2006). Science and Freedom: Science and Technology as a Policy of the New American States. In J. J. Saldaña (Ed.), *Science in Latin America: A History* (pp. 151–162). Austin: University of Texas Press.

Takayama, K., Sriprakash, A., & Connell, R. (2017). Toward a Postcolonial Comparative and International Education. *Comparative Education Review, 61*(S1), S1–S24. https://doi.org/10.1086/690455.

Thelin, J. R. (2011). *A History of American Higher Education*. Baltimore: The Johns Hopkins University Press.

Vessuri, H. (1994). The Institutionalization Process. In *The Uncertain Quest. Science, Technology, and Development* (pp. 168–200). Tokio: Universidad de las Naciones Unidas.

Vom Brocke, B. (1996). *Die Kaiser-Wilhelm-/Max-Planck-Gesellschaft und ihre Institut: Studien zu ihrer Geschichte das Harnack-Prinzip* [*The Harnack-Principle: The Kaiser-Wilmelm-Max Planck Society and Its Institutes: Studies About Their History*]. Berlin: Walter de Gruyter.

Ynalvez, M. A., & Shrum, W. M. (2011). Professional Networks, Scientific Collaboration, and Publication Productivity in Resource-Constrained Research Institutions in a Developing Country. *Research Policy, 40*(2), 204–216. https://doi.org/10.1016/j.respol.2010.10.004.

Zingerli, C. (2010). A Sociology of International Research Partnerships for Sustainable Development. *The European Journal of Development Research, 22*(2), 217–233. https://doi.org/10.1057/ejdr.2010.1.

INDEX[1]

NUMBERS AND SYMBOLS
501(c)(3) entities, 50

A
Ab inicio, 135
Abnormal Atrial Endocardial
  Electrograms, 157
Academic agreements, 18, 19
Academic alliances, 31, 66
Academic capacity, 76, 80
Academic collaborations, 31, 41, 42,
  56, 57, 137, 218
Academic community, 120, 123, 226
Academic connections, 90
Academic cooperation, 39
Academic cultures, 133, 187
Academic dialogues, 120
Academic exchanges, 25, 42, 117,
  123, 218, 251
Academic explorers, 233
Academic mobility, 162

Academic programing, 18, 64, 66, 82,
  117, 162
Academic structures, 28, 29, 149
Academic unit, 147, 150, 162
Acceleration, 160
Adgys System, 159
Advent of knowledge economy, 3
Advent of the Cuban Revolution, 55
Aerospace, 145
Agreement(s)
  of collaboration, 3
  parameters and publication, 2
  with USA, 17, 18, 22, 28
Agricultural Technology Institute, 228n2
Alliance Free from Violence, 159
Alliance of Progress, 235
Alpine tropical environments, 160
Alternative
  livelihoods, 47, 48
  principles, 118, 123–125
Amazon Tall Tower Observatory
  (ATTO), 268

[1] Note: Page numbers followed by 'n' refer to notes.

© The Author(s) 2018
G. Gregorutti, N. Svenson (eds.), *North-South University
Research Partnerships in Latin America and the Caribbean*,
https://doi.org/10.1007/978-3-319-75364-5

279

280 INDEX

América Economía magazine, 65
Americanists, 99, 100
Americas Barometer survey, 158
Amphibian, 161
*Anales de la Facultad de Ciencias
  Médica*, 153
Android Data Gathering System
  (Adgys), 159
Annotated Taxonomic Checklist, 161
Annual Latin America Forum, 70
Antarctica, 233
Anthropological, 108
APEX Telescope, 268
Apolobamba, 160
Applied Medicine Research Center, 221
Architects, 179, 192
Argentina, 5, 8, 9, 107, 129, 151,
  154, 162, 204, 208–211,
  216–219, 221, 223, 226, 228n4,
  234, 267, 268, 270
Argentina's macroeconomic
  instability, 223
Argentinian universities, 9, 203–227
Armed Forces Scientific and
  Technological Research Institute
  (*Instituto de Investigaciones
  Científicas y Tecnológicas de las
  Fuerzas Armadas*, CITEFA), 228n2
Artavia, Roberto, 67, 68, 71, 82
Article co-authorship, 142, 155–157,
  163, 165
Artificial photosynthesis, 269
Artistic University of Paraguay, 148
Arzt, Eduardo, 265
Associations, 2, 3, 7, 10, 30, 49, 63,
  69, 79, 80, 204, 205, 207, 210,
  211, 217, 218, 220, 221, 226,
  246, 251
Association to Advance Collegiate
  Schools of Business (AACSB),
  62, 65
Atacama Desert, 268
Atlantic Ocean, 40

Attentional resources, 207, 228n1
Austral Teaching Hospital, 213
Autonomous University Juan Misael
  Saracho (UAJMS), 146, 147
Axis/axes, 148, 180, 181, 189
Azanza, Julia, 6, 46

B
Baja California, 47
Baker, George P., 65, 75, 80
Barbero, Andrés, 162, 164
Barrett, Beverly, 6, 33n7
Belgium, 151
Belize, 63
Benchmarking, 184, 186
Ben-David, Joseph, 259, 261, 273
Benefits, 2, 4, 6, 22, 26–28, 31, 33,
  45, 54, 63, 73, 75, 77–79, 93,
  121, 134, 186, 190, 204, 205,
  207, 208, 215, 218, 219, 221,
  223, 226, 237, 241, 243, 245,
  248–249, 251, 252, 259, 260,
  263, 271, 272
Best system, 193
Bibliometric quantification, 3
Bilateral
  agreement, 24, 28, 29, 31, 217
  association, 220
  cooperation agreements, 217
  research, 15, 57
  research agreements, 23
Bi-national collaboration, 39, 43
Bi-national US–Cuba collaboration, 45
Biodiversity, 3, 54, 56, 147, 160
  patterns, 42
Biomass, 44
Biomedicine, 268
Biomolecular Electronics and
  Electrocatalysis
  (BIOMOLECTRONICS), 213
Biophysics of tropical diseases, 269
Biotechnology, 152

Bloqueo, 38
Bolivia, 8, 9, 141–165, 166n1, 268
Bolivian Academy of Economic
  Sciences (*Academia Boliviana de
  Ciencias Económicas*, ABCE), 151
Bolivian Association of Biomedical
  Journal Editors, 150
Bolivian Center for Multidisciplinary
  Research (*Centro Boliviano de
  Investigación Multidisciplinaria*,
  CEBEM), 158, 159
Bolivian innovation system, 147
Bolivian Institute for Advanced Studies
  in Development, 156
Boliviano, 158
Bolivian Society of Pediatrics, 152
Bolivian Society of Physics, 152
Bolivian think tank, 157–159
Bordeaux, 9, 160, 177, 179, 181,
  183, 189, 193, 195
Botanical gardens, 264
Brain circulation, 263
Brazil, 5, 8, 9, 143–146, 151, 154,
  156–158, 163, 175–198, 204,
  208, 234, 267, 268
Bretos, Fernando, 6, 46, 47
Buenos Aires, 265, 268
Bureaucratic, 10, 28, 42, 226, 227
  obstacles, 50, 219, 223
Bush, George W.
  administration, 41
Business Association of Latin American
  Studies (BALAS), 66

C
Capacity development, 3, 6, 77, 82,
  127, 185, 261
Capes, 186
Capital, 120, 142, 143, 180, 206, 216,
  217, 220–222, 225, 243, 249
Caribbean, 40, 43, 44, 48, 51, 56
Caribbean island, 56

Caribbean Sea, 40, 44, 56
Case study, 6, 9, 11, 15, 40, 62, 67,
  70, 81, 175, 178, 211, 212,
  215–225, 243, 273
  analysis, 2
Castro, Raul, 42
Catholic Church, 4, 17
Catholic University of Maule, 155
Catholic University of Our lady of
  Asuncion, 148, 157, 165, 235
Catholic University San Pablo
  (*Universidad Católica Boliviana
  San Pablo*, UCBSP), 147, 150,
  151, 155, 165
Cayo Largo, 44
Center for Global Development, 156
Center for Studies on Economic and
  Social Reality (*Centro de Estudios
  de la Realidad Económica y Social*,
  CERES), 158, 159
Central America, 7, 61–83, 130, 131
Central America and Caribbean Legal
  Pedagogy, 126–128
*Central American Agenda for the 21st
  Century*, 68, 69, 77
Central American Bank for Economic
  Integration (Banco
  Centroamericano de Integración
  Económica, BCIE), 65
Central American Free Trade
  Agreement (CAFTA), 77
Central American governments, 65,
  69, 77
Central American Institute of Business
  Administration (Instituto
  Centroamericano de
  Administración de Empresas,
  INCAE), 7, 61, 67
Central American Private Sector
  Initiative (CAPSI), 7, 69, 77, 82
Central Intelligence Agency, 188
Centre for Environmental
  Epidemiology Research, 155

282 INDEX

Challenges, 5, 7, 9, 22, 28, 30, 31, 33, 38–40, 42, 48, 51, 53, 54, 69, 70, 78, 80, 82, 83, 87–89, 93–95, 104–106, 109, 117, 118, 120, 131–133, 136, 143, 148, 165, 175, 178, 179, 187, 189–191, 196, 219, 252, 271
Champions, 80
Characteristics, 2, 3, 24, 25, 29, 50, 66, 73–75, 90, 93, 98, 109, 120, 127, 130, 132, 142, 150, 162, 163, 178, 179, 188, 193, 239, 252, 267
Charité – School of Medicine of Berlin, Germany, 214
Chemical Research Institute, 147
Chicago boys, 235
Chile, 8, 10, 151, 154, 155, 233–237, 240–243, 247, 248, 250, 251, 267, 268, 270
Cincinnati, 9, 179, 189, 190, 193
Cirugía Paraguaya, 154
Citations, 121, 213, 214, 223, 224, 228n9, 239, 240
Citizenship politics, 157–159
Ciudadanía, 157–159, 164, 165
Coastal marine ecosystems, 47
Co-authorship
  analysis, 205
  metrics, 3
Cochabamba, 146, 147, 157
Cochabamba: Equality, Identity, and Citizenship, 159
Cochabamba: Politics, Rights, and Daily Life, 159
Cocodrilo, 47
Cognitive dissonance, 116, 125, 129, 132
Cohort, 5, 250
Cold War, 265
Collaboration
  agreement, 18, 22, 26, 162
  facilitators, 247–248

models, 73, 77, 78
parameters, 2
Collaborative Approaches to Research, 73
Collaborative process, 8, 117, 206
Collaborative projects, 8, 42, 70, 115, 189, 242, 243, 248, 250, 251
Collaborative relationships, 3, 62, 80, 234, 239
Collaborative research, 10, 57, 63, 73, 81, 89, 100, 203–227, 234, 237, 239, 241–244, 247, 251, 252, 263
Colombia, 5, 7, 8, 87–109, 135, 154, 237, 267, 270
Colombian historical, 108
Colonial, 90, 118, 121, 125, 127, 132, 137, 137n1, 138n3, 260, 262, 263
Colonial model, 8, 116–121, 123, 126, 127, 130–132, 135, 136, 260
Commodity, 8, 115, 116
Communication and exchange, 187, 189–190, 206
Community education, 47
Comparison/comparing, 9, 32, 89, 95, 107, 175–198, 221, 261
Compatibility, 187–189, 238, 240–243
Compendio de Ciencias Veterinarias, 154, 156
Competency-based curriculum, 162
Competitiveness of Nations, The, 68
Complementarity, 238–240
Complementary institutional resources, 190–191
Comprehensive, 3, 16, 21, 32, 39, 42, 43, 138n4, 147, 176, 179, 185, 205, 250
Computational and microbial ecology, 269
Computational biophysics, 269
CONACYT Institute for Biological Research, 161
Concept of time, 119, 122

INDEX 283

Conceptual opposition, 119, 120, 137n1
Conditioning factors in research
  collaboration, 238–243
Conditions, 9, 28, 43, 55, 79, 83,
  116, 122, 123, 142, 163,
  176–178, 180–183, 185, 191,
  194, 196, 241, 250, 252, 261,
  262, 266
Condo, Arturo, 62, 69, 71, 77
Connection Emancipation Fund, 159
Conrad, Sebastian, 260, 263, 264, 272
Conservation of the interconnected
  ecosystems, 55
Conservation targets, 6, 38, 42
Considerations, 8, 93, 95, 120, 176,
  186, 194–198, 248
Consolidate, 19, 155, 211, 216, 220,
  222, 245
Constraints to collaboration, 248
Contexts, 2, 4–5, 8, 11, 16, 19–22,
  30, 32, 39–42, 49, 51, 63, 64,
  75, 88–92, 105, 115, 116, 119,
  123, 127, 128, 134, 135, 137,
  165, 176–179, 183–186, 188,
  190, 192, 195, 198n1, 204, 207,
  212, 225, 261, 271, 273
Contextualization, 178, 197
Contracts for oil, 57
Control, 10, 137, 191, 197,
  260, 262
Conventional research protocol, 9
Convention on International Trade in
  Endangered Species of Flora and
  Fauna (CITES), 47
Cooperation, 3, 9–11, 16, 19, 21, 22,
  26, 32, 39, 43, 46, 56, 62, 70,
  127, 164, 186, 192, 204–206,
  208, 210, 211, 215, 217,
  219–223, 225, 227, 238, 245,
  248, 259–273
  programs, 210, 222, 223
Cooperative agreements, 220, 266
Cooperative alliances, 225

Coordination of Women
  (Coordinadora de la Mujer), 158
Core elements, 238
Corengia, Angela, 9
Corporate partnership, 73, 75, 78, 81
Costa Rica, 5, 48, 63, 65, 154
Cost management, 80
Council of European Union, (2013), 3
Council of Rectors Cristiana de Araújo
  Lima study, 9
Counterpart, 16, 42, 51, 76, 103,
  104, 109, 126, 142, 153,
  209–211, 219, 225, 234, 235,
  246, 259, 270, 273
Crawford, Colin, 8, 260
Critical Component, 1
Cross-border, 2, 7, 10, 39, 205,
  206, 226
Cross-order research partnerships, 4
CubaMar, 38, 39, 42, 43, 46, 49–51,
  55, 57
Cuban archipelago, 45
Cuban Ministry of Science,
  Technology and Environment,
  50, 55
Cuban Revolution, 38
Cuba–US Marine Research and
  Conservation, 6
Cultural analysis of law, 8, 117
Cultural conditions, 179, 195
Cultural difference, 134, 185
Curitiba, 9, 177, 179, 185, 186, 189,
  190, 193

D

Daily life, 117
Danish Alianza Libres sin Violencia, 158
de Caldas, Francisco José, 264
de Fanelli, Ana Garía, 9
de Sola, Francisco, 71, 75, 80
Dean of Harvard Business School,
  65, 75, 80

284 INDEX

Decentralized, 4, 164
Decentralized management,
191, 192, 195
Declaration of Santiago, 3
Decolonial perspectives, 272
Decolonization, 3, 260
Definitions, 180, 205–208, 270
Delgado, Jorge Enrique,
8, 141–144, 150
Departmental management, 226
Department of Commerce, 41, 52
Department of Inorganic, Analytical
and Physical Chemistry at the
UBA School of Natural and Exact
Sciences, 213
De-territorialization, 196
Development Bank of Latin America
(*Corporación Andina de Fomento*,
CAF), 151
Diachronic analysis, 188
Dialogues, 82, 117, 120, 122, 124,
128, 135, 157, 271
Diaspora associations, 7
Diaspora networks, 88, 98, 107, 108
Digital communication, 190
Dimensions, 19, 81, 109, 178, 180,
186, 187, 195, 198n1, 206, 214,
215, 262, 274
Discourses, 3, 4, 49, 103, 118, 124,
125, 141, 180, 186, 264, 270
Dive compressor, 54
Doctoral, 66, 71, 72, 76, 80, 100,
101, 107, 144, 145, 162, 184,
198n2, 209, 210, 213, 220–222,
226, 246, 251, 252, 265, 266,
270, 273
Document analysis, 10, 62
Dominant global language, 131
Dominant global North partner, 8
Dominant languages, 120
Dominant models, 117, 124,
127–129, 132, 135–137
Dominant political economy, 124,
125, 128, 129, 131

Dominguez, Angeles, 6
Double-blindness of peer reviews, 219
Dry Tortugas and Biscayne National
Parks, 55
Dutch North-South cooperation, 261
Dynamics, 1, 7, 8, 10, 11, 40, 49, 73,
79, 81, 82, 88, 89, 94, 95, 98,
105, 117, 118, 123, 125, 127,
160, 178, 182–184, 196, 197,
208, 218, 221, 223, 225, 234,
260, 261, 272

E
Earth observation, 147
Ebola, 55, 56
Ecología en Bolivia, 152, 155
Ecological picture, 43
Economic development, 15, 30, 142,
144, 149, 163, 234
Economic development contexts, 2, 22
Economy, 3, 6, 8, 17, 30, 68, 115,
142, 143, 176, 196, 250
Ecosystem health, 43
Ecosystems, 3, 6, 38, 39, 43, 44, 47,
51, 52, 54, 55, 57, 160, 196
Ecuador, 72, 151, 160, 164, 268
El Salvador, 63, 64
Embargo, 38–42, 48, 51
Emblematic experiments, 184
England, 151
English, 6, 7, 17, 50, 57, 69, 90, 91,
120, 121, 126, 128–135, 138n5,
165, 189, 190, 240, 249, 250, 252
Enterprises, 78, 187, 208
Environment rehabilitation, 147
Environmental sustainability research, 51
Epistemic communities, 19, 39, 49
Epistemic justice, 117
Epistemological aims, 122
Espinoza, Oscar, 10
EuroAsianNet, 99, 100
Eurocentric, 262
EuroNet, 101

INDEX 285

European colonialism, 262
European colonizers, 4
European Foundation for
  Management Development
  (EFMD), 66
European Research Area (ERA),
  3, 21, 33n8
European Union (EU), 3, 99
Evidence, 5, 11, 44, 74, 93, 163, 205,
  207, 209, 211, 261
Evolution of circumstellar disks, 269
Exceptionalism characterizing, 120
Exchangeable legal knowledge, 126
Expansion, 31, 135, 209, 216, 227,
  237, 239, 248, 264, 271
Expenditure, 5, 64, 143, 208, 217, 221
Experiential learning, 77
Experimental
  development, 27, 143
  manipulations, 160
Experimental high school, 162
Extension, 196, 210, 234
External legitimization, 226
External Scientific Member, 265
Extrinsic rewards, 207, 226

F
Factors, 2, 10, 11, 48, 62, 63, 73,
  78–81, 83, 89–91, 105, 108, 109,
  123, 155, 177, 180, 182, 183,
  187, 191–194, 196, 207, 214,
  238–243, 248–250, 260, 273
Faculty, 5, 6, 17, 27, 31, 57, 66–68,
  70, 71, 73, 76, 79, 94, 104, 106,
  121, 126, 133, 153, 154, 162,
  164, 208, 216, 217, 227, 228n9
Fauna Paraguay, 161, 164
FCB Cellular and Molecular Medicine
  group, 214
Federal Technological University of
  Parana (Brazil), 157
Federal University of Paraiba, 156

Federal University of Parana (UFPR)
  (Brazil), 157
Federal University of Santa Maria
  (Brazil), 157
Fellows, 193, 210, 213, 220, 221, 223
Female participation, 194
Field, 21, 28, 32, 41, 47, 53, 54, 88,
  92, 130, 132, 133, 138n2, 144,
  146, 155–158, 163, 179, 180,
  184, 185, 192, 193, 196, 198n1,
  204, 205, 211, 212, 218–220,
  228n10, 238–240, 252, 260, 270
Financial agreements, 94
Financial Times, 65
Fitzsimons, Kent, 9
Florida, 22, 25, 38
Florida Keys National Marine
  Sanctuaries, 55
Florida Straits, 38, 40, 41, 51, 56
Flower Garden Banks, 55
Force, 2, 19, 33n1, 56, 80, 90, 116,
  137, 144, 184, 198n4
Ford Foundation, 77, 235
Foreign
  institutions, 103, 104, 210, 222
  partners, 226, 266
Formal agreements, 96, 235
Formal definitions, 2
Formalism, 123, 124
For-profit enterprise, 159
Foundation for Strategic Research in
  Bolivia, 153
Free market model, 118, 121, 123,
  126, 129–131, 134, 135
Free market model of legal ideas,
  116, 137
Fritz Haber Institute, 269
Fuenzalida, Edmundo, 235
Functional microscopy of cancer
  biology, 269
Fundraising, 66, 70, 71, 75, 80, 216
Furtado, Celso, 234
Future cooperation, 9

286 INDEX

G

Gaillard, Jacques, 3, 10, 205–207, 226, 260, 262, 263, 271
Galactic centers, 269
Genetic therapy, 221
Geochemical analyses, 43, 52
Geographic information system, 159
Geography of collaborations, 164
German-based institutes, 266
German Federal Ministry of Education and Research (*Bundes Ministerium für Bildung und Forschung,* BMBF), 214, 220, 264
German Research Foundation (*Deutsche Forschungsgemeinschaft,* DFG), 264
German Society for International Cooperation (*Deutsche Gesellschaft für Internationale Zusammenarbeit,* GIZ), 151
Germany, 67, 133, 151, 207, 211, 214, 216–218, 221, 225, 263, 266, 267
Glacial retreat, 160
Global, 1, 5, 9, 17, 21–23, 30, 31, 41, 45, 48, 49, 57, 62, 65, 67, 68, 70, 76, 88, 90, 108, 109, 119, 123, 124, 128, 130, 132, 135, 137, 147, 165, 175–178, 188, 190, 191, 196, 197, 266
Global bibliographic information services, 164
Global Competitiveness Report, 69
Globalized economy, 183
Global North, 117, 121, 123, 124, 135, 223, 260, 261
Global North legal production, 136
Global positioning systems (GPS), 53
Global scientific community, 3
Global South legal systems, 123
Global threats, 48
Godier, Patrice, 9, 178, 184
Goldberg, Ray, 67, 72, 76

González, Louis Eduardo, 10
Gonzalez, Patricia, 6, 148, 149
Governance, 149, 180, 181, 183, 189, 266
practices, 188
Government-University-Industry Research Roundtable, 4
Greenhouse gas emissions, 188
Gregorutti, Gustavo, 6
Gross domestic product (GDP), 5, 64, 93, 143, 144, 208
Grupo Tortuguero (GT), 47
Guanahacabibes Peninsula Marine Turtle Conversation Project, 6
Guatemala, 63, 64
Gulf of Ana María, 44, 54
Gulf of Batabanó, 44, 54
Gulf of Mexico, 40, 46, 54–56
Gulf of Mexico economic zone, 57

H

Habitats, 40, 44, 45, 48, 180
Harvard, 7, 18, 61–83
Harvard Business School (HBS), 62, 65, 67–71, 76, 79, 81
case-study methodology, 70
Harvard graduate education, 71, 76
Harvard Institute of International Development, 68
Harvard's Development Advisory Service, 68
Havana, 6, 38, 39, 42, 43, 45, 48, 50, 54–57
Hawksbill turtles, 46
Health Sciences Research, 162, 164
Hegemonic Northern knowledge production, 262
Helvetas Swiss Intercooperation, 159
Hepatic fibrosis, 221, 229n12
Hierarchical colonial teacher-student arrangement, 127
Hierarchical comparison, 197

Hierarchical relationship, 123
Hierarchical structures, 262, 267
Hierarchy of location, 126
Higher Education, 2, 4–5, 8, 16, 21, 22, 30, 31, 65, 66, 87, 95, 105, 109, 141, 142, 146–155, 161–163, 182, 191, 197, 204, 205, 208, 216, 227, 235, 259–261
Higher Education Personnel Improvement Coordinator (*Coordenação de Aperfeiçoamento de Pessoal de Nível Superior, Cap*), 186
Higher Institute of Bolivian Studies, 147
High technology exports, 142, 144, 145
Holistic, 43, 82
Holsboer, Florian, 265
Homogeneous, 8, 141, 188
Homogenize statistics, 189
Honduras, 63
Housing advocacy, 158
Human capital, 31, 142, 206, 220, 221, 249
Human development, 157–159
Humanity, 2, 93, 104, 105, 143–145, 162, 243, 264, 274n1
Human resources, 6, 29, 31, 64, 148, 204, 221, 227
Human rights, 135, 158
Hurricane Mitch, 68
Hydric resources, 147

I
Ibarra, María Elena, 45–47
Iberic-American, 142, 162
Iberoamerica, 66
Idiopathic Paroxysmal Atrial Fibrillation, 157
Ignis Mutat Res (2011), 9, 176, 182, 184

Impact, 27, 30, 32, 47, 62, 69, 93, 146, 160, 165, 177, 180, 184, 205–207, 219, 223, 226, 237, 239–241, 245, 249, 250, 252
Improved, 2, 6, 7, 41, 64, 75, 107, 137, 182, 196, 197, 207, 218, 252
INCAE-Harvard project, 64, 81
Incentives, 17, 22, 78, 108, 149, 212, 238, 246
Increased productivity, 2
Indicators, 8, 63, 90, 91, 105, 109, 142–146, 160, 163, 208, 212, 228n9, 239
Indirect members, 96, 97, 100
Industrialized, 1, 64, 204, 208, 209, 217, 219, 223, 225, 262
Industrialized countries, 1, 64, 204, 208, 209, 219, 262
Industrial Research Institute, 147
Industrial Revolution, 4
Industrial Technology Institute, 228n2
Inequality, 3, 63, 83n1, 123, 124, 156
Informal communications, 108, 207, 271
Informatics revolution, 41
Information and Resource Center for Development, 158
Information management, 238
Infrastructure, 16, 29, 43, 51, 53, 54, 57, 68, 75, 89, 145, 181, 215, 219, 223, 226, 227, 273
Innovation
  agenda, 4, 6, 15
  platforms, 147, 211
  systems, 8, 147
Innovative programming, 78
In situ, 132, 160, 185
Institute for Biomedical Research of Buenos Aires, 268
Institute for Health Science Research of UNA, 153
Institute of Atmospheric Sciences and Climate (Italy), 156

288 INDEX

Institute of Chemical Physics of Materials, Environment and Energy, 212
Institute of Latin American Studies of Stockholm University, 159
Institutional affiliation, 74, 76, 150, 245
Institutional agreements, 26, 96
Institutional documents, 214
Institutional relations, 96, 222
Institutional support, 225
Instituto Centroamericano de Administración de Empresas (INCAE), 7, 61–83
Institut Pierre Simon Laplace, 156
Intellectual collaboration, 234
Intellectual innovation, 4
Intense commercial fishing, 42
Intensive, 108, 145, 190, 191
Inter-American Development Bank (IDB), 67, 73, 77, 78, 156, 158
Interconnected ecosystems, 55
Interdependent, 118, 183
Interdisciplinarity, 192, 198n4
Interdisciplinary Program for Educational Research (PIIE), 235
Inter-institutional agreements, 248
Inter-institutional environmental studies, 156
Inter-institutional Research Collaboration on Fauna in Paraguay, 161
International agreements, 95
International ALMA telescope, 268
International Association of Academics (IAA), 2
International co-authorship, 3, 8, 143, 155–157
International collaboration, 8, 9, 22, 25, 43, 53, 142, 143, 147, 148, 150, 151, 155, 157–163, 165, 182–187, 204, 205, 207, 209, 210, 214, 215, 218, 219, 222, 224–226, 228n5, 236, 240, 272

International collaboration agreements, 162
International cooperation, 10, 32, 164, 186, 204, 219–221, 225, 266, 270
International Council for Science (ICSU), 2, 3
International development agencies, 67, 207
International Institute for Integration of the Andres Bello Agreement, 152
International institutions, 161, 211, 214, 250
Internationalization, 30, 87, 93, 95, 141–165, 205
Internationalization of SciELO Paraguay Journals, 153–155
International journals, 7, 91, 105, 160, 226
Internationally, 159
International networking, 223, 261
International North–South research partnership, 4
International Partnerships for Collaborative Research in Argentinian University, 9, 203–227
International partnerships policies, 214
International policies for assessment, 109
International projects, 23, 109, 217, 242
International research center projects, 164, 210, 211
International research collaboration (IRC), 2–4, 8, 10, 30, 87–96, 98–109, 142, 146, 149, 150, 156, 176, 204–211, 214, 236, 237, 243, 249–251, 271, 272
International Research Collaboration and Knowledge Production in Colombia, 7, 87–109
International research collaboration of Columbian universities, 7

INDEX   289

International Research Collaboration:
   Opportunities for the UK Higher
   Education Sector, 3–4
International Research Council, 2
International research groups, 155,
   187, 189, 210
International science policy, 146
International scientific cooperation,
   9, 215, 272
International Sea Turtle Learning
   Exchanges, 46
International Sea Turtle Symposium, 54
International universities, 146, 159,
   162, 226
Interpersonal collaboration, 73, 75–76
Introducing a Bilateral Research and
   Innovation Agendas, 6, 15
Invertebrates, 160
Isle of Youth, 44, 45, 47, 54
Isolationist, 124
Itauguá, 154
Itinerant seminar protocol, 195
Iuris Tantum Foundation, 152

J
Japan, 151, 157
Jardines de la Reina archipelago, 44
Joint research projects, 76, 79, 88, 103,
   187–191, 210, 211, 252, 263
Journal editorial boards, 142
Journal inspections, 142

K
Karolinska Institute
   (*KarolinskaInstitute,* KI),
   214, 220–222
Katz, J. S., 3, 63, 73, 76, 89, 90,
   205–207, 226
Kellogg Institute for International
   Studies, 158
Kennedy, John F. (President), 41, 65,
   71, 75, 79, 80, 235

Key concepts, 68, 205–208, 237
Key conduit, 48–52
Key success factors, 9, 79, 191–194, 197
KFW Bank for Development, 151
Kiel Institute for the World
   Economy, 151
Kilometers, 44, 63, 188
Knowledge generation, 2, 7, 30, 31,
   58n3, 62, 78, 122, 250
Knowledge production, 7, 39, 48–52,
   57, 81, 87–109, 183–186, 204,
   227, 260, 273
Knowledge transfer, 3, 72, 126,
   127, 135, 163, 164,
   234, 252
Knowledge transference, 142
Kyoto protocol, 181

L
Laboratoire de Météorologie Physique
   (France), 156
Laboratoire des Sciences du Climat et de
   l'Environnement (France), 156
LAC institutions, 1
Lanani, Alfredo, 212
Land-Grant universities, 30, 261–262
La Paz, 146, 147, 152, 153
Latin America, 1, 8, 10, 17, 23, 24,
   26, 31, 40, 61–63, 65–67, 70–72,
   81, 91, 94, 120, 124, 130–135,
   141, 143, 144, 150, 151, 154,
   157, 158, 163, 164, 203, 209,
   219, 234, 236, 239, 250,
   259–274
Latin American and Caribbean
   Pedagogical Institute, 151
Latin American Center for
   Competitiveness and Sustainable
   Development (Centro
   Latinoamericano para la
   Competitividad y el Desarrollo
   Sostenible, CLACDS), 7, 61–64,
   67–73, 76–82

290 INDEX

Latin American Council of Business Schools (Consejo Latinoamericano de Escuelas de Administración, CLADEA), 66
Latin American Council on the Social Sciences (Consejo Latinoamericano de Ciencias Sociales, CLACSO), 234
Latin American Faculty of Social Sciences (Facultad Latinoamericana de Ciencias Sociales, FLACSO), 234
Latin American Public Opinion Project (LAPOP), 158
Latin American University Network for Quality and Sustainable Development (Red Latinoamericana de Universidades por la Calidad y el Desarrollo Sostenible), 66
Latin legal awareness, 124
LatinNet, 101
Latin scholars, 121
Laval University, 158
Legal academies, 8, 117, 120, 121, 123, 127, 128, 133, 137
Legal barbarian, 118
Legal knowledge, 7, 8, 115, 116, 118–124, 126–132, 134–137
Legal knowledge production, 116, 118–122, 126, 127, 129–131, 136, 137
Legal production, 121, 136
Leibniz Institute for Tropospheric Research (Germany), 156
Limitations, 2, 6, 22, 28–30, 32, 41, 63, 73, 75, 81, 104, 105, 108, 117, 131, 133, 187–189, 204, 225, 227, 248
Linguistic communities, 189
Literature, 2, 3, 11, 53, 80, 128, 204, 226, 240, 248, 263, 270
Liver Fibrosis, 214

Lodge, George Cabot, 70–72, 75, 76, 82
London Metropolitan University, 151
Los Canarreos archipelago, 44
Los Colorados archipelago, 44
Los Tiempos, 158, 159
Loyola University, New Orleans, 151

M

Macroeconomic, 30
Macroeconomic instability, 223
Macrofauna, 160
Maldonado, Daniel Bonilla, 8, 116–119, 121–123, 136, 260
Major determinant, 1
Major trends, 4
Major University of San Andres (*Universidad Mayor de San Andrés*, UMSA), 146, 147, 150, 155, 156, 160, 164, 165
Management, 28, 41, 46, 51, 55, 56, 62, 65, 71, 75, 77, 80, 82, 150, 160, 164, 186, 187, 191, 192, 195, 206, 219, 223, 226, 237, 238, 243, 248, 249, 260, 271
Managua earthquake, 77
Mapping, 89, 94, 98, 190
Marie Curie International Research Staff Exchange program, 213
Marine health, 49
Marine protected areas (MPAs), 43, 44, 55, 57
Marine turtles, 45, 48
Max Planck (MP), 261, 263–268, 270–273
Max Planck Florida Institute for Neuroscience, 269
Max Planck Gesellschaft Institute, 213
Max Planck Institutes (MPIs), 10, 260, 263–266, 268, 270–272, 274n1
Max Planck Society (MPS), 10, 211, 259–274

INDEX 291

Max Planck Society for the
   Advancement of Science, 264
McGinn, Noel F., 10
Measuring, 90, 189
Measuring systems, 188
Medical research center, 222
Medical Research Institute Alfredo
   Lanani, 212
Medical sciences, 220, 226
Medicine, 56, 146, 161, 204, 209,
   212, 220
*Memorias del Instituto de
   Investigaciones en Ciencias de la
   Salud*, 157
Meritocracy, 122, 126, 270
Methodological device, 9, 185
Metropolis, 118, 119, 127, 137n1,
   138n3, 197
Metropolis time, 119
Metropolitanization, 189
Mexico, 5, 6, 8, 15, 33n1, 40, 46, 47,
   54–57, 105, 107, 135, 151, 154,
   159, 267
Microbiology, 43, 147
Microfauna, 160
*Migration and Citizenship in Bolivia
   in the Latin American Context,
   State of the Question*, 159
Military dictatorship (1973–1989),
   10, 236
Mimesis/autopoiesis, 116, 119, 137n1
Ministry of Culture and
   Communication, 176, 195
Ministry of Education (MEC), 147,
   148, 186
Ministry of Education and Culture of
   Paraguay, 148, 165
Miramar, 42
MIT agreements, 31
Mobilize, 80, 82, 88, 107, 109, 190, 195
Models of higher education, 191
Modern constitutionalism, 123
Molecular biosciences, 268

Monitoring, 7, 38, 46, 48, 82
Moot Court, 132–135
Mosquito, 269
Motivational factors, 182, 187
Motivations, 2, 7, 9, 11, 19, 22–26,
   29, 40, 43, 51, 55, 62, 63, 73,
   78–81, 88, 89, 94, 95, 102–104,
   109, 177, 182–187, 204,
   206–208, 212, 225, 226, 245,
   247, 248, 252, 262
MP agreement, 267
MP/CONICET Partner Institute in
   Biomedical Research in Buenos
   Aires, 265
MPI for Astronomy, 269
MPI for Biophysical Chemistry in
   Göttingen, 268
MPI for Chemical Ecology, 269
MPI for Comparative Public Law and
   International Law, 269
MPI for Developmental Biology, 269
MPI for Extraterrestrial Physics, 269
MPI for Infection Biology, 269
MPI for Intelligent Systems, 269
MPI for Medical Research, 269
MPI for Plant Breeding Research, 269
MPI of Molecular Physiology, 269
MPI of Molecular Plant Physiology, 269
MPI of Psychiatry in Munich, 265
MP Laboratory for Structural Biology,
   Chemistry and Molecular
   Biophysics in Rosario, 268
MP Liaison Office for Latin
   America, 265
MPU in Chemical Ecology, 269
Mucosal immunology, 269
Multi-decadal partnership, 37
Multidisciplinarity, 192
Multidisciplinary practices, 192
Multidisciplinary research team, 9
Multilateral, 221, 222
Multilateral research cooperation, 221
Multiplication of databases, 194

292 INDEX

Multi-sectoral networking, 80
Mutis, José Celestino, 263
Mutual communication, 102
Mutual recognition, 124, 125, 129

N
Nagasaki University School of
Medicine (Japan), 157
Nano bioengineering, 269
Nanoelectronics, 269
Nanotechnology, 31, 213
National academics, 108
National Aeronautics and Space
Administration (US), 156
National Agency for Higher Education
Evaluation and Accreditation, 148
National Agency for Science and
Technology Promotion (*Agencia
Nacional de Promoción Científica
y Tecnológica*, ANPCYT), 217
National Agency of Research and
Innovation (*Agencia Nacional de
Investigación e Innovación*,
ANII), 267
National Association of Schools of
Public Affairs and Administration
(NASPAA), 66
National Atomic Energy Commission
(*Comisión Nacional de Energía
Atómica*, CNEA), 228n2
National Biological Inventory, 161
National Commission for Scientific
and Technological Research
(Comisión Nacional de
Investigación Científica y
Tecnológica, CONICYT), 245
National Council of Higher
Education, 149
National Council of Science and
Technology (*Consejo Nacional de
Ciencia y Tecnología*,
CONACYT), 149, 161, 267

National Council of Scientific and
Technical Research (*Consejo
Nacional de Investigaciones
Científicas y Técnicas*,
CONICET), 268
National Education System, 149
National Fund for Science and
Technology (Fondo Nacional de
Ciencia y Tecnología,
FONDECYT), 245
National government, 164, 181, 214,
225, 243
support, 11, 271
National Hospital of Itauguá, 154
National Institute for Forestry,
Agriculture, and Livestock
Research (Mexico), 157
National Institute of Amazonian
Research (Instituto Nacional de
Pesquisas da Amazônia, INPA), 268
National Museum of Entomology, 151
National Museum of Natural History
of Paraguay (NMNHP), 161, 164
National policies to promote
international research
collaboration, 208–211
National reconstruction plans, 67
National research networks, 147
National Scientific and Technical
Research Council (*Consejo
Nacional de Investigaciones
Científicas y Técnicas*,
CONICET), 204, 208–211, 213,
217, 220–222, 226, 228n3,
229n12, 268
National Space Activities Commission
(*Comisión Nacional de
Actividades Espaciales*,
CONAE), 228n2
National University of Asunción
(*Universidad Nacional de
Asunción*, UNA), 148, 149, 153,
156, 157, 161–165

National University of the East, 157
Neocolonialism, 10, 259–274
Netherlands/Canadian *Conexión Fondo de Emancipación*, 158
Networking, 31, 66, 67, 75, 142, 165, 219, 223, 249, 261
Network of Argentinian Researchers and Scientists Abroad (*Red de Argentinos Investigadores y Científicos en el Exterior*, RAICES), 221
New Granada, 263
NGO Conservation International, 156
NGO/university collaboration, 49
Nicaragua, 63, 65, 67
Non-for-profit organizations, 50, 208, 209
Non-governmental research production-policymaking, 49
Non-monetized, 57
Normative criteria, 8, 117
North American, 21, 40, 124, 129, 151, 178, 234, 236, 240
North American Scholars, 10, 233–252
North and South, 28, 117, 123, 136, 137, 252, 265, 274
North and South scholars, 131
North-dominated, 240
Northern, 4, 10, 17, 25, 62, 105, 120, 121, 123, 127, 132, 134, 206, 218, 234, 241, 249, 259, 260, 262, 263, 270–273
Northern institution, 4, 28, 226, 236
Northern parent legal systems, 123
Northern university (*Universidad del Norte*), 148
North–South alliance, 80
North–South collaboration, 5, 204, 249, 263
North–South communication, 243
North–South partnership, 2, 204, 207
North–South partnership agreement, 217

North–South research partnership, 1, 2, 4, 9, 11, 206, 212
North–South university partnerships, 1–4, 9, 211
Nuclear, 147, 181, 185
Numerous, 3, 7, 50, 54, 62, 64, 70, 71, 76, 80, 88, 91, 184, 238

O
Obama administration, 41, 56
Observatoire des Sciences de l'Univers (France), 156
Obstacles, 4, 7, 9, 39, 40, 50, 51, 83, 94, 121, 177, 182, 187–191, 206, 207, 212, 214, 219, 223, 242, 251
Ocean Foundation Cuba Marine Research and Conservation Program, 6, 38
Operational mechanics, 2, 62, 73, 79
Organisation for Economic Co-operation and Development (OECD), 5, 188, 265
Organizational dynamics, 208
Organizational factors, 191–192
Organizational management, 3
Organized associations, 2
Our Lady of Asuncion, 148
Overfishing, 42, 44
Ownership, 3, 127, 205
Oxford University, 69

P
Paleontology, 147
Panama, 63
Paraguay, 8, 9, 141–165
Paraguayan fauna, 161, 164
Paraguayan higher education, 148–150
Paraguayan Society of Pediatrics, 154
Paraguayan Surgery Society, 154

294 INDEX

Parasitology, 152
Partnership agreements, 182, 198, 217, 221
Partnership contributions, 9, 211
Partnerships for International Research and Education (PIRE), 213
Patents, 142, 144, 145, 205
Pathogens, 269
Patterns of distribution of plants, 160
Peasant Carmen Pampa Academic Unit Foundation, 152
Pedagogical, 9, 179, 193, 198 innovation, 191
Pediatric medicine, 152
Peer pressure, 194
Peripheral role, 242
Perspective, 2, 4, 10, 20, 25, 47, 51, 64, 81, 88, 89, 92, 95, 100, 101, 103, 106, 108, 134, 177, 180, 183–185, 192, 196, 217, 227, 243, 262, 263, 271–273
Peru, 151, 162, 267
Phenomena/phenomenon, 2, 88, 90, 94, 109n1, 110n2, 176–178, 180, 183, 184, 190, 195, 198n1, 212
Philips, 69
Physical capital, 216, 217
Physical space, 129, 196
Physiological quality, 157
Phytochemistry, 152
Pineda, Pedro, 10, 261, 265, 272
Plant metabolomics, 269
Pluridisciplinarity, 185
Plurinational Science and Technology Award, 147
Plurinational State of Bolivia, 147, 148
Poey, Felipe, 53, 54
Policies, 3, 5–7, 9, 11, 16, 17, 19–22, 29, 30, 32, 40, 42, 43, 49, 55–57, 62, 68, 82, 88, 92, 93, 98, 105, 108, 109, 126, 130–132, 137, 146, 148, 149,

176, 178, 180, 181, 184, 188, 193, 196–198, 204, 208–212, 214, 217, 219, 222, 227, 237, 241, 249, 250, 259–274
Policies on Institutional Relations, 222
Policy advocacy, 40, 49
Political economy of legal knowledge, 8, 115–137
Political scenario, 108
Polytechnic, 148, 162
Pontifical Catholic University in Santiago, 235
Porter, Michael, 68, 69, 72, 76, 80
Positioning, 30, 31, 53, 56, 212
Positions, 26, 49, 55, 70, 71, 77, 82, 92, 110n5, 124, 127, 134, 177, 183, 209, 212, 217, 226, 227
Post colonialism, 109n1, 260, 262
Postdoctoral, 209, 210, 213, 218, 221, 222, 225, 227, 265–267
Postdoctoral fellowships, 220, 226, 227
Post-World War II, 3
Practices, 2, 8, 9, 21, 47, 81, 88–90, 92, 93, 99, 103, 106, 108, 116–118, 120, 123–125, 128, 131, 132, 136, 160, 164, 176, 180, 181, 184–186, 188, 192, 195, 196, 205, 207, 237, 238, 271, 272
Prebisch, Raul, 234
Precedents, 10, 56, 233–252
Princeton University, 158
Principal investigator, 177, 191, 229n12, 245
A priori, 121, 122, 128
Private enterprise, 50, 142, 215
Private sector, 5, 21, 29, 32, 49, 71, 77, 82, 204, 209, 215, 220
Private University of the Valley (*Universidad Privada del Valle*), 147

Processes, 7, 8, 16, 19, 20, 23–26, 28, 29, 31, 32, 39, 41–43, 50, 51, 68, 69, 88–90, 93, 95, 101, 105, 106, 109, 116–118, 122, 123, 129, 136, 144, 163, 178, 180, 183, 184, 187–190, 194, 197, 198, 206, 227, 238, 239, 251, 267, 273, 274
Prociencia, 149
Production, 5, 7, 8, 10, 49, 51, 64, 88, 90, 100, 102, 109, 115, 116, 118–121, 126, 134, 136, 137, 178, 179, 184, 188, 190, 193, 194, 203, 204, 209, 217, 218, 220, 223, 234, 236, 237, 262
Productive Agreements, 28
Professionalizing force for scientific production, 218
Program for Strategic Research in Bolivia (*Programa de Investigación Estratégica en Bolivia*, PIEB), 150, 158
Programmatic regional office, 10, 270
Projections, 10, 233–252
Protocol, 9, 55, 63, 71, 79, 179, 181, 194–196, 248
Public Action Community, 157
Publications, 1–4, 7, 27, 65, 68, 69, 76, 91, 98, 105, 106, 109, 117, 120–122, 129, 130, 142, 150, 153, 159, 161, 165, 186, 205–208, 211–214, 216, 219, 223, 224, 234, 237–243, 246, 248–250, 252, 260
Public health, 236, 237, 240, 243
Public opinion, 157–159, 164, 188
Public policy research axis, 189
Publish or perish dilemma, 219
Punta Frances, 44
Punto Cero, 152, 155
Purposive, 212
Pyriproxyfen and Diflubenzuron Effects on the Reproduction, 156

Q
QS World University Rankings, 212
Qualitative empirical evidence, 2
Qualitative Network Analysis approach, 7, 87–109

R
R&D products, 145
Rabossi, Marcelo, 9
Radio astronomy, 268
Ramos, Manuela, 158
Randomized sampling, 159
Rankings, 1, 61, 65, 109, 110n5, 146, 163, 165, 186, 228n9
Recipient country, 227, 262
Recycling, 48
Reflective scientist, 51
Regional, 5–7, 11, 17, 19–22, 25, 32, 33n1, 46, 62, 64, 65, 67–71, 73, 77–82, 90, 94, 108, 127, 130, 134, 142, 143, 146, 147, 150, 164, 183, 184, 188, 197, 234, 236, 239, 242, 245, 249, 250
Regional business enterprises, 65, 82
Regulation, 95, 104, 148, 178, 206, 214
Relationship, 2, 3, 15–17, 19–21, 23, 24, 26, 32, 49, 51, 55, 57, 62, 70, 72, 73, 75–81, 89, 90, 92, 94, 95, 98, 102, 106–108, 118, 119, 137, 176–178, 182, 183, 187, 197, 198, 205, 206, 216, 217, 220, 225–227, 234, 235, 237–243, 247, 248, 250–252, 260–263, 265, 270, 272–273
Reproductive biology, 269
Research
   centers, 24, 62, 67, 68, 82, 89, 142, 147, 157, 159, 164, 176, 183, 185, 204, 209–211, 215, 217, 218, 221–223, 225–227, 235, 263, 265–267, 271, 273

296 INDEX

Research (*cont.*)
  networks, 7, 87–98, 100–109, 110n3, 147, 207, 234, 240, 245, 260
  policies, 214, 222, 250
  productivity, 1, 2, 6, 22, 93, 145, 149, 163, 165, 182, 203, 207, 250, 261
  programs, 1, 9, 29, 62, 176, 177, 180, 182, 190, 194, 196, 197, 266
  publications, 237–243
  reports, 50, 214, 239, 247
Research and Development (R&D), 1, 4, 5, 8, 9, 11, 16, 19, 30, 64, 77, 91, 93, 142–144, 204, 208, 209, 211, 212, 214, 215
Research Collaboration to Institutional Partnerships, 175–198
Resource-constrained, 225
Re-territorialization, 196
Revista Boliviana de Física, 155, 156
Revista de la Sociedad Boliviana de Pediatría, 151, 155
Revista del Instituto de Ecología, 155
Revista Internacional de Investigación en Ciencias Sociales, 154
Revista Latinoamericana de Desarrollo Económico, 151, 156
Rights, 29, 56, 118, 135, 138n8, 145, 149, 183, 197, 263
Rio de Janeiro Earth Summit, 68
Roadmap for classification of books, 186
Rosario, 268
Royal Botanical Expedition, 263
Rural development, 67, 69, 72, 79, 158

S
Sachs, Jeffrey, 69, 72, 76, 80
Sajama, 160
Salto, Dante J., 9

Sandinista conflict, 65, 68
San Lorenzo, 154
Santa Cruz, 6, 146, 147
Santa Cruz de la Sierra Private University, 151
Satellite tags, 46
Scale-dependent studies, 43
Schmidheiny, Stephan, 68, 80
Scholars, 2, 8, 10, 21, 27, 48, 50, 62, 68, 70–72, 76–79, 81, 89, 91, 93, 95, 100–105, 107, 108, 117, 120, 121, 129–131, 136, 143, 158, 177, 195, 208, 210, 212, 216, 218, 219, 222, 223, 233–252, 260, 261, 272
School of Biomedical Science (FCB, *Facultad de Ciencias Biomédicas*), 212–214, 220–225, 229n12
School of law and legal postmodernism, 124
School of Medicine at Mount Sinai Hospital, 214
Science Beyond Politics, 37–58
Science Citation Index publications, 1
Scientific collaboration, 7, 37–39, 41, 228n4
Scientific colonialism, 264
Scientific community, 42, 55, 89, 90, 209, 246
Scientific cooperation, 9, 206, 211, 215, 217, 260, 264, 271, 272
Scientific journals, 53, 142, 150
Scientific partnerships, 2, 263
Scientific perspective, 2
Scientific production, 203, 209, 217
Scientific synthesis, 240
Seagrass ecosystems, 44
Sea Turtle Conservation project, 38, 45–48, 55
Sea Turtle Exchanges, 54
Sea Turtle International Learning Exchange, 52

Secretary of Environment of Paraguay, 161
Secret of Co-Responsible Care with We Effect, *The*, 159
Sector, 2, 4, 9, 16, 32, 44, 49, 50, 57, 66, 78, 80, 144, 145, 147, 148, 175, 197, 204, 208, 216, 273
Selva Andina Research Society, Department of Biochemical and Microbiological Teaching and Research, 152
Seminars, 9, 65, 67, 103, 106, 117, 120, 122, 127–130, 179–182, 184, 189–195, 197, 198, 211
Senior researchers, 214, 216–218, 221, 229n12
Seventh Framework Program of the European Community, 213
Shallow-water, 44
Simon Bolivar University, 155
Skills of compatibility, 240
Skoll World Forum, 69
Smith, D., 63, 73, 76, 88–90
Smithsonian Institute, 161
Snowballing, 142
Social Enterprise Knowledge Network (SEKN), 66
Social Network Analysis (SNA) approach, 7, 88, 89, 91–94, 97–99, 102, 109
Sociocultural, 2, 19, 22, 32
Sociologists, 160, 179, 192
Southern Cone, 264
Special Education, 147
State support, 10, 215
State University of Londrina (Brazil), 156
State University of Western Parana (Brazil), 157
STI Systems, 142, 143, 145, 146, 148–150
Strachan, Harry, 67, 68, 77, 81, 82

Strategic
fields, 147
plans, 31, 148
vision, 222
Streitwieser, Bernhard, 10
Student scientific Olympiads, 147
Studies in the Metropolitan Axis, 159
Subordinate global South partner, 8
Subordination, 123, 129
Subregion of Central America, 7
Subsidies, 251
Superficial sciences, 269
Supranational dynamics, 184
Surveys, 10, 38, 50, 70, 117, 158, 159, 163, 164, 188, 189, 243, 245–249, 270
Sustainability, 3, 9, 10, 40, 49, 50, 62, 133, 175, 205, 225, 273
of international partnerships, 227
Sustainable development, 7, 40, 51, 57, 65, 68, 70, 133, 159, 184, 236
Sustainable development action, 40, 49
A *stricto* sensu graduate program, 186, 198n2
Svenson, Nanette, 6, 64
Swedish Institute for Democracy and Electoral Assistance (IDEA), 159
Swedish International Development Cooperation Agency, 158
Swedish We Effect, 159
Synopsis, 6
Synthetic three-country database, 190

T
Tandem Groups, 266, 267
Tapie, Guy, 9, 178, 184
Tascón, C. I., 7, 88, 260
Team collaborations, 73, 74, 76–78
Tecnológico de Monterrey, 6, 33n5
Temperatures, 48, 160
Territorial boundaries, 55, 196

298 INDEX

Texas A&M University (Department of Wildlife and Fisheries Sciences), 161
Thematic national contacts for reporting on cooperation opportunities, 211
The Ocean Foundation (TOF), 6, 48–52
Theoretical, 2, 10, 116, 130, 192, 193, 204–206, 218, 245, 260–263
Third World Academy of Science (TWAS), 213
Three Gulfs Project, 6, 38, 42–45, 54
Time and space, 116, 127, 129, 131, 132
Trade liberalization, 57
Transcriptional control, 269
Transdisciplinary, 192, 198n4
Transformative evolutionary processes, 273
Translational Medicine Research Institute (*Instituto de Investigaciones de Medicina Traslacional*), 213
Transnational concerns, 196
Transnational logic, 183
Transnational migratory patterns, 46
Transparency, 129, 134, 270
Treasury Department, 41
Triennial cooperation projects, 210
Trinational Initiative, 46, 55, 58n2
Tropical High Andean Wetlands (BIO-THAW), 160, 164, 165
Tropicalize, 81
Tulane University Law School, 8
Tuni Condoriri, 160
Tutela action, 135
Twentieth century, 3, 129, 192, 196, 229n13, 264

U
UA Vice President of Research, 222
UBA Department of Chemistry, 216

UBA School of Exact and Natural Sciences, 216
UCBSP
  Department of Business, Economics, and Finance (Regional Academic Unit of Cochabamba), 153
  Department of Psychology, 153
  Institute for Socioeconomic Research Medical College of La Paz, 153
  Social Communication Sciences Undergraduate Program, 152
UK Higher Education International Unit, 3–4
UK universities, 4
UMSA
  Institute for Chemical Research, 152
  Institute for Ecology, 152
  Laboratoire de Glaciologie et Geophysique de l'Environnement, 156
  Physics Research Institute, 152
UMSS, School of Medicine, 152
UNA
  Institute for Research in the Health Sciences, 154
  School of Agricultural Sciences, 154
  School of Medical Sciences, 154
  School of Veterinary Sciences, 154
Under-report research publication, 240
UNESCO Biosphere Reserve, 45
United Nations Development Program (UNDP), 159
United Nations Economic Confederation for Latin America and the Caribbean (ECLAC), 234
United Nations for microfinance and sustainable development, 7
United Nations Organization, 188
Universalizable, 126
Universalizing default option, 131

INDEX   299

Universidad de los Andes School of Law in Bogota, 8
Universidad Nacional de Rosario and the University of Göttingen, 268
University Center for Higher Studies at UMSS, 158, 159
University Clinic of the University of Navarra, 221
University of Buenos Aires (UBA), 212, 213, 216, 217
University of California, 18, 235
University of California San Diego, 156
University of California Santa Cruz, 6, 38, 39, 42, 43, 48–50, 55, 57
University of Chile, 151, 155, 235
University of Cincinnati (UC), 25, 177, 182, 195, 214, 221
University of Granada, 155
University of Havana, 6, 38, 39, 42, 45, 48, 50, 54, 55, 57, 58n3
University of Michigan, 151
University of Pittsburgh, 165, 214
University of Valencia, 151
Urban development, 9, 62, 130–132, 175, 186
Urbanism, 176, 177, 185
Urbanization, 196, 197
Urban lifestyles, 198
Urban mobility, 9, 175–198
Uruguay, 5, 154, 267
US Agency for International Development (USAID), 65, 67, 68, 73, 77, 78, 82, 151, 158, 207
US/USA
  bank-issued credit, 41
  Department of State, 16, 50
  Department of Treasury, 50
  embargo, 39
  embassy in Havana, 42
  institutions, 6, 18, 31, 54, 121, 234, 237, 243, 250
  national academics, 4
  National Park Service, 52

  Office of Foreign Assets Control, 42
  partners, 18, 158
  Southern Association of Colleges and Schools (SACS), 65
  State Sponsors of Terrorism, 50
  universities, 4, 6, 10, 16, 18, 19, 29, 31, 42, 50, 237
  US–Cuba academic collaboration, 56

V
Vanderbilt University, 158, 159
Vegetal development, 269
Vehicle, 87, 120, 127, 188, 193
Venezuela, 5, 154, 155, 268
Versailles, France, 182
Veterinary sciences, 154
Vice Ministry of Science and Technology, 147, 150
Vice Provost for Research, 225
Vice rectors, 243, 265
Virtual libraries, 147
Virtual platform, 195
Volkswagen, 213
von Humboldt, Alexander, 263–266

W
Wall Street Journal, 65
Walmart, 69
Water run-off inputs, 160
Website reviews, 142
WEF Global Agenda Council on Philanthropy and Social Investing, 69
West Africa, 56
Wetlands, 160
Wharton, 76
Women rights, 158
Woods Hole Oceanographic Institution (WHOI), 43, 55
World-consciousness signals, 178
World Council of Credit Unions, 151

300 INDEX

World Economic Forum and Social Progress Index, 7
World-Wide Fund for Nature, 161

X
Xenophobia, 270

Y
York University (Canada), 158

Z
Zea, Francisco, 264

CPSIA information can be obtained
at www.ICGtesting.com
Printed in the USA
LVOW13*1605100618

580224LV00012B/500/P